Sericulture Handbook

– Study Material Book –

Part I

Sericulture Handbook

– Study Material Book –

Part I

Dr. Amardev Singh (*M.Sc., Ph.D*)

State Sericulture Development Department
Poonch – 185 101 (J&K)

Dr. Ravinder Sharma (*M.Sc., Ph.D*)

Skaust-K, Mirgund, Kashmir (J&K)

BIOTECH

2013

BIOTECH BOOKS®

ISBN 978-81-7622-293-5

Published by: **BIOTECH BOOKS®**
4762-63/23, Ansari Road, Darya Ganj,
New Delhi - 110 002
Phone: +91-011-23262132
E-mail: biotechbooks@yahoo.co.in

Printed at: **Chawla Offset Printers**
Delhi - 110 052

PRINTED IN INDIA

Preface

It is our great pleasure to present this book **"Sericulture Handbook: Study Material Book, Part I"**. In this book, we have incorporated answer to all the units of **Paper-A & B,** as students of sericulture always faced difficulty in findings the answers as per the syllabus guidelines and this book definitely will serve an effective tool.

We are highly grateful to Biotech Books Publisher for publishing this book within a very short period of time and also those who gave us suggestions regarding publishing of the book. Suggestions to improve this book into a more effective tool for performance will always be welcome from all quarters.

Grateful acknowledgment is made to the publishers of vaiours books, research articles *etc.,* from which information have been included in the text with due references of the respective authors.

Last, but not least, the usefulness of this book, we dedicate to our beloved parents who reared us with absolutely love and always watched our success.

Finally, we thank the **"Almighty"** for giving us an opportunity to write this book especially for students.

Dr. Amardev Singh

Dr. Ravinder Sharma

Foreword

The present title **"Sericulture Handbook: Study Material Book, Part I"** is intended to provide most of the guidance of sericulture, always faced difficulty in findings the answers for the students. The book is prepared as per the syllabus guidelines of University of Jammu and I have no doubt that this book will be immense helpful for the students as the text has been written on the basis of original research work, papers and specialized books.

This text claims to be a complete, thorough and authentic exposition of the topic dealt with. I am especially grateful to Dr. Amardev Singh and Dr. Ravinder Sharma who have taken considerable pains to bring out this valuable book in a short period.

Dr. A.P. Goswami

(M. Sc., Ph. D., F. I. S. C. A., F. I. S. S. T.)
Associate Professor and Head
Department of Biology
M.V. Mahila Science and Home Science College
Kalawad Road, Rajkot, Gujarat – 360 007

Contents

— PAPER-B —

Biology of Mulberry and Biology of Silkworm and Rearing Technology

— *PAPER-A* —

Introduction of Sericulture and Soil Sciences

Unit-I

Dr. Ravinder Sharma

1.1. Introduction to Sericulture, What is Sericulture, Scope of Sericulture, Science of Sericulture, Origin and History of Sericulture Industry in India Other Countries, Silk Route

Introduction to Sericulture

Sericulture is derived from the word 'Su (Si)' meaning silk. It is usually associated with the socio- economic life of many countries. The word 'Silk' spells comfort and class, and the 'Silk Fibre' is a protein produced by silk glands of silkworms. According to Confucius, it was in 2640 B.C., once upon a time Chinese Emperor, Chin Shin Huang Ti, ordered his wife, Si Ling Shi, to find out what was damaging his mulberry trees. The empress found worms eating the leaves and spinning shiny cocoons, some of which accidentally dropped into a cup of hot water. A delicate cocoon bave separated itself from the cocoon, as she played with the cocoons in the water and on unwinding one slender thread or silk was discovered. It was kept as a national secret and the knowledge of sericulture remained unknown to the rest of the world for about 300 years. From that historic moment, that Chinese discovered the life cycle of the silk worm and for the 3000 years were kept their monopoly of silk Chinese silk fabrics were beginning to find their way throughout the whole of Asia, and were transported overland to the west, and by sea to Japan, in those long itineraries known as the silk roads. It was in Asia that the Romans discovered these wondrous fabrics but they knew nothing of their foundation. In 1552 A.D., the Emperor Justinian sent two monks on a assignment to Asia, and they came back to Byzantium with silkworm eggs hidden inside their bamboo walking sticks. From then on, sericulture spread throughout Asia Minor and grace. In the 7th century, the Arabs occupied the Persians, capturing their magnificent skills in the process, and helped to spread sericulture and silk weaving as they swept victoriously through Africa, Sicily and Spain. In the 10th century, Andalusia was Europe's main silk- producing centre. Then the Crusaders, the formation of the Mongol Empire, Marco Polo's journeys in china led to the development of commercial exchanges between East and West, and to an ever-increasing use of silk. In this way, Italy started a silk industry as early as 12th Century in the period 1450-1466, Lyon became a major warehouse for foreign silks, but these imports caused a harmful outflow of capital, and in 1466 Louis XI declared his intention to "introduce the art and craft of making gold and silk fabrics in our city of Lyon" Many expert throwers and weavers contributed in a very large degree to the development of the silk industry in Germany, Great Britain, Italy and Switzerland. Throughout the 18th Century, silk continued to prosper in Europe, Japan and above all in China. European missionaries to China reported, "Even the simplest soldiers are dressed in Silk". In 1804, Jacquard perfected the method of producing figured fabrics, by the use of perforated cards. This was a revolution in weaving techniques and gave a tremendous impetus to the creating of silk industry in Lyon and then in other European countries. The 19th Century is characterized by two contradictory trends; increased mechanization and increase in productivity in the silk industry, and on the other hand on beginning the decline of European sericulture in the last quarter of the century. In the 3rd century B.C., from china it spread to Rome and other European countries through 'Silk Road' which was opened in 138-118 B.C. by the Chinese Emperor 'Wu Ti. It started from Xian in Shanxi province of china and passed through Khotan, Yunnan, Burma, India, Pakistan, Afghanistan, Mary, Iran, Iraq, Turkey and ultimately reached Rome.

From 1872, and the opening of the Suez Canal, raw silk imported from Japan became more competitive. Diseases effected silkworm, although overcome by Pasteur, made silk- reeling a less reliable source of income and the first man- made fibres were beginning to make into the markets traditionally reserved for silk. The early part of the 20th Century, whereas European sericulture continued its slow decline, the silk industry succeeded in maintaining a strong position through its technical innovations and the development of silk blended with other fibres. The major turning point was to be the Second World War. Raw –silk supplies from Japan were cut off; synthetic fibres captured many of silk's markets, such as stockings and parachutes. After the war Japan resorted her silk production, with vastly improved with reeling inspection and classification of her raw silk. Japan was to remain the world's biggest producer of raw silk, and practically the only major exporter of raw silk, then china remarkable effort of organisation and planning, gradually re-captured her historic position as the world's biggest producer and exporter of raw silk, in 1985, world production of raw silk was about 56000 tonnes (the same as in 1938) of which over 50 per cent were produced in China.

What is Sericulture?

The term "Sericulture" is used to denote both the industry concerned with Silkworm rearing and the science which provides the technical basis for the industry.

There are more than twenty countries in which Silkworms are reared for commercial purposes. The commercial species of silkworms are *Bombyx mori (Linnaeus),* Antheraea pernyi,(Guerin-Meneville), Antheraea yamamai (Guerin-Meneville), Antheraea mylitta (Drury) *etc.*, among these, *Bombyx mori* is the most widely used, intensively studied, and the techniques for its rearing are the most improved. In this review, only this species will be considered.

The objectives of the scientific studies in sericulture are concerned with solving the problems that arise from the practical side. Most important among such problems are those of increasing the productivity of land as well as labour, stabilization of the cocoon crop, and improvement of the quality of silk and silk fabrics.

Scope of Sericulture

Sericulture has been identified as an occupation of low investments, employment creating and income generating. It has been found that sericulture is highly profitable as compared to many other crops. Sericulture involves simple technologies, easy to understand and adopt even by illiterate farmers and it gives returns in quick succession yielding income in every two or three months. Sericulture does not involve hard labour and rearing of silkworms is generally attended to by women and old people. Sericulture does not require sophisticated machinery and it involves use of simple appliances. Mulberry plants can be grown in any type of soil even in forest fringes, hill slopes and watershed areas. Sericulture ideally suits even in rain fed conditions because of its low cost of production and higher returns than any other crop. Mulberry plant withstands severe drought conditions and gives at least some income for sustenance while other agriculture crops wither away. Sericulture would be a more advantageous industry for improving the economy of retarded section of the society like scheduled caste and scheduled tribes. Non-mulberry sericulture is largely practiced by the tribals. Sericulture ideally suits small and marginal farmers.

In developing countries like India, agriculture and agro-based industries play a vital role in the improvement of rural economy. The limited availability of land, the limited cash returns, and agriculture being confined to one or two seasons in the year, have made villages to look for supporting rural industries, such as sericulture. Agriculture and sericulture are adopted simultaneously by the agriculturists in regions where the ecological conditions are favorable. In India, over three million people are employed in various fields of sericulture. It is a cottage industry and provides ample work for the womenfolk in the rural areas in rearing silk worms, while the male members work in the fields. Recently the enforcing of new ideas by research institutions both in mulberry cultivation and silk-worm-handling among sericulturists, the industry is now practiced as a main profession and as a major cash crop of the country. It is estimated that Sericulture can generate employment @ 11 man days per kg of raw silk production (in on-farm and off-farm activities) throughout the year. This potential is *par-excellence* and no other industry generates this kind of employment, especially in rural areas, hence, sericulture is used as a tool for rural reconstruction. Now due to enhancement of import duty on silk from 5 to 15 per cent the sericulture industry will further boost in the country.

The strengths of silk industry can be summarized as follows:

- ✰ Enormous production capacity
- ✰ Efficient raw material manufacturing capacity
- ✰ Large pool of skilled and cheap labour
- ✰ Entrepreneurial skills
- ✰ Enormous export potential
- ✰ Large domestic market

Science of Sericulture

The domesticated silkworm, *Bombyx mori* has been the target of intensive scientific study. Since, the drawn of human civilization, the silkworm has been used as a source of silk for procuring exquisite textiles and dress material. Because of its industrial importance, the study of insect has been encouraged by governments in several countries. The scientific achievement on *Bombyx* is thus different from those achieved with the widely used experimental organism, *Drosophila.* The characteristics of the former are economic, *i.e.,* efficiency of silk production per unit amount of food plant, pest prevention, etc. However, extensive scientific studies have also been carried out on fundamental problems to support the development of agricultural technology. Studies on the physiology and endocrinology of metamorphosis, nutrition, and synthesis of silk protein are noteworthy among these achievements in the sense that

valuable generalizations have been based on findings obtained originally with this insect. Other studies, for instance, those on radiation and chemical mutagenesis have been carried out with the intention to explore a new frontier by utilizing characteristic features of the silkworm. Other studies on the culture of tissues and cells have contributed to our knowledge of the mechanism of virus infection as well as to the improvement of culture techniques of insect cells.

Origin and History of Sericulture Industry in India Other Countries

History of Sericulture

Sericulture or silk production has a long and colorful history. Pliny, the Roman historian, wrote in his Natural History in 70 BC "Silk was obtained by removing the down from the leaves with the help of water...".

Origin of Silk: Legend of Lady Hsi-Ling-Shih

Chinese legend gives the title **Goddess of Silk** to Lady **Hsi-Ling-Shih**, wife of the mythical Yellow Emperor, who was said to have ruled China in about 3000 BC. She is known for introducing silkworm rearing and the invention of the loom.

Silkworm cocoon unearthed in 1927 from the soils of Yellow River in Shanxi Province (northern China), indicated that silk was existing during 2600 - 2300 BC. In another excavation in Zhejiang province, the presence of ribbons, threads and woven fragments, indicated the use of silk in 3000 BC. More recent archeological finds like a small ivory cup carved with a silkworm design and spinning tools, silk thread and fabric fragments from sites along the lower "Yangzi", reveals that the origin of sericulture to be even earlier, which may be 6000 to 7000 years old.

The Secret of Sericulture

Now let us know about the stages, the silkworm pass through during its life cycle. After the eggs hatch, the baby worms feed day and night on fresh, hand-picked leaves until they pass second moult. A fixed temperature has to be maintained throughout. After the second moult whole branch of mulberry has to be fed to the worms on the shoot rearing racks. Thousands of feeding worms are kept on these racks. A roomful of worms eating mulberry leaves in the fifth instar sounds like heavy rain. The newly hatched silkworm multiplies its size 10,000 times within a month, changing color and shedding its whitish-gray skin *four* times. The silkworms feed until they enter the cocoon (also called Pupal stage) stage. When it is time to build their cocoons, the worms produce a jelly-like substance in their silk glands, which hardens when it comes in contact with air. Silkworms spend three or four days spinning a cocoon around themselves until they look like puffy balls (Cocoons). After four to nine days in a warm, dry place the cocoons are ready to be unwound.

First they are steamed or baked to kill the worms, or pupas. The cocoons are then dipped into hot water to loosen the tightly woven filaments. These filaments are unwound onto a spool. Each cocoon is made up of a filament between 600 and 900 meters long! Between five and eight of these super-fine filaments are twisted together to make one thread. Finally the silk threads are woven into cloth or used for embroidery work. Clothes made from silk are not only beautiful and lightweight they are also warm in cool weather and cool in hot weather.

Reeling silk and spinning were always considered household duties for women, while weaving and embroidery were carried out in workshops as well as the home. In every silk-producing province the daughters, mothers and grandmothers of every family devoted a large part of the day for six months in a year to the feeding, tending and supervision of silkworms and to the unraveling, spinning, weaving, dyeing and embroidering of silk. By the fifth century BC, at least six Chinese provinces were producing silk. Each spring, the empress herself inaugurated the silk-raising season, for silk production was the work of women all over China. The technique and process of sericulture were guarded secrets and closely controlled by Chinese authorities. Anyone who reveals the secrets or smuggle the silkworm eggs or cocoons outside China would be punished by death.

Sericulture in India

India is one of the 58 sericulture industries. It has the unique distinction of being the only country in the world producing all the four varieties of silk, namely mulberry, tasar, eri and muga. No one really knows when sericulture came in India, but it existed in the Ganga Brahmaputra bells from time immemorial. The word Saree is derived from Sanskrit shatto or Shatika, which was later abbreviated as Shadi or Sari. While some believe that it is derived from Seres meaning silk.

According to one view all domesticated forms of mulberry came from China. A Chinese princess got married to a king in Tibet in 140 B.C. She brought some eggs of silkworms and some mulberry seeds hidden in her headdress. According to second view, put forward by N.G. Mukerjee, all mulberry insects originated somewhere on the slopes of Himalayas on the skirts of Mount Everest, from where they spread to warmer regions.

The chronology of events regarding the history of sericulture in India is summarized below.

- ☆ **4000 B.C**. Ericulture existed even before the Aryans migrated to India. It has been almost a prerogative to the tribal of Northeast India.
- ☆ **1400 B.C**. Traces of tasar silk have been excavated from a burial mound in an urn in Nevassa in Maharashtra *i.e.*, even before China started producing tasar around 100 A.D.
- ☆ **321-296 B.C** Kautiylyas 'Arthashastra' of Chandragupta's time reveals that patrona (a variety of silk) was obtained from the country of magadh. Pundrya and Subarakundya. Silk obtained from Naga trees was yellow and that obtained from Artocarpus lakooch vern. Lokucha was of the colour of wheat. Silk obtained from M musops elengi vern. Vakula was white and that obtained from Ficus bengalensis and Ficus religliosa vern. Veta was the colour of butter. Arthashastra also made distinction between cultivated and wild varieties of silk. Theophillareligiosae (wild mulberry silkworm) still feeds on mulberry, Artocarpus lakoocha and Ficus religiosa.

- **150 B.C.** Reshma shawls and woven silks were quite popular in kings courts of Kashmir, which was also known for its wonderful mulberry trees.
- **58 B.C.** According to some historians raw silk was exported from India to Rome during the regin of Kanishka.
- **629-645 A.D.**The Harisharita written by Bana Bhat reveals that during the Hiun Tsang's visit to India, great monarch Bhaskara of Pragiyotishpura sent silk clothes of all varieties produced in kampura, Assam to king Harsha of Kanyanubja (Kanyakubja). The gift included chinapatta (figured textile), kauseya (textile from kosaor cocoon), khsauma (fine silk), and jattipatka (woollen silk0. During this period the people knew the art for the production of silks from wild silkworms, such as Muga, Deomuga, Kotkari Muga *etc.*, the Catterpillars which feeds on Litsaea salicfolia, L. citrate vern. Mejankari and L. champaca vern. Chapa.
- **1526-1857 A.D.** Sericulture industry flourished during the mughal period.
- **1603-1641 A.D** During the reign of Pratap Singh in Northeast India, the golden hued Muga silk, the costliest and most precious of all silks.
- **1869 A.D.** Maharaja Ranbir Singh built 127 rearing houses in Kashmir state.
- **1878 A.D.** Sericulture industry received a setback due to pebrine disease.
- **1900-1930 A.D.** Britishers (East India Company, which came to India six filatures in 1900) and the industry once again started prospering. They also set up at Patna. Many silk centres like filature were also set up at Patna. Many silk centres like Maldaha, Murishidabad, *etc.*, came up.
- **April 1949 A.D.** Act No. LXI of 1948 was passed by Parliament by which a statutory body called Central Silk Board under the administrative control of Ministry of textiles, Government of India was constituted.

Present Status of Sericulture in India

Sericulture, it is an effective tool for rural development as it generates income and employment. Out of the 576,000 villages providing employment to about six million persons, most of them belonging to the weaker sections of the society including scheduled caste scheduled tribes.

Silk Varieties

There are four kinds of commercial exploitation in the world, Mulberry, Tasar, Eri and Muga. India has the unique distinction in the field of sericulture, as it is the only country producing all the four commercial varieties of silk. The differentiation is based on the race, species of the worms and the food plants led them.

India's Position in World Silk Production

The world silk production in the year 2010-2011 was about 103,627 metric tonnes of which India share was 16.632 tonnes according to the international Silk association. India ranked among top three which includes China and Japan amounting for as much as 84 percent of the total global silk production India ranks second among mulberry silk producers with a share of 14 percent of the global production and second largest producer of Tasar Silk in the world. India has monopoly in the golden-yellow muga silk, which is obtained mainly from Assam and adjoining states.

Mulberry Sericulture

Mulberry sericulture is practiced mainly in the states of Karnatka, Andra Pradesh, Tamil Nadu, Jammu and Kashmir and West Bengal. These states account for about 98 percent of the total mulberry raw silk produced in the country. Karnatka has the unique distinction of producing 60 percent of the mulberry sericulture has also been introduced in the states of Maharashtra, Kerla, Gujarat, Rajasthan, Bihar and Orrisa, where a vast potential exist for its growth, Present scenario of mulberry silk production given in Table 1.1.

Non-Mulberry Silk

Non–mulberry sector, tasar culture is practised in the states of Bihar, Madhya Pradesh, Orrisa, West Bengal, Uttar Pradesh, Rajasthan and Andra Pradesh. Muga culture is practised mainly in the state of Assam and to some extent in Mizoram, Megalaya and Nagaland. Ericulture is practised in the northeastern states namely Assam, Manipur and also in Bihar and Orrisa.

Area and Production

Presently 242,000 hectares are available under mulberry cultivation, producing about 86,525 of cocoons and 8,455 tonnes of raw silk. Production of non- mulberry silk is to over 1000 tonnes which includes 463 tonnes of tasar, 522 tonnes of eri and 58 tonnes of muga.

Silk Reeling and Weaving

Silk reeling capacity in India consists of 21,983 charkhas, 6,955 cottage basins and 8,879 filatures. Raw silk is twisted in small factories except those produced in Kashmir and west Bengal. Twisted yarn is used in both handlooms and power looms. There are about two lakh spindles in India. Indian silk is essentially woven on handlooms. About 65 per cent of the Indian woven on the handlooms and 30 per cent on power looms. The power looms are also organized on a small scale cottage pattern. The modern silk weaving factories having better power looms may account for about five percent of the silk production. There are about 182,000 silk handlooms and 31,000 silk power looms in India. Indian silk fabrics, mainly sari materials which are produced such as Kancheepuram, Kumakonam and Arni in Tamil Nadu, Mysore and Bangalore in Karnataka, Dharavaram and Pochampilli in Andhra Pradesh, Varanasi in Uttar Pradesh and Murishidabad and Birbhum in West Bengal.

Spun Silk Industry

The processing of silk waste of spun silk yarn and noil yarn, which had been confined to the three public sector mills up to 1984. The three public sector spun silk mills are located at Channapatana (Karnataka), Jagi road (Assam) and Bhagalpur

(Bihar). The total installed capacity of the spun silk yarn and 3,462 spindles for nylon yarn.

Table 1.1: Mulberry Silk Production in India

Year	*Area Under Mulberry (Hectares)*	*Reeling Cocoons (Tonnes)*	*Raw Silk*	*Silk Waste (Tonnes)*	*Rendita (Tonnes)*
1980-81	170	58	4593	1376	12.70
1981-82	180	55	4801	1523	11.50
1982-83	197	55	4801	1523	11.50
1983-84	207	71	5681	2017	12.50
1984-85	215	75	6895	2464	10.90
1985-86	218	77	7029	2504	10.90
1986-87	230	82	7905	2837	10.30
1987-88	242	87	8455	3086	10.20
1988-89	268	96	9683	3399	10.00
1989-90	294	110	10805	3921	10.10
1990-91	317	117	11486	33953	10.20
1991-92	331	107	10658	3544	10.10
1992-93	343	130	13000	4513	9.98
1993-94	319	117	12550	4518	9.34
1994-95	283	123	13450	4501	9.15
1995-96	289	116	12884	4022	9.03
1996-97	281	116	12954	4000	8.93
1997-98	282	127	14048	4250	9.08
1998-99	270	127	14048	4250	9.08
1999-00	227	125	13994	4153	8.96
2000-01	216	125	13994	4153	8.96
2001-02	232	140	14432	4237	8.66
2002-03	193	128	14617	4385	8.79
2003-04	185	117	13970	3,765	8.41
2004-05	172	120	14,620	3,587	8.21
2005-06	179	126	15,445	3,749	8.17
2006-07	192	135	16,525	4055	8.20
2007-08	185	135	16,245	3,416	8.12
2008-09	178	125	15,610	3,746	8.00
2009-10	184	132	16,322	4.080	8.07
2010-11	170	131	16,360	4090	7.99
2011-2012	181	140	18,272	4568	7.66

Compiled by: Economic Division, Updated on 27.09.2012 (*Source*: Central Silk Board).

Large Scale Silk Producing units

In recent years, several large scales silk manufacturing enterprises have been set up in the private sector. Hitherto only one major silk have been set up in the govt. sector- under Karnataka Silk producing unit at Mysore. The new companies include Richimen Silks Limited, Hindupur (A.P) Himatsinka seide Ltd., Doddaballapur and indosaka Silk Ltd., Hyderabad, which are 100 percent export oriented.

Domestic Market

The domestic market for silk is essentially for sarees. About 90 percent of the silk produced for domestic market goes for production of sarees. Only the balance 10 percent is used for other products like dress material, men's wear etc. Indian silk market is estimated to be around Rs 2000/- crores and the saree market about Rs. 1800 crores.

Export Market

India has achieved good results in silk exports in recent years. The main items of export are silk fabrics, ready-made garments, carpets made up clothes and Silk waste. The silk export from India has been steadily increasing at the rate of over 25 percent per annum.

The Indian Silk Export Council

The Indian Silk Export Promotion Council established by the Government of India in 1983. Its headquarters established in Bombay. Its prime objectives are to undertaken export promotion measures for silk goods, generic promotion of silk, liaison between the exporters and Government, assign small scale and now exporters in exporting silk goods and advising the Government of India in export promotion strategies for the silk sector. It is the link between the buyers and the sellers the weavers and weavers.

Silk Development in China

Do you know how Sericulture Industry Flourished in China during Ancient Time?

When silk was first discovered, it was reserved exclusively for the use of the ruler. It was permitted only to the emperor, his close relations and the very highest of his dignitaries. Gradually the various classes of society began wearing tunics of silk, and silk came into more general use as well as being used for clothing and decoration. Silk was quite quickly put to industrial use. Silk, indeed, rapidly became one of the principal elements of the Chinese economy. Silk was used for musical instruments, fishing-lines, bowstrings, bonds of all kinds, and even rag paper, the world's first luxury paper. Eventually today even the common people were able to wear garments of silk.

The chronological events of the history of Sericulture in China are summarized below:

☆ **1600 B.C.** Breeding of silkworms was started during Shang times

- ☆ **1200-1058** B.C. Silkworms were domesticated.
- ☆ **1027 B.C.** During chow Dynasty there was there were well organized breeding programmes.
- ☆ **1000-77 B.C.** A necklace with silkworm motif was unearthed in Baoji near Xian Shamshi province
- ☆ **206 B.C.-8 A.D.** During Han Dynasty weaving and printing had attained a high degree of perfection and it was considered as the 'Golden Age of Sericulture' in Chinese history.

(Maximum traffic was observed on Silk Road and silk was smuggled out to Constantinople (Now called as Istanbul).

Sericulture in Europe

Silk was smuggled out to Istanbul in 6th century. During this period sericulture was spread to Europe and the Balkan Countries. In the 8th and 9th centuries Thebes, Greek and Syria cities increased their silk production as the looms of Constantinople declined. The name Morus is derived from Morea, a place in Peloponnesian of Greece, where mulberry tree were abundant.

In 740 A.D. sericulture was introduced in Spain by the Arab conquerors and it brought prosperity in Almeria, Murcia, Malaga, Saragossa, Valencia, etc. Soon it began to export healthy silkworm seeds to Portugal and neighboring countries, but during the second half of last century the industry declined rapidly.

In 1146 A.D. Norman King Roger II (Ruggero II), the king of Sicily introduced sericulture into Italy. He captured many slaves and artisans while conquering Athens. Later on it spread to Bologna first made a reeling machine.

Sericulture was introduced into France during the reign of Clement V around 1260 A.D. and by 1480 A.D. weaving of silk was started. From 1515-1541 Francis I, 'Father of Silk Industry in Europe' the industry flourished during the reigns of Louis XIII and Louis XVI, In 1725-1803 a number of looms including 'Jacquard Loom' Were invented for Silk weaving.

In 1598 A.D. sericulture was introduced in Germany during the region of Frederick and in 1616 A.D. it was introduced into England during the reign of Elizabeth I. Sericulture was encouraged by Michael I in Russia in 1880 A.D.

Sericulture in Southeast Asia

Sericulture in Southeast Asia was introduced in 11th century. Atjek and Palembang towns in Sumatra and Pensutran, Madjalenka, Garut, Sala and Djeunbu town in java are associated with silk. Bugin and Makasser tribes in celebes (Sulawasi) are ancient Sericulturist. Their normal attiries 'Sarong and 'Hujubodo' are made of silk. Thailand is famous for hand- woven silks, the Thai silk. In Myanmar (Burma) local Burmese tribes, Yabein, Shah, Wa, Lisu, Kachin, Akha, Mon, Meo, etc. rear indigenous silkworms and dye their own silk from local vegetable products.

Sericulture in America

Spanish conquistador Cortes in 1552 introduced sericulture in Mexico. James I introduced it in American colonies in 1600. In Brazil sericulture was introduced in Parana and Sao Paolo districts. Here Italian and Chinese silkworms were crossed to obtain two varieties.

Sericulture in Middle East

In Iran reeling of cocoons and rearing of silkworms were started in the sixth century. From 1500-1700 under the dynasty of safavis great progress was made. Guilan and Mazandaran situated on the shores of the Caspian Sea are the important provinces.

Sericulture in Japan

The chronological events of the spread of sericulture in Japan are summarized below:

- ☆ **199 A.D**. During the reign of Chi, Ai, one of the descendents of Chinese Emperor named Kama-O. came over to Japan and brought some silkworm eggs.
- ☆ **462 A.D.** During the reign of a Mikado, named Yu-Lyak rearing of silkworms was done on a large scale by his queen. Four Korean girls were brought to Kyushu Island along with some eggs.
- ☆ **1500 A.D**. Silk weaving techniques reached to the highest point producing a popular textile called Nishijin for the warrior's called Samurai's
- ☆ **1869 A.D.** Epidemic of pebrine disease in Europe.
- ☆ **1870-1890 A.D.** Raw silk was exported to the west and it helped to gain foreign exchange.
- ☆ **1893-1914 A.D**. Triumph of filature over the hand reels.
- ☆ **1930 A.D.** Golden year for country's Sericulture industry as a multiple reeling machines and power looms enhanced the production of silk.
- ☆ **1957-till date** Japan is the 3rd largest silk producing country in the world.

Silk Route

The Han Emperor Wu Ti opened the silk Road from China to Rome in 138-118 B.C. It started from Xian in Shanxi province and passed through Lanchou to Dun Huang, where it divided into two:

I. The Northern Road crossing the Pamir Mountains passed through Turfan and led to Ferghana to Kazhakh stepee.

II. The southern Road went past the southern edge of Taklamakan desert; through Yarkhand and across Pamir Mountains continuing to Bactria and from there to Parthia India and to Antioch (Antakya) of modern Turkey. During Tang Dynasty (618-907 A.D.) China and Rome reigned at each end of the Silk Road.

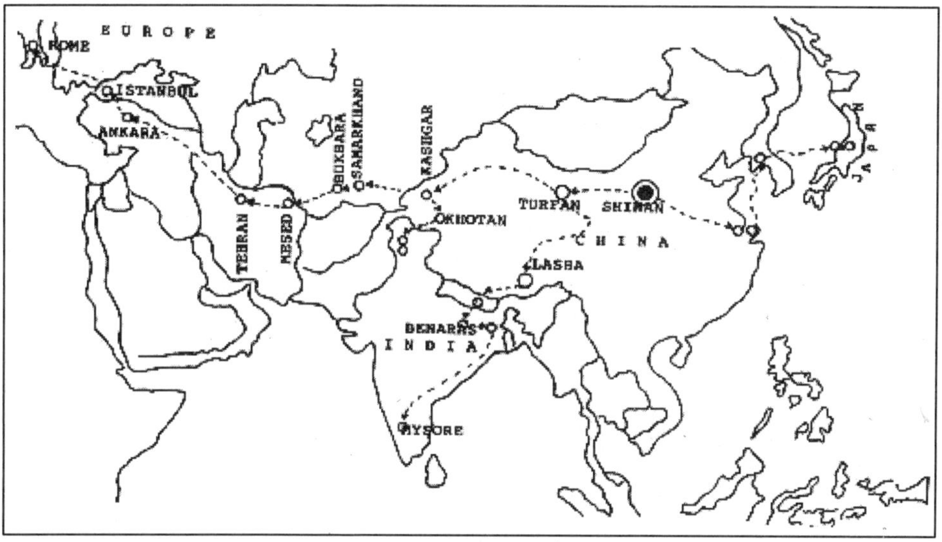

The Great Silk Route and Spread of Sericulture (Ancient) from China

Silk Road

The trade between China and India existed even before the establishment of 'Silk Road' It followed a south-western route starting from Dali in Yunna to North Burma and from there it proceeded in two directions:

I. One route going southward along rivers Salween and Irrawaddy to the seaports.

II. Second route went across India via Kamrup (Assam). Patliputra (Patna), Aryavartha (The Gangetic Plains), Takshashila (Rawalpindi), Purushpura (Peshawar), Ganddhara (Afghanistan) and many, where it joined Silk Road. Trade between China and India at many established spiritual and cultural contacts besides spreading Buddhism.

During Ming Dynasty (1368-1644 A.D.) Silk Road was nearly died a quiet death. This was the period when Vasco da Gama of Portugal rounded Africa to reach India in 1498 and Christopher Columbus of Italy discovered America. Thus Alexandria became the centre of silk distribution, when oriental trade routes were changed to water routes. Palmyria (Syria) became the clearinghouse for the silk brought from china and India.

Sericulture spread to India from China through Tibet during 140 BC. Sericulture reached Korea around 200 BC, when groups of Chinese immigrants arrived there. Silk reached the West through a number of different channels. Shortly after AD 300, sericulture traveled westward and the cultivation of the silkworm was established in India. It is also said that in AD 440, a prince of Khotan (today's Hetian)–a kingdom on the rim of Taklamakan desert – courted and won a Chinese princess. The princess smuggled out silkworm eggs by hiding them in her voluminous hairpiece.

Then around AD 550, two Nestorian monks appeared at the Byzantine Emperor Justinian's court with silkworm eggs hid in their hollow bamboo staves. Under their supervision the eggs hatched into worms, and the worms spun cocoons. Byzantium was in the silk business at last. The Byzantine church and state created imperial workshops, monopolizing production and kept the secret to themselves. Thus silk industry established in the Middle East, limiting the market for ordinary-grade Chinese silk. However high-quality silk textiles, woven in China especially for the Middle Eastern market, continued to bring high prices in the West, and trade along the Silk Road therefore continued as before. By the sixth century the Persians, too, had mastered the art of silk weaving, developing their own rich patterns and techniques. It was only in the 13th century that Italy began silk production with the introduction of 2000 skilled silk weavers from Constantinople. Eventually silk production became widespread in Europe.

Silk and its Trade

Here we will be learning about the spread of silk trade in the world.

- ☆ Silk trade was actually started before the Silk Road was officially opened in the second century BC.
- ☆ During the second century BC, the Chinese emperor, Han Wu Di's ambassadors traveled as far west as Persia and Mesopotamia, bearing gifts including silks.
- ☆ A Han embassy reached Baghdad in AD 97, and important finds of Han silks have been made along the Silk Road.
- ☆ From about the fourth century BC, the Greeks and Romans began talking of Seres, the Kingdom of Silk.
- ☆ The Roman Emperor Heliogabalus (AD 218 - 222) wore silk.
- ☆ By 380 AD, Marcellinus Ammianus reported, "The use of silk which was once confined to the nobility has now spread to all classes without distinction, even to the lowest." The craving of silk continued to increase over the centuries.

1.2. World Output of Silk, Other Natural Gibres, Need for Textile Fibres-Different Types of Textile Fibres Production from 1938 Onwards and Present Status, Importance of Natural Fibres *vis-a-vis* Man Made, Role of Silk Fibres amongst Batural Fibres

World Output of Silk

World silk production has approximately doubled during last 30 years in spite of man-made fibers replacing silk for some uses. China and Japan during this period have been the two main producers, together contributing for more than 50 per cent of the world production each year.

Country-wise Growth of Raw Silk Production in the World

[Metric tones]

Year	*Country*						
	China	*India*	*Japan*	*Brazil*	*South Korea*	*Others*	*Total*
1970	10200	2258	20515	240	2846	4195	40254
1975	15000	2434	20169	930	5545	4622	48700
1980	23485	4193	16155	1284	3279	7104	55500
1985	32000	6895	9592	1558	1850	6805	58700
1990	43800	10805	5700	1680	780	7320	70085
1995	64613	13450	3228	2468	643	7115	91517
1996	59000	12954	2580	2270	146	8242	85192
1997	55117	14048	1920	2120	146	6239	79590
1998	49430	14260	1080	1821	146	4990	71727
1999	55990	13944	650	1554	50	2119	74307
2001	58600	15857	431	1484	–	–	80774

World Mulberry Raw Silk Production

Unit-Tonnes

Country	*1995*	*1996*	*1997*	*1998*	*1999*	*2000*	*2001*	*2002*	*2003*	*2004*	*2005*
China	64613	59000	52700	49430	55990	60000	62560	64100	76324	85000	
India	12884	12954	14048	14260	13944	14432	15842	14617	13970	14620	
Japan	3240	2580	1920	1080	650	557	431	394	287	263	
Brazil	2468	2270	2120	1821	1554	1389	1485	1607	1563	1512	
Korea Republic	946	506	272	210	200	165	157	154	150	150	
Uzbekistan	1320	2500	2000	1500	923	1100	1260	1260	950	950	
Thailand	1313	1144	1039	900	1000	955	1510	1510	1500	1420	

Contd...

Table–*Contd...*

Country	*1995*	*1996*	*1997*	*1998*	*1999*	*2000*	*2001*	*2002*	*2003*	*2004*	*2005*
Vietnam	2100	1500	1000	862	780	780	2035	2200	750	750	
Others	2967	2766	2117	1684	1250	1952	1692	3814	1500	1500	
Total	**91851**	**85220**	**77216**	**71747**	**76291**	**81330**	**86972**	**89656**	**96994**	**106165**	

World Raw Silk Production

Unit-Tonnes

Country	*1995*	*1996*	*1997*	*1998*	*1999*	*2000*	*2001*	*2002*	*2003*	*2004*	*2005*
China	67113	68500	60300	57500	56959	61648	64567	68600	94600	102560	
India	13909	14126	15236	15544	15214	15857	17351	16319	15742	16500	
Japan	3240	2580	1920	1080	650	557	431	394	287	263	
Brazil	2468	2270	2120	1821	1554	1389	1485	1607	1563	1512	
Korea Republic	946	506	272	210	200	165 *	157 *	154 *	150	150	
Uzbekistan	1320	2500	2000	1500	923	1100	1260	1260 **	950	950	
Thailand	1313	1144	1039	900	1000	955	1510	1510 **	1500	1420	
Vietnam	2100	1500	1000	862	780	780 **	2035	2200	750	750	
Others	2967	2766	2117	1572	1250	1952	1692	3814	1500	1500	
Total	**95376**	**95892**	**86004**	**80989**	**78530**	**84403**	**90488**	**95858**	**117042**	**125605**	

Source: 2004-Sericollgia 44(3) and ISCC-20005

Note: Figures of India is for financial year April to March.

The silk production in China has increased steadily. The silk production in India also registered a growth rate of 602.25 per cent in the same period. India is the only country, which registered a growth rate of above 100 per cent during the eighties and the highest growth rate in the last three decades because of the evolution of new tropical sericulture technologies. The production growth rates in Japan, South Korea and other countries for the reference period were found negative.

At present, India is the second largest producer of mulberry silk, next only to China, accounting more than 15 per cent of the global raw silk production. Mulberry sericulture is practiced in almost all the states in the country but Karnataka, Andhra Pradesh, West Bengal and Tamil Nadu together account for about 98.20 per cent of the total mulberry silk production in the country.

Sericulture has attained a significant growth in the past four decades in India. The mulberry area increased steadily from 83 thousand hectares in 1960-61 to 3418 thousand hectares in 1993-94, but there was decline in the mulberry area in the ensuing years and so reduced to 2271 thousand hectares during 1999-2000. The growth rate of raw silk production reduced in the later part of the last decade due to the reduction in mulberry area, but still there was improvement in the silk production due to increased productivity and so the silk production reached to 13.94 thousand tonnes in 1999-2000.

Silk productivity in India between 1960 and 1970 was very low and ranged from 14 kg to 20 kg per hectare. However, a significant leap in productivity was observed in the eighties and nineties and at present it is 85 kg per hectare. The improvement in productivity was due to the adoption of improved practices for mulberry cultivation and silkworm rearing in the field through the efforts of Central Silk Board and the State Sericulture Departments.

Though, India has achieved a significant leap in silk production and productivity, Indian sericulture industry is facing with certain problems. Some of them are taken into stock here under:

Bulk of the silk produced in the country is of the cross breed of multivoltine and bivoltine breeds, which is low in quality by international silk standards and cannot be used in high-speed looms.

There was a sharp decline in mulberry area due to uprooting of mulberry.

Comparative Account of Sericulture Productivity of China and India (1993-94)

Sl.No.	*Particulars*	*China*	*India*	*India (2005-06)*
1.	Leaf yield/Ha/year (MT)	25-30	20-30	40-50
2.	Races reared	All bivoltine	Predominantly CB	2-3 per cent bivoltine
3.	Egg production	All government	Both private and Govt.	Both private and Govt.
4.	Supply system	Chawki reared	Majority supplied as eggs	10-15 per cent chawki reared
5.	Rearing pattern	Batch wise	Throughout year	Throughout year
6.	Dfls brushed/Ha/year	4000	2500	2800-3500
7.	Cocoon yield (kg/100 dfls)	60-65	35-40	40-60
8.	Leaf cocoon ratio (kg)	16-18	26-28	16-18
9.	Cocoon yield (kg/Ha)	2200-2400	1000-1200	1400-1800
10.	Cocoon weight (g)	1.9-2.0	1.6-1.7	1.8-2.0
11.	Shell percentage	21-23	17-19	18-22
12.	Filament length (m)	> 1000	< 800	>1000
13.	Renditta	6-7	8.5-9.5	7-8
14.	Grade of silk	1, 2A, 3A	E, F, C	E-2A
15.	Cost of cocoon production (Rs./kg)	40-45	65-75	70-80
16.	Raw silk production (kg/ha/yr.)	300-350	60-80	175-250
17.	Average crop loss per year	3-5 per cent	20-25 per cent	10-15 per cent

Though attempts were made to introduce sericulture in many states in a big way through World Bank aided National Sericulture Project (NSP) during the 1990s, sericulture production is still limited to the traditional silk producing states.

The cost of production of silk in India is much higher than that of China. Hence, the imported Chinese silk is available to Indian weavers at a cheaper price

The production system of China is far superior to that of India. Thus there is a scope for a lot of improvement in the production system to improve the quality and productivity of Indian silk.

The reeling sector is unorganized in India. Sixty per cent of Indian raw silk is produced in age-old charka technology and 35 per cent of the production is in cottage basin and only 5 per cent is in filature.

The current production of silk in the country cannot cater the demand for silk in the country. Hence, India had to import raw silk.

Trade liberalization due to implementation of WTO agreement possesses threat to sericulture industry due to high cost and low quality of Indian silk.

This clearly indicates that there is a scope to improve the productivity and quality of silk in the country. In this context, extension management is necessary for the all round development of sericulture industry in the country.

Need for textile fibers-Different types of textile fibers Production from 1938 onwards and present Status, Importance of natural fibers *vis-a-vis* man made, Role of silk fibers amongst natural fibers

What is Textile Fibre?

A **textile** or **cloth** is a flexible woven material consisting of a network of natural or artificial fibres often referred to as thread or yarn. Yarn is produced by spinning raw fibres of wool, flax, cotton, or other material to produce long strands. Textiles are formed by weaving, knitting, crocheting, knotting, or pressing fibres together (felt).

The word **fabric** and **cloth** are used in textile assembly trades (such as tailoring and dressmaking) as synonyms for *textile*. However, there are subtle differences in these terms in specialized usage. *Textile* refers to any material made of interlacing fibres. *Fabric* refers to any material made through weaving, knitting, spreading, crocheting, or bonding that may be used in production of further goods (garments, etc.). *Cloth* may be used synonymously with *fabric* but often refers to a finished piece of fabric used for a specific purpose (*e.g.*, *table cloth*).

Different Types of Textile Fibres

Textiles can be made from many materials. These materials come from four main sources: animal (wool, silk), plant (cotton, flax, jute), mineral (asbestos, glass fibre), and synthetic (nylon, polyester, acrylic). In the past, all textiles were made from natural fibres, including plant, animal, and mineral sources. In the 20th century, these were supplemented by artificial fibres made from petroleum.

Textiles are made in various strengths and degrees of durability, from the finest gossamer to the sturdiest canvas. The relative thickness of fibres in cloth is measured in deniers. Micro fibre refers to fibres made of strands thinner than one denier.

Animal Textiles

Animal textiles are commonly made from hair, fur or skin.

Wool refers to the hair of the domestic goat or sheep, which is distinguished from other types of animal hair in that the individual strands are coated with scales and tightly crimped, and the wool as a whole is coated with a wax mixture known as lanolin (aka wool grease), which is waterproof and dirt proof. Woollen refers to a bulkier yarn produced from carded, non-parallel fibre, while worsted refers to a finer yarn which is spun from longer fibres which have been combed to be parallel. Wool is commonly used for warm clothing. Cashmere, the hair of the Indian cashmere goat, and mohair, the hair of the North African angora goat, are types of wool known for their softness.

Other animal textiles which are made from hair or fur are alpaca wool, vicuña wool, llama wool, and camel hair, generally used in the production of coats, jackets, ponchos, blankets, and other warm coverings. Angora refers to the long, thick, soft hair of the angora rabbit. Qiviut is the fine inner wool of the musk ox.

Silk is an animal textile made from the fibres of the cocoon of the Chinese silkworm which is spun into a smooth fabric prized for its softness. There are two main types of the silk: 'mulberry silk' produced by the Bombyx Mori, and 'wild silk' such as Tussah silk. Silkworm larvae produce the first type if cultivated in habitats with fresh mulberry leaves for consumption, while Tussah silk is produced by silkworms feeding purely on oak leaves. Around four-fifths of the world's silk production consists of cultivated silk.

Plant Textiles

Grass, rush, hemp, and sisal are all used in making rope. In the first two, the entire plant is used for this purpose, while in the last two, only fibres from the plant are utilized. Coir (coconut fibre) is used in making twine, and also in floor mats, doormats, brushes, mattresses, floor tiles, and sacking.

Straw and bamboo are both used to make hats. Straw, a dried form of grass, is also used for stuffing, as is kapok.

Fibres from pulpwood trees, cotton, rice, hemp, and nettle are used in making paper.

Cotton, flax, jute, hemp, modal and even bamboo fibre are all used in clothing. Piña (pineapple fibre) and ramie are also fibres used in clothing, generally with a blend of other fibres such as cotton. Nettles have also been used to make a fibre and fabric very similar to hemp or flax. The use of milkweed stalk fibre has also been reported, but it tends to be somewhat weaker than other fibres like hemp or flax.

Acetate is used to increase the shininess of certain fabrics such as silks, velvets, and taffetas.

Seaweed is used in the production of textiles. A water-soluble fibre known as alginate is produced and is used as a holding fibre; when the cloth is finished, the alginate is dissolved, leaving an open area.

Lyocell is a man-made fabric derived from wood pulp. It is often described as a man-made silk equivalent and is a tough fabric which is often blended with other fabrics – cotton for example.

Fibres from the stalks of plants, such as hemp, flax, and nettles, are also known as 'bast" fibre.

Mineral Textiles

Asbestos and basalt fibre are used for vinyl tiles, sheeting, and adhesives, "transite" panels and siding, acoustical ceilings, stage curtains, and fire blankets.

Glass fibre is used in the production of spacesuits, ironing board and mattress covers, ropes and cables, reinforcement fibre for composite materials, insect netting, flame-retardant and protective fabric, soundproof, fireproof, and insulating fibres.

Metal fibre, metal foil, and metal wire have a variety of uses, including the production of cloth-of-gold and jewellery. Hardware cloth (US term only) is a coarse weave of steel wire, used in construction. It is much like standard window screening, but heavier and with a more open weave. It is sometimes used together with screening on the lower part of screen doors, to resist scratching by dogs.

Synthetic Textiles

All synthetic textiles are used primarily in the production of clothing.

Polyester fibre is used in all types of clothing, either alone or blended with fibres such as cotton.Aramid fibre *(e.g.,* Twaron) is used for flame-retardant clothing, cut-protection, and armor. Acrylic is a fibre used to imitate wools, including cashmere, and is often used in replacement of them. Nylon is a fibre used to imitate silk; it is used in the production of pantyhose. Thicker nylon fibres are used in rope and outdoor clothing. Spandex (trade name *Lycra*) is a polyurethane product that can be made tight-fitting without impeding movement. It is used to make active wear, bras, and swimsuits.

Olefin fibre is a fibre used in active wear, linings, and warm clothing. Olefins are hydrophobic, allowing them to dry quickly. A sintered felt of olefin fibres is sold under the trade name Tyvek.

Ingeo is a polylactide fibre blended with other fibres such as cotton and used in clothing. It is more hydrophilic than most other synthetics, allowing it to wick away perspiration.

Lurex is a metallic fibre used in clothing embellishment.

Milk proteins have also been used to create synthetic fabric. Milk or casein fibre cloth was developed during World War I in Germany, and further developed in Italy and America during the 1930s. Milk fibre fabric is not very durable and wrinkles easily, but has a pH similar to human skin and possesses anti-bacterial properties. It is marketed as a biodegradable, renewable synthetic fibre.

Carbon fibre is mostly used in composite materials, together with resin, such as carbon fibre reinforced plastic. The fibres are made from polymer fibres through carbonization.

Textile Fibres

Lichens

Fibre is obtained from the stalk of a plant (*Linum ustiatissimum*) that is from 80 to 120 cm high, with few branches and small flowers, of a colour that varies from white to intense blue, which flowers only for one day. The lichen plant is uprooted in such a way as to obtain the maximum length of the fibres. The stalks left to macerate so that the fibres can free themselves of the rubber like substances that cover them tying them into bundles. After the maceration separation of the textile fibres from the woody residues occurs and then the carding which eliminates the shorter fibres and impurities. At this point the fibre is ready for spinning, which can be dry or humid, *i.e.*, with the passage of the fibres in water. Humid spinning produces a finer, more regular and resistant thread, above all suitable for the production of cloths for clothing. Linen fibres are mixed with cotton, wool, silk, viscose, and polyester and this mixed thread allows many types of cloth. The combination of two fibres allows one to obtain a different "hand", *i.e.*, a consistency and aspect different from those obtained with simple threads. Linen is cultivated in Eastern Europe, Russia, Brazil, China and the Baltic countries, but its quality is not comparable to that of Western Europe France, Belgium and Holland.

Properties

70 per cent composed of cellulose, it absorbs humidity and allows the skin to breathe and therefore it is very indicated in the manufacture of summer clothes. Very resistant, if wetted it can be washed many times without alteration. It becomes softer, sometimes very important for clothes of clothing and for daily use which require frequent washing such as shirts etc.

Treatment of Linen Clothes

White clothes should be washed in the washing machine at 600C, whilst colored ones at a lesser temperature. White clothes should be ironed damp with a very hot iron, even stern, first on the inside, then on the right side. Colored clothes, above all if dark, should be ironed only on the inside. Starching is not needed as with ironing linen returns to being stiff. If you hang the articles folded in a suitcase over a bath of hot water, they will return to their original state the steam will help to stolen the folds.

Cotton is a soft, fluffy staple fibre that grows in a boll, or protective capsule, around the seeds of cotton plants of the genus *Gossypium*. The fibre is almost pure cellulose. Under natural condition, the cotton balls will tend to increase the dispersion of the seeds.

The fibre is most often spun into yarn or thread and used to make a soft, breathable textile. The use of cotton for fabric is known to date to prehistoric times; fragments of cotton fabric dated from 5000 BCE have been excavated in Mexico and the Indus Valley Civilization (modern day Pakistan). Although cultivated since antiquity, it was the invention of the cotton gin that so lowered the cost of production that led to its widespread use, and it is the most widely used natural fibre cloth in clothing today.

Current estimates for world production are about 25 million tonnes annually, accounting for 2.5 per cent of the world's arable land. China is the world's largest producer of cotton, but most of this is used domestically. The United States has been the largest exporter for many years.

There are four commercially grown species of cotton, all domesticated in antiquity:

- ☆ *Gossypium hirsutum* – upland cotton, native to Central America, Mexico, the Caribbean and southern Florida, (90 per cent of world production)
- ☆ *Gossypium barbadense* – known as extra-long staple cotton, native to tropical South America (8 per cent of world production)
- ☆ *Gossypium arboreum* – tree cotton, native to India and Pakistan (less than 2 per cent)
- ☆ *Gossypium herbaceum* – Levant cotton, native to southern Africa and the Arabian Peninsula (less than 2 per cent)

The two New World cotton species account for the vast majority of modern cotton production, but the two Old World species were widely used before the 1900s. While cotton fibres occur naturally in colours of white, brown, pink and green, fears of contaminating the genetics of white cotton have led many cotton-growing locations to ban the growing of coloured cotton varieties, which remain a specialty product.

Uses

Cotton is used to make a number of textile products. These include terrycloth for highly absorbent bath towels and robes; denim for blue jeans; cambric, popularly used in the manufacture of blue work shirts (from which we get the term "blue-collar"); and corduroy, seersucker, and cotton twill. Socks, underwear, and most T-shirts are made from cotton. Bed sheets often are made from cotton. Cotton also is used to make yarn used in crochet and knitting. Fabric also can be made from recycled or recovered cotton that otherwise would be thrown away during the spinning, weaving, or cutting process. While many fabrics are made completely of cotton, some materials blend cotton with other fibres, including rayon and synthetic fibres such as polyester. It can either be used in knitted or woven fabrics, as it can be blended with elastine to make a stretcher thread for knitted fabrics, and apparel such as stretch jeans.

The cottonseed which remains after the cotton is ginned is used to produce cottonseed oil, which, after refining, can be consumed by humans like any other vegetable oil. The cottonseed meal that is left generally is fed to ruminant livestock; the gossypol remaining in the meal is toxic to monogastric animals. Cottonseed hulls can be added to dairy cattle rations for roughage. During the American slavery period, cotton root bark was used in folk remedies as an abortifacient, that is, to induce a miscarriage.

Silk

Silk is a natural protein fibre, some forms of which can be woven into textiles. The protein fibre of silk is composed mainly of fibroin and produced by certain insect larvae to form cocoons. The best-known type of silk is obtained from the cocoons of the larvae of the mulberry silkworm *Bombyx mori* reared in captivity (sericulture). The shimmering appearance of silk is due to the triangular prism-like structure of the silk fibre, which allows silk cloth to refract incoming light at different angles, thus producing different colours.

Silks are produced by several other insects, but generally only the silk of moth caterpillars has been used for textile manufacturing. There has been some research into other silks, which differ at the molecular level. Many silks are mainly produced by the larvae of insects undergoing complete metamorphosis, but some adult insects such as web spinners produce silk, and some insects such as raspy crickets produce silk throughout their lives.

Silk production also occur in hymenoptera (bees, wasps and ants) silverfish, mayflies, thrips, leafhopper, beetles, lacewings, fleas files a and midges. Other types of arthropod produce silk, most notably various arachnids such as spider.

Physical Properties

Silk fibres from the *Bombyx mori* silkworm have a triangular cross section with rounded corners, 5-10 μm wide. The fibroin-heavy chain is composed mostly of beta-sheets, due to a 59-mer amino acid repeat sequence with some variations. The flat surfaces of the fibrils reflect light at many angles, giving silk a natural shine. The cross-section from other silkworms can vary in shape and diameter: crescent-like for *Anaphe* and elongated wedge *fortussah*. Silkworm fibres' are naturally extruded from two silkworm glands as a pair of primary filaments (brin), which are stuck together, with sericin proteins that act like glue, to form a bave. Bave diameters for tussah silk can reach 65 ìm. See cited reference for cross-sectional SEM photographs.

Silk has a smooth, soft texture that is not slippery, unlike many synthetic fibres. Silk is one of the strongest natural fibres but loses up to 20 per cent of its strength when wet. It has a good moisture regain of 11 per cent. Its elasticity is moderate to poor: if elongated even a small amount, it remains stretched. It can be weakened if exposed to too much sunlight. It may also be attacked by insects, especially if left dirty.

Silk is a poor conductor of electricity and thus susceptible to static cling.Unwashed silk chiffon may shrink up to 8 per cent due to a relaxation of the fibre macrostructure, so silk should either be washed prior to garment construction, or dry cleaned. Dry cleaning may still shrink the chiffon up to 4 per cent. Occasionally, this shrinkage can be reversed by a gentle steaming with a press cloth. There is almost no gradual shrinkage no shrinkage due to molecular-level deformation.

Natural and synthetic silk is known to manifest piezoelectric properties in proteins, probably due to its molecular structure. Silkworm silk was used as the standard for the denier, a measurement of linear density in fibres.

Chemical Properties

Silk emitted by the silkworm consists of two main proteins, sericin and fibroin, fibroin being the structural centre of the silk, and sericin being the sticky material surrounding it. Fibroin is made up of the amino acids Gly-Ser-Gly-Ala-Gly-Ala and forms beta pleated sheets. Hydrogen bonds form between chains, and side chains form above and below the plane of the hydrogen bond network.

The high proportion (50 per cent) of glycine, which is a small amino acid, allows tight packing and the fibres' are strong and resistant to breaking. The tensile strength is due to the many interceded hydrogen bonds, and when stretched the force is applied to these numerous bonds and they do not break.

Silk is resistant to most mineral acids, except for sulphuric acid, which dissolves it. It is yellowed by perspiration. Chlorine bleach will also destroy silk fabrics.

Wool is the textile fibre obtained from sheep and certain other animals, including cashmere from goats, mohair from goats, qiviut from muskoxen, angora from rabbits, and other types of wool from camelids.

Wool has several qualities that distinguish it from hair or fur: it is crimped, it is elastic, and it grows in staples (clusters). In the United States the term wool is usually restricted to describing the fibrous protein derived from the specialized skin cells called follicles in sheep, although in the UK it may be used of any long curling fibre such as wood wool, wire wool, etc.

Characteristics

Wool's scaling and crimp make it easier to spin the fleece by helping the individual fibres attach to each other, so they stay together. Because of the crimp, wool fabrics have a greater bulk than other textiles, and retain air, which causes the product to retain heat. Insulation works both ways: Bedouins and Tuaregs use wool clothes to keep heat out and protect the body.

Felting of wool occurs upon hammering or other mechanical agitation because the microscopic barbs on the surface of wool fibres hook together, somewhat like Velcro.

The amount of crimp corresponds to the fineness of the wool fibres. A fine wool like Merino may have up to 100 crimps per inch, while the coarser wools like karakul may have as few as 1 to 2. Hair, by contrast, has little if any scale and no crimp, and little ability to bind into yarn. On sheep, the hair part of the fleece is called kemp. The relative amounts of

Kemp to wool vary from breed to breed, and make some fleeces more desirable for spinning, felting, or carding into batts for quilts or other insulating products, including the famous tweed cloth of Scotland.

Wool fibres' are hydrophilic, meaning they readily absorb moisture, but are not hollow. Wool can absorb moisture almost one-third of its own weight. Wool absorbs sound like many other fabrics. It is generally a creamy white colour, although some breeds of sheep produce natural colours, such as black, brown, silver, and random mixes.

Wool ignites at a higher temperature than cotton and some synthetic fibres'. It has lower rate of flame spread, low heat release, low heat of combustion, and does not melt or drip it forms a char which is insulating and self-extinguishing, and contributes less to toxic gases and smoke than other flooring products, when used in carpets. Wool carpets are specified for high safety environments, such as trains and aircraft. Wool is usually specified for garments for fire fighters, soldiers, and others in occupations where they are exposed to the likelihood of fire.

Wool is resistant to static electricity, as the moisture retained within the fabric conducts electricity, so wool garments are much less likely to spark or cling to the body. The use of wool car seat covers or carpets reduces the risk of a shock when a person touches a grounded object. Wool is considered by the medical profession to be hypoallergenic.

Properties of Wool

The properties of wool result in a material that is multifaceted and multipurpose. It is one of the few **natural products** available that can be made use of in a myriad of ways. From providing the sheep with a house on its back to providing us with insulating wool garments, art products and tree mulches.

The specific properties of wool vary from breed to breed. The variation is why we have a grading system. In understanding the properties we'll take a look at the various characteristics that make wool what it is.

If you are researching wool you will see such terms as fibre and staple, length, coarseness, strength and brightness.

Fibre

Fibre is an individual strand of wool, just like a single strand of hair from your head.

Staple

A staple is a cluster of many, many fibres, like a lock of hair.

Fine or Coarse Fibres can have varying diameters according to the breed of sheep and type of wool. Like human hair, on some individuals the hair is fine (smaller diameter) and on others it is very coarse (larger diameter).

The diameter of the fibre accounts for the durability of wool. Wool can withstand a lot of wear and tear without the fibres breaking. The fineness or coarseness of the wool ultimately determines its end use.

Crimp

Each individual fibre is crimped (picture corrugated cardboard) and the crimp is easy to see in the collective staple.

The crimp varies according to the breed of sheep. Typically if the individual fibres of wool are fine the crimp will be fine. If the crimp is fine there are more crimps (ridges in the cardboard) per length of fibre than if the crimp was heavier.

Wool is **naturally woven** by longer fibres that run across several staples thus holding the fleece together. This is why it is possible to throw the fleece after shearing without it falling apart like hair would. Throwing the fleece is the act of tossing the wool clip up and out to spread it onto a table for skirting (removal of dirty or damaged wool pieces).

Count

If you are looking at yarns you will come across the term 'count'. The count is the spinning quality and is determined by the diameter of the fibre. Since it is not feasible to measure the diameter of individual fibres, the crimp as visually seen in the collective staple is used to make an assumption on the spinning quality.

Length

For spinning, wool has to have length. Fine wool of considerable length will be a highly sought after product. Length is a measurement of the staple without stretching out the crimp.

When processed wool is stretched at several stages. The amount of crimp determines how much the piece of wool can stretch and this is a very important feature. The more stretch wool can give the tighter it can be when returned to original length.

What all this means when speaking of the properties of wool, is that generally a shorter staple with deeper crimp is preferred over a longer staple with flatter crimp that will not stretch as much.

The length of the fibre is one of the properties of wool that will vary significantly from breed to breed. The fibre length plays a role in determining if the wool can be combed or carded. The longer fibres are suitable for combing while the shorter ones are suitable for carding. Wool that is combed will serve a different purpose than the shorter varieties that are carded.

Importance of Natural Fibre

Natural fibres' are major source of livelihoods and food security for millions of small-scale farmers and processors in the world. This has high economic importance in terms of contribution in GDP for many of developing countries. However due to the lack appropriate research and information dissemination, only a few species are identified and extracted commercially leaving many more fibre containing species not identified leading to extinct and disappear in future. Thus awareness in harvesting natural fibre is an issue of global concern not only to the producers and industry but also to the consumers, conservationists and the environmentalists

Celebration of 2009 as the "International Year of Natural Fibber" has grown interest and importance of natural fibre leading to the better market opportunities in local and global arena. Being renewable resource and the carbon neutral, natural fibre products are eco-friendly and also vital to promote in the context of growing global environmental crisis.

Being basically organic, products from natural fibres' are getting attractions throughout the world.

Nepal has comparative advantage on fibre containing non-timber forest species. Due to the variation in climate, topography and vegetation, we have diversity and abundance of fibre containing plants that could be utilized to promote micro and small businesses. It is estimated that in Nepal more than 200 thousands family rely on natural fibre for livelihood and they utilize only 15-20 percent out of total of fibre containing plants. We know these readily available local resources have a huge potential for local as well as international market which can invariably foster local economic growth and create green jobs. Thus sustainable utilization of these not only contribute to national economy but also vital to improve economic base of local people.

Traditionally Nepalese people have been extracting fibres' from a few known plants for producing fabric, clothes, mattresses, ropes etc. Because of the limited knowledge on availability of such plants and technology and skill to commercialize such fibres' we have been loosing its economic value for a long. Hence it is an urgent to step ahead to commercialize the natural fibres' in Nepal.

Manmade Fibre

Man-made fibre industry is an essential part of the textile industry. Such fibres' are more durable, easily washable and free from shrinkage. These are mass produced and their production is not affected by the vagaries of the nature.

These fibres' are mainly divided into two groups: (a) cellulose (rayon an acetate), and (b) non-cellu-lose (nylon polyester, etc). Of these cellulose fibres' are mainly derived from wood pulp (from bamboo, eucalyptus, etc).

History and Development

In India man-made fibre weaving units using imported rayon and synthetic yarns came into being between 1925 and 1935. But the first indigenous rayon manufacturing plant was established by the Travancore Rayons Ltd at Rayapuram (Kerala) in 1945 (production started in 1950).

Two other plants were set up at Mumbai and Hyderabad in the next year. In 1954 fourth plant was set up at Nagada (Madhya Pradesh) by Birla Brothers in 1954. In 1961 the Century Rayon Mills was set up at Mumbai. At present there are about 50 units producing cellulosic and synthetic fabrics. These units have total installed capacity of 1.47 lakh tones with employment potential of30, 000 persons. The industry has an investment of over Rs.280 crores and provides yarns to 1, 10,000 power looms and over 4 lakh handlooms.

Raw Materials

Cellulose pulp derived from bamboo, euca-lyptus and other woods is the basic raw material for producing viscose or acetate rayon yarns. The coun-try produces about 75 per cent of the rayon-grade pulp indigenously and the remaining need is met through import.

The raw materials (caprolactum, naphtha, pollster chips, ethylene, glycol, etc.) re-quired for the production of synthetic fibres' (nylon, pollster, and acrylic) are mostly imported. Recently two public sector plants have been set up at Vadodara (capacity 44,000 tones) to manufacture polypropylene.

Distribution

The man-made fibre industry is capital-inten-sive and is mainly based on imported raw materials.

The industry is mainly associated with large textile houses. Their largest concentration is noticed in Maharashtra, Gujarat, Uttar Pradesh, West Bengal, Tamil Nadu and Delhi. Mumbai and its suburbs (Kalyan, Thane and Goregaon have a large number of man-made fibre units. Other important centres include Vadodara, Kanpur, Kolkata, Chennai, Modinagar, Pune, Hyderabad, Ujjain, Nagpur, Kota, Rayapuram etc. Besides, there are a large number of power looms and handlooms in the decentralised sector associated with man-made fibres'. The impor-tant units manufacturing rayon, nylon filament yarn, nylon tire cord and other types of yarn fibre are as follows:

1. Rayon units-Kagaznagar (Andhra Pradesh), Udhn (near Surat, Gujarat, Junagarh (Gujarat), Rayapuram (Kerala), Birlagram (Himachal Pradesh), Nagda (Madhya Pradesh), Kalyan (near Mumbai, Maharashtra), Pimpri-Pune (Maharashtra), Goregaon (Maharashtra), Kota (Rajasthan), Mettupalayam (Tamilnadu), Kanpur (Uttar Pradesh), and Tribeni (West Bengal).
2. Nylon filament yarn units-J.K. Synthetics, Kota; Garware Nylons Ltd. Pimpri-Pune; Modipan Ltd. Modinagar; Century Enka Ltd. Bhosari-Pune; Stretch Fibres, Nagpur; and the Industrial Develop-ment Corporation of the states of Gujarat (Vadodàra), Haryana(Chandigarh), Karnataka (Bangalore), Tamil Nadu (Chennai), Andhra Pradesh (Hyderabad), Kerala (Thiruvananthapuram), Bihar (Barauni), West Ben-gal (Kolkata), and U.P. (Kanpur).
3. Nylon staple fibre units-J.K. Synthetics, Kota; Arthur Import and Export, Mumbai; and Indian Petrochemical Corporation Ltd. Vadodara
4. Nylon tyre cord units-J.K. Synthetics, Kota (1972); Nirlon, Mumbai; Shree Ram Fibres, Chennai (1975); National Rayon, Kalyan; and Baroda Rayon's, Udhn.
5. Polyester stable fibre units-Chemical and Fibres India Ltd., Thane (1965); Ahmadabad Manufacturing Ltd., Vadodara (1974); Swadesh Polytecs, Ghaziabad (1973), Indian Organic Chemicals, Manali (1973), J.K. Synthetic Ltd., Kota (1972).
6. Polyester filament yarn units-Nylon (Mumbai, 1967); J.K. Synthetics, Kota (1967), Garware Nylons, Pune (1973); Modipon Ltd., Modinagar (1973); Shree Synthetics, Ujjain (1973); Baroda Rayon, Udhna (1976); Petrofils Corporation Ltd. Vadodara.

Production

India produced 61,000 tons of rayon fila-ment yarn; 1, 78,000 tonnes of rayon viscose staple fibre; about 34,000 tonnes of acetate yarn; 29,000 tonnes of nylon filament yarn; and 5, 23,000 tonnes of pollster staple fibre in 1998-99.

Role of Silk Fibers amongst Natural Fibers

Silk fibre is the finest and also quite strong amongst the natural fibre. Besides, its fineness, it has a very good lusture, smoothness, and elastic and that is why silk fibre is known as "Queen of fibre". It has more value than any other natural fibre. The tenacity of silk fibres is from 3 to 4 gm per denier. Elongation of silk is from 16 to 22. A highly valued animal fibre, silk has long been used for the production of luxurious textiles for the finest quality. It is one of the most ancient and preferred fibre in the world due to its natural texture, strength and fineness. Silk has an economic value that is higher than that of other natural fibres such as cotton and wool because of its superior characteristics. The steadily growing demand for silk in the silk consuming countries indicates excellent opportunities for any country to increase her silk production. The importance of silk as a regrowing raw material for textiles and other goods cannot be appreciated from its minute based share in the world fiber production, but rather from its value trade and processing. Despite the triumphal advance of synthetic and other natural fibres, silk maintain its place in the raw material market, in the textile and clothing industries, and in retail trade because of its unique properties.

Silk cover a wide range of applications from ready-to-wear articles and home textiles to technical fabrics and cosmetic fibres. Ready-to-wear articles include mainly mens and womens wear such as shirts, blouses, scarves, shawls ties and high quality evening clothes, as well as lining materials, underwear, night clothes, national dress (kinonos and sarongs). In home textiles, silk is most often used for furnishing fabrics, upholstery, wallpaper, velvet, carpet etc. in technical fabrics, silk is employed for typewriter ribbon, insulating material for cable covering and surgical articles. Silk powder is added to lipstick, skin cream, and shop; fibroin or sericin is added to shampoos and lotions. Silk is also a very suitable material for sewing and embroidery thread because it can be dyed to give any shade.

1.3. Silk Industry in World with Special Reference to China, Japan and India. Present status and trends of developments, Silk industry in silk producing states of India *viz.*, Bengal, Karnataka, Tamil Nadu, Andhra Pradesh and Jammu and Kashmir, mulberry areas, sericulture villagers, no. of families, cocoon and silk production

Silk Industry in World

Thailand

Silk is produced year round in Thailand by two types of silkworms, the cultured Bombycidae and wild Saturniidae. Most production is after the rice harvest in the southern and northeast parts of the country. Women traditionally weave silk on hand looms, and pass the skill on to their daughters as weaving is considered to be a sign of maturity and eligibility for marriage. Thai silk textiles often use complicated patterns in various colours and styles. Most regions of Thailand have their own typical silks. A single thread filament is too thin to use on its own so women combine many threads to produce a thicker, usable fibre. They do this by hand-reeling the threads onto a wooden spindle to produce a uniform strand of raw silk. The process takes around 40 hours to produce a half kilogram of Thai silk.

Many local operations use a reeling machine for this task, but some silk threads are still hand-reeled. The difference is that hand-reeled threads produce three grades of silk: two fine grades that are ideal for lightweight fabrics, and a thick grade for heavier material.

The silk fabric is soaked in extremely cold water and bleached before dying to remove the natural yellow colouring of Thai silk yarn. To do this, skeins of silk thread are immersed in large tubs of hydrogen peroxide. Once washed and dried, the silk is woven on a traditional hand operated loom.

Middle East

In Islamic teachings, Muslim men are forbidden to wear silk. Many religious jurists believe the reasoning behind the prohibition lies in avoiding clothing for men that can be considered feminine or extravagant. There are disputes regarding the amount of silk a fabric can consist of (*e.g.*, whether a small decorative silk piece on a cotton caftan is permissible or not) for it to be lawful for men to wear but the dominant opinion of most Muslim scholars is that the wearing of silk by men is forbidden. Modern attire has raised a number of issues, including (for instance) the permissibility of wearing silk neckties, which are masculine articles of clothing.

Despite injunctions against silk for men, silk has retained its popularity in the Islamic world because of its permissibility for women. The Muslim Moors brought silk with them to Spain during their conquest of the Iberian Peninsula.

Medieval and Modern Europe

Italy was the most important producer of silk during the Medieval age. One notable centre was the Italian city-state of Lucca which largely financed itself through silk-production and silk-trading, beginning in the 12th century. Other Italian cities involved in silk production were Genoa, Venice and Florence.

The Silk Exchange in Valencia from the 15th century, where previously in 1348 also *perxal* (percale) was traded as some kind of silk, dramatically illustrates the power and wealth of one of the great Mediterranean mercantile cities.

France

In France, since the 15th century silk production was cantered around the city of Lyon where many mechanic tools for mass production were first introduced in the 17th century.

James attempted to establish silk production in England, purchasing and planting 100,000 mulberry trees, some on land adjacent to Hampton Court Palace, but they were of a species unsuited to the silk worms, and the attempt failed. in 1732 John Guardivaglio set up a silk throwing enterprise at Logwood mill in Stockport, and in 1744, Burton Mill was erected in Macclesfield and in 1753 Old Mill was built in Congleton. These three towns remained the centre of the English silk throwing industry until silk throwing was replaced by silk waste spinning. British enterprise also established silk filature in Cyprus in 1928. In England in the mid 20th century, raw silk was produced at Lulling stone in Kent. Silkworms were raised and reeled under the direction of Zoe Lady Hart Dyke.

North America

King James introduced silk-growing to the American colonies around 1619, ostensibly to discourage tobacco planting. The Shakers in Kentucky adopted the practice. In the 19th century a new attempt at a silk industry began with European-born workers in Paterson, New Jersey, and the city became a US silk centre. Manchester, Connecticut emerged as centre of the silk industry in America from the late 19th through the mid-20th century. The Cheney Brothers Historic District showcases mills refurbished as apartments and includes nearby museums.

World war II interrupted the silk trade from Japan. Silk prices increased dramatically and US industry began to look for substitutes, which led to the use of synthetics such as nylon. Synthetic silks have also been made from lyocell, a type of cellulose fibre, and are often difficult to distinguish from real silk.

Malaysia

In Terengganu, which is now part of Malaysia, second generation of silkworm was being imported as early as 1764 for its silk textile industry, especially songket. However, since the 1980s, Malaysia is no longer engaged in sericulture but does only plant mulberry trees.

Vietnam

According to Book of Han, in Lac Viet people have known the process of making silk since 2000 BC: "In a year, they have two rice crops and eight silk crops.In Vietnamese legend, silk had appeared at the sixth dynasty of Hung Vuong.

Silk Industries in China

According to Chinese tradition, the **history of silk** began in the 27th century BCE. Its use was confined to China until the Silk Road opened at some point during the latter half of the first millennium BCE. China maintained its virtual monopoly over silk for another thousand years. Not confined to clothing, silk was also used for a number of other applications, including writing, and the colour of silk worn was an important indicator of social class during the Tang Dynasty.

Silk cultivation spread to Japan in around 300 CE, and by 522 the Byzantines managed to obtain silkworm eggs and were able to begin silkworm cultivation. The Arabs also began to manufacture silk during this same time. As a result of the spread of sericulture, Chinese silk exports became less important, although they still maintained dominance over the luxury silk market. The Crusades brought silk production to Western Europe, in particular to many Italian states, which saw an economic boom exporting silk to the rest of Europe. Changes in manufacturing techniques also began to take place during the Middle Ages, with devices such as the spinning first appearing. During the 16th century France joined Italy in developing a successful silk trade, though the efforts of most other nations to develop a silk industry of their own were unsuccessful.

The Industrial Revolution changed much of Europe's silk industry. Due to innovations in spinning cotton, it became much cheaper to manufacture and therefore caused more expensive silk production to become less mainstream. New weaving technologies, however, increased the efficiency of production. Among these was the Jacquard loom, developed for silk embroidery. An epidemic of several silkworm diseases caused production to fall, especially in France, where the industry never recovered. In the 20th century Japan and China regained their earlier role in silk production, and China is now once again the world's largest producer of silk.

Spread of Production

Although silk was well known in Europe and most of Asia, China was able to keep a near monopoly on silk production. The monopoly was defended by an imperial decree, condemning to death anyone attempting to export silkworms or their eggs. Only around the year 300 CE did a Japanese expedition succeed in taking some silkworm eggs and four young Chinese girls, who were forced to teach their captors the art of sericulture. Techniques of sericulture were subsequently introduced to Japan on a larger scale by frequent diplomatic exchanges between the 8th century and 9th centuries.

Starting in the 4th century BCE silk began to reach the West by merchants who would exchange it for gold, ivory, horses or precious stones. Up to the frontiers of the Roman Empire, silk became a monetary standard for estimating the value of different products. Hellenistic Greece appreciated the high quality of the Chinese goods and made efforts to plant mulberry trees and breed silkworms in the Mediterranea basin. Sassanid Persia controlled the trade of silk destined for Europe and Byzantium.

Much later, following the Crusades, techniques of silk production began to spread across Western Europe. In 1147 while Byzantine emperor Manuel I Komnenos was focusing all his efforts on the Second Crusade, the Norman king Roger II of Sicily attacked Corinth and Thebes, two important centres of Byzantine silk production. They took the crops and silk production infrastructure, and deported all the workers to Palermo, thereby causing the Norman silk industry to flourish. The sack of Constantinople by the Fourth Crusade in 1204 brought decline to the city and its silk industry, and many artisans left the city in the early 13th century. Italy developed a large domestic silk industry after 2000 skilled weavers came from Constantinople. Many also chose to settle in Avignon to furnish the popes of Avignon.

The sudden boom of the silk industry in the Italian state of Lucca, starting in the 11th and 12th centuries was due to much Sicilian, Jewish, and Greek settlement, alongside many other immigrants from neighbouring cities in southern Italy. With the loss of many Italian trading posts in the Orient, the import of Chinese styles drastically declined. Gaining momentum, in order to satisfy the rich and powerful bourgeoisie's demands for luxury fabrics, the cities of Lucca, Genoa, Venice and

Florence were soon exporting silk to all of Europe. In 1472 there were 84 workshops and at least 7000 craftsmen in Florence alone.

Silk Since the Industrial Revolution

The start of the Industrial Revolution was marked by a massive boom in the textile industry, with remarkable technological innovations made, led by the cotton industry of Great Britain. In its early years, there were often disparities in technological innovation between different stages of fabric manufacture, which encouraged complementary innovations. For example, spinning progressed much more rapidly than weaving.

The silk industry, however, did not gain any benefit from innovations in spinning, as silk is naturally already a thread. Making silk, silver, and gold brocades is a very delicate and precise process, with each colour needing its own dedicated shuttle. In the 17th century and 18th centuries progress began to be made in the simplification and standardization of silk manufacture, with many advances following one after another.

Bouchon and Falcon's punched card loom appeared in 1775, later improved on by Jacques de Vaucanson. Later, Joseph-Marie Jacquard improved on the designs of Falcon and Vaucanson, introducing the revolutionary Jacquard loom, which allowed a string of punched cards to be processed mechanically in the correct sequence. The punched cards of the Jacquard loom were a direct precursor to the modern computer, in that they gave a (limited) form of programmability. Punched cards themselves were carried over to computers, and were ubiquitous until their obsolescence in the 1970s. From 1801 embroidery became highly mechanized due to the effectiveness of the Jacquard loom. The mechanism behind the Jacquard loom even allowed complex designs to be mass-produced.

The Jacquard loom was immediately denounced by workers, who accused it of causing unemployment, but soon it had become vital to the industry. The loom was declared public property in 1806, and Jacquard was rewarded with a pension and a royalty on each machine. In 1834 there were a total of 2885 Jacquard looms in Lyon alone. The Canut revolt in 1831 foreshadowed many of the larger worker uprisings of the Industrial Revolution. The canuts occupied the city of Lyon, and would not relinquish it until a bloody repression by the army, led by Marshal Soult. A second revolt, similar to the first, took place in 1834.

Decline in the European Silk Industry

The first silkworm diseases began to appear in 1845, creating an epidemic. Among them are pébrine, caused by the microsporidia *Nosema bombycis*, grasserie, caused by a virus, flacherie, caused by eating infected mulberry leaves or white muscardine disease, caused by the fungus *Beauve bassiana*. The epidemic grew to a massive scale, and after having attacked the silkworms, other viruses began to infect the mulberry trees. The chemist Jean-Baptiste Dumas, French minister of agriculture, was charged with stopping the epidemic. In face of sericulturers' call for help, he asked Louis Pasteur to study the disease, starting in 1865. For many years, Pasteur thought that pébrine was not a contagious disease. In 1870 he changed his view, and measures were enacted that caused the disease to decline.

Nevertheless, the increase in the price of silkworm cocoons and the reduction in importance of silk in the garments of the bourgeoisie in the 19th century caused the decline of the silk industry in Europe. The opening of the Suez Canal in 1869 and the silk shortage in France reduced the price of importing Asian silk, particularly from China and Japan.

Starting from the Long Depression (1873 – 1896), Lyonnais silk production had become totally industrialized, and hand looms were rapidly disappearing. The 19th century saw the textile industry's progress caused by advances in chemistry. The synthesis of aniline was used to make mauveine (aniline purple) dye and the synthesis of quinine was used to make indigo dye. In 1884 Count Hilaire de Chardonnet invented artificial silk and in 1891 opened a factory dedicated to the production of artificial silk (viscose), which cost much less and in part replaced natural silk.

The Silk Industry in Japan in The 1800s

In one of its publications, the Japan Society presents its views on how silk originated in China. Around 1700 BC, the fourteen-year-old Queen of the third Emperor of China, began the cultivation of wild silkworms at the suggestion of her husband. The Emperor wanted to know how silkworms were raised and whether the Chinese people could raise them generally so that they might make garments. So successful were the Queen's experiments that she was named "The Goddess of the Silk Worm". This story seems more or less consistent with what we have read and learned in class.

It was not long before the Chinese were weaving gorgeous garments from silk. However, the garments were so expensive that only the Emperors of China could afford them. In any event, the silk industry thrived and China began to sell her silks to Persia. The Persians were the people who introduced silk to the rest of the world. At that time, the Persian's didn't have a clue about the origins of silk. This was natural, since death was the penalty for anyone caught sneaking silk worms out of the borders of China, or revealing the process by which silk was obtained.

Many were the theories in Europe as to just where silk came from. Some thought beetles were the source, some wondered if it came from sheep, and still others marvelled whether it could be a kind of earth that was combed out fine! Soon people began to wonder how to weave it. According to popular belief, Pamphila, daughter of the Greek king Platoes of the Island of Cos, discovered in 400 BC the art of unravelling the heavy Chinese silk and re-weaving it to understand how it was woven. For almost nine centuries after that, silk in Europe was manufactured by unraveling and reweaving the Chinese silk products.

The existence of such a valuable and exquisite commodity naturally led other countries to be curious about the secret behind its making.

The silkworm is mentioned in the oldest Japanese myths, but its historical record only begins with the naturalization of a Chinese man, who came to Japan in 199 AD, carrying with him a cluster of silkworm eggs. It is not known whether these eggs were smuggled in or not. However, we assume they were in fact smuggled in, due to the fear of the death penalty. According to the Japan Society, ninety years later, several other Chinese experts went to Japan and engaged in the rearing of silkworms in various districts. This account of the Japan Society seems rather inconsistent since the Chinese guarded their secret rather fiercely. Perhaps by then, the Chinese allowed the spread of this precious knowledge. In any case, the sericulture industry in Japan can be assumed to have dated from between the second and the third century AD.

In 600 AD, a new tax system was initiated in Japan, whereby people had to pay taxes in silk textures. We are familiar with this system since many countries, including China, followed this system of paying taxes using silk. This system automatically brought about a dramatic increase in the production of silk fabrics. A law in 701 AD ordered that every family should plant a certain number of mulberry trees according to its socioeconomic standing.

Besides clothing, silk also had other uses. The parasol and fan, both of which were considered a part of any respectable lady's costume at a social event, were both made of silk stretched over a delicate bamboo framework. Silk was also employed in the making of lanterns. Instead of using wax in their lanterns, the Japanese used a type of vegetable fat that was coated on to a paper cylinder wrapped in silk.

Japan however, did maintain relations with two countries during the early part of the Tokugawa reign. These two countries were Holland and China, the latter from which she imported silk since domestic production didn't satisfy domestic demands.

During the Tokugawa period, the Fukushima Prefecture's Shindatsu district was the most important silk producing region in Japan during the period in question. This was not the only silk producing region at the time. Both Nagano and Gumma prefectures also produced silk, but on a smaller scale.

In order to make silkworm egg cards, the very best cocoons were selected for breeding purposes. The moths were permitted to break through the cocoons, mate and lay eggs. These eggs were placed on a sheet, which was hung up to dry for a few days, until their colour turned black (the eggs are sticky and hence adhere to the sheets). After the eggs turned black, lime powder would be sprinkled over them and the sheets would be folded up and stored until the following winter. These sheets were then taken out and rinsed in either salt water or cold tea for about 10 days to kill off the weaker eggs. (How the silk producers knew which eggs were weaker and which eggs could be disposed of is quite a mystery, especially since the 'strong' eggs didn't hatch till the following year either! Alternatively, maybe they didn't know which eggs were weaker beforehand, but rinsed them so that the weaker ones wouldn't hatch, and the peasants ''t produce lower quality silk). In any event, the eggs would then be stored again until spring, when they were taken out to hatch. In the latter part of the eighteenth and the early part of the nineteenth century, wholesale trading houses in important metropolitan areas established branches in Shindatsu and contracted with local merchants to buy these egg cards and raw silk on consignment.

Practices developed during the reign of the Shogunate however, were not mechanized, and sericulture was highly labour-intensive. Feeding the silkworms, cleaning the rearing trays several times a day to prevent disease to both the worm and those involved with the raising of the worms, and regulating the temperature all demanded a large number of laborers. As a result of high labour costs, the economies of scale were severely limited.

A look at the sericulture industry during the first half of the nineteenth century also suggests that small-scale production was more the norm than the exception. Most people had a small room at home that was well ventilated and had sufficient light to rear the silkworms. Large trays were stacked on one side of the room, and silkworms were fed with mulberry leaves on these trays. When the worms reached their full size, they were placed on twigs and branches and allowed to spin their cocoons. The cocoons were picked from the branches and silk was reeled off them using both hand and foot power. The most important reason that silk rearing was undertaken by a large number of small peasants was that small families could contribute the labour of its members, rather than hire additional workers and add to their costs. Women tended to do most of the sericulture work in addition to housework, while men worked in the rice fields. The fact that silkworm rearing did not require large tracts of land further enabled small families to engage in the production of silk. Moreover, the fact that technology about genetic improvements in both mulberry and silkworm strains was freely disseminated, drove a large number of small farmers to rear the silkworms in their homes.

Until 1860, sericulture was taxed at a low rate during the reign of the Shogunate, and this was another reason that attracted small peasants to this occupation. Crops grown on unirrigated and comparatively infertile soil were not taxed as much as those grown on highly fertile soils. Villages specializing in egg-card manufacture began to pay an annual fee, and braziers used to boil cocoons were taxed lightly, but for the most part, sericulture was not taxed directly, which contributed to its being a family cantered industry.

As mentioned earlier, the Tokugawa government was formed in an atmosphere in which foreigners were mistrusted due to the fear of the insurgence of Christianity and as a result, the Japanese restricted their foreign contacts to the Chinese and Dutch. Russian and British efforts to end Japan's policy of national seclusion had as yet achieved little but news of China's defeat by Great Britain in the Opium War (1839-1842) gave confirmation of the fears of Japan's ruling elite about Western power and intentions.

While insecurity was creeping up amongst the officials, problems began in the villages. Peasants produced raw silk, and sold them at local fairs in the villages while large producers engaged in the manufacture of silkworm egg cards. In the 1860s, several silk taxes were imposed and had important repercussions on the sericulture industry which led to widespread revolts among the peasants. In the autumn of 1864, two wealthy peasants, who were spokesmen for large-scale producers in Shindatsu wrote to the Bakufu, complaining about the declining standard in silkworm egg card production and calling for rigorous inspection to enforce the high quality needed to protect their trade. The two peasants proposed to be the inspectors of locally produced silkworm eggs, and they also asked to be the ones to collect the taxes directly.

Firstly, in Europe (1855 -1870) the silkworm disease had produced such ravages in the silk industry that the end of the industry seemed not far off. Many expedients and remedies were tried. Fresh silkworms were brought from China and Japan numerous times but even they succumbed to the disease. It was the great French scientist, Louis Pasteur, who rescued the silk industry in 1870. He found out that the silkworms had been suffering from two diseases, pebrine and flacherie, and that the spread of these two diseases could be prevented by careful segregation of healthy worms from those diseased.

Secondly, the Taiping Rebellion (1850-1864) in China did great damage to the sericulture districts as well as the urban silk weaving industry when its forces struck the lower Yangtze valley in the early 1860s. The extent and nature of this damage was believed to have been disastrous for silk exports.

As a result of these two catastrophes, the Japanese silk industry received hardly any competition and flourished and even spread to new areas where they had not been as profitable.

By the end of the 1860s and the beginning of the 1870s, the silk industry in China and Europe began to recover while the quality of Japan's silk deteriorated. As a result, the Ministry of Civil Affairs took up the matter and concluded that there were two main reasons for the decline of the silk industry. One of the reasons was the fact that producers were only exporting as much as possible to get the highest profit and disregarding the quality of their silk and its production methods. The other reason was the fact that the nation did not have good machinery and the necessary skills required to produce superior quality silk. The ultimate solution given was simply to acquire the Western techniques and machinery.

This marked the beginning of the mechanization of the silk industry in Japan. This mechanization was technically simple. The process consisted merely of turning the reel by steam or water-power instead of by hand or foot, thus producing a silk filament of brighter luster, of more uniform size and of greater strength, with greater speed. The Western-style mechanization also did not cause a cut down on the labour force as the skills of the handicraft veterans were still required as the cocoons still had to be prepared, the filaments started on the reel and splices made when breaks occurred by hand. Women comprised the majority of the employees in the silk factories, thus continuing the tradition. With the introduction of more advanced methods of production and the setting up of numerous silk-reeling mills and factories throughout Japan, sericulture progressed greatly under the Meiji rule.

Sericulture Industry in India

The technique of Silk production is an agro-based industry, playing an eminent role in the rural economy of India. Silk-fibre is a protein produced from the silk glands of silkworms. The annual production of silk in the world is estimated at 103,627 tonnes of which china contribute 84,000 tonnes respectively. South Korea, USSA and India are the other leading Sericulture countries in the world. To meet the domestic demand of raw silk, India imports silk from Chin, Uzbekistan, Vietnam and other countries. The total volume of imports during 2010-2011 was 5870 tonnes valued at Rs 9384.4 million as can be observed.

Apart from raw silk, India also imports natural silk yarn and silk and silk fabrics. India imported natural silk yarn worth Rs 1473.7 million and Rs 6201.6 million of fabrics during 2010-2011.

Among the developing countries, India enjoys a very favourable position for the present status of silk production of 16,322 (metric tonnes) because the low cost of labour. Sericulture is ideally suited for improving the rural economy of the country; it is practiced as a contributory industry to agriculture.

Background of the Industry

In developing countries like India, agriculture and agro-based industries play a vital role in the improvement of rural economy. The limited availability of land and agriculture being confined to one or two seasons in the year, have made villages to look for supporting rural industries, such as sericulture. The agriculturists in regions where the ecological conditions are favourable adopt agriculture and sericulture simultaneously. It is a cottage industry and provides work for the womenfolk in the rural areas in rearing silk worms, while the male members work in the fields.

Five varieties of silkworms are reared in India for producing this natural fibre. *Bombyx mori,* the silk worm, feeds on the leaves of *Morus alba* to produce the best quality of fibre among the different varieties of silk produced in the country. *Antherea assama* is confined to only Brahmaputra Valley of India of India in the world. It produces the famous muga silk. Tasar silk is a product of Antherea mylitta, which feeds on *Terminalia tomentosa* grown in the thick jungles of Bihar, Madhya Pradesh and Orissa. The recent introduction of Antherea royeli and Antherea perniyi has enabled the country to produce the oak tasar silk, *Phylosamia ricini*, the eri silkworm, which feeds of Ricinus communis, is raised in Assam and Orissa commercially.

Mulberry silk is produce extensively in the states of Karnataka, West Bengal and Jammu and Kashmir. About 85 percent of the country's production is contributed by the Karnataka state by rearing multivoltine hybrids of silkworm and this activity enables the sericulturists to harvest five to six crops in a year. Jammu and Kashmir reared during autumn and spring, producing silk by rearing pure bivoltine silkworms. Other states, namely, Andhra Pradesh, Assam, Tamil Nadu, Uttar Pradesh, Himachal Pradesh and Punjab, contribute only 1.8 percent to the total production of mulberry Silk in India.

Silk Industry in Silk Producing States of India *viz.*, Bengal, Karnataka, Tamil Nadu, Andhra Pradesh and Jammu and Kashmir, Mulberry Areas, Sericulture Villagers, No. of Families, Cocoon and Silk Production

Sericulture which was practiced only in the traditional states of Karnataka, Jammu and Kashmir, Tamil Nadu, Andhra Pradesh and West Bengal has now spread to the other non- traditional states. The combination of factors including the new awareness of the economics of Sericulture operations and the thrust given by government agencies including CSB backed multi-lateral aid has resulted in a near uniform spread of this industry in new areas all over the country. In the recent years a number of schemes have been initiated for the propagation of mulberry silkworm rearing in the non- traditional areas using highly disease resistant silkworm races, developed indigenously in the government owned research institutes.

West Bengal

West Bengal is the third largest mulberry silk producing state after Karnataka and Andhra Pradesh. Mulberry sericulture is traditional industry in famous for the handloom woven designs.

Mulberry sericulture is practised in Malda, Murshidabad, Birbhum and West Dinapur districts. Sericulture development project is being implemented in West Bengal by the CSB and the state Govt. at a total cost of Rs. 966.44 lakh for a period of five years. The project aims at increasing the production of raw silk by 390 tonnes per annum in West Bengal. Tasar silk worm rearing is practiced in the district of purulia, Midnapur, and Birbbum. Eri culture is confined to coochbihar and jalpaiguri districts. Efforts are being made to introduce muga silkworm rearing by exploiting the nature grown muga food plants in Coochbihar district.

The state Government has proposed implementation of a National Sericulture project with external assistance at a total cost of 52.23 crores over a period of five years. The project covers 7,200 hectares of area under mulberry for production of additional 8,320 tonnes Cocoon and 770 metric tonnes of raw silk. The various infrastructure facilities proposed under the project are 15 seed farms, nine P2/P1 grainages, 500 chawkie rearing centres, 11 cocoon market, 59 technical service centres, two training schools, one silk exchange and eight cocoon testing units.

Karnataka

The state is considered to be the "Silk bowl "of the country accounting for 60 percent of total raw silk production. Presently sericulture is being practiced in about 14,500 villages covering almost all the districts of the state. Karnataka is the number one silk producing state, contributing two-third of the total raw silk output (Datta, 2005). In Karnataka, 1, 78,904 farmers, cultivated 91,434 hectares mulberry distributed in twenty-eight districts. Inspite of severe drought persisted in some parts of the state, 10,544 hectares mulberry was newly planted. During 2007-08, cross breed cocoon production was 58,211 MT and 2,585 MT of bivoltine cocoon were produced, totaling to 60,796 MT. Cross breed raw silk production was 7838.870 MT and bivoltine raw silk production was 400.775 MT, totaling to 8239.645 MT. The average cocoon yield for cross breed was 53.80Kg and 44.38Kg for bivoltine per100 dfls and the overall yield was 53.31Kg/100dfls (*Source*: Annual Report for the year 2007-08 Department of Sericulture, Karnataka).

The production of raw silk in Karnataka is mainly confined to traditional belt comprising Kolar, Mandya, Tumkur, Chammarajnagar, Mysore, Bangalore urban and Ramanagaram districts covering 81.18 percent of mulberry area producing 93.14 percent of raw silk. In these districts, sericulture is being practiced as a major commercial crop (Madhu Prasad, 2002).

Kolar

In Karnataka, Kolar district stands first in the state in activities related to sericulture. Sericulture in the Kolar district has long history dating back to the earlier part of the 19th century. Kolar district belongs to semi arid drought-prone region. The major source of employment is from agriculture, dairy and sericulture, hence it is popularly known as the land of "Silk, Milk and Gold". The district of Kolar in Karnataka has the honour of being one of the producers of the highest quantity of cocoons in the state. Now, sericulture has deep roots in almost all the taluks of the district. Kolar district is comprised of 05 taluks, which are found practicing sericulture for livelihood. In Kolar, the acreage under mulberry is 20130 hectares. The cocoon production of cross breed was 14083 MT and bivoltine was 469 MT during the year 2007-08. The raw silk production of cross breed was 1904.50 MT and bivoltine was 72.12 MT. Mulberry is the major commercial crop practiced in the area followed by sugarcane and vegetables under irrigated and Ragi, Groundnut, pulses are grown under rainfed conditions in the district.

Mandya

According to Hindu legend, sage Mandavya had performed penance in this land. Since then, this place is called as Mandya. Mandya district popularly known as "land of Sugar" come in to existence on 1st of July 1939. Mandya is about 90 Kms from Bangalore, on Bangalore-Mysore highway. This district is very much prosperous with sizable area in both agriculture as well as sericulture under irrigated conditions. The rich endowment of resources enables the sericulture and agriculture on commercial venture too. Mandya district consists of seven taluks. The acreage under mulberry was 15008 hectares. Cross breed cocoon production was 10087 MT and bivoltine cocoon production was 390 MT. The cross breed raw silk production was 1363.10 MT and bivoltine raw silk production was 60.46 MT during the year 2007-08.

Tumkur

It is one of the progressive districts of Karnataka situated in the southern part of Karnataka. Tumkur is 70 Kms from capital city of Bangalore. It consists of 10 taluks and has an area 10606 sq. kms. The prominent crops are coconut, Paddy, Groundnut, Sericulture, Jowar and Ragi. Coconut is the commercial crop and in recent days sericulture place a vital role in improving the economy of the district. In Tumkur district, the mulberry acreage is 2511 hectares. The cocoon production of cross breed was 11850 MT and bivoltine cocoon production was 230 MT during the year 2007-08. The raw silk production of cross breed was 250 MT and bivoltine was 35.65 MT.

Bangalore Urban

Bangalore lies in the south-east of the state of Karnataka. The majority of the city of Bangalore lies in the Bangalore urban district of Karnataka and the surrounding rural areas are a part of the Bangalore rural district. Bangalore Urban district came into being in 1986, with the partition of the erstwhile Bangalore district into Bangalore urban and Bangalore rural districts. The agricultural activity in this district is less in comparison to Bangalore rural district. The area under mulberry was 1556 hectares and cross breed cocoon production was 685 MT and bivoltine cocoon production was 252 MT. The cross breed raw silk production was 92.56 MT and bivoltine cocoon production was 39.07 MT during the year 2007-08.

Ramanagaram

Ramanagaram district is located in the south-eastern corner of Karnataka state. Ramanagaram and Kanakapura are major silk producing areas in the district. By and large Ramanagaram district is agricultural based and Ragi is the main crop though mulberry is raised over considerable tracts. Ramanagaram has 8808ha area under mulberry. The cross breed cocoon production was 8861 MT and bivoltine cocoon production was 109 MT during the year 2007-08.The cross breed raw silk production was 1197 MT and bivoltine raw silk production was 16.99 MT.

Andhra Pradesh

Andhra Pradesh is the second largest producer of mulberry silk with 5375 MT in the country after Karnataka (8239.665 MT). The area under mulberry is 37,000 hectares covering one lakh farmers. In Andhra Pradesh, sericulture is a sustainable economic activity and is practiced in almost all the districts. However, Chittoor and Anantapur districts of Rayalaseema region adjacent to Karnataka contribute to more than 80 per cent of total raw silk production in the state.

Tamil Nadu

Tamil Nadu occupies fourth position in the country in silk production. Now it is working with an aim to occupy third position. At present 30,000 farmers are practicing sericulture in the state and area under mulberry cultivation is 14126 hectares. The total dfls consumed during the year 2007-08 was 151.40 lakhs and cocoon production was 9675.7 MT. The raw silk production was 321.8 MT. Sericulture provided employment opportunities to around 1, 75,600 persons as on 31.03.2008 (Source: Annual Report, DOS, Tamil Nadu). Now the sericulture has taken roots in almost all districts, more particularly in Salem, Dharmapuri, Erode, Coimbatore, Namakal, Vellore etc.

The state government had proposed to implement a national sericulture project in the state with external assistance at a total cost of Rs 40.71 corers over a period of five years. The project covers 1200 hectare area under mulberry production of additional 7,938 tonnes of cocoons and 860 tonnes of raw silk. The project is implemented from 1989-90. The various infrastructure facilities was proposed under this project are 11 seed farms, p2/p1 grainages, 100 chawkie rearing centres, 15 cocoon markets, 82 technical service centre, one training school, five reelers training centres and four reeling units.

Jammu and Kashmir

Sericulture is traditional industry in the state of Jammu and Kashmir. The state with favourable climate is highly congenial for production of bivoltine silk. Presently in state about 3,806 acres cultivation that is of bushes type. Today the sericulture industry is providing part time employment to about 30,000 families in the state besides whole time employment to over 5,000 persons in different sectors of sericulture industry paving the way for the speedy development of the sector. Jammu and Kashmir is the only state where entire raw silk is produced in the government filatures.

The central silk board has drawn a project for development of oak tasar industry in North Eastern and North Western states including Jammu and Kashmir. The project of Rs. 45.51 crores for additional raw silk production of 137 tonnes annually.

The state has proposed implementation of National sericulture development project of Rs 25.93 crores a period of five years. The project covers 2,750 hectare of area under mulberry production of additional 420 tonnes of cocoons and 40 tonnes raw silk. The various infrastructure facilities proposed under the project are eight seed farms, six P2/P1 grainages, 450 Chawki rearing centres, 3 cocoons markets, 30 technical service, 10 nursery farms, 2 training schools, 10 green houses, 2 training centres for reeling and one silk exchange.

Area Cultivated with Mulberry in India

Mulberry foliage is the only food for the silkworm (*Bombyx mori*) and is grown under varied climatic conditions ranging from temperate to tropics. Mulberry leaf is a major economic component in sericulture since the quality and quantity of leaf produced per unit area has a direct bearing on cocoon harvest. In India, most states have taken up sericulture as an important agro industry with excellent results. The total acreage of mulberry in India is around 282,244 ha. The details of area under mulberry cultivation in different states in India are shown in the table given below:

Area Under Mulberry Cultivation in different States

States	Area (ha)
ANDHRA PRADESH	38,084
ASSAM	2,813
JAMMU and KASHMIR	4,717
KARNATAKA	166,000
KERALA	1,164
MADHYA PRADESH	2,043
MANIPUR	*25,975
TAMIL NADU	9,491
UTTAR PRADESH	5,665
WEST BENGAL	21,358
OTHER	4,934
TOTAL	282,244

1.4. Characteristics of Sericulture Industry, International Demand of Silk and Constraints in Silk Production like Labour and Environmental Conditions

The Indian silk industry is preparing to witness sweeping changes. What the Indian silk industry will look like after a decade from now is more unpredictable than it used to be a decade ago. The world's second largest silk producer, recipient of lavish attentions of royalty until the British raj, carefully nurtured by the British rulers until 1930s, recognized as a thrust area in the post independent regime, subject of protectionist government policies even in the post liberalization period... the distinctions of silk sector are many.

In India, sericulture is not only a tradition but also a living culture. It is a farm-based, labour intensive and commercially attractive economic activity falling under the cottage and small-scale sector. It particularly suits rural-based farmers, entrepreneurs and artisans, as it requires low investment but, with potential for relatively higher returns. It provides income and employment to the rural poor especially farmers with small land-holdings and the marginalized and weaker sections of the society.

Characteristic of Sericulture Industry

High Employment Potential

60 lakh persons are engaged in various sericulture activities in the country. It is estimated that Sericulture can generate employment @ 11 man days per kg of raw silk production (in on-farm and off-farm activities) throughout the year. This potential is par-excellence and no other industry generates this kind of employment, especially in rural areas, hence, sericulture is used as a tool for rural reconstruction.

Provides Vibrancy to Village Economies

About 57 per cent of the gross value of silk fabrics flows back to the cocoon growers with share of income to different groups as under:

- ☆ 56.8 per cent to cocoon grower
- ☆ 6.8 per cent to the reeler
- ☆ 9.1 per cent to the twister
- ☆ 10.7 per cent to the weaver
- ☆ 16.6 per cent to the trade

Thus, large chunk of income goes back to the villages from the cities.

Low Gestation, High Returns

Mulberry takes only six months to grow for commencement of silkworm rearing. Mulberry once planted will go on supporting silkworm rearing year after year for 15-20 years depending on inputs and management provided. Five crops can be taken in one year under tropical conditions. By adopting stipulated package of practices, a farmer can attain net income levels up to Rs.30000 per acre per annum.

Women friendly Occupation

Women constitute over 60 per cent of those employed in down-stream activities of sericulture in the country. This is possible because sericulture activities starting from mulberry garden management, leaf harvesting and silkworm rearing is more effectively taken up by the women folk. Even silk reeling industry including weaving is largely supported by them.

Ideal Programme for Weaker Sections of the Society

Sericulture can be practiced even with very low land holding. ¾ acre of mulberry garden and silkworm rearing can support a family of three without hiring labour. Features such as low gestation, high returns make sericulture an ideal programme for weaker sections of the society. Vast tracts of forest based tasar food plants are available in the country, It can be judiciously used for rearing tasar silkworms which can offer supplementary gainful employment for the tribes.

Eco-friendly Activity

As a perennial crop with good foliage and root-spread, food plants contribute to soil conservation and provide green cover. Waste from silkworm rearing can be recycled as inputs to garden. Dried twigs and branches are used as fuel in place of firewood and therefore reduce the pressure on vegetation/forest. Being a labour intensive and predominantly agro-based activity, involvement of smoke-emitting machinery is minimal. Developmental programmes initiated for tasar/mulberry plantation are mainly in upland areas where un-used cultivable land is made productive. Mulberry can also be cultivated as intercrop with numerous plantations. Mulberry and tasar being a deep-rooted perennial plant can be raised in vacant lands, hill slopes and watershed areas.

Satisfies Equity Concerns

Benefits of sectoral value-addition primarily accrue to rural households. As the end-product users are mostly from the higher economic groups, the money flows from high end groups to low end groups. Cases of landless families engaged in cocoon production using mulberry contracted from local farmers are common in some states.

International Demand of Silk and Constraints in Silk Production like Labour and Environmental Conditions

No doubt there has increasing demand for quality bivoltine silk in domestic and in international market. India, in spite of being the second largest producer of silk in the world, has been striving hard to meet the demand of quality silk as more than 90 percent of its production comprises of ungraded silk. Of the late bivoltine sericulture technologies were stabilized and the country first time could crosses 1000 MT mark in bivoltine raw silk production recently. Though there has been perceptible improvements in cocoon production and reduction in crop losses due to new sericulture technologies developed by various research institutes in various aspects of sericulture. But, still there is lot more to be done to meet the international demand of silk. Despite, there are various bottlenecks coming in the way to produce the raw silk in bulk to meet the quality as well as quantity silk at the international level.

A far as demand and supply of raw silk, the production of raw silk shows an increasing trend since over the last decades. The raw silks produced in different countries are mainly exported to USA. Even in terms of fibre quality silk occupies the highest position. Therefore, as compared to others fibres its value is very high. The demand for raw silk is primarily in the USA. On the other hand, considering the supply position of raw silk it is extremely difficult to suddenly increase or decrease the production of cocoon and therefore, it is very difficult to strike a balance between the supply and demand. This ultimately affects the price of cocoons and silk yarn and this is indeed a difficult problem.

Some of the constraints in the silk production are discussed as under:

Labour

There is a dearth of trained manpower in sericulture in the early stage. Trained manpower plays a vital role in productivity. The main factors for low productivity are geographic variability in different regions of the country, lack of knowledge, skill in adoption of various technologies and poor trained manpower. In order to enhance the qualitative and quantitative production and also to meet the future demands of raw silk production, it was felt to strengthen the human resource development in sericulture in the country.

Environmental Conditions

At the foremost, an organization should be aware/understand the changes that take place in and around the world, for its survival. The production/services have to be changed relevance to socioeconomic conditions and whims and fancies of consumer's taste and user habits. In such the condition, the training needs are to be changed scientifically and meaningfully.

Unit-II

Dr. Amardev Singh

2.1. Role of Central Silk Board in Research and Development of Sericulture in Different States of India; Sericulture Research and Development in Jammu and Kashmir State

Central Silk Board (CSB) is an apex body for silk in India and is one of the oldest commodity Board in the country set up as early as in 1948 by an act of parliament. The silk procurement committee that existed during World War II for parachute production was converted into (CSB) by an act of parliament. Government of India has identified sericulture as one of the agro-based cottage industry for the development of rural economy. Besides, being an employment oriented industry, it is export oriented too. Realizing the importance of sericulture a developing country economy like India, the Government of India had constituted the (CSB) for the planned development of the silk industry, under the Stewardship of none other Pandit Jawarhar Lal Nehru, the architect of modern India.

The Central Silk Board (CSB) is constituted for every three years and has 36 members including the Chairman and Member Secretary representatives of the Lok Sabha, Rajya Sabha, the industry and trade besides the representation of central and state government, CSB has been entrusted with the overall responsibility of developing the silk industry with manner it think fit. Some of the major function of the Board as envisaged in its act.

Central Silk Board Vision

See India emerged as the leader in the world market for silk

Our Mandate

- Promoting the development of Silk Industry by such measures as it thinks fit.
- To create greater opportunities for gainful employment and improved levels of income in sericulture through spread of scientific sericulture practices
- Undertaking, assisting or encouraging scientific, technological and economic research.
- Devising means for improved methods of mulberry cultivation, silkworm rearing,developing and distribution of healthy silkworm seeds, improved methods of silk reeling and spinning of the cocoons and silk-waste, improving the quality and production of raw silk, if necessary by making it compulsory, for all the raw silk to be marketed,only after the same has been tested and graded in properly quipped raw Silk Testing and Conditioning Houses.
- Improving the marketing of raw silk.
- The collection of statistics.
- See India emerge as the leader in the world market for silk.
- To advise the Central Government on all matters relating to the development of silk industry including import and export of raw silk.
- To prepare and furnish such other reports relating to the silk industry as may be required by the Central Government from time to time.

Our Mission

- Make continuous efforts in Research and Development and Technology Transfer.
- To create greater opportunities for gainful employment and improved levels of income in sericulture through spread of scientific sericulture practices.
- To improve productivity in all stages of silk production.
- Strengthen levels of efficiency through a commitment to quality.

Our Clients

- Departments concerned with sericulture development in all states of the country.
- Non-Government Organizations (NGOs).
- Farmers practicing sericulture.
- Silk reelers.
- Silk spinners.
- Private silkworm seed producers.
- Exporters.

- ☆ Entrepreneurs interested in taking up
  - Cocoon growing.
  - Silk reeling/spinning.
  - Silkworm seed production.
  - Manufactures of chemicals and bio-pesticides for controlling pests and diseases of silkworm and its food plants.

Services Offered

To State Sericulture Department, and NGOs

- ☆ Basic planting materials of high-yielding varieties of silkworm food plants.
- ☆ Region and season-specific package of practices for food plant cultivation and silkworm rearing.
- ☆ Collaboration in pest and disease surveillance and control.
- ☆ Technology packages for reeling and spinning.
- ☆ Post-cocoon research support.
- ☆ Assistance in supply of inputs to rearers and reelers.
- ☆ Implementation of centrally sponsored Catalytic development Programme (CDP) in collaboration with all the state sericulture departments to provide central share of subsidy to the stakeholders of silk industry.

Research and Development

The main Research and Training Institutes of the CSB function to provide research and development and training support for the development of sericulture. The Institutes at Mysore (Karnataka), Berhampore (West Bengal) and Pampore (J&K) deal with mulberry sericulture and the one at Ranchi (Bihar) deals with Tasar. A main Research Institute has been established at Ladoigarh Jorhat (Assam) for Muga and Eri. Regional Sericultural Research Stations (RSRS/RTRS) for mulberry and non-mulberry have been functioning for the dissemination of research findings and tackling the regional field issues of the industry. Besides, a network of Research Extension Centres (RECs) for mulberry and non-mulberry are also functioning to provide extension support to sericulturists. In order to provide R and D support in post-cocoon processing, the Board has established a Central Silk Technological Research Institute (CSTRI) at Bangalore. In addition, the CSB has also set up a Silkworm Seed Technology Laboratory (SSTL) in Bangalore (Karnataka), a Central Sericultural Germplasm Resources Centre (CSGRC) at Hosur, (Tamil Nadu) and a Seri-Biotech Research Laboratory (SBRL) at Bangalore.

Research work on the on-farm side continued to be directed mainly at (i) evolving stress tolerant mulberry, eri and muga plant varieties, which give high leaf yield, breeding superior silkworm races; (ii) evolving improved techniques of silkworm rearing to give higher productivities; and (iii) control of pests and diseases of both plant and silkworms. During the year 2000-2001, 4 mulberry silkworm hybrids were developed and are put under field trial at 25 Race Authorization Test Centres.

On the post-cocoon side The Central Silk Technological Research Institute, Bangalore has developed a multiend reeling package for reeling quality silk from bivoltine and crossbreed cocoons. It has also fabricated a low-cost multifuel drying chamber, a tail end cutter and slit buttons; cooking technologies of different commercial tasar cocoons for reeling on tasar reeling charkha (TRC); low-cost improved pedal-cum-motorized reeling-cum-twisting devices for tasar and muga; and improved spinning wheel for muga and eri, which will produce better quality silk/spun yarn with less wastage, thereby fetching higher

2.2. Introduction to Mulberry Silkworm and its Food Plants, What is Mulberry Sericulture, Silkworm Races

Introduction to Mulberry Silkworm and its Food Plants

Mulberry constitutes the only satisfactory food of the silkworm, Bombyx mori. Mulberry silk is produced by the silkworm *Bombyx mori* which fed on mulberry leaves. *Bombyx mori* is a domesticated silkworm and is commercially reared to produce mulberry silk. Mulberry is a very hardy plant belonging to the genus *Morus* under the family Moraceae. There are more than twenty species under the genus Morus among which *Morus alba; Morus indica; Morus serrata; Morus levigata; Morus latifolia etc.,* may be mentioned. The alternative host plants are osage, orange, junifer, peepul and some other leaves have tried to fed the silkworms, the results was not encouraging. These could at best be regarded as make shifts only and can never become a satisfactory substitute for mulberry. They can be used to keep the silkworms alive when, due to some reasons, mulberry cannot be got. Food on these leaves, the silkworms would soon suffer in growth and vigour, and fall an easy prey to diseases. Even the survivors would be miserable specimens, spinning flimsy cocoons if they do spin cocoon at all.

Mulberry being practically the sole food source of the silkworms, it is at once obvious that the quality of mulberry leaf has a predominant influence on the development of the silkworms and the quality of cocoons. If silkworms rearing and cocoon production are to be a success, it is necessary that mulberry leaf to be fed to the silkworms is very nutritive fresh. Mulberry is very quick growing plant and its leaves can be harvested several times in a year in tropical countries like India. Silkworm too grows fast. In order to make the maximum use of these two quick growing living beings, a delicate technique is required.

What is Mulberry Sericulture

Cultivation of mulberry (*Morus* sp.) and rearing of silkworm (*Bombyx mori* L.) are the basis of mulberry sericulture that is entirely dependent primarily on mulberry leaves, the only source of nutrition for silkworms, the growth and development of the larvae and the subsequent cocoon production are very much influenced by the nutritive value of mulberry leaves. After rearing of silkworms, the matured silkworm spin the cocoons and when the cocoons are subjected to boiling will loosen up its silk filament and make it easier to reel out the silk using charka and other improvised mechanism.

The mulberry sericulture is divided into three different sections

1. Production of reeling cocoons.
2. Production of raw silk.
3. Utilization of byproducts such as pupae, silk waste *etc.*, while the first sector is agriculture in nature, the other two are cottage industry based.

Producing of reeling cocoons involves cultivation of mulberry plantations and rearing of silkworms. Production of raw silk is carried out by reeling of cocoons. The byproducts are utilized by the subsidiary industries like the spun silk industry for making different goods.

Silkworm Races

Broadly the silkworm races are classified into two categories *viz.*, temperate and tropical. Based on the geographical distribution the silkworms races are grouped into:

- ✰ **Japanese races:** are univoltine producing white dumbbell/spindle shape cocoon. The larval duration is usually larger. The larvae are slow in their early habits. The occurrence of double cocoon is high.
- ✰ **Chinese races:** are in general uni/bi and polyvoltine. The larvae are fast growing and the larval duration is short. They produce golden, yellow, pink or white cocoons. The shape of the cocoon varies elliptical/oval and occasionally spindle in some exceptional aces.
- ✰ **European races:** are in general univoltine and produce white or cream color cocoon. they produce large eggs and larvae that eat voraciously. the larval duration, especially in the 5th instar stage is long. The ratio of the double cocoon in the breed is low.
- ✰ **Tropical races:** These are polyvoltine having a short larval duration, except in the case of the some Mysore breed. They produce spindle/shaped cocoons (Indian races).

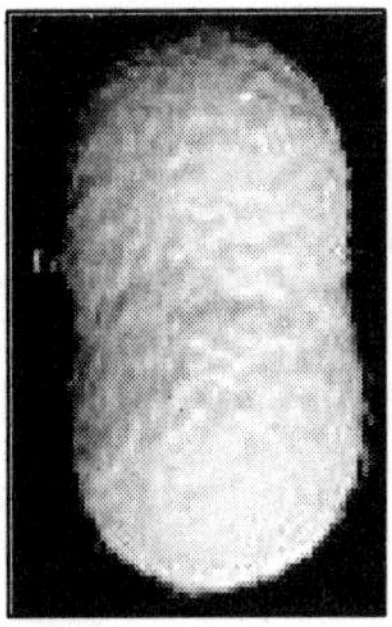

Dumbell Shape (Japanese races)

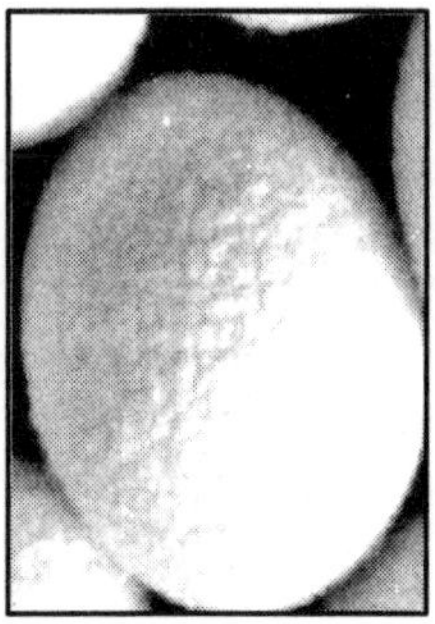

Oval Shape (Chinese races)

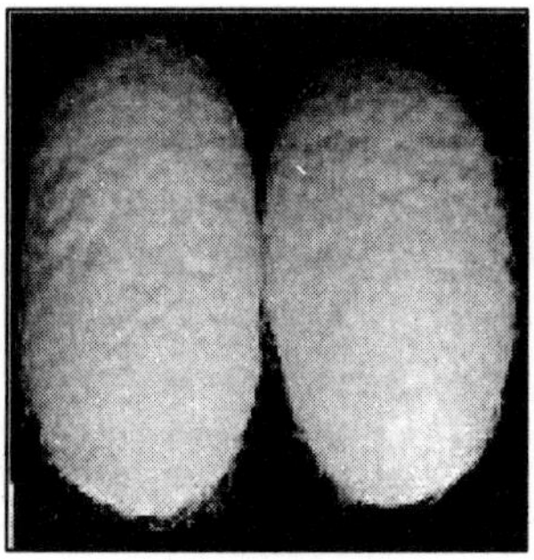

Normal Shape (European races)

Pointed shape Tropical races

2.3. Characteristic Features, Different Varieties of Mulberry-Different Uses of Mulberry

Characteristic Features, Different Varieties of Mulberry

In India, there are many species of Morus, of which *Morus alba, Morus indica, Morus serrata* and *Morus laevigata* grow wild in the Himalayas. Several varieties have been introduced belonging to *Morus multicaulis, Morus nigra, Morus sinensis* and *Morus phillippinensis*. Most of the Indian varieties of mulberry belong to *M.indica*.

Different Mulberry Varieties Under Cultivation in different States of India

Variety	*Region*	*Developed at*	*Origin*
Kanva-2	South India Irrigated	CSRTI, Mysore	Selection from natural variability
S-36	-do-	-do-	Developed through EMS treatment of Berhampore Local
S-54	-do-	-do-	-do-
Victory-1 or V-1	-do-	-do-	Hybrid from S30 x Ber 776
DD	South India Irrigated	KSSRDI, Thalaghattapura	Clonal selection
S-13	South India rainfed	CSRTI, Mysore	Selection from polycross (mixed pollen progeny)
S-34	-do-	-do-	-do-
MR-2 hybrids	-do-	-do-	Selection from open pollinated
S-1	Eastern and N.E. India irrigated	CSRTI, Berhampore	Introduction from (Mandalaya) Burma
S779 hybrids	-do-	-do-	Selection from open pollinated
S1635	-do-	-do-	Triploid selection
S146	North India and Hills of J&K irrigated	-do-	Selection from open pollinated hybrids
Tr-10	Hills of Easter India	-do-	Triploid of ber.S1
BC 259	-do-	-do-	Back crossing of hybrid of Matigare local x Kosen with kosen twice
Goshoerami	Temperate	CSRTI, Pampore	Introduction from Japan
Chak Majra	Sub-temperate	RSRS, Jammu	Selection from natural variability
China White	temperate	CSRTI, Pampore	Clonal selection

Kanva-2

Belongs to *Morus indica*-Diploid. Widely cultivated in southern India after the same was recommended for cultivation in 1969 by CSR and TI, Mysore. Selection from population of Mysore Local variety.

Flower and Sorosis

Female, profuse flowering, many sorosis.

Economic Characters

Medium leaf maturity, yields about 30 to 35 MT/ha/year under irrigated condition. Leaf moisture content 70 per cent protein content 21 per cent and sugar content 11.5 per cent.Resistant to leaf spot. Moderately resistant to leaf rust and powdery mildew. High rooting ability (80 per cent) and wide adaptability.

S-36

Belongs to *Morus indica.* Developed at CSR and TI, Mysore and recommended during 1984.evolved from Berhampore local by chemical mutagenesis. Cultivated in southern India. Moderate rooting ability.

Economic Characters

yields about 38/45MT/ha/year under assured irrigated conditions of south India. Moisture content 76 per cent, protein content 22 per cent and carbohydrate content 28 per cent. Tolerate to leaf spot and powdery mildew. Moderately susceptible to leaf rust and to tukra infestation. Most suitable to **young age silkworm rearing**. Sapling plantation recommended due to moderate rooting ability.

S-54

Belongs to *Morus indica.* Developed at CSR and TI, Mysore and recommended during 1984. Selected from Berhampore local by chemical mutagenesis (EMS). Recommended for assured irrigated conditions of south India.

Economic Characters

Yield about 45MT/ha/year under assured irrigated conditions. Highly responsive to agronomical input. Moisture content of leaf 70.5 per cent, protein content 23.9 per cent and sugar content 13.8 per cent.Moderately resistant to powdery mildew and leaf rust and resistant to leaf spot. Looses moisture very quickly. Good rooting ability.

DD

Selected from natural population of Dehra Dun variety and recommended by Karnataka State Sericultural Research and Development Institute, Thalaghattapura. Recommended for southern India.

Erect, thin branches, coarse leaves, greenish grey colour bark. Lower branches spreading, leaves unlobed, big size, ovate shape. Yields 35-40Mt/ha/year under irrigation condition.

MR-2

Belongs to *Morus sinensis*-Diploid. Selection from open pollinated hybrid population. Developed at CSRTI, Mysore and recommended for propagation in Tamil Nadu. Mainly cultivated in Tamil Nadu under both irrigated condition in plains and rainfed conditions in hilly region.

Economic Characters

Yield about 30-35 Mt/ha/year under irrigated conditions of Tamil Nadu. Moisture content 68 per cent, protein content 23.2 per cent and sugar content 13.2 per cent. Resistant to powdery mildew disease, suitable for hilly areas.

V-1

Belongs to *Morus indica*.Developed at CSRTI, Mysore from a cross of S-30 x Ber.776.Recommeded during 196 for assured irrigated conditions

Flower

Male, profuse flowering, occasionally few sorosis.

Economic Characters

Yields about 70 MT/ha/year under assured irrigated conditions.

Very high sprouting. Moisture content 78.9 per cent and 72.5 per cent in young and matured leaves respectively. Protein content 24.6 per cent and total sugar content 16.98 per cent.

Moderately resistant to leaf rust and tukra infestation and resistant to leaf spot. Quick sprouting ability and very high rooting ability (Ø 94 per cent) high photosynthetic rate and higher water use efficiency are additional advantages. Moreover, leaves are suitable for both young and late silkworm larvae.

S-34

Belongs to *Morus indica*. Diploid. Selection from progeny of S30 x Berc 776. Recommended during 1990 for rainfed areas with black cotton soils of South India

Flower and Sorosis

Male, profuse flowering, occasionally few sorosis.

Economic Characters

Under rainfed conditions, yields about 15 MT/ha/yr. Moisture content 70 per cent, crude protein content 23.7 per cent. Soluble sugar content 13.2 per cent. Resistant to powdery mildew and leaf rust. Moderately resistant to leaf spot and susceptible to tukra infestation.

Goshoerami

Goshoerami was introduced in the valley several decades ago from Japan and with the passage of time, it fascinated sericulturists, general public, gardeners and foresters alike due to its sheer large attractive leaves, good canopy and ability to develop into tree. As a high yielding variety, it is suitable for tree as well as dwarf type of cultivation for sericultural purpose as well as for greening the landscape. It also grows well as bush. It is cultivated mostly in temperate areas of Jammu and Kashmir.

It grows luxuriantly under rainfed conditions in Kashmir as trees besides dwarf and bush and hence suitable for road side plantation, on ponds and river dykes and other places both as block and scattered tree.

Economic Characters

It gives a leaf yield of 21 tons as dwarf and 16 tons as tree per hectare/year which is remarkable under rainfed conditions, that too by way of just two crops –one each in spring and autumn seasons. Overall leaf yield ranges between 15-20 MT/ ha/year. The Fresh weight of 100 leaves 0.555g, moisture content 75.34 per cent.

China White

It is a temperate variety originates through clonal selection developed at CSRTI, Pampore.

Chak Majra

It is cultivated mostly under sub-temperate zone of Jammu and Kashmir state. This variety is developed at RSRS, Jammu trough selection from natural variability.

Tr-10

This variety was developed by polyploidy breeding (T4 x Mandalaya). Average leaf yield is 18-19Mt/ha/year. The area for cultivation is eastern hills of India. Triploid developed from S1 at CSRTI, Pampore

Varieties	*Leaf Yield (tons/ha/yr)*		*Fresh Weight of 100 Leaves (kg)*		*Moisture Content (per cent) in Fresh Leaves*		*Moisture Content (per cent) After 12 hrs Harvest*		*Evaluation Index*	
	Tree	*Dwarf*	*Tree*	*Dwarf*	*Tree*	*Dwarf*	*Tree*	*Dwarf*	*Tree*	*Dwarf*
Chinese White	4.860	9.680	0.280	0.307	72.71	72.59	61.94	61.81	40.72	**40.18**
Ichinose	15.924	20.186	0.306	0.304	72.23	72.40	63.57	63.06	46.72	**47.94**
KNG	17.220	20.415	0.316	0.308	72.50	73.12	63.65	63.96	48.62	**49.01**
Goshoermi	**15.960**	**20.964**	0.591	0.555	**73.99**	**75.34**	**68.22**	**69.02**	**63.88**	**64.36**

Different Uses of Mulberry

For sericulture operation, mulberry trees are cultivated, mulberry leaves are harvested, silkworms are reared and cocoons are produced. Besides the cocoons, various other products are also attained. In the case of mulberry, the most important use in globally is for the production of the silkworm that feeds exclusively on its leaves, instead, it also used in different purposes is discussed as under:

Fruit

All throughout Asia, but in particular in Central Asia delicious fruit, which is consumed fresh, or in the form of juice or conserves. A few mulberry orchards also exist in Latin America. Ripen mulberry fruit is also used in the preparation of jam, jelly *etc.*Naturopaths recommend mulberry fruit in lower bad cholesterol level, reduction in body weight, strengthening bone and fight osteroporosis.Recent studies

S_{36}

V_1

S_1

K2

S13

DD-Vishwa

Picture Depicting Different Mulberry Varieties

indicate that premature graying of hair may be stopped with mulberry and even increasing low libido is possible with its fruit (Sreekumar *et al.*, 2012).Besides, it is also good for brain heart, spleen and helps curing diarrhoea and intestinal ulcers. It is considered as a laxative and oral juice administration good drink during convalescence after a febrile illness (Shailesh *et al.*, 2009). A new UK fruit juice company "Fairjuice" has launched a super fruit drink prepared from pure fresh pressed mulberry fruits which is full of antioxidants. It is also a source of resveratrol which is considered to be beneficial for heart health. It also suppresses the appetite, which is why it has been reported as a useful drink against obesity (Fairjuice, 2008). Mulberry fruits can be dried and stored as a powder. About 10 g of dried fruits provides about 100 mg of anthocyanins. As it contains resveratrol, fruit powder works as an anti-mutagen which can inhibit the mutation of healthy normal cells into cancerous cells (Hou, 2003). It is believed to prevent heart disease, cancer and other diseases associated with chronic inflammation. The fruit powder has an anti-aging effect on cells because it combats free radical damage. Fruit powder promotes healthy cholesterol and controls carbohydrate digestion in the human body (www.znaturalfoods.com, 2009; www.yourhealthyourherbs.com, 2009; Liu *et al.*, 2009). Over-ripened and sour fruits can be converted into mulberry wine (Ehow, 2009). The wine has a sweet and sour taste. A glass of mulberry wine a day helps get rid of impurities and coprostasis (faecal residue in the intestines) in the body which can help make the body slim. Habib (2004) has reported that a multi-nutrient feed block prepared from mulberry fruits has increased milk production from 30 per cent to 50 per cent in livestock with low disease incidence. It is found that a farmer can earn about US $ 17-26 per month

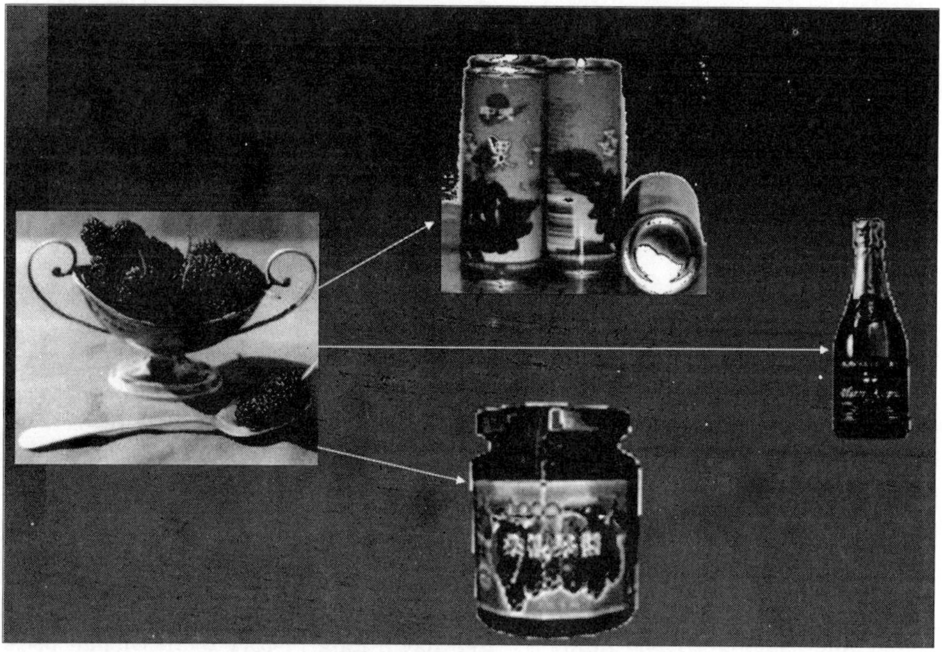

Mulberry Fruit Products

Mulberry Jam

during the mulberry season from commercial preparation of mulberry fruit blocks. It is mentioned that the technology of utilizing mulberry fruits as feed blocks for animals can be exploited as an income-generating micro enterprise.

Wood

Especially in the Indian subcontinent, mulberry wood is used for handicrafts, and for sporting woods (*e.g.* Grass-hockey sticks and tennis rackets). Its thin branches are woven into baskets.

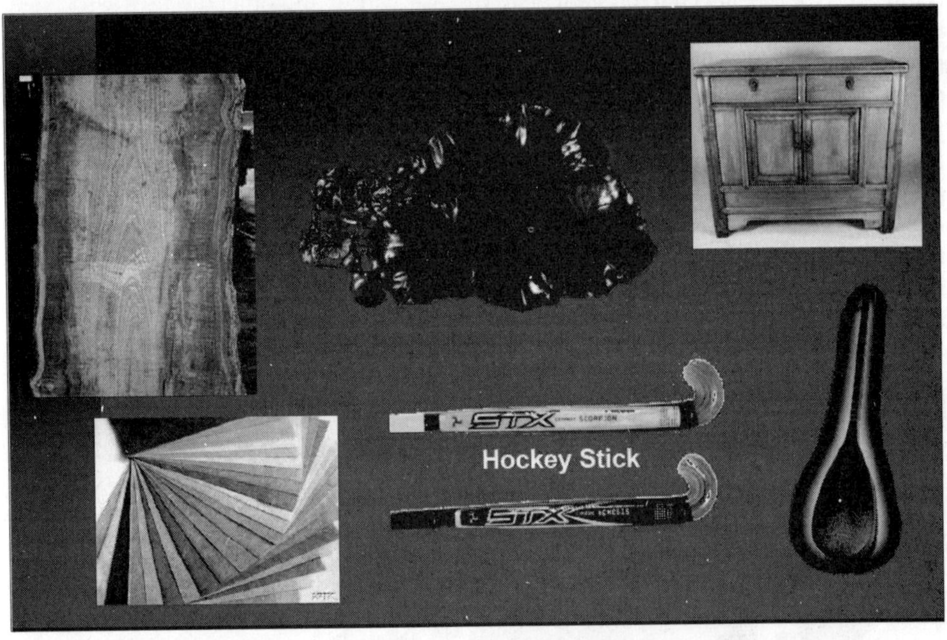

Mulberry Wood Product

Landscaping

In Asia, Southern Europe and in Southern U.S.A. (Tipton, 1994), mulberry trees are utilized for landscaping. Their resistance to pruning and their low water requirements make them very suitable plants for urban conditions, house gardens, street shade and city embellishment.

Medicine

A variety of medicinal properties have been attributed to the different parts of the mulberry plant (Datta, 2000). Leaves are also dried and used in infusions in Asia (*e.g.*, China, Thailand).The mulberry tree has a long history of medicinal uses.

Medicinal Product made from Mulberry

According to the theories of traditional Chinese medicine, mulberry leaves are effective in controlling disease because the leaves have calming properties. It works by removing the symptoms of lung heat like cough, fever and sore throat and can also clear up the fiery heat in our liver (Jane and Merlita, 2012). One case study reported recently in the healthy life style magazine showed that mulberry leaves are beneficial in controlling bronchitis. Based on Toshiyuki Kimura (2011) in a study on the mulberry extract for diabetes in Japan, the study has shown the newly developed 1-deoxynojirimycin (DNJ)-enriched powder can be used a dietary supplement for preventing diabetes mellitus.

Use of Mulberry Shoots

The mulberry shoots are widely used in agricultural farms as firewood and fuel. The shoots are either used as they are or after changing them into mulberry coal. Artificial leather can also be made by processing the mulberry bark and can be used for making ropes nets, *etc.*

Use of Mulberry Leaves

Besides, used for silkworm feeding its leaves are used for preparation a decoction known as mulberry tea. Usually the tea is prepared with mulberry leaves but some people prefer to boil mulberry roots and stems to prepare a broth, which is said to be effective in lowering the blood pressure. In India, a tea known as **"Spoorthi"** which is readily available in market is prepared from mulberry leaves and it is very effective against diabetes, hypertension, gastric trouble, constipation etc. In Chinese markets, mulberry is often provided in the form of a paste called sangshengao. The paste is mixed in hot water to make a tea to improve the liver and kidney and sharpen the

Mulberry as Cattle Feed

Liking of Mulberry Leaves

hearing and brighten the eyes (Singhal *et al.*, 2010).Mulberry leaves are used as cattle feed as it contents crude protein 15 to 28 per cent. Rabbits for example have a great liking for mulberry leaves and they grow well when fed on them.

Use of Mulberry Root

The surface of mulberry roots has a constituent which can effectively lower the blood pressure. This constituent is soluble in water as well as in alcohol and is fairly heat stable. Study conducted with rabbits reveal that there is an increase in the rate of lowering of blood pressure as the quantity of mulberry root peel fed to them is increased and the lower blood pressure condition remains stable for a considerable length of time. One medicine prepared from the root is called *Glucosidae* which can be administered to the patients suffering from high blood pressure (Tewary and Rao, 1990). Japanese have already isolated a hormone called *Moranoline* which contains 5 carbon atoms and one nitrogen atom. Its use as medicine is yet to be confirmed.

Left over Mulberry Leaves

The left leaves and silkworm litter are used for preparation of compost.

Despite, different uses of mulberry, the health benefits of mulberry are largely linked with the elements composing its chemical structure. Mulberry contains large amount of vitamin C and K, and minerals like magnesium, phosphorus, potassium, calcium and iron. It is rich in proteins, pectin, fiber, free acids (tartaric acid and malic acid), fatty acids (linoleic, stearic and oleic), fructose and glucose. Strengthening the immune system of body, relieving pain from chronic inflammation caused by arthritis or atherosclerosis and nourishing the blood have a long history of treatment with mulberry. Besides, maintaining healthy liver and kidneys, soothing the nerves, eliminating weakness, fatigue and anemia is possible with them.

2.4. Introduction to Non-Mulberry Silkworm and their Food Plants, Different Species of Non-Mulberry Silkworm their Habit and Habitat

Introduction to Non-Mulberry Silkworm and their Food Plants

The natural silk is broadly classified as mulberry and wild or non-mulberry. On-mulberry sericulture is universally known as forest or wild sericulture.Trpoical and Temperate tasar, Eri and Muga are the principle non-mulberry silk. Other varieties *i.e.*, fagara, coan, mussel and spider silk are limited interest. Nearly 95 per cent of the global production of non-mulberry silks is tasar.

All branches of sericulture require food plants and manpower. In mulberry sericulture over 60 per cent of the cost of production goes into raising and maintaining the food plants, besides, a heavy initial investment is necessary for rearing houses, rearing appliances and other essentials. Likewise, among the non-mulberry varieties, eri has the disadvantages of higher production costs. Tasar is endowed by nature with vast potential. But continuous deforestation resulted in depletion of non-mulberry food plants. One should not forget that non-mulberry sericulture holds great promise for the world forestry as a supplementary activity.

Non-mulberry sericulture is a forest-based industry uniquely suited to the economy and social structure of developing countries because of its minimum investment requirement, high employment, and foreign exchange earning potential.

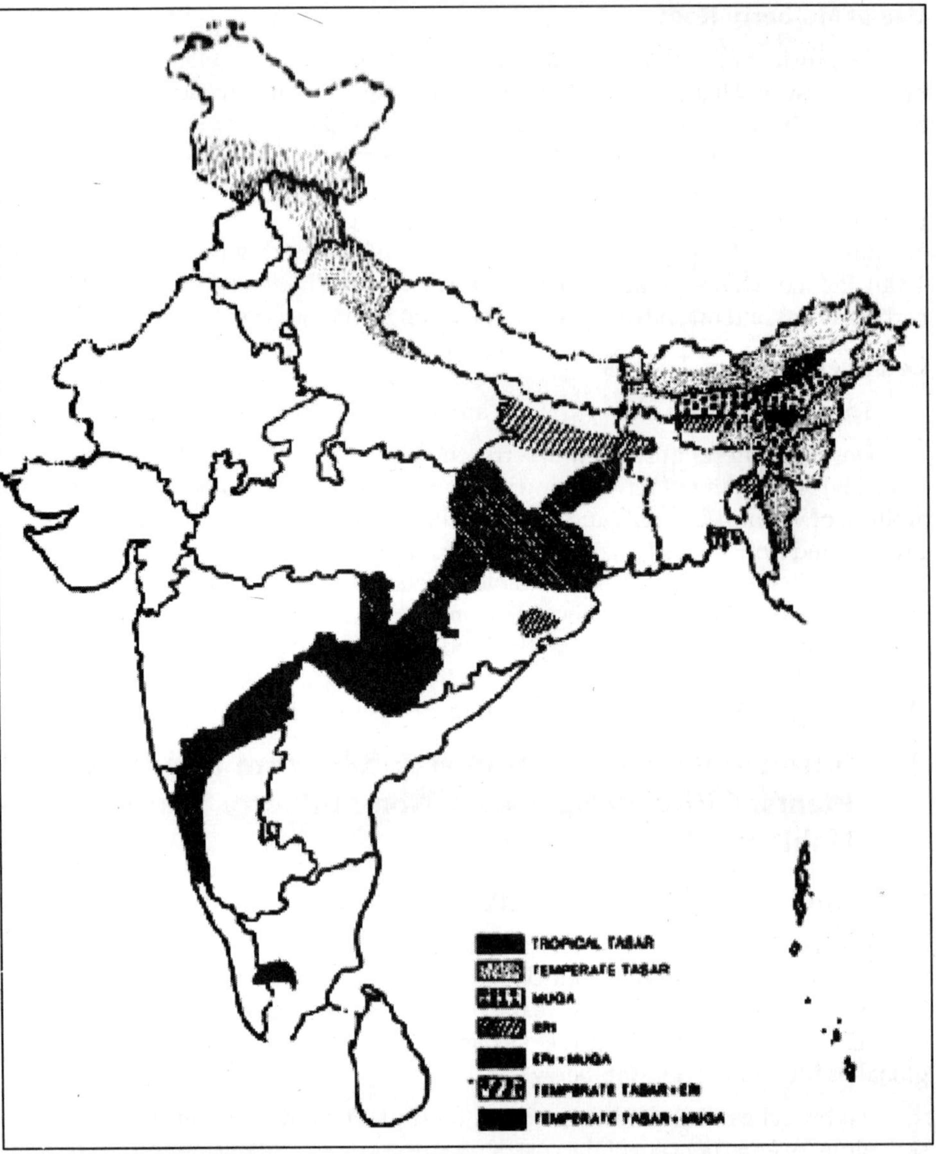

Non-Mulberry Silk Production in different States of India

In India about 12, 43 million hectares of unexploited tasar food plants in the tropical and temperate belts could b put to use without investment. Moreover, unlike large industries in which heavy investments indispensable and the employment potential is limited, tasar culture requires a very low investment for net high returns. Various operations of tasar production can be carried out even in remote forest villages as they do not require electricity, complex machinery, specialized skills etc. Non-mulberry production offers rural population an attractive source of income, arrests their migration to urban areas, thereby pre-serving their traditional skill and way of life.

Food Plants of Non-Mulberry Silkworms

As it is discussed earlier there are four different species of non-mulberry silkworms being reared in India. All these species have different food plants which are mentioned below:

Tropical Tasar Silkworm and its Food Plants

Tasar silkworm is polyphagous.The primary food plants are eight types. Besides, more than two dozens of secondary food plants.

Primary Food Plants

- ☆ *Terminalia tomentosa*
- ☆ *T. arjuna*
- ☆ *Shorea robusta*, Roxb
- ☆ *Lagerstroemia parviflora*, Roxb.
- ☆ *L. Speciosa*, Pers.
- ☆ *L. indica*, Linn.
- ☆ *Zizyphus mauritiana*, Lam.
- ☆ *Hardwickia binata* Roxb

T. tomentosa

T. arjuna

Secondary Food Plants

Of the more than two dozen secondary food plants so far reported, the most important are:

- ☆ *Terminalia chebula*
- ☆ *T.belerica*

- *T.catappa*
- *T.paniculata*
- *Anogeissus latifolia*
- *Syzygium cumini*
- *Careya arborea*
- *Shorea taliura*

Temperate Tasar Silkworm and its Food Plants

The food plant for temperate tasar silkworms is oak plant. The primary food plants are

- *Quercus incana*
- *Q. Serrata*
- *Q. delabata*
- *Q. himalayana*
- *Q. semiserrata*

Muga Silkworm and its Food Plants

The polyphagous silkworm feeds on

- *Machilus bombycina* King (Som) and
- *Litsaea monopetala,* Pers. (Scalu)

Other Food Plants include

- *Litsea citrata* Blume
- *L. salicifolia,* Roxb. Ex.Wall
- *Michelia oblonga,* Wall
- *Cinnamomum obtusifolium,* Nees
- *Symplocos grandiflora,* Wall.

Eri Silkworm and its Food Plants

The silkworm feeds mainly on

- *Ricinus communis* (Caster oil plant).

Other Important Secondary Food Plants are

- *Heteropanax fragrans,* Seem
- *Manihot utilissima,* Phol
- *Carica papaya,* L
- *Evodia faxinifolia,* Hook
- *Ailanthus excelsa,* Roxb.

Different Species of Non-Mulberry Silkworm their Habit and Habitat

India is the only country producing all the four types of commercially important wild silks (Vanya silks) namely tropical tasar, temperate tasar, eri and muga. Tasar culture and other associated activities have been extensively practiced in Jharkhand, Madhya Pradesh, Chhattisgarh, Orissa, Uttar Pradesh, North Eastern and sub-Himalayan belts of India since many decades. Due to ethnic, aesthetic and eco-friendly values, wild silk has a strong demand in the national and international market.

Tropical Tasar Silkworm Habit and Habitat

These are reared in the tropical and temperate zones. Four species for the genus ***Antherea*** (Hubner) are used for commercial production. They are as follows.

- ☆ Tropical tasar silkworm *A. Mylitta*, D (India)
- ☆ Temperate Silkworm *A. Proyli*, J. (India)
- ☆ *A. Pernyi*, G.M. (China, USSR)
- ☆ *A. Yamamai*, (G.M. Japan)

Antherea comprises more species than any other genus of sericigenous insects. So far thirty five species have been recorded (31 in the Indo-Asutralian biogeographic region, 3 in Palearctic region, one in USA). These are uni or bivoltie types. The dense, humid forest sprawling over the central and southern plateau is the habitat of tropical tasar.

Larvae of *Antherea mylitta*

Temperate Tasar Silkworm Habit and Habitat

This is an hybrid worm. The oak tract extending from Jammu and Kashmir in the West to Manipur in the east, embracing Himachal Pradesh, Uttar Pradesh, West Bengal, Sikkim, Assam, Arunachal Pradesh, Meghalaya, Mizoram and Nagaland inhabits the temperate tasar silkworm. There are five species in temperate tasar.

- ☆ *Antherea proylei*, Jolly
- ☆ *A. roylei*, Moore

- ☆ *A. pernyi*, Guerin-Meneville
- ☆ *A. yamamai*, Guerin-Meneville
- ☆ *A. polyphemus*, Cramer

Muga Silkworm Habit and Habitat

The muga silkworm is largely cultivated only in Assam, possibly its characteristic ecological requirements are found only in its natural abode. The Muga silk worm, *Antheraea assama* is mainly confined to the Brahmaputra valley of Assam and foothills of East Garo hills of Meghalaya. Its distribution in the wild state, however, extends from western Himalaya to Nagaland, Cachar district of Assam and south Tripura. However, commercial exploitation is restricted only to north eastern India.

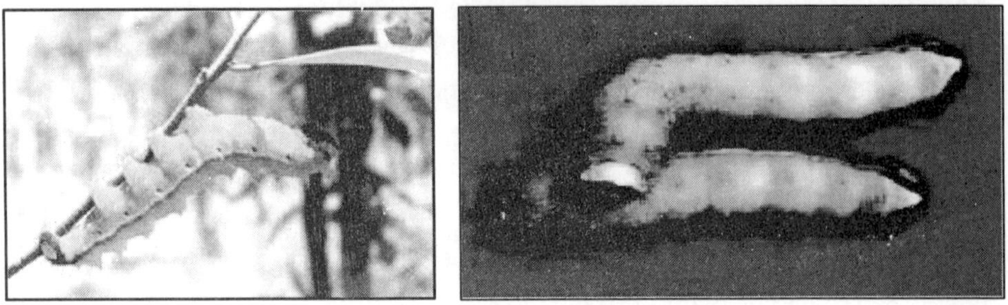

Muga Silkworm Larva

Eri Silkworm Habit and Habitat

The white or brick–red eri silk (endi, errandi) is produced by *Philosamia ricini*, B. a domesticated multivoltine silkworm. It is widespread in Assam and also practiced in Bihar, West Bengal, Manipur, Orissa and Tripura. Among the non-mulberry varieties, eri has the disadvantage of higher production costs because it is made from domesticated silkworms. Like mulberry silkworm it is also reared under optimum environmental conditions.

Eri Silkworm Larva

2.5. Brief account of

a. Tasar food plants, *Terminilia* species, *Shorea robusta*

b. Muga food plants, *Litsea polyantha*

c. Eri food plants (Castor, Tapioca)

d. Types of cocoons and silk produced by them

a. Tasar Food Plants, *Terminilia* species, *Shorea robusta*

Non-mulberry silkworms are polyphagous. Nevertheless, certain plants have been observed to yield a better crop of cocoons with superior technological properties. These are referred to as primary food plants, while the others are known as secondary food plants.

Primary Food Plants

Eight primary food plants for tropical tasar silkworms have been reported these include:

I. *Terminalia tomentosa*

II. *Terminalia arjuna*

III. *Shorea robusta*

IV. *Lagerstroemia parviflora*

V. *Lagerstroemia speciosa*

VI. *Zizyphus mauritiana*

VII. *Hardwickia binata*

Secondary food plants

Of the more than two dozen secondary food plants so far reported, the most important are *Terminalia chebula, T.belerica, T.catappa, T. paniculata, Anogeissus latifolia, Syzygium cumini, Careya arborea* and *Shorea tailura.*

The food plants of temperate tasar silkworm are mainly of the genus *Quercus* Linn. (oak). This very large genus of nearly 300 species is distributed throughout the temperate regions of the northern hemisphere and extends into the tropics and subtropics of South America, India, Malayasia and Australia, often above 600m above sea level.

In India about 58 better know species of the genus are distributed all along the western sub-Himalayan range at 1200 to 2100m and in the eastern hill traces 700 to 1500m above sea level.

Primary Food Plants

The oak flora consists mainly of *Q.incana, Q. glauca, Q. semicarpifolia, Q. himalayana* in the western sub-himalayan belt and *Q.serrata, Q.semiserrata and Q.dealbata* in the eastern belt. Of these, *Q.incana, Q,dealbata, Q.himalayana and Q.semiserrata* are the primary food plants of the temperate tasar silkworm

b. Muga Food Plants, *Litsea polyantha*

The polyphagous muga silkworm feeds primarily on the leaves of *Machilus bombycina* (som) and *Litsaea monopetala* (scalu). The other food plants of muga include *Litsaea citrate, L.salicifolia, Michelia oblonga, Cinnamomum obtusifolium and Sympocos grandiflora. Machilus bombycina* (som) is classified on the basis of leaf shape into sixteen morphotypes, of which the three more significant are Naharpatiya, Azarpatiya and Jampatiya. Naharpatiya is considered the best by muga rearers.

Distribution

M.bomycina and *L.monopetala* are distributed in India, Nepal, Burma, Malaysia and Indonesia. In India, these plants are common in Assam, Meghalaya, Arunachal Pradesh, Tripura, Nagaland, Manipur and North Bengal L. citrate is found throughout the sub-Himalayan belt.

Som Plant

Soalu Plant

c. Eri Food Plants (Castor, Tapioca)

CASTOR (*Ricinus communis*)

It is an evergreen, bush or small tree, shoots and panicles glaucous, leaves green, 30-45 cm diameter, membranous, lobes from oblong to linear acute, gland serrated, petiole m12-30 cm., racemes stout, erect, male flower 1.5 cm in diameter, female calyx nearly oblong, styles often highly colored, capsules 1.5 to 3.0 cm, long globosely oblong, smooth or echinate, seeds oblong, smooth and mottled.

Method of Propagation

Castor is grown generally through seeds, which are sown during March-April and September-October in N-E India. Perennial varieties are recommended to be

Seed of *Ricinus communis*

Plant of *Ricinus communis*

sown at a spacing of 1 X 1.5 meter spacing while annual in 1 X 1 meter spacing. Both pit and furrow method of planting could be adopted for castor cultivation.

Tapioca or Cassava: *Manihot esculenta*

Tapioca is a perennial shrub with variously branched stems growing to a height of 3-4 meters and produces enlarged tuberous roots. It grows best in warm and humid climate, soils of all types except in saline or alkaline having pH within 5.5 to 7.0, but could not withstand water logging. The leaves of this plant are very large with long petioles, having 5-10 lobes or sometimes more, dark green in colour but red, yellow and purple colour leaves are also found.

Plant of *Manihot esculent*

Method of Propagation

Tapioca is propagated through cuttings. Stems of 8-10 months old with a diameter of 2-3 cm are selected for preparation of cuttings. Discarding the upper immature and lower mature base, the stem is cut into pieces of 20 cm which are used as planting material.

d. Types of Cocoons and Silk Produced by them

Tasar Silk

The cocoon is single shelled, pendent, oval, closed and reelabe, having a hard non-flossy shell with fine grains. At the anterior end there is a well-formed dark brown peduncle with a ring at the distal end. The cocoons are generally yellow or grey. The female spin larger cocoons than the males. Silk reeled from cocoons of silkworms belonging to saturniidae family, which are fed on leaves of Oak, Asan and Arjuna trees. Tasar silk is mainly produced in Jharkhand, Bihar, Chhattisgarh, Madhya Pradesh, Orissa and West Bengal and Andhra Pradesh. Coarse quality silk from silkworms raised on Arjuna/Asan trees in natural forests; constitutes a minor share (2 per cent) in total silk.

Muga Silk

Coarse spun silk from northeast India, from silkworms reared on Som (*Persea bombycina king*), Soalu (*Litsaea polyantha*) leaves collected from forests; constitutes a negligible share (<1 per cent) of total silk. It is silk produced only in Assam from cocoons of silk worms belonging to saturniidae family, which are fed on Som and Soalu leaves. It has a rich golden colour.

Tasar Cocoons

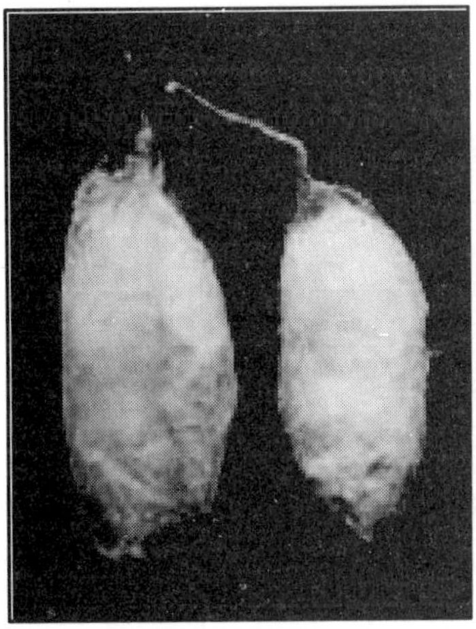

Muga Cocoons

Muga Silk

Eri Silk

It is spun from cocoons of silkworms belonging to saturniidae family, which are fed on castor leaves. Eri yarn is produced in Assam, Bihar, Manipur, Meghalaya, Nagaland and West Bengal. Eri cocoons are open ended cocoons utilized for spinning purpose. Cocoon is not compact, but loosely spun. Silk is white or brick red in colour and not as glossy as mulberry silk. It is not in one single strand and therefore not reelable. Fine quality silk from silkworms reared on Castor (*Ricinni communis*) leaves; has about 8 per cent share in total silk. Household activity in the northeast states of India. Cocoon colors are white, off-white and brick red. White colour cocoon is

Different Types of Cocoons Spun by Eri Silkworm

available in whole North East India. In Kokrajhar of Assam, eri silkworm is reared exclusively for brick red cocoons. Cocoons are oval in all cases.

Unit-III

Dr. Amardev Singh

3.1. Cocoon and Silk Grading, Brief Account of Silk Conditioning and Testing

The objective of cocoon testing and grading is to judge the quality of the cocoon lot. Cocoon testing means the procedure under which the nature and behavior of cocoons are tested concerning their consumptive value, and are graded according to the result of tests. In Japan, the raw silk industry law provides that the transaction of cocoons is to be conducted according to the result of tests performed by the pre-factual cocoon testing station (Tammanna, 2001).

Items of Cocoon Testing

i. **Percentage of rejected cocoons:** The ratio of rejected cocoons in a lot is expressed in percentage. Rejected cocoons include: double cocoon, inside soiled cocoon, outside soiled cocoon, thin-end cocoon, thin-shell cocoon, cocoon with points of cocooning frame, malformed cocoon, perforated cocoon *etc.*

ii. **Length of cocoon filament:** The length of filament taken from a cocoon is expressed in metre.

iii. **Reelability percentage:** It represents how many times the cocoon filament has been broken during reeling. The reciprocal of the average end-feeding times per cocoon is expressed in percentage.

iv. **Raw silk percentage of cocoon:** The conditioned weight of raw silk that has been produced from the reelabe cocoons is divided by the total weight of cocoons submitted for testing (including rejected cocoons). The result is shown in percentage

$$\text{Raw Silk \%} = \frac{\text{Silk weight}}{\text{Green cocoon weight}} \times 100$$

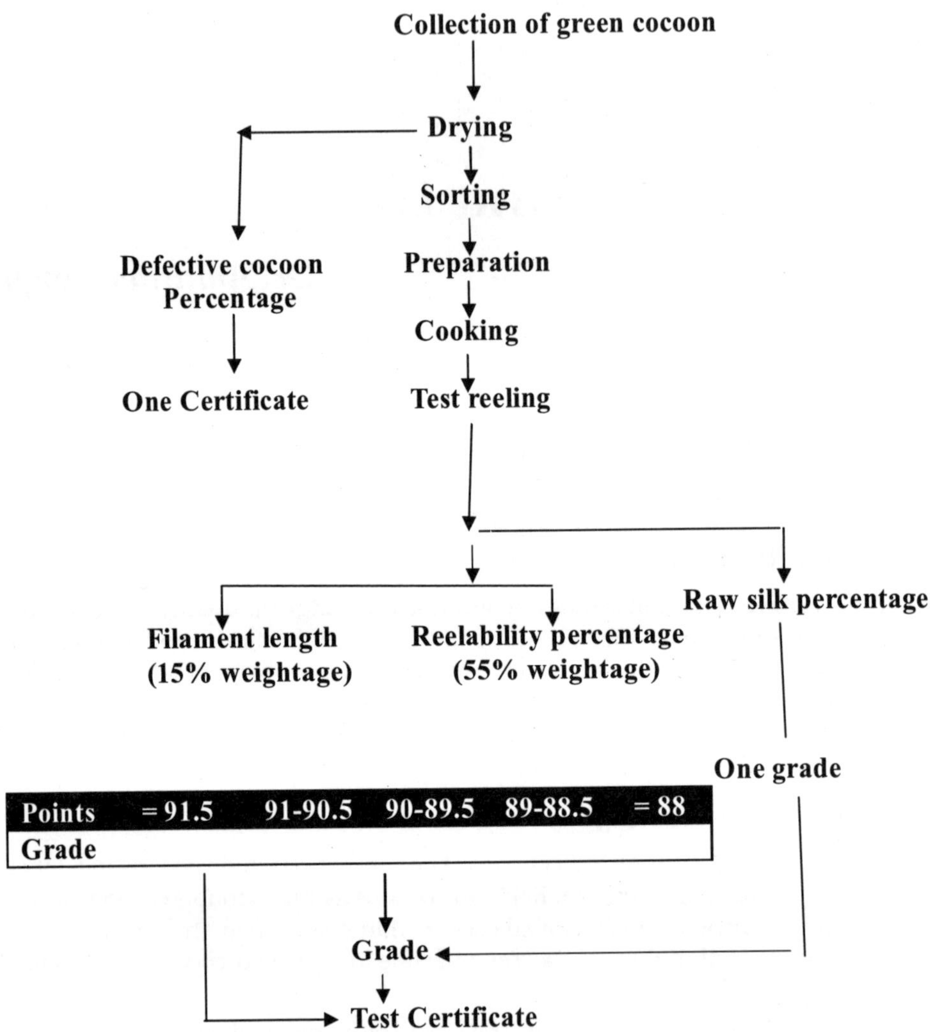

Cocoon Testing Method Adopted in Japan

Indian System of Cocoon Testing and Grading

In India there is no standard method of cocoon testing and grading. In maximum cases the grading is done by ceiling directly the defective cocoon percentage within the cocoon lot. Whereas, in the southern region Reelability percentage and raw silk percentage are generally taken additionally into consideration for cocoon grading.

Grading of Cocoon

The results of the testing of the length of the cocoon filaments and the Reelability are given marks according to the table of marks respectively. The sum of both marks (called the grading marks) is compared with the classification table. The grade on the table corresponding to the grading marks is given to the lot of the cocoons. The grade is divided into 5: Excellent to the 4th.

Classification of Cocoons by the Result of Testing

Sl.No.	Classification/Test Items	Good	Medium	Inferior
1.	Reelability-average	76%	73%	69%
2.	Reelability-range	Above 75.1%	75.0-70.1%	Below 70.1%
3.	Length of cocoon filament	Above 1,201m	1200-1,051m	Below 1,050m
4.	Rejected cocoon ratio	Below 0.7%	0.71-1.0%	Above 1.1%
5.	Size of cocoon filament-average	2.74d	2.57d	2.48d
6.	Grade of cocoon	Extra-1st	2nd	3rd-4th
7.	Raw sill percentage of cocoons-average	18.84	18.00	17.19

Degree of Cooking

The degree of cocoon cooking is measured by the cocoon shell weight, whole cocoon weight and swelling rate of cocoon.

A standard measurement is as following:

i. **Cooked cocoon shell weight:** 5-6 times as heavy as the original shell weight is desirable.4-5 times or below under cooking while 6 times or above is overcooking.

ii. **Cooked cocoon lot:** 10-11 times he lot of the original (dried) cocoons.

iii. **Swelling rate of the cocoon shell:** 1.7-2 times as thick as that of the original cocoon shell.

Brief Account of Silk Conditioning and Testing

Quality of raw silk can affect the variety and quality of fabric. Good quality will be given the high price. The standard is from the government, and the raw silk is tested and classified by the special testing centres. The quality of raw silk consists mainly of two items:

i. Visual inspection.

ii. Mechanical tests

Visual Inspection

Before the raw silk is subject to mechanical test, the sample lot is visually and tactually examined for commercial characteristics such as:

- Uniformity in colour, lusture and hand.
- Condition of general finish and,
- Nature of the lot.

Mechanical Tests

The mechanical test to which the raw silk is subjected to are: winding size, evenness, cleanness, neatness, dynamometric properties and cohesion. Besides these, the other tests which are also in practice for raw silk are the determination of its commercial weight (conditioned weight), loss in degumming and specification of loading.

Winding Test

The test is established in order to determine the winding quality of the skein, when the thread is transferred from hank to the bobbin during the throwing process prior to weaving. More number of breakage per unit time during winding obviously means loss of production and more wastage and naturally the quality of woven product is affected on account of more number of knots in the silk thread.

Average Size, Size Deviation and Maximum Deviation Test

Thickness of raw silk thread is expressed in terms of Tex or Denier and it is as important as the counts of any other textile yarns. Actual count (size) should be very close to the nominal count which is required by the weavers. Besides attaining the nominal count, variation of the thickness (size) all along the length of the thread must be within an acceptable range. Raw silk thread is composition of a number of individual filaments. Variations of thickness in the individual filament and variation in maintenance of required number of cocoons at each end of the reeling basin throughout the reeling process influence the variation in size (thickness) of the raw silk thread. Hence, the size test is considered to be one of the important characteristics of raw silk. The test to determine standard deviation in size (or size deviation) and maximum deviation within the sample are necessary.

Evenness, Cleanness and Neatness Test

Evenness, cleanness and neatness characteristics have direct influence on the weaving quality of fabrics. Hence, considerable importance is attached to these tests in grading of raw silk. Short ranged irregularities shall be measured by evenness test, whereas the long ranged irregularities are measured by the size (count) deviation test. Actually, these are visual tests. The raw silk thread is wrapped on the black board, so as to have a uniform panel and this panel of raw silk is visually examined and directly compared individually with the standard photographs in a dark-room under specified intensity of light whereby average percentage of evenness, neatness and cleanness are determined.

Tenacity and Elongation Test

The unique synthesis of strength and fineness make silk very useful in certain important sectors, such as, surgical field and fabrication of precision equipments.

Silk fibre is also highly extensible. Therefore, the determination of strength and elongation of raw silk is an important test. Breaking load *i.e.,* the load the thread can withstand just when it breaks is expressed in terms of grams per tex or per denier and is known as tenacity. Normally, the tenacity and elongation test is carried out on the serigraph strength tester or the serimeter. The tester works on the principle of constant rate of traverse, pendulum type of yarn strength testing machine, graduated in grams and capable of recording simultaneously the breaking load and the corresponding elongation of the threads. Normally, the tenacity and elongation percentage of mulberry raw silk are in the range of 3.5-4.5g/d and 18-22 per cent respectively.

Cohesion Test

Composite raw silk thread is not twisted during reeling. The individual filaments are combined mainly by the sericin content in the silk fibre. When the cocoons are cooked in boiling water, the sericin is softened and it will be in softened condition during reeling as the reeling is done in hot water. The sericin adhering to the filaments dries after reeling *i.e.,* on exposure to air and causes the filaments to agglutinate in the thread. Thus, the raw silk thread is compact and strong enough to with stand friction during the later processes

Silk Conditioning

Silk is highly hygroscopic in nature. Therefore, it absorbs moisture to the extent of 15-20 per cent during the days of high humidity like rainy season etc. During dry season, the moisture content in the silk will be very low. However, at standard atmospheric conditions *i.e.,* at 27°C temperature and 65 per cent relative humidity, silk absorbs about 11 per cent moisture. So, in order to avoid loss/gain either to the seller or buyer, the silk is conditioned to have standard moisture content of 11 per cent in it.

To start with, silk is subjected to heat treatment at 140°C so as to remove all the moisture content and then add 11 per cent moisture to oven dry weight to find out the conditioned weight of silk.

$$\text{Conditioned Weight of Silk} = W_D + \frac{W_D \times 11}{100}$$

where, W_D = Oven dry weight of silk

All the tests except evenness, cleanness and neatness should be undertaken in air conditioned room with a standard temperature of 27°±2°C and relative humidity of 65 per cent ±2 per cent. However, our silk testing houses are not fully air conditioned for the purpose. Similarly, raw silk is not transacted on the basis of conducted weight in India unlike in sericulturally advanced countries like Japan and China.

Grading of Silk

For classification purposes raw silk shall be divided into three categories according to size.

- ☆ 1st category: 18 denier and below
- ☆ 2nd category: 19 to 33 denier
- ☆ 3rd category: 34 denier and above

The grades shall be expressed in the following order in all categories of raw silk 4A, 3A, 2A, A, B.

Method of Classification

The grade of a lot shall be determined in the following manner.

1) Grading in Accordance with the Major Tests

The grade of a lot in size 33 denier and finer (categories 1 and 2) shall be determined according to the lowest percentage of its size deviation. Evenness variation II, cleanness, average neatness and low neatness, whereas the grade of a lot in sizes 34 denier and coarser (category 3) shall be determined according to the lowest respective percentage of its size deviation, maximum deviation, evenness variation I, evenness II, cleanness, average neatness and low neatness, as tabulated in the classification table for each category.

2) De-grading in Accordance with the Auxiliary Tests

a. If any one of the maximum deviation, evenness variation III, winding, tenacity, elongation or cohesion tests of a lot in sizes 33 denier and finer, or if any one of the evenness variation III, winding, tenacity or elongation tests of a lot in sizes 34 denier and coarser, is found to be lower than the corresponding value listed in the class of auxiliary tests, then the grade provisionally established in accordance with the preceding paragraph shall be lowered by as many grades as the difference exists between required auxiliary test class and the class actually found, provided that any difference more than one class shall be deemed as one class difference with respect to the maximum deviation and evenness variation III of a lot in sizes 33 denier and finer and evenness variation II of a lot in sizes 34 denier and coarser. In case two or more auxiliary test classes are found to be lower than the corresponding values listed in the classes of the auxiliary tests, then the lot shall be declassed to the lowest auxiliary test class actually found.

b. In case the result of the visual inspection of a lot is found to be "Slightly Inferior" in the general finished and/or the result of the skein finish inspection in the winding test of a lot is found to be "Poor" the grade of the lot shall be one below that as determined in accordance with the preceding paragraphs.

c. In case the result of the visual inspection of a lot is found to be "Inferior" in its general finish, or in case the number of breaks in the winding test exceeds the limits mentioned the lot shall be determined as **B** grade.

	Breaks
12 denier or finer	50
13 to 18 denier	40
19 to 33 denier	35
34 to 69 denier	25
70 denier or coarser	20

3) Average Size Variation

The conditioned average size of a lot shall not vary more than the following limitations either way from the arithmetical mean of the size limits specified in the contract.

20/22 denier and finer	4 per cent either way
21/23 to 26/28	3.5 per cent either way
27/29 and coarser	Unless by special agreement, the Average size shall fall within the Size limits specified in the contract.

3.2. Employment Potential of Sericulture Industry in Rural India, with Special Reference to J&K State

Silk is a way of life in India. Over thousands of years, it has become an inseparable part of Indian culture and tradition. No ritual is complete without silk being used as a wear in some form or the other. Sericulture and Silk Textiles Industry is one of the major sub-sectors comprising the textiles sector. Sericulture is an agro-based cottage industry. Sericulture refers to the mass-scale rearing of silk producing organisms in order to obtain silk. The major activities involved in a sericulture industry are:

a. Cultivation of silkworm food plants
b. Rearing of silkworms for the production of raw silk
c. Reeling the cocoons for unwinding the silk filament and
d. Other post-cocoon processes such as twisting, dyeing, weaving, printing and finishing.

Sericulture is one of the most labour intensive sectors, combining activities of both agriculture (sericulture) and industry. India is ranked as the second major raw silk producer in the world. It is this position along with its immense employment potential that makes sericulture and silk, indispensable in the Indian textile map. Sericulture is an eco-friendly agro-based labour intensive rural cottage industry providing subsidiary employment and supplementing the income of rural farmers especially the economically weaker section of the society. Sericulture generates a higher income and employment per unit area and ensures a continuous and assured flow of income to the farmer throughout the year. The changes in employment and income opportunities in rural areas may be brought about by selecting a highly labour intensive and high income generating cropping system and sericulture has been identified as one such sector which plays a vital role in generating gainful employment opportunities to the villages (Ahsan, 2000). It is a highly remunerative occupation requiring little capital investment. It is estimated that sericulture can generate employment @11 man days per kg of raw silk production (in on-farm and off-farm activities) throughout the year. In China 20 million farmers and 5 lakh people are occupied by sericulture and silk processing industry. In India 59000 villages providing employment to 6 million people from the farm sector and silk processing industry are practicing sericulture. Employment and income generation is primarily among the disadvantageous groups, *i.e.*, women, SCs, STs and minorities and other marginalized groups are also substantially involved. In the year 2010-11 the employment in sericulture sector was 72.5 lakh persons (*i.e.*, 52.20 lakh farmers, 3.70 lakh reelers and 16.60 lakh weavers) when compared to 68.17 lakh persons during 2009-10. Moreover, 55-60 per cent of the Sericultural activities are undertaken by rural women. CSB has in its CDP programme designed for XI Plan period, a special scheme for Women in Sericulture *viz.*, Women Empowerment (CSB, 2011).

Income among Different Crops in One Hactera of Land (US$/ha)

J&K state is known for producing bivoltine silk of international quality. Being one of the traditional agro based industries of the state, producing high quality bivoltine silk comparable to international quality helps in improving the economic condition of the landless farmers and weaker sections of the society and providing employment opportunities during pre and post cocoon activities. Presently about 25500 rural families generating income worth Rs.1100 lakhs annually and 1 lakh mandays in private reeling sector are associated with this profession (Dhar *et al.*, 2011). With the increased economic needs due to changing social status and unpredictable market trend of different kinds of produces by the farmers of the state, sericulture has assumed special significance as an important subsidiary occupation which supplements the income of the farmers in addition to their returns from the other crops. Basic feature of this farm based economic enterprise is the involvement of women. However, production of quality bivoltine silk is still a challenge in J&K having enormous potential to produce bivoltine silk of international grade can help to reduce the import of bivoltine silk in the country.

Statistics of Sericulture in J&K for the Year 2010-11

An analysis of trends suggests that the main objective of increasing cocoon production, income generation, productivity and the number of silkworm rearers has been achieved.

Year	*Cocoon Crop (MT)*	*Income Generation (Lakhs)*	*Avg. Price for "A" Grade Silk (Rs.)*	*Productivity per Oz (Kg)*	*Silkworm Rearer Popn (no's)*	*No. of Sericulture Villages*	*No. of mulberry Trees (000 no's)*	*Raw Silk Prod. (MTs)*
2008-09	738	455.67	192.00	32.00	19700	2420	8100	82
2009-10	810	800.00	300.00	35.00	22800	2421	8100	100
2010-11	860	1100.00	400.00	40.00	23500	2500	8690	110

Source: Economic Survey, 2010-11

3.3. Introduction to Seed Organization, What is Seed Organization. Need for Seed Organization, Seed Cocoon Production at different Levels: Silkworm Egg Production (a) Pure (b) Hybrid

Introduction to Seed Organization, What is Seed Organization?

Seed organization in India is well conceived, planned and takes care of production of quality P_1 seed required for raising seed cocoons of component races of either sex *i.e.*, males and females for hybrid silkworm seed production. Seed organization can be defined as structured production of silkworm P_1 seed for raising seed crops successfully to support the projected commercial seed production. Seed organization consists of maintenance of breeder's stock and its multiplication for the ultimate production of large quantity of commercial hybrid seeds. Three distinct levels of handling and multiplication of silkworm races are involved in seed production, namely breeder's stock, basic seed multiplication and industrial seed. The maintenance of breeder's stock should be the responsibility of breeders of Research Institute, which in turn should supply the basic seed for further multiplication. The breeders stock will be multiplied 3-4 times in a year and the different multiplication levels are designated as P_3, P_2 and P_1. However, a three tier system is considered more ideal and efficient which is followed in all sericultural advanced countries. The breeder's stock and multiplication centers should be under the control of govt. agencies and well rained persons.

Need for Seed Organization

The most vital step in silkworm rearing is the production of the silkworm eggs (seed) required for rearing. The silkworm eggs (seeds), required for commercial rearing should be of high quality and free from disease. On innumerable occasion the entire sericulture industry has been ruined through lack of appreciation of the need for healthy high-quality silkworm seeds. The production and supply of disease-free silkworm eggs is highly specialized work involving technical and scientific skills. To produce quality seed there must be a sound seed organization. Realizing the importance of quality seeds in the development of the sericulture industry, sericulture countries all over the world have established a network of institutions both for research on egg production for commercial production of quality eggs.

Seed Cocoon Production at Different Levels: Silkworm Egg Production (a) Pure (b) Hybrid

Multiplication of Basic Seed Stock at P4, P3 P2 and P1

Procedure for Multiplication of Basic Stocks at P4 and P3

i. Plan and programme the basic seed production based on the requirement of eggs for next level of multiplication. There should be an integrated programme to supply the eggs to various multiplication centers.

ii. Prepare a flow chart and supply programme for one year in advance for effective monitoring of the production and supply of basic seed.

iii. Brush 10-30 Dfls of each breed in cellular batches (individual laying) depending upon their demand and supply of laying.

iv. Count all the larvae after third moult and retain till spring

v. Sort out dead pupae-cocoons, malformed cocoons, stained cocoons, thin shelled cocoons etc., after the cocoon harvest.

vi. Calculate pupation rate on the bases of live pupae.

vii. Calculate the pupation rate for the number of larvae brushed. Deduct the number of uzi infested larvae and muscardine affected if any, from the original number and calculate the pupation rate only for the remaining basic number of larvae.

viii. Take 50-60 cocoons at random in each batch and sex them, then record mass cocoon weight, shell weight and cocoon shell percentage separately for both male and female cocoons. Take the mean of both the sexes in each batch. Calculate the mean of various characters.

ix. Select only the batches above average for pupation in each race.

x. For every rearing the P_3 layings should be obtained from P4 stock. The selected batches of each breed both in P_3 and P_4 are to be interbred or inter-batch crossing for raising next generation.

xi. Depending upon the required number of Dfls, keep equal number of male and female pupae for egg production.

xii. After egg laying, mother moths are subjected for perbrine examination.

xiii. Make provision to preserve P3 and P4 eggs under different hibernation schedule.

xiv. Replace the breeder's stock from breeders once or twice in a year.

P_4 and P_3 stations are the race breeding experimental stations and their aim is to maintain the purity of the races. 25 per cent of the selected cocoons from P_3 are sent to the P_2 stations. The eggs produced in P_3 centers are called Breeders Stock Eggs. These centers are the germ banks for many races.

P_2 Stations

They get seed cocoons from P_3 stations and rear them by cellular method.

Multiplication of Silkworm Breeds at P2 Stations

i. For every rearing, the P_2 layings should be obtained from P3 stock.

ii. Depending upon the requirements of P_1 Dfls, the P_2 Dfls rearing should be prepared. To produce-1000 P_1 Dfls, 6000 pupae are required *i.e.*, 3000 males and 3000 female. The survival rate is 50 per cent of the total larvae brushed.

iii. 5-10 Dfls are brushed in mass.

iv. After cocoon harvest, sort out dead pupae, cocoons, malformed cocoons, stained cocoons, thin shelled cocoons *etc.*, live-pupae-cocoons are only taken for calculation of pupation rate.

v. Use mass cocoons assessment of 50 males and 50 females in each batch to record cocoon weight, shell weight and shell percentage.

vi. Record data systematically.

vii. Utilize all good cocoons for P_1 laying production.

viii. After egg laying, all the mother moth should be subjected for perbrine test individually

ix. Create data base systematically in Basic Seed Farms (BSF).

P_1 Stations

These produce reproductive seed cocoons from the cocoons received from P_3 stations. The seed cocoons are mass reared and the first hybridization of double crosses is done here and the hybrids produced are called foundation hybrids. They send 25 per cent of the cocoons produced to grainages or to seed cocoon rearers for rearing the seed cocoon which acts as parents for commercial eggs. Polyhybrids are superior to monohybrids. If grainages are situated in places where there is little space/mulberry/labour for mass rearing of parental cocoons, P_1 send seed cocoon to License Seed Cocoon rearers. They sell their seed cocoons at a premium prices to the grainages.

P_4 and P_3 level

↓

Individual laying/cellular brushing

↓

Batch-(bed) wise cocoon harvest

↓

Calculation of pupation rate

↓

Assessment of 50-60 cocoons (male and female) bed-wise for cocoon weight, Shell weight and shell percentage

↓

Calculation of mean values of all the batches of the breed for cocoon weight, shell weight and shell percentage

↓

Selection of batches above average in P4 nearer to average in P3

↓

Culling undesirable cocoons

↓

Cocoon cutting and sexing

↓

Inter-batch (bed) crossing

↓

Preparation of P_3 layings from P_4 and P_2 layings from P3

↓

P_2 level

↓

Mass rearing of 5-10 Dfls

↓

Batch-wise cocoon harvest and assessment

↓

Mixing of good cocoons from all the batches

↓

Preparation of P_1 Dfls

FLOW CHART FOR MULTIPLICATION OF $P_{4,}$ P_3 AND P_2

Silkworm Egg Production (b) Hybrid

Reproductive seeds, or eggs, are those intended for producing the seed cocoons which are required in large numbers for producing commercial hybrid eggs or industrial seed. These pure lines are difficult to rear and so special care and attention must be taken and ideal rearing conditions provided. These are sold at premium price of 30-50 percent more than reeling cocoons.

Industrial seeds are generally specific hybrid between two or more pure lines of races of silkworms and are reared by the sericulturists for producing cocoons on a commercial scale for reeling purposes. After multiplying the reproductive seeds to meet the needs of the industrial seeds the latter are prepared by crosses between parental races for producing the hybrid seed.

3.4. Role of Women in Sericulture-Women Participation in Mulberry Garden and Rearing Management-Silk Reeling-Twisting, Weaving and Finishing

Women workers constitute one third of the world labour force performing nearly two thirds of aggregate working hours but their contributory role in vital productive work-share remains still invisible. It is estimated that India is home of 12.7 crores of working women while 90 per cent of them are working in the unorganized sector. Specifically they are found in marginal and casual employment in agriculture, where the gender-bias wage differential is substantial. In India, women are also concentrated in agro-based household activities, where they often serve as unpaid family labour and thereby remain imperceptible.

Sericulture is one of such activities where most of the works are carried out by women alone, both in terms of operations performed and time invested. Thus in a way, they contribute a significant role in different spectrum of work-activities as well as in decision-making. The women of rural areas in particular are quite adept in farm related activities both within and outside the household. All activities in sericulture are mostly indoor except land preparation for mulberry plantation, which are best suited to women folk. Moreover women can concentrate and accomplish the work with their full sincerity and devotion while at home.

The sericultural activities like sapling/nursery raising, leaf harvest, silkworm rearing, cocoon harvesting, marketing, entire grainage operations for disease free layings preparation (pupae sexing, coupling, covering and microscopic moth examination, surface sterilization of layings, incubation, preservation and disposal of layings to the rearers etc.), silk reeling and weaving are being attended independently by women. Recently the participation of women in cultural practices of mulberry like weeding, manuring, pruning are also increasing day by day. Women are equally expert as artisan of rearing appliances, handicraft materials and selling of patented products. It is a proven fact that women constitute sixty percent of the work force engaged in various sericulture activities.

We can depend on the women folk to run the entire sericulture industry, production in particular if they are helped and trained as they require. Because, women constitute 48.2 per cent of the total population (49.6 crores as per 2001 census) in India, at least if we can utilize even 1 per cent of this huge women population for the sericulture, it would be a real boost to the rural development.

Simultaneously, we are to ensure the necessary support to them through access to rearers such as land, input, technology and training. Training regarding women's participation in group formation and leadership development, group economic activity, development in decision making, access to sericulture income through savings accounts in their name is most essential to benefit the whole sector.

Usha Rani (2007) in one of her studies showed that the establishment of one acre mulberry garden for rearing 300 Dfls (disease free layings) of silk worms in two months generates 96.36 man days of employment, of which 72.70 percent are women. Not only this, she has also shown that cocoon cutting, sexing and egg incubation is exclusively done by women labour. According to one statistical analysis submitted at a National Conference on "Women in Sericulture" (held at Mysore on 16th and 17th March, 2007), it can generate employment up to 11 persons of every kg of raw silk produced, out of which more than 6 persons are women. In India, more than 60 lakh persons are employed as full time workers in the production chain out of which 35-40 lakh persons are women. Ever-increasing demand to meet the domestic handloom

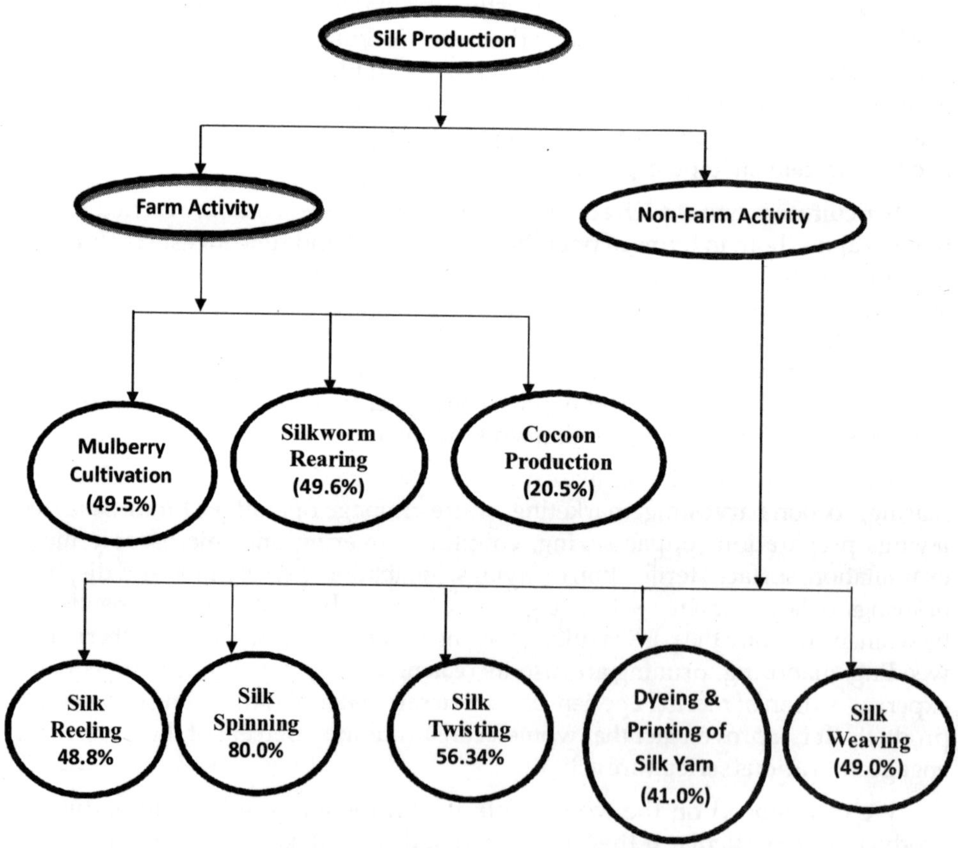

Women Involvement in Silk Production (Flow Chart)

industry requirements and equally increasing potentials for exports provide tremendous opportunity for the women to avail sustainable income generating activities.

Participation of Women in Various Sericulture Activities

Sl.No.	Sericulture Activity	Per cent of Women Participation (Som and Eri Cultivation)
1.	Land Preparation	25
2.	Collection of Planting Material	10
3.	Procurement of Fertilizers and Manure	10
4.	Planting	78
5.	Application of Manure	65
6.	Application of Fertilizer	70
7.	Pest and Disease Management	20
8.	Transportation of Leaf	40
Sl.No.	*Sericulture Activity*	*Per cent of Women Participation (Silkworm Rearing)*
9.	Chawki Rearing	88
10.	Leaf Preservation	80
11.	Maintenance of Hygienic Conditions	94
12.	Pest and Disease Management	50
13.	Maintenance of Environmental Conditions	70
14.	Bed Cleaning	88
15.	Spinning	90
16.	Harvest Sorting	94
17.	Marketing	06
18.	Finance and Account Keeping	08

Source: Chandrama Goswami and Manisha Bhattacharya, 2013: International Journal of Scientific and Research Publications. 3(3):1-6.

Reasons for Dominance of Women Workers in Sericulture

Sericulture is practiced in villages of India as a family-based occupation and thereby provides women a major role to play with, in various activities of this household-industry. Nearly 60 per cent of the labour requirement is met by the women in almost all the traditional sericulture agencies in the world. Women's precision and patience make their presence more invincible in silk-worm handling. Since, traditions and customs of society in Indian rural context do not encourage the majority of rural women to work outdoors, sericulture proves to be a boon. It gives a wide opportunity where women can carry all their contributory work even after attending to their own regular household chores. Thus, sericulture is ideally suited for family women in the rural areas.

Farm women have certain unique attributes, which are of special relevance to sericulture development and that these characteristics make the female dominance in sericulture indispensable:

i. A farm woman is the sheet anchor of the farm family. She is the foremost member who is concerned all the time about the well being of the family. So when women dominance is seen in any activity that has to be turned out to be a successful one. Poverty in rural India is another key feature that makes the women from lower class more intensive and serious to the work and this also enhances their productivity.

Women Participation in Different Activities of Sericulture since Ancient Time

ii. Women are proved to be an efficient home-maker from the time immemorial. So whether as an artisan or a household industrial worker, she is supposed to give her best as it is involved with her family. Sericulture is such farm enterprises that have a great share of indoor components and demand enough tenacity and sufficient attention. Thus female dominances in sericulture become quite natural.

iii. According to the analysts, women have proven themselves to be better learners. They are easily adaptable which is important for a dynamic world where better sericulture technologies are about to pay better dividends.

3.5. Import and Export Potential and Policies of Sericulture *viz.*, Seed, Silk Thread and Finished Garments

India exports considerable quantity of silk goods and the value of these silk goods is more than 15 per cent of the total raw silk production. India's export includes Dress Materials, Readymade Garments, Saris and Made-up articles for interior decoration. India's export has adequately progressed during the study period with both quantity and value of export showing high and significant growth. This increased growth is also accompanied by higher volatility. India exports mainly to 10 countries *viz.*, USA, UK, Hong Kong, German People Republic, Italy, France, Spain, Saudi Arabia, UAE and Singapore. The share of total Indian exports to these 10 countries constitutes 80 per cent.

Export of Silk from India

Year	*Exports (Rs)*	*Trend Value (Rs in crores)*
1997-98	1006.43	1422.85
1998-99	999.45	1593.74
1999-00	1755.55	1764.64
2000-01	2421.98	1935.53
2001-02	2359.56	2106.43
2002-03	2294.05	2277.32
2003-04	2779.19	2448.22
2004-05	2879.56	2619.11
2005-06	3194.20	2790.01
2006-07	3338.35	2960.90
2007-08	2727.87	3131.80
2008-09	3178.19	3302.69
2009-10	2892.44	3473.59
2010-11		3644.48
2011-12		3815.38
2012-13		3986.27
2013-14		4157.17

Source: CSB, Bangalore; Including Silk Yarn, Fabrics and Made-ups, Silk Waste and silk RMG.

The above table shows the export of silk goods from India and trend value estimated from the year 1997 to 2014. The trend value for the years 1997-98, 1998-99, 1999-2000, 2007-08, 2008-09 and 2009-10 are more than the actual value. In these years, silk goods exports show an unsatisfactory trend. The trend value of Growth of silk exports in India 2005-06 and is less than the trend value in the periods, 2000-01, 2001-02, 2002-03, 2003-04, 2004-05 and 2006-07. It shows the satisfactory trend in

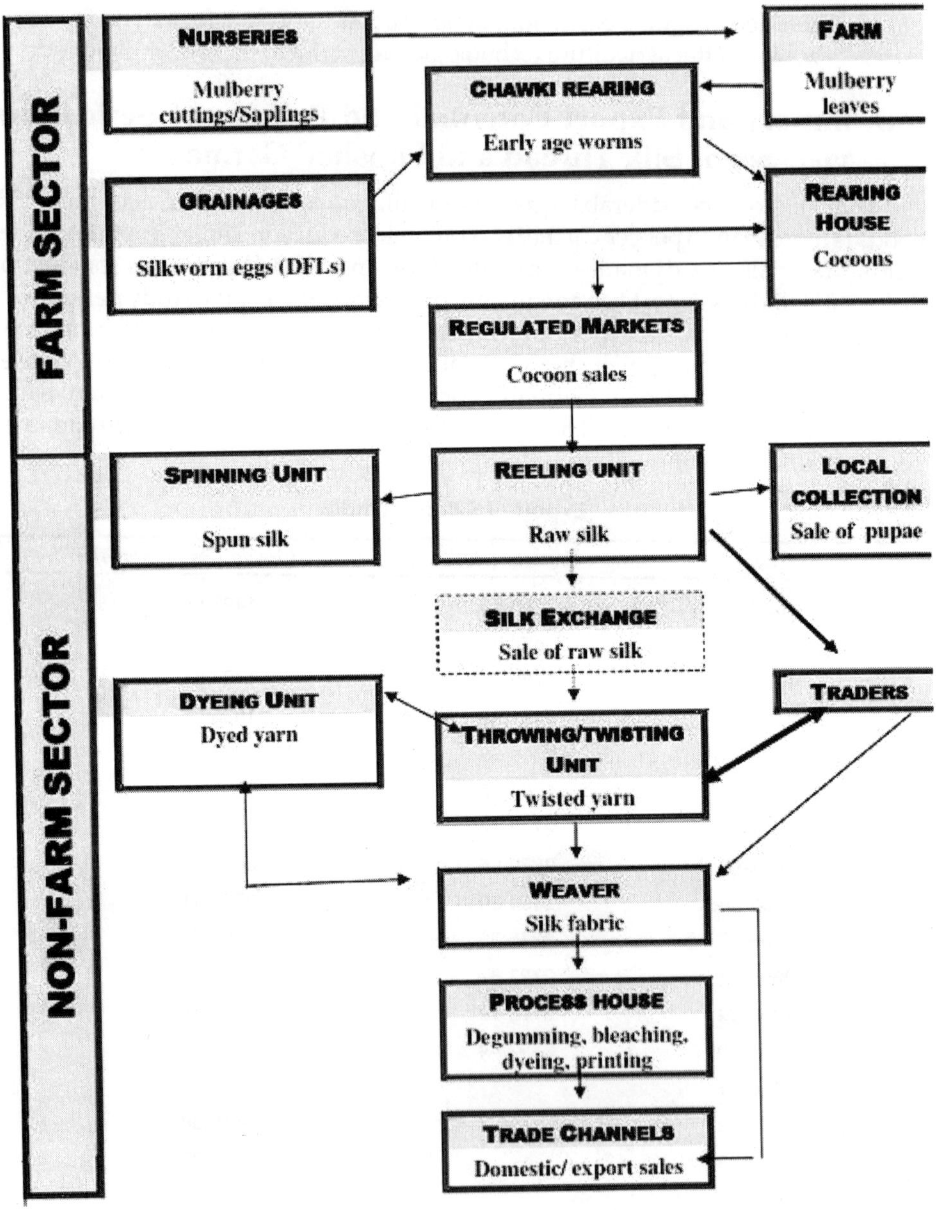

Activity Chain in Silk Industry

these periods. In case of future prediction, the estimated growth of silk exports from India will be 4157.17 cores of silk exports in the years 2014. The major silk trading countries in the world are India, United States, Germany, Italy, France, Australia, Japan, China, and Thailand. Germany is the largest consumer of Indian silk. With substantial government and international subsidies for silk projects and marketing schemes, the industry has been expanding rapidly over the last few years. Silk exports too are growing rapidly.

Import of Raw Silk

Year	*Quantity in tonnes*	*Value (Rs in millions)*
1997-98	1876	2183.31
1998-99	1984	2593.64
1999-00	5018	4127.44
2000-01	4713	4732.61
2001-02	6808	6247.30
2002-03	9054	6471.50
2003-04	9258	6291.7
2004-05	7948	6374.3
2005-06	8383	7797.1
2006-07	5565	6733.7
2007-08	7922	7344.4
2008-09	8392	9030.6
2009-10	7338	9337.0

Source: Ministry of Textiles in India.

The above Table shows the import of raw silk between 1997-98 and 2009-10. The year to year continuous increase in imports of silks shows that domestic production of raw silk is not adequate to meet the domestic and export demand. It is estimated

Import of Silk Yarn and Fabrics (Value in Rs. million)

Year	*Silk Yarn and Fabrics*	*Per cent of Import*
1999-00	619.75	1.62
2000-01	910.21	2.38
2001-02	1729.94	4.53
2002-03	2930.4	7.68
2003-04	5298.9	13.88
2004-05	8030.6	21.04
2005-06	9645.8	25.27
2006-07	9004.9	23.59

Source: Ministry of Textiles in India.

that against the demand of around 26,000 ton per annum the domestic production is around 17300 tonnes. The gap of nearly 8700 tones in demand is mainly on account of the fact that high-grade quality mulberry raw silk is not being produced in the country to the extent required by the industry. This mulberry raw silk is basically required in the power loom industry, for export purposes, and to some extent in the handloom industry for warp purposes.

Above Ttable shows an increase in the import of silk yarn and fabrics from the year 1999-00 to 2006-07. The import of silk yarn and fabrics was 1.62 in the year 1999-00 and it rose to 23.59 per cent in the year 2006-07.

Export and Import of Silkworm Seed

Conditions and Standards for Export and Import of Silkworm Seed

No person shall export or import the silkworm seeds unless:

- ☆ He is a registered seed producer or a registered dealer; and
- ☆ He possesses export or import license as the case may be;
- ☆ He has obtained prior permission of the Committee or its authorized representative.
- ☆ He possesses valid quarantine certificate issued by the Quarantine Authority.
- ☆ Every exporter or importer shall abide by the terms and conditions of silkworm seed export and import laid down by the Government of India from time to time.
- ☆ Every exporter shall export only hybrid silkworm seed, and shall not export silkworm seed of pure races in any form.
- ☆ Every exporter shall get the seed permitted for export, inspected by the quarantine authority who shall seal and mark the same as "Inspected and certified" and such seal shall not be altered or mutilated before exporter.
- ☆ Every importer of silkworm seed shall submit a report of the performance of the imported seed to the Committee.

Demand for Silk and Silk Fabrics

The demand for sericulture activity is a derived demand as it emanates from the demand for finished silk fabric from the consumers. This link is all the same more important because of high value of the silk fabric and silk goods. There are two market segments for silk goods–domestic and export sectors. Idea about domestic demand pattern can be obtained from the annual surveys of the Textile Committee, Ministry of Textiles, Government of India. Information about export market can be obtained from foreign trade statistics. The domestic demand of raw silk when compared to other fibres.

Domestic Demand of Silk and Other Fibres

The latest survey of Textile Committee covered 11,860 households spread in 112 urban and 211 rural areas across the country. The survey brought out that the per capita purchase of silk in the year 2002 declined drastically by about 52 per cent to 0.13 meter compared to 0.27 meter purchased in 2001. The consumption of synthetic blends grew faster compared to cotton. Consumption of silk declined at 1.09 per cent per annum and the share of silk in total fabric consummation also declined. Closer examination, however, revealed that but for steep decline in 2002, the consumption of silk in both absolute and relative terms increased annually at 6.28 and 2.57 per cent, respectively. The declining trend in the year 2002 can be due to general drought condition in the country and related slump in demand for non-farm outputs such as silk.

Consumption of Silk, Cotton and Synthetic Blend Fabric in India

Year	*Per capita Consumption of Fabric (meters)/Annum*				*Per cent of Silk to Total Consumption*
	Silk	*Cotton*	*Synthetic+Blend*	*Total Cloth*	
1995	0.19	7.02	7.41	14.62	1.3
1996	0.21	6.93	8.00	15.14	1.4
1997	0.25	7.07	9.64	16.96	1.5
1998	0.26	6.39	9.42	16.07	1.6
1999	0.22	7.06	9.06	16.34	1.3
2000	0.31	7.11	10.31	17.73	1.7
2001	0.27	7.45	10.84	18.56	1.5
2002	0.13	7.77	10.98	18.88	0.7
Exponential growth rate perannum (per cent)	–1.09 (6.28*)	1.43	5.42	3.58	–4.54 (2.57)*

* Growth upto 2001.

In monetary terms, an average Indian spent Rs 122.38 in 2001 on silk fabric which declined to Rs.71.50 in 2002, compared to Rs.41.65 in 1995, thus, registering annual compound growth of a wee bit below 12 per cent. The growth is higher than that for cotton and synthetic blends.

Export Market for Silk in the World

China has been the undisputed leader in silk production and its share in World exports. India, in spite of being second largest producer, shares only 1/5th of the World's production of raw silk. Incidentally, hardly any major new producer has emerged in the World silk market. This may be on account of two factors namely the price and the quality. While the raw silk price in the International market are at their lowest in twenty years, the demand for quality raw silk is soaring high due to modernisation of textile machinery that works at higher speeds.

Production of Raw Silk in different Countries (tonnes)

Country	*2005*	*2006*	*2007*	*2008*	*2009(P)*	*Per cent Share*
China	105360	130000	108420	98620	104000	81.95
India	17305	18475	18320	18370	19600	15.44
Japan	150	150	105	95	90	0.07
Brazil	1285	1387	1220	1177	811	0.64
Korea Republic	150	150	150	135	135	0.11
Uzbekistan	950	950	950	865	750	0.59
Thailand	1420	1080	760	1100	665	0.52
Vietnam	750	750	750	680	550	0.43
Others	1500	1000	500	350	304	0.24
Total	**128870**	**153942**	**131175**	**121392**	**126905**	**100.00**

The countries participating in the international silk trade can be classified into four types as below:

Category	*Countries*
Mainly Raw Silk Producers	Vietnam
Raw Silk Producers and Manufacturers of Processed Silk Goods	Brazil, China, India, Japan, Republic of Korea, The Commonwealth of Independent States, Thailand, Bangladesh, Armenia, Bulgaria, Egypt, Nigeria, Uganda, etc.
Silk Converting Countries using imported raw silk	France, Germany, Italy, Switzerland and United Kingdom
Countries which neither produce raw silk nor process it, *i.e.*, pure consumers	Australia, certain European countries,New Zealand, Canada, the United States and most of Africa and Latin America

Two groups of products are traded internationally:

1. Raw silk, silk waste, silk yarn and create fabric which need further processing.
2. Finished silk fabric, readymade garments, made up goods, interior decoration items etc.

Hongkong and China, taken together, are the World's largest converter of silk fabric into industrially processed garments.

The situation in India is completely different. Here almost all the raw silk produced is consumed domestically and there has been a wide gap between supply and demand of raw silk, which necessitated imports of silk yarn, primarily from China. As of today, many of India's leading exporters of silk goods depend entirely on imports for their raw material. Thus, we have two segments within the Indian Silk Industry, one depending on the domestic supply of raw material, which is not adequate for its needs, and the other export oriented segment, which totally depends on imports for its raw material needs. Now the Govt of India, Ministry of Textiles, has enhanced the custom duty on silk from 5 per cent to 15 per cent and it will help the sericulture industry to become self sufficient in producing the raw silk for meeting the domestic as well as international demand.

Unit-IV

Dr. Ravinder Sharma

4.1. Definition of Soil, Introduction to Soil Forming Factors, Soil Classification

"The soil was deep, it absorbed and kept the water in the loamy soil, and the water that soaked into the hills fed spring and running streams evergreen"

– Plato

Soil, in its traditional meaning, is the natural medium for the growth of land plants, soils are all unconsolidated material of the earth's crust in which land plants can grow, if water and temperature are adequate, at least the minimum nutrients are available, and toxic substances are in low concentration. According to Joffe (1949), the soil is a natural body of mineral and organic materials differentiated into horizons which differ among themselves as well as from the underlying material in morphology, physical make-up, chemical composition and biological characteristics (i) natural formation (ii) Differentiation into horizons and (iii) morphological, chemical and biological differences between parent material and soil horizon.

All soils develop from weathered rock, volcanic ash deposits, or accumulated plant residues. There are two approaches for study of soil- Pedology and Edaphology. Pedology includes the study of origin of soil, its classification and its description. Edaphology includes the study of soil in relation to plant growth.

Definition of Soil

To define soil is not an easy task in view of the heterogeneity and complexity of the soil system. This is clearly evident from the different definitions put forth from time to time ever since soil has been considered a scientific entity. A definition becomes difficult when we have to describe soil as a natural three dimensional body of the landscape and attempt to adequately describe the characteristics. It is probably worthwhile therefore to quote the definition of soil given by Joffe (1949) who stated; "The soil is a natural body of mineral and organic constituents, differentiated into horizons of variable depth, which differs from the material below in morphology, physical makeup, chemical properties and composition, and biological characteristics" The limitations of this definition lie in the fact that in many cases, soil horizons may be absent and the material below may be hard to find.

Soil is a dynamic natural body developed as a result of pedogenic processes during and after weathering of rocks, consisting of mineral and organic constituents, possessing definite chemical, physical, mineralogical and biological properties, having a variable depth over the surface of the earth and providing a medium for plant growth for land plants.

It may be of interested to distinguish between a soil and soil. A soil is situated as a natural body from the point of view of pedology, and as part of the landscape. Soil is a material whose physical, chemical mineralogical and biological characteristics are studied in relation to plant growth or to any other use. Thus emerged the different branches of soil science. They are soil physics, Soil Chemistry, Soil Biology, Soil mineralogy, Soil Fertility, Soil Genesis and classification, Soil survey and Soil Technology Technology. The Scope of each of these may be inducted but not exactly defined because of their overlapping domains.

Factors of Soil Formation

Studies of soils have shown that all kind of soils are formed under the influence of five factors of thousands of years.

Active Factors

1. Climate
2. Living organisms

Passive Factors

3. Nature of parent material
4. Topography or Relief
5. Time

Climate and Soil Formation

Climate is an increasingly dominant active factor in soil formation mainly because of the effects of precipitation and temperature. Some direct effects of climate on soil formation include the following:

1. A shallow accumulation or retention of lime (carbonates) in areas having low rainfall occurs because calcium bicarbonate (from dissolving carbon dioxide, minerals, and lime) are not leached if sufficient water is not present. Such soils are usually alkaline.

2. Acidic soils from in humid areas due to intense weathering and leaching out of basic cations (calcium, sodium, magnesium, potassium).
3. Erosion of soils on sloping lands constantly removes developing soil layers.
4. Weathering, leaching, and erosion are more intense and of longer duration in warm and humid regions.

Moisture is important in soil formation. A soil is said to be "developed" when it has detectable layers (horizons), such as of accumulated clays, organic colloids, carbonates, or soluble salts that have been moved downward by water. The extent of colloid movement and the depth of deposition are determined partly by amount and pattern of precipitation, which produce the leaching action.

Climate also influences soil formation indirectly through its action on vegetation. Semiarid climates encourage only scattered shrubs, and grasses. Arid climates supply only enough moisture for spars, short grasses or shrubs, which may not be dense enough to protect the soil against wind and water erosion. Many arid soils exhibit only slight organic matter accumulation and small amounts of profile development.

Changes during Soil Formation or Types of Soil Forming Processes

Soil formation- the processes of weathering and of change within a soil mass is caused by many factors. The processes involved in soil formation include additions, losses, transformations and translocations occur constantly.

1. Additions are made by water (rainfall, irrigation), nitrogen from bacterial fixation, energy as sunlight, sediment from wind and water, salts, organic residues, and fertilizers, and in other ways.
2. Losses result from chemicals soluble in soil water, eroded small- sized fractions, nutrients in grazed and harvested plants, water losses, carbon losses as carbon dioxide, and denitrification loss of N^2.
3. Transformations happen because of the many chemical and biological reactions that decompose organic matter, from insoluble materials from soluble substances, and alter or dissolve some materials.
4. Translocations are movement of soil material within the soils. As water and organisms move within the soil, many substances are translocated to different depths. This may be in the form of suspension or solution, for example, clays to deeper layers, and soluble salts into the groundwater or to the soil surface as water evaporates. Even localized sorting is active, such as forming deposits of carbonates or iron oxides in portions of the profile.

The above changes bring out by various geochemical cycle soil forming processes which are also known as pedogenic processes.

Soil Forming or Pedogenic Processes

The soil forming processes are complex and dynamic involving various chemical and biological reactions and usually operate simultaneously in a given area. One process may counter ac another, or two different processes may work out simultaneously to achieve the same result. The soil forming processes are fundamental or specific in nature. The fundamental processes provide a base for later operation of more specific processes.

Fundamental Soil Forming Processes

A. Humification (Organic Changes)

Humification is the process of transformation of raw organic matter into humus. These transformations occur mainly on the surface and follow a specific sequence. Degrading or break down of the organic material by algae, fungi, insects and worms causes humification which leaves behind a dark, amorphous humus releases nitrogenous compounds into the soil. This stage is called mineralization. The organic changes thus refer to the accumulated effect produced by these processes.

Degrading --- Humification --- Mineralization

B. Eluviation

The meaning of eluviation is washing out. It is the process of removal of constituents in suspension or solution by the percolating water from the upper to lower layers. In other words it refers to the down wash of clay and other soluble material, leaving behind a deprived or alluvial horizon.

C. Leaching

It is the downward movement of material-clay, bases or organic stuff, in solution or colloidal form. Leaching is more pronounced in humid areas than in dry areas.

Soil Classification

In the ancient period (2500 B.C.–1200AD.), we find reference to two classes of soil. *viz.*, urvara (fertile) and anurvara or usara (barren). The earliest attempt to classify the soils of India was on the basis of productivity of soil for a specific crop of economic importance. The land classification for revenue purposes, probably in the recent centuries, and soil classification used by the settlement officers for this purpose were based on suitability of soils for certain crops under local conditions and yield of crops, soil water status and water availability, texture, colour, etc. from the productivity point of view, they were given local names by the farmers.

Local Names

Experienced cultivators recognized the difference in soils by giving them local names. One example of classification are the Bhata, Matasi, Dorsa and Kanhar found in catenary sequence in the Chhattisgarh basin of Madhya Pradesh. Red Bhata is the poorest soil in the region, full of stones and ferruginous gravels, without any consistence; yellow Matasi, clay loam in texture, is famous for rise cultivation; Kanhar is dark brown to black clay soil which is suitable for rabi crops and resembles the Vertisols. Brown Dorsa is intermediate between Matasi and kanhar and is also suited for rice cultivation. In Andhra Pradesh, red sandy loam soils on a permeable murrum base, developed on the sides and the foot- hills are locally called chalk soils.

Another significant fact is the classification of soils as Reh, showing salt efflorescence (in morden terminology, the saline soils) and the formation of an Indian Reh committee in 1877 with the objective of investigating the causes of the deterioration of such lands. The other non-productive soil is the Kallar (acidic soil or alkali soil).Both the Reh and kallar lands are even today known in local parlance by a variety of names in different parts of India and the common term used for both is ussar (barren).

Kari soil is a name for acid sulphate soil, covering about 50,000 ha in Kerala; this typically peaty saline soil is highly acidic (ph around 3.5), deep black in colour, high in organic matter, poorly drained, remains submerged in water during the monsoon and is put to rise cultivation as soon as the water recedes. It is also known as pokkali soil.

Regular (derived from the Telugu word Nullah regarding meaning black clay),a local name for black soils was previously described in literature as black cotton soil as cotton was the major crop grown on these soils in Peninsular India. It I now called black soil or Vertisols in modern terminology. A group of very dark coloured and fine textured soils occurring in the basin area in Uttar Pradesh is popularly known as Kargil (meaning black) soils, which have some characteristics similar to those of regurs. In the black soil zone of south India, there is a peculiar type of saline and acidic soils, called chopan, which is extremely hard and impermeable to water and occasionally shows the presence of salt deposits on the surface.

These are only a few examples in point. There are a number of other local names by which the soils are classified by local farmers in India.

Geological Approach

Geologists were the earliest workers to study and classify soils, evidently from the geological point of view. Studies by various workers of the Geological Survey of India brought out important contributions to the knowledge of soils in India. Wadia, Krishana and Mukherjee in 1935 prepared a soil map of India on the basis of geological formations – generalizations put forth by the examination of lithographic materials on a very board scale. The map and classification were further improved by Wadia in 1945 and soils shown on to the map were red soils, black soils (regurs), laterite and lateritic soils, desert soils, bhbar and tarai soils.

Genetical Approach

The earliest scientific soil studies date back from 1898, when J.W. Leather, the first imperial Agricultural Chemist of the Imperial (now India) Agricultural Research Institute, New Delhi did pioneering work on soils of India. Leather distinguished four major soil groups, *viz.*, the Indo-Genetics alluvium the regurs or black soils, red soils lying on metamorphic rocks and the lateritic soils. These soils received major area of India. These generalized soil groups cover wide areas having divergent climate, vegetation and physiographic; there are other soil groups covering not- so- wide areas. Further attempts were mainly concentrated on the subdivisions of these groups and their geographical location.

By this time the Russian concept of soil was gaining ground workers in India, Z.J. Schokalsky of the Dokuchaev Institute of Soil Science, Leningard, and U.S.S.R.

prepared in 1932 a soil map of India showing the above major four soil groups and their subdivisions. In this classification, natural condition of soil formation was the main consideration. Subsequent approach to soil classification was largely influenced by the then American system of classification, mainly the genetical approach. In 1943, Viswanath and Ukil, of the Indian Agricultural Research Institute, New Delhi, in consultation with a number of soil scientists all over the country, prepared a soil map of India which showed 14 soil classes. Although this was based on scanty data, it was the beginning of soil classification and soil mapping on scientific lines.

For accurate soil map and soil classification detailed soil surveys and supporting soil data of a large number of soil samples are essential. As a first step, the All India Soil Survey Scheme was started in 1942 with its headquarters at the Indian (then Imperial) Agricultural Research Institute, New Delhi, with the object of collection and critical examination of available soil information in the different parts of country and the preparation of a preliminary soil map of India. It was published in 1957. The soil groups show map were (1) alluvial soil, (2) alluvial soil impregnated with varying amount of salt, (3) coastal sandy alluvium, (4) old alluvial soil, (5) saline and deltaic soil, (6) calcareous soil, (7) deep black soil, (8) medium black soil, (9) shallow black soil, (10) mixed red and black soil, (11) red sandy soil, (12) mixed red loam and red sandy soil, (13) lateritic soil, (14) forest and hill soil, (15) gravelly soil, (16) submontane soil, (17) Tarai soil,(18) marshey land, (19) peat soil, (20) desert soil, (21) red loam soil.

(*Source*: Final Report of the All India Soil Survey Scheme, ICAR, New Delhi, 1957.)

A second phase of the scheme was from 1958 to 1960. Detailed information on soil maps of states were published in the form of a book entitled, Soils of India by S.P. Raychaudhuri *et al.* (1963). The soil map of India, based on this information is included in Land Resources of India (vol. 1); Indian soils—Their classification, Occurrence, and properties by S.P. Raychaudhuri (1963). The soil map has 27 broad soil classes. This was revised in 1968 by Govindarajan *et al.* (1968), and was appended in the Review of soil Research in India published by the Indian Society of Soil Science in 1971. This includes 24 broad soil classes. The extent and distribution of the soil classes are presented in below in the Table.

Soil Taxonomy

The earlier classification and preparation of soil maps had a genetical bias. As soil survey progressed in the country, soil variation related to relief or physiographic were recognized and mapped. The concept of Benchmark soils for identifying and describing soil series was adopted. The Benchmark Soils of India published by Murthy *et al.* (1982) records such as 64 Benchmark soils. The concept of identifying and describing soil series was adopted in mapping and classification was according to the Soil Taxonomy. The latest Soil map of India published in 1983 by the national bureau of Soil Survey and land Use planning shows the distribution of soils classified up to suborder level and their associations. The map is, however, based on soil Surveys of about 33 percent of the total area of the country and the rest by extrapolation. As the soil survey programme in the country progresses in the regions not yet covered by actual soil survey, a more accurate soil map of India will be available.

Soil Group of India

Soil Groups of India and their Distribution*

Sl.No.	Soil Group	Area (km²)	Distribution in the State**	Soil Order (Soil Taxonomy)
1.	Red loamy	2,13,271	AP,TN,KT,KR,MP,O,R	Alfisols
2.	Red sandy	3,30,590	TN,KT,AP,B,WB	Alfisols
3.	Laterite	1,30,066	TN,KR,KT,AP,O,M,G, AWB,AN,GJ	Ultisols Oxisols
4.	Red and yellow	4,03,651	MP,O,B	Ultisols
5.	shallow black	31,532	M	Entisols
6.	Medium black	4,30,383	M,MP,GJ,AP,KT,R	Vertisols
7.	Deep black	1,12,060	M,AP,KT,MP,GJ,R	Vertisols
8.	Mixed red and black	1,62,255	KT,TN,M,MP,AP,B	Association of Alfisols and vertisols
9.	Coastal alluvium	54,403	TN,KR,KT,AP,M,GJ, WB,AN	Entisols
10.	Coastal sands	4,534	O,TN,AP,PO	Entisols
11.	Deltaic alluvium	87,045	TN,AP,O,WB	Entisols
12.	Alluvial Khadar (recent) Bhangar (old)	3,56,720	P,P,B,WB,A,H,AP,GJ, JK,KR,MPR,D	Entisols, Inceptisols Alfisols
13.	Alluvial (highly calcareous)	13,611	UP,B	Entisols
14.	Calcareous	45,080	P,H,R	Aridisols
15.	Grey brown	1,01,572	GJ,R	Aridisols
16.	Desert–Regosolic	1,54,423	R,G,H	ArdisolsEntisols
17.	Desert–Lithosolic			Entisols
18.	Tarai	28,919	UP,B,WB,AN	Mollisols
19.	Brown hill	81,242	UP,S,HP,GJ,JK,KR,P,WB	Ultisols
20.	Sub –montane(Podzolic)	76,695	UP,JK,HP	Alfisols
21.	Mountain meadow	59,790	JK	Mollisols
22.	Saline and alkali	17,377	UP,HP,M,KR,T,GJ,R	Aridisols, Entisols Vertisols
23.	Peaty and saline peaty	2,720	KR,WB	Histosols
24.	Skeletal	79,151	MP	Entisols
25.	Glaciers and eternal snow	29,335	UP,JK	

(Note: The area indicated is approximate)

* Adapted from soils of India by Raychaudhuri and Goviand Rajan, 1971 and Studies on soils of India by Govind Rajan and Gopal Rao.1978.

** Symbol for the states and Union Territories: AN: Andaman and Nicobar Island; AP: Andra Pradesh; A: Assam; B: Bihar; D: Delhi; G: Goa; GJ: Gujarat; H: Haryana; HP: Himachal Pradesh; JK: Jammu and Kashmir; KT: Karnataka; KR: Kerala; MP: Madhya Pradesh; M: Maharashtra; O: Orissa; PO: Pondicherry; P: Punjab; R Rajasthan; TN: Tamil Nadu; UP: Uttar Pradesh; WB: West Bengal.

4.2. Soil Properties, Physical *viz.*, Texture, Structure, Colour, Permeability and Air Contents, Soil Water-Importance, Physical and Biological Classification, Moisture Content, Soil Water Management for Mulberry Growth

Soil Properties, Physical *viz.*, Texture, Structure, Colour, Permeability and Air Contents

Soil is comprised of minerals, soil organic matter (SOM), water, and air. The composition and proportion of these components greatly influence soil physical properties, including texture, structure, and porosity, the fraction of pore space in a soil. In turn properties affect air and water movement in the soil, and thus the soil's ability to function. Although SOM comprises a relatively small portion of soil, typically only 1-4 per cent in Montana and Wyoming agricultural soils, it plays a key role in many soil processes and will be discussed throughout the module.

Soil physical properties

The physical properties of soils- texture, structure, density, porosity, water content, strength (consistency), temperature, and colour are dominant factors affecting the use of a soil. These properties determine the availability of oxygen in soil, the mobility of water into or through soils, and the ease of root penetration.

What is Soil Texture?

Soil texture is the "feel" of the soil when a moist quantity is manipulated between thumb and forefinger. It is one of the more useful test in evaluating soil.

Some soils are sticky others will not stick together at all, and others feel "doughy" or "spongy". Some can be manipulated like plasticine. These differences in properties gave rise in agriculture, to soils being called clays, loams or sands. Clays stick to your boots, looms are easily moulded but non-sticky, and sands are not cohesive at all and cannot be moulded when moist.

There are 19 grades of texture that can be simplified into six major groups: Sands, Sandy Loams, Loams, Clay Loams, Light Clays and Medium to Heavy Clays. These texture differences are the result of fineness or coarseness of particles in the soil. Texture will have a definable range of clay (*i.e.* d" 0.002 mm), silt (*i.e.* 0.002-0.02mm) and sand (*i.e.*, 0.02-2mm). A special triangular graph is available where texture can be related to likely clay per cent, slit per cent and sand per cent.

Soil Texture

Natural soils are comprised of soil particles of varying sizes. The soil- size groups, called **soil separates,** are sands (the coarsest), silts, and clays (the smallest). The relative proportions of soil separates in a particular soil determine its soil texture.

Texture is an important soil characteristics because it will, in part, determine water intake rates (infiltration), water storage in the soil, the ease of tilling the soil, the amount of aeration (vital to root growth), and will influence soil fertility. For instance, a coarse sandy soil is easy in till, has rapidly and easily loses plant nutrients, which are drained away in the rapidly lost water. High- clay soils (over 30 percent clay) have very small particles that fit tight together, leaving little open pore space, which means there is little room for water to flow into the soil. This makes high-clay soils difficult to wet, difficult to drain, and difficult to till.

Soil Separate Sizes

The U.S. Department of Agriculture (USDA) has established limits of variation for the soil separates and has assigned a name to each size class.

Soil Separates and their Diameter Ranges

Soil Separate Name	*Diameter Range (mm)*	*Visual Size Comparison of Maximum Size*
Very coarse sand	2.0-1.0	House key thickness
Coarse sand	1.0-0.5	Small or salt crystals
Medium sand	0.5-0.25	Sugar or salt crystals
Fine sand	0.10-0.10	Thickness of book page
Very fine sand	0.05-0.002	Visible to the eye
Slit	0.05-0.002	Visible under microscope
Clay	Less than 0.002	Most are not visible even with a microscope

Soil Textural Classes

Textural names are given to soils based on the relative proportions of each of the three soil separates- sand, slit and clay. Soils that are preponderantly clay are called clay (textural class); those with high slit content are silt (textural class); those with a high sand percentage are sand (textural class). A soil that does not exhibit the dominant physical properties of any of these three groups (such as a soil with 40 percent sand, 40 percent silt and 20 percent clay) is called loam. Note that loam does not contain equal percentages of sand, silt and clay. It does, however, exhibit approximately equal properties of sand, silt and clay.

The Textural Classes along with Relative Percentages of Sand, Silt and Clay Separates

Textural Group	*Sand*	*Slit*	*Clay*
Sand	80-100	0-20	0-20
Sandy loam	50-80	0-50	0-20
Loam	30-50	30-50	0-20
Slit loam	0-50	50-100	0-20
Sandy clay loam	50-80	0-30	20-30
Silty clay loam	0-30	50-80	20-30
Clay loam	20-50	20-50	20-30
Sandy clay	50-70	0-20	30-50
Silty clay	0-20	50-70	30-50
Clay	0-50	0-50	30-100

The Textural Triangle

A triangle (Fig) is used to determine the soil textural name after the percentages of sand, silt and clay are determined from a laboratory analysis. Since the soil's textural classification includes only mineral particles and those of less than 2mm diameter, the sand plus silt plus clay percentages equal 100 percent (Note that organic matter is not included)

Determination of Textural Class

Two methods employed for the determination of textural class.

Feel Method

In the field, texture is commonly determined by the sense of feel. The foil is rubbed between thumb and fingers under wet conditions. Sands feel gritty and its particles can be easily seen. The silt when dry feels like flour and talcum powder and is slightly plastic when wet. Clayey particles feel very plastic and exhibit stickiness when wet and are hard under dry conditions.

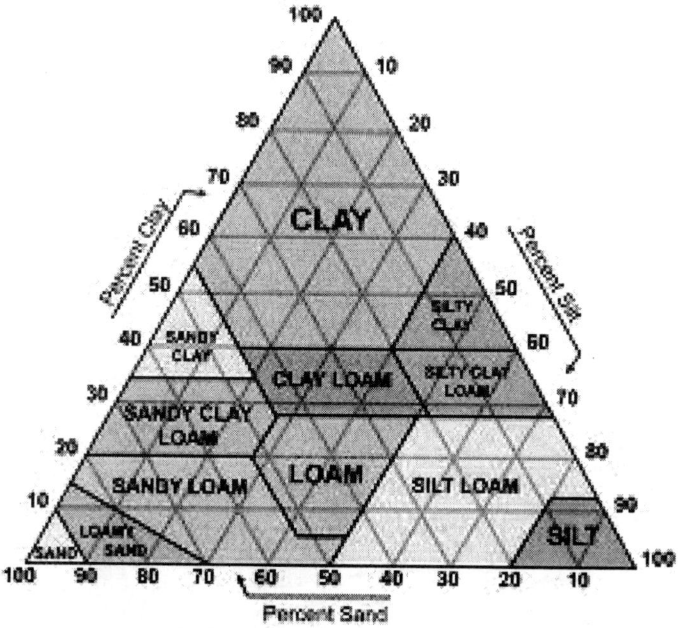

Triangle to know the Soil Texture

Laboratory Method

A more accurate and fundamental method has been devise by the U.S. Department of Agriculture for the naming of soils based on a mechanical analysis. From the **Fig** mentioned earlier the determination of textural class names can be easily made. The diagram re-emphasizes that a soil is a mixture of different sizes of particles. This figure also suggests a gradual change of properties with change in particle size since it has not sharp line of demarcation in the distribution of sand, silt and clay fractions.

Soil structure

Soil texture is the relative proportion of sand, silt and clay in a soil, how these particles are grouped together into stable collection of aggregate is soil structure. So soil structure is defined as the arrangement of primary particles (sand, silt and clay) and their aggregates into a certain definite pattern. Natural aggregates are called peds and vary in their water stability; the word cold is used for a coherent mass of soil broken into any shape by artificial means such as by tillage.

Structure Class

Soil structure units (peds) are described by their characteristics: Type (shape), Class (Size), and Grade (Strength of cohesion).

Types of Structure

It is determined by the general shapes and arrangement of peds. There are mainly four types of soil structure:

1. Plate like
2. Prism like
3. Block like
4. Spherical.

Plate Like

The horizontal dimensions are much more developed than the vertical axis resulting a flattened, compressed or lens like appearance to the peds. When the units are thick, they are called platy and when the units are thin, they are called laminar. The platy type is often inherited from the parent materials. In addition frost heaving; fluctuating water tables, compaction and thin layering of different textured alluvium or lacustrine material can from platy type of soil structure.

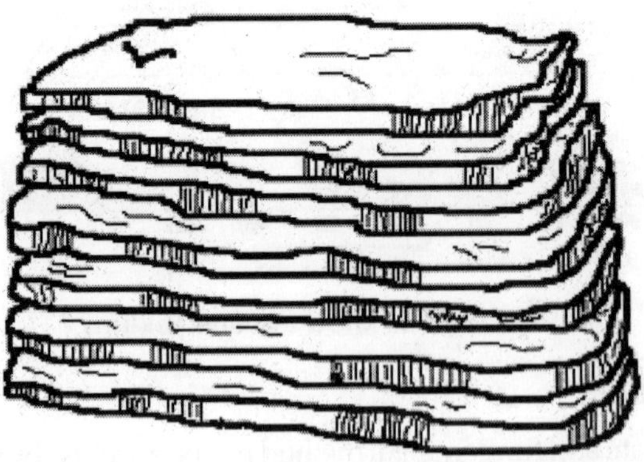

Platy

Prism Like

The vertical axis is more developed than others, with flattened sides, giving a pillar-like shape. It has also two sub types: columnar- when the top of such ped is rounded, and prismatic- when the tops of the peds are plane, level and clean cut. The prism like structures are commonly found in sub-soil horizons in arid and semiarid regions.

Prismatic

Block Like

All three dimensions are about the same size and the peds are cube-like with flat or rounded faces. Block like structure has also two sub- types: angular blocky when the faces and edges of the cubes are sharp and sub-angular blocky when the faces and edges are mainly rounded. The block like soil structures are usually found in the sub-surface horizons and their characteristics have much to do with soil drainage, aeration, and root penetration.

Angular Blocky Soil

Spheroidal (Sphere Like)

All axes are developed equally with the same length, curved and irregular faces. Generally all rounded or sphere like peds (aggregates) may be placed in this type of soil structure. Spheroidal type of soil structure has two structural sub –types: granular the aggregates of this type are usually less porous, and crumb when the granules are especially porous. The term Spheroidal more appropriately refers to those sizes of aggregates not exceeding inch in diameter. Granular and crumb structures are characteristic of many surface soils. In spheroidal soil structure, the physical properties of soil like, infiltration, percolation and aeration *etc.*, are not affected by wetting of soil.

Sphere Like

Soil Colour

After texture, soil colour is the most significant and important physical feature. From colour we can conclude a number of very important soil attributes includes:

- ☆ How well the soil allows gases and water to flow
- ☆ The extent of chemical weathering that goes on
- ☆ The soil's overall productivity

Soil colour does not affect the behaviour and use of soil, however it can indicate the composition of soil and give clues to the conditions that the soil is subjected to. Soil can exhibit a wide range of colour; gray, black, white, reds, browns, yellow and under the right conditions green. Varying horizontal bands of colour in the soil often identify a specific soil horizon. The development and distribution of colour in soil results from chemical and biological weathering, especially redox reactions. As the primary minerals in soil parent material weather, the elements combine into new and colourful compounds. Aerobic conditions produce uniform or gradual colour changes, while reducing environments results in disrupted colour flow with complex, mottled patterns and points of colour concentration.

Causes of Soil Colour

Soil colour is influenced by the amount of protein present in the soil. Yellow or red soil indicates the presence of iron oxides. Dark brown or black colour in soil indicates that the soil has high organic matter content. Wet soil will appears darker than dry soil. However the presence of water also affects soil colour by affecting the oxidation rate. Soil that has a high water content will have less air in the soil, specifically less oxygen. In well drained(and therefore oxygen rich soils) red and brown colours caused by oxidation are more common, as opposed to in wet (low oxygen) soils where the soil usually appears grey.

The presence of specific minerals can also affect soil colour. Manganese oxides causes a black colour glauconite makes the soil green, and calcite can make soil in arid regions appear white.

To ensure that colour definition is consistent, the Munsell colour Notation used. This standardization system was developed by Albert Munsell in the early 20th century and is used by all soil scientist as the basis of soil colour classification. Munsell broke down colour into 3 parameters

1. **Hue:** The system recognizes 5 dominant colours with 5 additional "half way' colours such as yellow-red. These are referred to as the Hues.
2. **Value:** The Value describes the brightness of the colour from black (0) ti white(10) and 5 being natural grey.
3. **Chroma:** Chroma is a measure of "purity" or strength of the colour on a scale from 0(weak) to 12 (very strong)-although the later applies to some colours.

Soil Air Contents

Soil pores, the voids between minerals, organic matter, and living organisms, are filled with air or water. There is a dynamic

Soil Air

Soil pores, the voids between minerals, organic matter, and living organisms, are filled with air or water. There is a dynamic equilibrium between water and air content within a soil. When water enters the soil, it displaces air from some of the pores.

- ☆ Composition of soil air.
- ☆ Movement of gasses within soil.
- ☆ Soil porosity

Composition of Soil Air

The composition of soil air is different from that of the atmosphere because it cannot readily mix with air above the soil. The metabolic activity of plant roots, microbes and soil fauna all affect the composition of soil air. For example, the concentration of carbon dioxide (CO_2) in soil (between 0.3 and 3 per cent) is often several hundred times higher than the 0.03 per cent found in the atmosphere. In extreme cases oxygen can be as low as 5-10 per cent, compared to 20 per cent in the atmosphere. Soil air has higher moisture content than the atmosphere, with relative humidity approaching 100 per cent under optimum conditions. (Humidity is not as variable in soil as it is in the atmosphere). The amount and composition of air in soil are dynamic and to a large degree are determined by water content and activity of soil organisms.

Soil Water

No living organism can survive without water. Water is the chief constituent of plants. It is essential for certain vital processes like photosynthesis and is also responsible for maintaining the turgidity of plant cells. Nutrients are dissolved in the soil water and absorbed by the crop. The soil water containing nutrient ions is known as the soil solution. Water effects weathering of rocks and formation of soil. Soil water regulates the physical, chemical and biological properties of the soil. Although plants absorb some water directly from rain and dew, the major portion of water utilized by the crop comes from soil.

Source of Soil Water

The original source of soil water is rainfall, which occurs during the months of June to September and December- January. All parts of India do not receive equal rainfall. The moisture bearing south-west monsoon wind blows over to the Arabian sea and the Bay of Bengal and strikes the Western Ghat mountains on the west coast of India and the Himalayan mountain ranges at Assam. Thus it rains heavily on the western side of the Western Ghat Mountains, ranges and Assam beginning from the last week of May. A broad and rather irregular belt of low rainfall exist on the eastern side of the Western Ghat mountains, which stretches from the interior of Tamil Nadu to the Deccan Plateau and Madhya Pradesh. The south – west monsoon wind is deflected by the Himalayan mountain ranges towards upper India, during June to September when it rains heavily in West Bengal, Bihar, Uttar Pradesh and northern Punjab. Since the Aravalli mountain ranges lies parallel to the direction of the south-west monsoon wind, so it passes over Gujarat, Rajasthan and Haryana where it rains little during the latter part of the monsoon season. This obstructs and pushes back the monsoon wind towards southern India. So heavy rainfall occurs on the east coast of Tamil Nadu during October-November.

The original source of irrigation water is the river system. The six major river systems of India have been assessed to supply the following quantities of water.

Sl.No.	*River System*	*Estimated Water in million cubic meters*
1.	The Indus River System	49300
2.	The Ganges River System	1850000
3.	The Brahamaputra River System	12300
4.	The Mahanandi and other following rivers.	123400
5.	The Narmada, Tapti, Godaveri, Krishna Cauvery and other southern rivers	246700
6.	The west flowing rivers excluding Narmada and Tapti	49300
	Total	**666000**

Irrigation systems are being developed in order to utilize the above water resources of the river system. Well water and pond water are also used for irrigation at many places of India.

Forms of Soil Water

Soil water is commonly of the following three forms:

1. Gravitational or free water than moves under the influence of gravity, down the macropores. It is held by the soil with a force of less than bars. It is harmful to crops because it removes air and moisture from the soil. Hence crops suffer from lack of enough oxygen and nutrient. Moreover, they cannot use this kind of water.
2. Capillary water is held on the surface of the soil particles and within the micropores by surface tension forces (0.1 to 31 bars). Plant can use it.
3. Hygroscopic water is held with a force greater than 31 bars, mostly in non-liquid or vapour from. Higher plants cannot absorb it.

Movement of Water in the Soil

A Movement of Liquid Water: Liquid water moves in the soil under saturated and unsaturated conditions.

Saturated Flow of Water

Soil is saturated with water which means that even the macropores are full of water, and water at the surface of the soil possesses a high positive potential with respect to the water located at the lower level of the soil profile. As water moves from the state of higher positive potential to the state of lower the adjacent drier soil. But water can only flow through the pore spaces which are very irregular or even discontinuous in shape.

Saturated flow of water depends on the difference of potential which the force is causing the flow of water between different points the soils and the case with which the soil allows the ready movement of water. This latter factor is called the Hydraulic conductivity of the soil which depends on the micropores and the viscosity of water.

Unsaturated Flow of Water

The soil is unsaturated with water which means that the micropores are filled up with air and the micropores are filled up with water. Water flows through micropores and the surface of the soil particles from a zone of lower negative potential to another zone of a higher negative potential. Clay and humus attract water molecules. Water moves from moist soil where it is under a lower negative potential to dry soil. The water absorbed by dry clay possesses a very high negative potential.

4.3. Soil Properties, Chemical *viz.*, Ion Exchange (Anions and Cations) and its Significance, Soil Organic Matter, Carbon-Nitrogen Ratio and its Significance

Chemical Properties of Soils

The chemical properties of soils refer to the nature of the chemical changes taking place in them. These chemical changes taking place in them. These chemical changes depend upon their chemical compositions and the nature of the inorganic and organic materials contained in them, which have originated from the gradual decomposition of the soil and organic materials, mainly of plant origin.

Chemical Composition of soil

Since the soil is mainly made up of oxygen (46.7 per cent), silicon, (27 per cent), aluminum (8.1 per cent) and iron (5.0 per cent), the inorganic component of soils are mainly made up of them. Plant nutrients like calcium, magnesium, potassium, sodium, phosphorous and sulphur are present in the minerals and the soil solution. The elemental composition of different soils very due to the differences in the rates of chemical weathering and leaching. Oxygen, silicon and aluminum occur as constituents of minerals and as oxides. Iron occurs mainly in the form of oxides and ferromagnesium minerals. The proportion of titanium in soils increases when the intensity of chemical weathering increases, because the titanium containing minerals, rutile and anatase are resistant to weathering. Calcium occurs mainly in calcite, gypsum, apatite, dolomite, while magnesium is present mainly in dolomite, hornblende, augite etc. Potassium occurs mainly in orthoclase, microcline, mica and illite, some of which slowly weather to release potassium in the soil solution. These potash bearing minerals are present in the fine sand and silt fraction of most soils. Aerable soils usually contain insignificant amounts of sodium, which, however, is present in high quantities in saline and alkaline soils such as chloride, sulphate and carbonate. The major portion of inorganic phosphorous occurs as iron and aluminum phosphate in the acidic soils and calcium phosphate in the alkaline soils. Phosphorous also occurs in the organic form, *e.g.*, phospholipids, inositol etc. All micronutrients *i.e.* iron, manganese, zinc, copper, boron and molybdenum mainly occur in the inorganic form.

Ion Exchange

Ion exchange is an exchange of ions between two electrolytes or between an electrolyte solution and a complex. In most cases the term is used to denote the processes of purification, separation and decontamination of aqueous and other ion-containing solutions with solid polymeric or mineralic "ion exchangers'

Typical ion exchangers are ion exchange resins (functionalized porous or gel polymer), zeolites, montmorillonite, clay, and soil humus. Ion exchangers are either cation exchanger that exchange positively charged ions (cation) or anion exchangers that exchange negatively charged ions (anions). There are also amphoteric exchangers that are able to exchange both cations and anions simultaneously. However, the simultaneous exchange of cations and anions can be more efficiently performed in *mixed beds* that contain a mixture of anion and cation exchange resins, or passing the treated solution through several different ion exchange materials.

Ion exchangers can be unselective or have binding preferences for certain ions or classes of ions, depending on their chemical structure. This can be dependent on the size of the ions, their charge, or their structure. Typical examples of ions that can bind to ion exchangers are:

- ☆ H^+ (proton) and OH^- (hydroxide)
- ☆ Single-charged monatomic ions like Na^+, K^+, and Cl^-

- Double-charged monatomic ions like Ca^{2+} and Mg^{2+}
- Polyatomic inorganic ions like SO_4^{2-} and PO_4^{3-}
- Organic bases, usually molecules containing the amino functional group -NR_2H^+
- Organic acids, often molecules containing -COO^- (carboxylic acid) functional groups
- Biomolecules that can be ionized: amino acids, peptides, proteins, etc.
- Along with absorption and adsorption, ion exchange is a form of sorption.

Ion exchange is a reversible process and the ion exchanger can be *regenerated* or *loaded* with desirable ions by washing with an excess of these ions.

Application

Ion exchange is widely used in the food and beverage, hydrometallurgical, metals finishing, chemical and petrochemical, pharmaceutical, sugar and sweeteners, ground and potable water, nuclear, softening and industrial water, semiconductor, power, and a host of other industries.

Most typical example of application is preparation of high purity water for power engineering, electronic and nuclear industries; *i.e.* polymeric or mineralic insoluble **ion exchangers** are widely used for water softening, water purification, water decontamination, etc.

Ion exchange is a method widely used in household (laundry detergents and water filters) to produce soft water. This is accomplished by exchanging calcium Ca^{2+} and magnesium Mg^{2+} cations against Na^+ or H^+ cation.

Industrial and analytical ion exchange chromatography is another area to be mentioned. Ion exchange chromatography is chromatographical method that is widely used for chemical analysis and separation of ions. For example, in biochemistry it is widely used to separate charged molecules such as proteins. An important area of the application is extraction and purification of biologically produced substances such as proteins (amino acids) and DNA/RNA.

Ion exchange processes are used to separate and purify metals, including separating uranium from plutonium and other actinides, including thorium, and lanthanum, neodymium, ytterbium, samarium, lutetium, from each other and the other lanthanides. There are two series of rare earth metals, the lanthanides and the actinides, both of whose families all have very similar chemical and physical properties. Using methods developed by Frank Spedding in the 1940s, ion-exchange used to be the only practical way to separate them in large quantities, until the advent of solvent extraction techniques that can be scaled up enormously.

A very important case is the PUREX process (plutonium-uranium extraction process), which is used to separate the plutonium and the uranium from the spent fuel products from a nuclear reactor, and to be able to dispose of the waste products. Then, the plutonium and uranium are available for making nuclear-energy materials, such as new reactor fuel and nuclear weapons.

The ion-exchange process is also used to separate other sets of very similar chemical elements, such as zirconium and hafnium, which is also very important for the nuclear industry. Zirconium is practically transparent to free neutrons, used in building reactors, but hafnium is a very strong absorber of neutrons, used in reactor control rods.

Ion exchangers are used in nuclear reprocessing and the treatment of radioactive waste.

Ion exchange resins in the form of thin membranes are used in chloralkali process, fuel cells and vanadium redox batteries. Ion exchange can also be used to remove hardness from water by exchanging calcium and magnesium ions for sodium ions in an ion exchange column.

Other Applications

- In soil science, cation exchange capacity is the ion exchange capacity of soil for positively charged ions. Soils can be considered as natural weak cation exchangers.
- In pollution remediation and geotechnical engineering, ion exchange capacity determines the swelling capacity of swelling or Expansive clay such as Montmorillonite, which can be used to "capture" pollutants and charged ions.
- In planar waveguide manufacturing, ion exchange is used to create the guiding layer of higher index of refraction.
- Dealkalization, removal of alkali ions from a glass surface.
- Chemically strengthened glass, produced by exchanging K^+ for Na^+ in soda glass surfaces using KNO_3 melts.

Cation Exchange Capacity (C.E.C) of Soils

The total number of cation adsorption sites per unit weight of soils is called the cation exchange capacity of soils. The cation exchange capacity of the soil may also be defined as the total number of negative charges per unit weight of the soil. It is expressed in Mill equivalent per 100 gms of soil.

$$\text{Mill equivalent} = \frac{\text{Milligram}}{\text{Equivalent weight}}$$

Or Milligram = Mill equivalent x Equivalent weight

Factors Affecting Cation Exchange Capacity of Soils

1. *Soil texture*: Since the negatively charged clay include clay micelle attracts positively charged clay micelle attracts positively charged cations, and holds them, the cation exchange capacity of soils increases when their percentage of clay increases i.e their texture becomes finer.
2. *Soil humus content*: Since a negatively charged humic micelle attracts cations and holds them, the cation exchange capacity of soils increases when their

percentage of humus increases. The cation exchange capacity of humus varies from 200 to 400 milliequalvent per 100 gms. So C.E.C. of soils also depends on the nature of humus they contain.

3. *Nature of clay*: the cation exchange capacity of soil also depends on the nature of clay minerals which constitute them. The cation exchange capacity of different clay minerals are as follows:

Clay Mineral	*Cation Exchange Capacity*
Montmorillonite	80 to 150 meg/100 gms
Vermiculture	100 to 150 meg/100 gms
Illite	15 to 40 meg/100 gms
Kaolinite	3 to 15 meg/100 gms

Hence the cation exchange capacity of a soil dominated by montmorillonite or vermiculture is much higher than the cation exchange capacity of another soil dominated by lllite or kaolinite.

4. *Soil reaction*: When the pH of soil increases more hydrogen ions dissociate from the hydroxyl group located on the broken edge of clay minerals especially Kaolinite exposing more hydroxyl groups. Hence the cation exchange capacity of soils dominated especially by Laolinite increased when the pH of the soil increased

Anion Exchange Capacity (AEC)

Anion exchange capacity should be thought of as the soil's ability to remove anions from the soil water solution and sequester those for later exchange as the plant roots release carbonate anions to the solution. Those colloids which have low CEC tend to have some AEC. Amorphous and sesquioxide clays have the highest AEC, followed by the iron oxides. Levels of AEC are much lower than for CEC. Phosphates tend to be held at anion exchange sites.

Iron and aluminum hydroxide clays are able to exchange their hydroxide anions (OH^-) for other anions. The order reflecting the strength of anion adhesion is as follows:

$$H_2PO_4^- \text{ replaces } SO_4^{2-} \text{ replaces } NO_3^- \text{ replaces } Cl^-$$

The amount of exchangeable anions is of a magnitude of tenths to a few mill equivalents per 100 g dry soil. As pH rises, there are relatively more hydroxyls, which will displace anions from the colloids and force them into solution and out of storage; hence AEC decreases with increasing pH (alkalinity).

Soil Organic Matter

Soil organic matter is the fraction of the soil that consists of plant or animal tissue in various stages of breakdown (decomposition). Most of our productive agricultural soils have between 3 and 6 per cent organic matter. Soil organic matter contributes to soil productivity in many different ways. In this fact sheet, we describe the various components of organic matter and the different roles organic matter plays in soil productivity. We also discuss field management practices that will help preserve or increase soil organic matter levels over time.

What is Soil Organic Matter?

Organic matter is made up of different components that can be grouped into three major types:

1. Plant residues and living microbial biomass.
2. Active soil organic matter also referred to as detritus.
3. Stable soil organic matter, often referred to as humus.

The living microbial biomass includes the microorganisms responsible for decomposition (breakdown) of both plant residues and active soil organic matter or detritus. Humus is the stable fraction of the soil organic matter that is formed from decomposed plant and animal tissue. It is the final product of decomposition.

The first two types of organic matter contribute to soil fertility because the breakdown of these fractions results in the release of plant nutrients such as nitrogen, phosphorus, potassium, etc. The humus fraction has less influence on soil fertility because it is the final product of decomposition (hence the term "stable organic matter"). However, it is still important for soil fertility management because it contributes to soil structure, soil tilth, and cation exchange capacity. This is also the fraction that darkens the soil's colour.

Benefits of Stable Soil Organic Matter

There are numerous benefits to having a relatively high stable organic matter level in an agricultural soil. These benefits can be grouped into three categories:

Physical Benefits

- ☆ Enhances aggregate stability, improving water infiltration and soil aeration, reducing runoff.
- ☆ Improves water holding capacity.
- ☆ Reduces the stickiness of clay soils making them easier to till.
- ☆ Reduces surface crusting, facilitating seedbed preparation.

Chemical Benefits

- ☆ Increases the soil's CEC or its ability to hold onto and supply over time essential nutrients such as calcium, magnesium and potassium.
- ☆ Improves the ability of a soil to resist pH change; this is also known as buffering capacity.
- ☆ Accelerates decomposition of soil minerals over time, making the nutrients in the minerals available for plant uptake.

Biological Benefits

- ☆ Provides food for the living organisms in the soil.
- ☆ Enhances soil microbial biodiversity and activity which can help in the suppression of diseases and pests.
- ☆ Enhances pore space through the actions of soil microorganisms. This helps to increase infiltration and reduce runoff.

Organic Materials

Over time, the application and incorporation of organic materials can result in an increase in stable soil organic matter levels. Sources of organic materials include:

- ☆ Crop residues.
- ☆ Animal manure.
- ☆ Cover crops (green manure).
- ☆ Perennial grasses and legumes.

The quickest increases are obtained with sources that are high in carbon such as compost or semi-solid manure.

Organic Matter Management

Farm practices that help to maintain or increase soil organic matter levels: • Use of conservation tillage practices (for example zone tillage or no-till). Tillage exposes the organic matter to air and will result in the lowering of stable organic matter due to increased mineralization rates and erosion losses. • Rotation of annual row crops with perennial grass or legume sods will reduce erosion and build up organic matter as a result of the decomposition of the root mass.

- ☆ Avoiding soil compaction which increases water logging, and maintaining proper pH to enhance microbial activity and decomposition of freshly added materials.

Actual build up of stable organic matter will, in addition to the amount and source of organic material added, and tillage and rotation practices, also depend on:

- ☆ Soil temperature.
- ☆ Precipitation and soil moisture holding capacity.
- ☆ Soil type and drainage class.
- ☆ Existing microbial community.
- ☆ Soil fertility status and soil pH.

Carbon Nitrogen Ratio in the Soil

The objective of this lesson is to learn the importance of the carbon: nitrogen ratio in the soil. The knowledge is important for practical farming.

The ratio of carbon to nitrogen is the carbon: nitrogen ratio or the C:N ratio. The C: N ratio of the organic material added to the soil influences the rate of decomposition of organic matter and this result in the release (mineralisation) or immobilization of soil nitrogen. If the added organic material contains more nitrogen in proportion to the carbon, then nitrogen is released into the soil from the decomposing organic material. On the other hand, if the organic material has a less amount of nitrogen in relation to the carbon then the microorganisms will utilize the soil nitrogen for further decomposition and the soil nitrogen will be immobilized and will not be available. The following lesson will give you an opportunity to learn what happens when different quantities of organic material with varied C:N ratios are added to the soil.

The computer will randomly generate the values for a C:N ratio from many possible combinations.

Calculation Procedures of Carbon Nitrogen Ratio

Example

A farmer incorporated 2560 kg of fresh organic matter into the soil. It contained 55 per cent carbon with a carbon nitrogen ratio of 20:1. As this material decomposes, will there be a decrease (immobilization) or an increase (release) in soil nitrogen? And by how many kg?

Let us calculate the soil nitrogen status

Fresh organic matter added = 2560 kg Carbon content of organic matter= 55 per cent Carbon: nitrogen ratio = 20:1

Step I The amount of carbon present in the organic matter added to the soil. 2560 kg of fresh organic matter x 0.55 carbon content =1408 kg of carbon in organic matter

Step II The amount of nitrogen present in the organic matter added to the soil. Fresh organic matter contains 1408 kg of carbon and its C:N ratio is 20:1. The nitrogen content of the organic matter is 1408 kg = ——— = 70 kg 20

Step III The amount of C and N required for the microbes to form new tissues: As fresh organic matter is decomposed, the microbes use 75 per cent of the carbon for energy and, the remaining 25 per cent of the carbon is used to form their new tissue. To form their new tissue, microbes use nitrogen from soil or from the added organic matter. Microbes require 1 kg of N for every 8 kg of carbon as the C:N ratio of microbes is 8:1.

Carbon content in fresh organic matter is 1408 kg. Of this one fourth is used for new tissue. The amount of carbon used by 1408 kg microbes for forming new tissue is —— = 352 kg 4

The amount of nitrogen required by microbes to form the new tissues: Microbes require 1 kg of N for every 8 kg of carbon to form the new tissue. Therefore the amount of Nitrogen required for microbes using 352 Kg of Carbon is 352 k = —— = 44 kg 8

Step IV Finally we compare the two nitrogen values. Fresh organic matter contained 70 kg of N, and microbes used 44 kg of N to form new tissue.

The balance nitrogen available is = 70 - 44 = 26 kg

4.4. Important Soil Types of India *viz.*, Alluvial, Black, Red, Laterites and Latertic Soils. Acidic and Alkaline Soils and their Problems; Reclamation and Management of Holomorphic Soil; Importance of Soil with Reference to Mulberry Cultivation

Soils of India

The Indian subcontinent from 8° to 37° North latitudes and from 69° to 93° East longitudes and covers an area of 32, 74, 90 square kilometres (327.46 million hectares). It has the monsoon type of climate, there being two distinct periods of heavy annual rainfall. The south –west monsoon is active during June to September and the North –east monsoon during the winter. The rainfall, is however, controlled by the relief. The Himalayas and the western Ghat mountain ranges lying across the path of the south-west monsoon winds are responsible for precipitating their moisture as rain on the wind-ward side. The Himalayas also deflect the south-west monsoon towards upper India. Consequently, the area extending from Assam to Punjab receives goods rainfall. Rajasthan dose not experience good rainfall because the south-west monsoon winds pass unobstructed over it as the aravallis lie along its path. Another dry zone extends from the interior of Tamil Naidu to central Gujarat.

The Indian subcontinent is characterized by a great diversity of parent rocks which have weathered under different climate, vegetation and topography to from soils with different characteristics in different regions of the Indian Union.

J.A. Voelekar (1893) and J.W. Leather (1893) recognised four major soil groups; the Indo- Gangetic Alluvium, Black soil, Red soil and Laterite soil. These are four other groups of soils which include forest and Hill soils, the Desert and Semi Desert soils, the Saline and Alkali soils and Peaty and Marshy soils.

Major Groups of India

Soil of India have been broadly classified into the major groups: (i) Alluvial soils, (ii) Black soils, (iii) Red soils, (iv) Laterite soil, (v) mountain and hill soil, (vi) Arid and Desert soil, (vii) Saline and Alkali soil; and (viii) Peaty and other organic soil.

Alluvial Soil

These soils have been found in Major parts of Punjab, Haryana, U.P. Bengal. Assam, North Bihar and small areas in the other States of the Indian Union. The main features of alluvial soils have been derived as silt deposition laid down by the Indian river systems like the Indus, the Ganges, the Brahmaputra and the rivers like Narmada, Tapti, Mahanandi, Godaveri, Krishna and Cauvery. These rivers carry the products of weathering of rocks constituting the mountains and deposit them along their path as they flow down the plain land towards the sea. Most of the alluvial soils do not posses well developed horizons. Geologically alluvial soils have been divided into two broad groups, namely old and new alluvium, which are also called Bangar and Khadar respectively in North India. Some of the old alluvial soils are reddish brown of grey brown sandy loam or loomy in texture, and the sub-soil contain more clay than the surface soil. The texture of the new alluvium is very coarse on the river banks and very fine in the low lying marshly lands. Alluvial soils usually contain lime nodules intermixed with soil at different depth. Frequently drainage is restricted and soluble salts accumulate in the soils of more arid regions *i.e.* Uttar Pradesh, Punjab and Haryana. Alluvial soils are usually deficient humus and nitrogen, occasionally in phosphorous but not in potash and lime.

Black Soil

Almost the whole of Maharashtra, the western half of Madhya Pradesh, the southern parts of Gujarat and some areas in Andhra Pradesh, Karnataka and Tamil nadu and Bundi and Tonk district of Rajasthan and Bundelkhand division of U.P. are covered by black soil which have been divided into three broad groups *i.e.* (i) shallow black soil of depth of 35-50 cms, (ii) medium black soils of depth of 50-120 cm, and (iii) deep black soil of a depth of more than 120 cms. In many places, black soils often occur in close proximity to red soils. In the vicinity of the hills, the red soils merge imperceptibly into the black soil.

Shallow black soils of a texture that varies fom silty loam to loam and colour that varies from dark yellowish brown to dark brown, have formed from basalts of the Deccan trap.parent materials of medium black soils include basaltic trap, Dharwar Schist, basic granite gneisses, hornblended and chlorite schist, whereas deep black soils consist of basaltic trap. The soil texture in both cases varies from silty clay to clay. Both contain 40 to 60 percent or more clay. Gypsum accumulates in association with lime in some of the soil profiles.

The colour of these soils varies from deep black to light black. The exact cause of the black colour of these soils is unknown. Probably it is due to the presence of titeniferous magnetite, organic compounds of iron and aluminium, humus and colloidal hydrated double iron and aluminium silicate.

Black soils are rich in the smectite group of clay minerals and therefore possess a high cation exchange capacity (40to60meg/100gms) and high base status. They are very sticky and plastic when wet and from very wide and deep cracks when dry. Black soils are very rich in iron, lime, magnesia and alumina. They are deficient in organic matter, nitrogen and phosphorous but not in potash. Soluble salts alkaline in reaction accumulate in medium and deep black soils. Black soils, especially deeper ones, can retain a high amount of moisture and are fairly fertile, giving reasonably good yields of crops despite continued cultivation without proper manuring. These soils are well suited from cultivation of cotton, cereals and oil seeds. Deep black soils are often called black cotton soils because cotton is most extensively grown on them.

Red Soils

Red soils cover almost the whole of Tamil Nadu, Karnataka, Andhra Pradesh, Orissa, Nagaland, Mizoram and Tripura, eastern and southern parts of Madhya Pradesh, Bundelkhand division and Mirzapur district in Uttar Pradesh, Chhota Nagpur division and Santhal Parganas districts in Bihar, parts of west Bengal, Arunchal Pradesh and maghalaya, Karbianglong districts of Assam, Thane and Kolaba districts of Maharashtra and also parts of Rajasthan.

Red soils include (i) red loam soils, (ii) red and yello soils, and (iii) red sandy soils. Red soils have been formed from varieties of rocks which include granite, gneiss, schist, sandstone, hornblende, shales etc. under a forest of broad leaved trees in warm humid climate. As basic elements have been leached from most of these soils, they are poor in humus, and nitrogen, phosphorous and lime. Whenever water soluble phosphate are added to these soils, they react with ferric and aluminium ions and their hydrous oxides and are precipitated as insoluble ferric and aluminium hydroxyl phosphate. Kaolinite and hydrous oxides of iron and aluminium are the dominant clay minerals in red soils, responsible for the excellent physical condition of red soils. A number of kharif crops are thus grown on these soils, even though cannot retain enough moisture for their growth. These soils differ greatly in fertility and depth.

Laterite Soils

Laterite soils occur in small patches in almost all the states of north- eastern, eastern, southern and western India. They are formed from several kinds of rocks like basalt under a hot, humid climate when the basic elements and silica have been washed down and iron is precipitated and oxidized. Whenever drainage is restricted, a soft deposit of iron oxide occurs at or near the water table, which hardens when it dries. In some places like Malabar, this is cut in the form of bricks and used as a building material. The word Laterite has originated from Latin word "Later" which means bricks. This possesses and indurated honey combed mass of iron oxides.

Laterite soils are usually shallow and gravelly at higher lands, but are very deep loam to clay soils in the valleys where good paddy crops are produced on them. Laterite soils are deficient in basic elements like lime, magnesia, potash and nitrogen and available phosphorus. These soils are not sticky and plastic when wet. They are in excellent physical condition due to the presence of hydrous oxides of iron and aluminium and kaolinite as the dominating clay minerals.

Acidic and Alkaline Soils and their Problems

Soil Alkalinity (Alkaline-Sodic Soils)

Definition

Alkaline soils are soils (mostly clay soils) with a high pH (>9) and a poor soil structure and a low infiltration capacity. They are not saline, *i.e.* the total amount of soluble soils, especially sodium chlorides, is not excessive (ECe < 4 to 8 dS/m). Often they have a hard calcareous layer at 0.5 to 1 m. depth.

Causes

The causes of soil alkalinity are natural or they can be man-made. The natural development is due to the presence soil minerals producing sodium carbonate upon weathering. The man-made development is due to the application of irrigation water (surface or ground water) containg a relatively high proportion of sodium bicarbonates).

Where

The extent of alkaline soils is not precisely known. Important research on alkaline soils has mainly occurred in Central Europe and North India (above the Ganges river), where alkaline soils occur frequently.

Problems

Alkaline soils are difficult to take into agricultural production. Rainwater stagnates on the soil easily and, in dry periods, irrigation is hardly possible. Agriculture is limited to crops tolerant to surface water logging (*e.g.* rice, grasses) and the productivity is low.

Details

Soil alkalinity is associated with the presence of sodium carbonates (Na_2CO_3) in the soil, either as a result of natural mineralization of the soil particles or brought in by irrigation and/or floodwater. The sodium carbonate, when dissolved in water, dissociates into $2Na^+$ (two sodium cations, *i.e.*, ions with a positive electric charge) and CO_3 – (a carbonate anion, *i.e.*, an ion with a - double - negative electric charge). The sodium-carbonate can react with water to produce carbon-dioxide (CO_2), escaping as a gas, and sodium-hydroxide ($Na^+ OH^-$), which is alkaline and gives high pH values (pH>10). To understand this reaction, we may consider the water (H_2O) as being partly dissociated into H^+ (hydrogen) and OH- (hydroxyl) ions. In pure, neutral water, the concentration of H^+ and OH^- ions equals 10-0.7 eq/l each (respectively 10^{-7} g/l and $17x10^{-7}$ g/l), a very small concentration.

The pH, being the negative log value of the H^+ concentration in eq/l, is 7. Similarly, the p OH is also 7. Please note that each unit decrease in pH indicates a tenfold increase of the H^+ concentration. Similarly, each unit increase in pH indicates a tenfold increase of the OH^- concentration. In water with dissolved salts, the concentrations of the H^+ and OH^- ions may change, but the sum of pH and pOH remains equal to 14.

Water with excess H+ ions is called acid (pH < 6), and water with excess OH^- ions is called alkaline (pH > 8). Soil moisture with pH < 4 is called very acid and with pH > 10 very alkaline.

The reaction between Na_2CO_3 and H_2O can represent as follows:

$2na^+ + co^-_3 + 2H^+ + 2OH^- — 2Na^+ 2oH^- + H_2 CO_3$

The acid H_2CO_3 is unstable and produces H_2O and CO_2 (carbon dioxide gas, escaping into the atmosphere). This explains the remaining alkalinity in the form of soluble sodium hydroxide. Not all sodium carbonate follows the above chemical reaction. The remaining sodium carbonate, and hence the presence of CO_3^- ions, causes $CaCO_3$ (which is only slightly soluble) to precipitate as solid calcium carbonate (limestone). Hence, the calcium ions Ca^{++} are immobilized: The presence of abundant Na^+ ions and the precipitation of Ca^{++} ions cause the clay particles, which have negative electric charges along their surfaces, to absorb more Na^+ and, in exchange, release Ca^{++}, by which their exchangeable sodium percentage (ESP) is increased as follows:

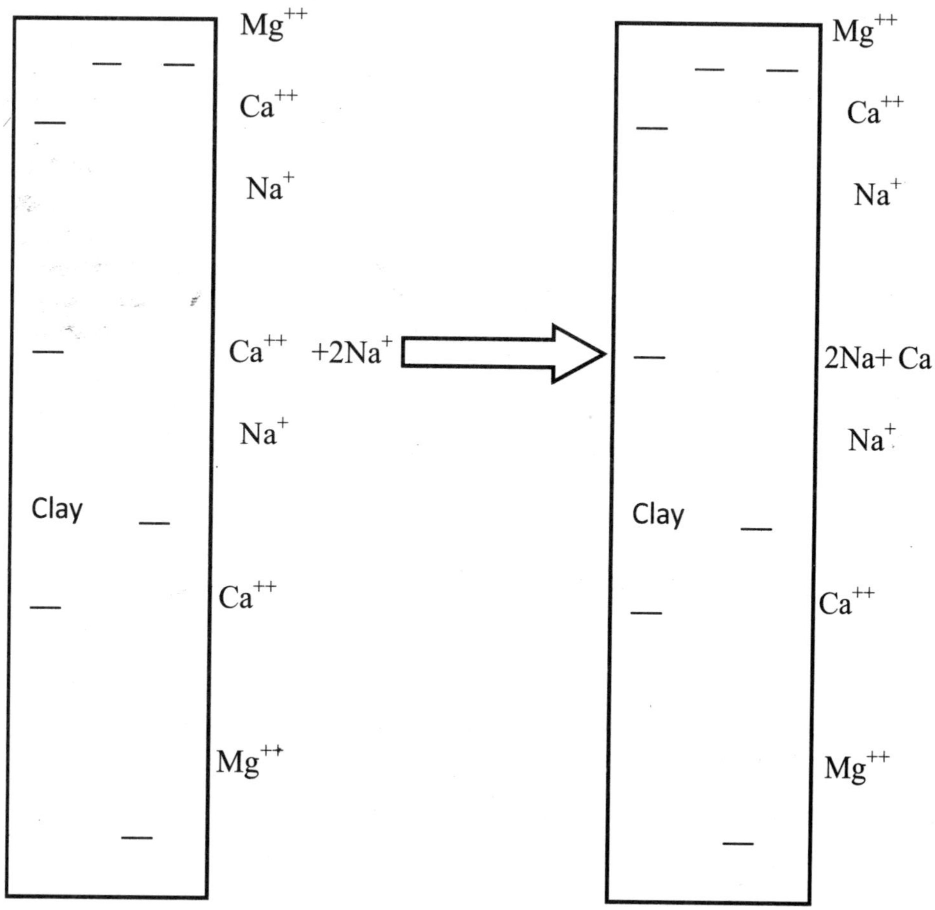

Clay particles with considerable ESP (> 16), in non-saline conditions, and in contact with non-saline water occupy a larger volume than otherwise, because the Na^+ ions are quite mobile and have smaller electric charges than Ca^{++} ions, hence they are adsorbed less coherently to the surface of the clay particle and they float farther away: the soil swells.

The phenomenon is called sodicity and results in deterioration of the soil structure, and especially crust formation and compaction of the top layer.

Hence the infiltration capacity of the soil and the water availability in the soil is reduced, whereas the surface-water-logging or runoff is increased. Seedling emergence and crop production are badly affected.

Under saline conditions, the many ions in the soil solution counteract the swelling of the soil.

Certain clay minerals with 100 per cent ESP (*i.e.* fully sodium saturated) are called bentonite which is used in civil engineering to place impermeable curtains in the soil, *e.g.* below dams, to prevent seepage of water.

The problems of alkalinity and sodicity go hand in hand. Alkaline/sodic soils are not necessarily saline, and the alkalinity problem is worse as the salinity is less. Alkalinity problems are more pronounced in clay soils than in loamy, silty or sandy soils. The clay soils containing montmorrillonitic or smectitic minerals (swelling clays) are more subject to alkalinity problems than illitic or kaolinitic clay soils. The reason is that the former types of clay have larger specific surface areas (*i.e.* the surface area of the soil particles divided by their volume).

Solutions

Alkaline/sodic soils with solid $CaCO_3$ can be reclaimed with grass cultures, ensuring the incorporation of much acidifying organic material into the soil, and leaching of the excess sodium. Deep ploughing and incorporating the calcareous subsoil into the topsoil also helps.

It is also possible to reclaim alkaline soils by adding acidifying minerals like pyrite (see next section on acid sulphate soils).

If necessary, gypsum (calcium sulphate, $CaSO_4$) can also be applied as a source of Ca^{++} ions.

To reclaim the soils properly one needs prohibitively high of doses of amendments. Most efforts are therefore directed to improving the top layer only (say the first 10 cm of the soils), as the top layer is most sensitive to structure deterioration. The treatments, however, need to be repeated in a few (say 5) years time.

It will be important to refrain from irrigation with poor quality water.

The quality of the irrigation water in relation to the alkalinity hazard is expressed by the following two indices:

1. The sodium adsorption ratio (SAR)

$$SAR = \frac{[Na^+]}{\sqrt{[Ca^{++}/2 + Mg^{++}/2]}} = \frac{[Na^+/23]}{\sqrt{\{Ca^{++}/40 + Mg^{++}/24\}}}$$

where,

[ ]: Stands for concentration in meq/l, and

{ }: Stands for concentration in mg/l.

It is seen that Mg (Magnesium) is thought to play a similar role as the Calcium.

The SAR should not be much higher than 20 and preferably less than 10.

When the soil has been exposed to water with a certain SAR value for some time, the ESP value tends to become about equal to the SAR value.

1. The residual sodium carbonate content (RSC, meq/l):

$$RSC = [HCO_3^- + CO_3^{--}] - [Ca^{++} + Mg^{++}]$$

$$= \{HCO_3^-/61 + CO_3^{--}/30\} - \{Ca^{++}/20 + Mg^{++}/12\}$$

This must not be higher than 1 and preferably less than 0.5 Note that the above expression recognises the presence of bi-carbonates (HCO3), the form in which most carbonates are dissolved. For simplicity reasons, this was not considered in the foregoing explanations.

Comment

Saline soils are mostly also sodic (the predominant salt is sodium chloride) but not very alkaline. However, upon leaching they are usually converted into non-sodic soils as the Na^+ ions are easily removed. Therefore, the sodic problem is more acute in non-saline sodic soils, and mostly they do not need gypsum applications.

Soil Acidity (Acid-sulphate soils)

Definition

Acid sulphate are drained coastal wetland soils that have become acid (pH<4) due to oxidation of the pyritic minerals in the soil. Un drained soils containing pyrites need not be acid and they are called potential acid sulphate soils.

Causes

The cause of the formation of acid sulphate soils is the drainage and flood control effectuated to permit agricultural or sedentary activities.

Where

(Potential) Acid sulphate soils are found coastal lowlands, especially in the (semi) humid tropics, but not exclusively. In the tropics the soils are often related to mangrove vegetations under tidal influence. The soils are found extensively in South-East Asia, West Africa, and North-East South-America, but also in other regions.

Problems and Solutions

Acid sulphate soils are unproductive. The lands look barren and the water is very clear, devoid of silt and life. The soils can be colourful.

Indigenous populations have managed to develop acid sulphate soils, *e.g.*, for rice cultivation.

It has taken them many years of careful management and toil (Oosterbaan 1981). The soils are hardly attractive for large scale and commercial exploitation. However, there have been efforts in that direction at deplorable loss of environmental quality and of financial resources.

The best cure would be to restore the original conditions. Unfortunately most undertakers are not interested to spend additional funds in repairing of what was damaged already at a large expense.

The indigenous efforts have led to soils that are no longer acid due to long lasting drainage and removal of the acids. These soils have acquired an excellent and stable soil structure coupled with a high permeability. Their fertility, however, has gone. Continued cultivation requires frequent application of organic manure and fertilizers.

In tropical humid climates with high rainfall rice yields in acid coastal lowlands can benefit from restricted subsurface drainage during a short time (< 1 month) in a relatively dry period (Oosterbaan 1992).

Details

When draining pyrite (FeS_2) containing soils (also called cat-clays), the soil may become extremely acid (pH < 4) due to oxidation (reaction with oxygen, O_2, gas) of pyrite into sulphuric acid (H_2SO_4), giving acid sulphate soils. In its simplest form, the chemical reaction is:

$$2FeS_2 + 9O_2 + 4H_2O \rightarrow 8H^+ + 4SO_4^{--} + 2Fe(OH)_3 \text{ (solid)}$$

The product Fe $(OH)_3$, iron (III) hydroxide (orange), precipitates as a solid, insoluble mineral, by which the alkalinity is immobilized and the acidity remains active. In alkaline soils, in contrast, it is the escape of CO_2 gas and the precipitation of $CaCO_3$ that causes the removal of acidity from the system whereby the alkalinity remains active.

The process of acidification is accompanied by the formation of high amounts of aluminium (Al^{+++} ions, released from clay minerals under influence of the acidity), which are harmful to the crop.

Other Products of the Chemical Reactions are

- H_2S: hydrogen sulphide, a smelly gas
- S: sulphur (yellow)
- FeS: iron (II) sulphide (black/grey/blue)
- Fe_2O_3: (haematite, iron (III) oxide, red coloured)
- FeO.OH: Goethite (brown)
- Fe Compounds: (*e.g.*, jarosite, yellow)
- Hi Clay mineral: (hydrogen clay with a large fraction of adsorbed H^+ ions, a stable but poor in nutrient)

It can be seen that the iron can be present in bi-valent (II) and tri-valent (III) forms (Fe^{++}, the ferro ion, and Fe^{+++}, the ferri ion respectively). The ferro form is soluble, whereas the ferri form is not. The more oxidised the soil becomes, the more the ferri forms will dominate.

Acid sulphate soils exhibit an array of colours ranging from black, to brown, blue-grey, red, orange and yellow. The hydrogen clay can be improved by admitting sea water: the Mg and Na present in the sea water will replace the hydrogen adsorbed.

Cat-clays occur mainly in coastal lowland (Beek *et al.*, 1980) and are often not cultivated or, if they are, planted under rice, so that the soil can be kept wet preventing oxidation. Subsurface drainage of these soils is normally not advisable. However, cultivated acid sulphate soils can often not be kept wet continuously because of climatic dry spells and shortages of irrigation water. In such a situation, surface drainage may help to remove the acidic and toxic chemicals (formed in the dry spells) during rainy periods. On the long run surface drainage can help to reclaim acid sulphate soils (Oosterbaan 1981). In the short run, careful and restricted use of subsurface drainage in humid climates can help to improve rice yields (Oosterbaan 1992).

For additional information reference is made to Dent (1986). See also the following table:

Drainage and Yield of Malaysian Oil Palm on Acid Sulphate Soils (after Toh Peng Yin and Poon Yew Chin 1982)

	Yield in Tons of Fresh Fruit per ha											
Year:	60	61	62*	63	64	65	66**	67	68	69	70	71
Yield:	17	14	15	12	8	2	4	8	14	19	18	19

*: Drainage depth and intensity increased.

**: Water table raised again to counter negative effects of a)

Note that subsurface drainage can be harmful, but that soils can recover after reducing drainage again.

Importance of Soil with Reference to Mulberry Cultivation

Mulberry, being a perennial crop, it is all the more important to know the soil fertility where it is to be cultivated and make it fit for plantation in the beginning itself. Soil of very acidic or alkaline nature is not suitable for mulberry cultivation. Mulberry flourishes well in soils which are flat, deep, fertile, well drained, loamy to clayey, porous with good moisture holding capacity. The ideal range of soil pH is 6.2 to 6.8. The optimum pH required for mulberry is 6.5 to 6.8. Soil amendments may be used to correct the soil to get required pH. The quantities of gypsum or lime to be applied in different cases are as mentioned below:

Soil Amendments (To be taken up after soil test)

pH range (To bring pH to 6.8)	*Quantity of gypsum/ha*
7.4 to 7.8	2.0 MT
7.9 to 8.4	5.0 MT
8.5 to 9.0	9.0 MT
9.1 to above	14.0 MT

pH Range Quantity of Lime/ha (to bring pH to 6.8)

pH Range	*Quantity of Lime/ha (To bring pH to 6.8)*		
	Plain	*Hilly Areas*	*Soil Type*
5.5 to 6.5	1.25 MT	2.5 MT	Sandy
	2.50 MT	5.0 MT	Sandy loamy
	5.0 MT	7.5 MT	Loamy
	7.5 MT	8.75 MT	Clay loamy

Method of Application

The powdered gypsum/lime is mixed well with soil with soil of the garden and irrigated to stagnation for 48-72h. Later the water is leached out by drainage and dried (suitable for ploughing and intercultural operations).

Unit-V

Dr. Ravinder Sharma

5.1. Mulberry Growth and Nutrition, Essential Elements, their Types. Mechanism of Absorption and Utilization

5.2. Source of Nutrient Elements in Soil and their Role in Plant Growth, including their Deficiency and Toxicity

Mulberry Growth Nutrition

Several factors are responsible for successful cocoon crop *i.e.*, mulberry leaf (38.2 per cent), climate (37 per cent), rearing technique (9.3 per cent) and silkworm race (4.2 per cent) etc. It is therefore clear that mulberry leaf play a major role in cocoon production as a source of nutrition of silkworm. The bulk of the silk goods produced in the world are made up of mulberry silk is directly dependent upon the leaf quality, which influence the healthy growth of silkworm larvae and quality of cocoons. In the event of miner changes in climate and rearing practices, the quality of leaf nutrition that helps in getting a good cocoon crop. It is the quality of leaf that stabilize cocoon crop at former's level.

The quality of leaf is dependent on mulberry variety, climatic condition, soil type and it innate fertility, cultivation practices, the fertilization management (source, time method) irrigation (water quality, interval, etc) and harvesting method (age of leaf, time, method, transportation, storage etc). The soil fertility has direct bearing on nutrient status of leaf.

It is note that the plant leaf tissue analysis has revealed the presence of some sixty (60) elements in the leaf. But research carried out on the aspects of plant nutrition has established the essentiality of only sixteen elements. Of these sixteen, six element *viz.* nitrogen (N), phosphorous (P), Potassium (K) as primary nutrients, Calcium (Ca), Magnesium (Mg), and Sulphur (S) are used in large quantities by the plants as a secondary nutrients, while seven other *viz.*, Zinc (Zn), Iron (Fe), Copper (Cu), Manganese (Mn), Boron (B), Molybdenum (Mo) and Chloride (Cl) are required in relatively smaller quantities and are called as micronutrients or minor nutrients. In addition, there are five more nutrient like Cobalt (Co), Nickel (Ni), Sodium (Na) and sometimes Vanadium (Va) and Iodine (I), which do play a role in governing the quality of mulberry leaf and are known as beneficial nutrients.

According to them Arnon and Stout (1939), an element is essential when:

1. Its deficiency prevents the plant from completing the vegetative or reproductive stage of its life cycle.
2. The shortage is specific for a given element being corrected only when the same is supplied.
3. The element has to directly involved in the metabolism of the plant; its effect is not a result of an eventual collection of unfavorable physical, chemical or Microbiological condition in the soil or in the culture medium.

It is essential to know that each of these elements plays a specific function in the plant growth. Hence these nutrients have to be in the soil in the available form to enable the plant to absorb them in required amount for higher production of leaf.

Mobility Status of Various Nutrients

The mobility of nutrients in the plant is the normal function of the plant in order to its growth and development requirement. The mobility of the nutrient is grouped into four categories based on their mobility.

1. Highly mobile (N,P,K)
2. Moderately mobile (Zn)
3. Less mobile (S, Fe, Mn, Cu, Cl.)
4. Immobile (Ca and B)

Forms of mineral elements absorbed by mulberry and the forms in which the nutrients are absorbed from the soil:

Mineral Elements	*Ionic Forms*	*Non-Ionic Forms*
N	$NH_{4,}NO_3$	$CO(NH_4)^2$
P	$H_2 PO_4 HPO_4^2$	Nucleic acids and Phytin
K	K+	
Ca	Ca_2^{++}	
Mg	Mg_2	
S	So_4^{++}	SO_2
Fe	$Fe^{2-}Fe^{3-}$	Fe So^4 with EDTA(Ethylene Diamine Tetracetic Acid)

Mineral Elements	Ionic Forms	Non-Ionic Forms
Mn	Mn^{2+}	$MnSO_4$ with EDTA
Zn	Zn^{2+}	$ZnSO^4$ with EDTA
Cu	Cu^{2+}	$CuSo_4$ with EDTA
B	$B_2O_7^{2-}H_2BO^{3-}HBO^{3-}$	
Mo	MoO_4^{2-}	
Cl	Cl^-	

For mulberry the sandy soil is most preferred compared to the heavy texture soil like black (Vertisols). The red soil (alfisols) is low in certain nutrients. The nutritional stress in soil is often related to the type of parental materials and soil forming process. Therefore, many nutrient deficiencies or toxicity can often be known from the parental material and the soil type (Dudal, 1976 and Clark, 1982 a,b).

In India the deficiency of major and micronutrients has been observed in the light textured acid calcareous soil. This situation has been aggravated with the introduction of high yielding mulberry variety as they required balanced nutrients under intensive cropping system. In recent years majority of soil have turned in to hard/compact and low in exchangeable base due to inadequate use of organic manures. Continuous use of high analysis fertilizers like Urea and DAP has led to increase in the soil acidity due to more soluble iron, Aluminum and Manganese. The increase concentration of these elements in the soil sometimes also reaches toxic levels in highly acidic soils leading to deficiencies of calcium, phosphorus, magnesium, molybdenum and zinc.

In order to maintain the high level of leaf productive and its quality, the soil has to be managed suitably with suitable and efficient crop management practices. The mulberry crop gains large quantities of nutrients from the soil. Many of the nutrients would become less available to mulberry due to monocrops either under irrigated or rainfed condition, results in reduction of leaf yield and quality. Such nutrients stress may also be due to the use of high dose of fertilizer in the cultivation of high yielding varieties of mulberry. So lack of recycling crop of residue of organic matter may also contribute for deficiency of nutrients in soil.

Identification of Nutrient Deficiency and its Symptoms

Deficiency symptoms of various micro and macronutrients can be categorized and distinguished based on following symptoms manifested on leaf/leaves.

1. Region and location of occurrences.
2. Presence or absent of the dead spot.
3. Chlorosis of the entire leaf or intervienal chlorosis.

Mineral Deficiency in Mulberry

The assessment of the nutrient status of the crop is a method of clarifying the nutritional and physiological state of the crop, for obtaining data for formulating strategies to attain optimum nutrient balance and optimum productivity. Normally, for this purpose, the nutrient contents of the crop are measured and visible symptoms caused by deficiency or toxicity because of excessive supply are also looked for. Symptoms of deficiency or toxicity are often caused by lack of balance among two or more elements and are therefore difficult to interpret precisely.

Deficiency Symptoms occur in mulberry mainly due to the non-availability of minerals, like nitrogen, phosphorous, potash, calcium, sulphur, zinc and magnesium. Disorders caused by the mineral deficiency can be overcome by the application of suitable fertilizers/chemicals to the soil.

Nitrogen

Symptoms

Spindly yellow plants or yellow leaves, sometimes with pink tints.

Nitrogen Deficiency in Young and Top Leaf

Cause

Nitrogen promotes green, leafy growth and deficiency results in yellowing and stunted growth. Nitrogen is very soluble, so is easily washed out of the soil in winter rains, leaving the soil deficient in spring, just when plants are putting on new growth. Nitrogen deficiency is a common cause of yellow leaves in spring.

Remedy

In the long term, mulching with organic matter (such as well rotted garden compost or manure) provides a steady trickle of nitrogen to stabilise levels. In the short term, applying high nitrogen fertilisers such as sulphate of ammonia or poultry manure pellets will remedy the problem.

Phosphorus

These phosphorus-deficient leaves show some necrotic spots. As a rule, phosphorus deficiency symptoms are not very distinct and thus difficult to identify. A major visual symptom is that the plants are dwarfed or stunted. Phosphorus deficient plants develop very slowly in relation to other plants growing under similar environmental conditions but without phosphorus deficiency. Phosphorus deficient plants are often mistaken for unstressed but much younger plants. Some species such as tomato, lettuce, corn and the brassicas develop a distinct purpling of the stem, petiole and the under sides of the leaves. Under severe deficiency conditions there is also a tendency

Phosphorous Deficiency

for leaves to develop a blue-gray luster. In older leaves under very severe deficiency conditions a brown netted veining of the leaves may develop.

Potassium

Potassium deficiency, also known as **potash deficiency,** is a plant disorder that is most common on light, sandy soils, because potassium ions (K^+) are highly soluble and will easily leach from soils without colloids Potassium deficiency is also common in chalky or peaty soils with a low clay content. It is also found on heavy clays with a poor structure.

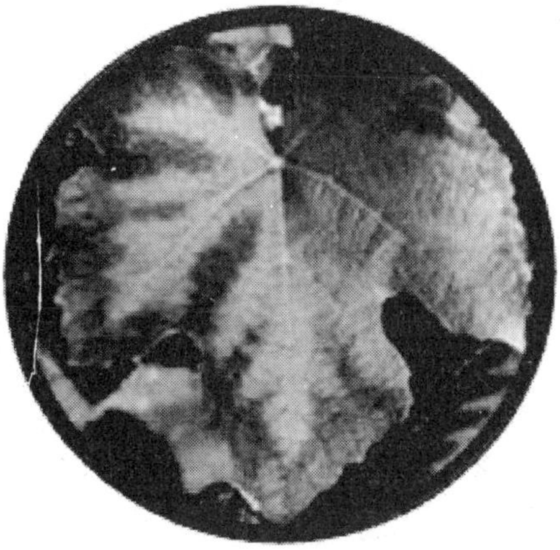

Potassium Deficiency

Yellow chlorosis, necrosis of marginal leaf area is noticed and in severe cases it occurs on both younger and old leaves. Marginal scorching of leaves in younger stage and later become coarse, non- juicy and necrotic. Stem and root systems becomes weaker. Application of potassium fertilizer at appropriate dose is recommended for correction.

Calcium

Necrosis, curling of narcotic leaf downwards and black coloration could be as in younger leaves and buds. Defoliation of young leaves with necrosis along the veins. The stems become woody and short with yellowish tips. Roots become stubby and dry. Application of calcium nitrate at appropriate dose is recommended for correction

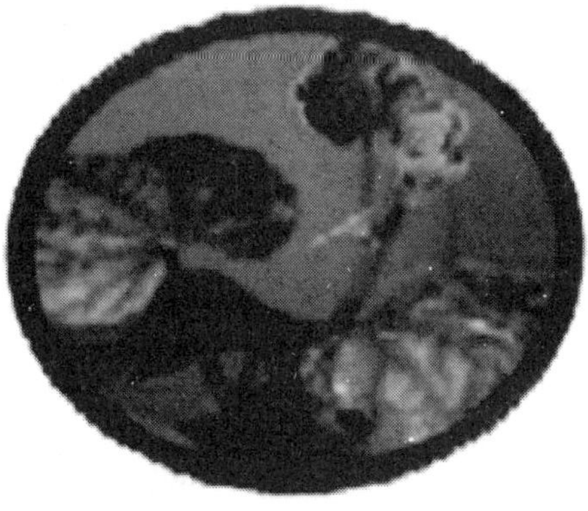

Calcium Deficiency

Magnesium

Symptoms

Yellowing between the leaf veins, sometimes with reddish brown tints and early leaf fall. Magnesium deficiency is common in tomatoes, apples, grape vines, raspberries, roses and rhododendrons.

Cause

Magnesium is needed for healthy leaves and for plants to harness energy from the sun (photosynthesis). Soil shortages of magnesium are more common on light, sandy soils. Over-use of high-potassium fertilizers (such as tomato feed) can cause magnesium deficiency, as plants take up potassium in preference to magnesium.

Remedy

In the short term, apply Epsom salts as a foliar feed in summer. Dilute the salts at a rate of 20g of Epsom salts per litre of water (1/3oz per pint) plus a few drops of liquid detergent. Apply two or three times at fortnightly intervals, spraying in dull weather to avoid leaf scorch. In the long term apply to the soil around the roots either Dolomite limestone (calcium-magnesium carbonate) at 100g per sq m (4oz per sq yd) or Epsom salts (magnesium sulphate) at 30g per sq m (1oz per sq yd). Dolomite limestone will make the soil more alkaline, so should not be used around ericaceous (acid-loving) plants such as rhododendrons or camellias, or where the soil is already alkaline.

Magnesium Deficiency

Sulphur

It is similar to N deficiency but the young leaves show a general overall chlorosis while still retaining some green colour. The veins and petioles show a very distinct reddish colour. The visual symptoms of sulphur deficiency are very similar to the chlorosis found in nitrogen deficiency. However, in sulphur deficiency the yellowing is much more uniform over the entire plant including young leaves. The reddish colour often found on the underside of the leaves and the petioles has a more pinkish tone and is much less vivid than that found in nitrogen deficiency. With advanced sulphur deficiency brown lesions and/or necrotic spots often develop along the petiole, and the leaves tend to become more erect and often twisted and brittle.

Sulphur Deficiency

Iron

These iron-deficient leaves show strong chlorosis at the base of the leaves with some green netting. The most common symptom for iron deficiency starts out as an interveinal chlorosis of the youngest leaves, evolves into an overall chlorosis, and ends as a totally bleached leaf. The bleached areas often develop necrotic spots. Up until the time the leaves become almost completely white they will recover upon application of iron. In the recovery phase the veins are the first to recover as indicated by their bright green color. This distinct venial re-greening observed during iron recovery is probably the most

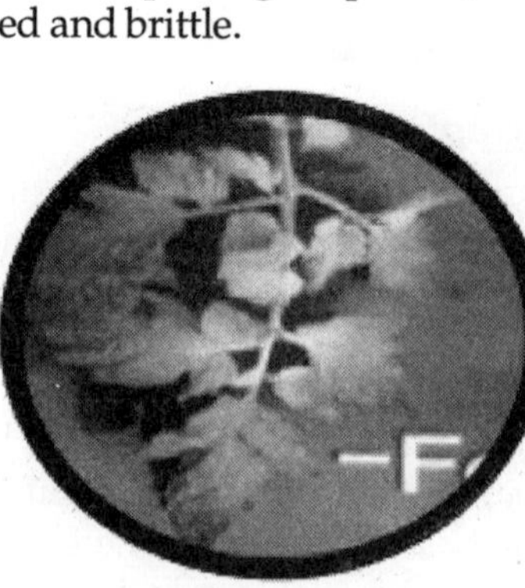

Iron Deficiency

recognizable symptom in all of classical plant nutrition. Because iron has a low mobility, iron deficiency symptoms appear first on the youngest leaves. Iron deficiency is strongly associated with calcareous soils and anaerobic conditions, and it is often induced by an excess of heavy metals.

Zinc

Zinc Deficiency

This leaves show an advanced case of interveinal necrosis. In the early stages of zinc deficiency the younger leaves become yellow and pitting develops in the interveinal upper surfaces of the mature leaves. Guttation is also prevalent. As the deficiency progress these symptoms develop into an intense interveinal necrosis but the main veins remain green, as in the symptoms of recovering iron deficiency. In many plants, especially trees, the leaves become very small and the internodes shorten, producing a rosette like appearance.

Manganese

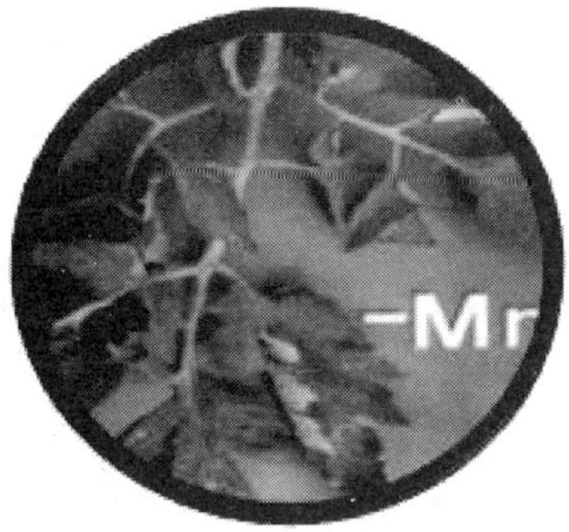

Manganese Deficiency

These leaves show a light interveinal chlorosis developed under a limited supply of Manganese. The early stages of the chlorosis induced by manganese deficiency are somewhat similar to iron deficiency. They begin with a light chlorosis of the young leaves and netted veins of the mature leaves especially when they are viewed through transmitted light. As the stress increases, the leaves take on a gray metallic sheen and develop dark freckled and necrotic areas along the veins. A purplish lusture may also develop on the upper surface of the leaves. Grains such as oats, wheat, and barley are extremely susceptible to manganese deficiency. They develop a light chlorosis along with gray specks which elongate and coalesce, and eventually the entire leaf withers and dies.

Copper

Copper Deficiency

These copper-deficient leaves are curled, and their petioles bend downward. Copper deficiency may be expressed as a light overall chlorosis along with the permanent loss of turgor in the young leaves. Recently matured leaves show netted, green veining with areas bleaching to a whitish gray. Some leaves develop sunken necrotic spots and have a tendency to bend downward. Trees under chronic copper deficiency develop a rosette form of growth. Leaves are small and chlorotic with spotty necrosis.

Chloride

Chloride Deficiency

These leaves have abnormal shapes, with distinct interveinal chlorosis. Plants require relatively high chlorine concentration in their tissues. Chlorine is very abundant in soils, and reaches high concentrations in saline areas, but it can be deficient in highly leached inland areas. The most common symptoms of chlorine deficiency are chlorosis and wilting of the young leaves. The chlorosis occurs on smooth flat depressions in the interveinal area of the leaf blade. In more advanced cases there often appears a characteristic bronzing on the upper side of the mature leaves. Plants are generally tolerant of chloride, but some species such as avocados, stone fruits, and grapevines are sensitive to chlorine and can show toxicity even at low chloride concentrations in the soil.

Molybdenum

Molybdenum Deficiency

These leaves show some mottled spotting along with some interveinal chlorosis. An early symptom for molybdenum deficiency is a general overall chlorosis, similar to the symptom for nitrogen deficiency but generally without the reddish coloration on the undersides of the leaves. This result from the requirement for molybdenum in the reduction of nitrate, which needs to be reduced prior to its assimilation by the plant. Thus, the initial symptoms of molybdenum deficiency are in fact those of nitrogen deficiency. However, molybdenum has other metabolic functions within the plant, and hence there are deficiency symptoms even when reduced nitrogen is available. In the case of cauliflower, the lamina of the new leaves fail to develop, resulting in a characteristic whiptail appearance. In many plants there is an upward cupping of the leaves and mottled spots developing into large interveinal chlorotic areas under severe deficiency. At high concentrations, molybdenum has a very distinctive toxicity symptom in that the leaves turn a very brilliant orange.

5.3. Soil and Water Conservation including Types and Causes of Soil Erosion, Soil and Water Conservation including Agronomic and Mechanical Measure

Soil Conservation

Soil conservation is a set of management strategies for prevention of soil being eroded from the Earth's surface or becoming chemically altered by overuse, acidification, salinization or other chemical soil contamination. It is a component of environmental soil science.

Decisions regarding appropriate crop rotation, cover crops, and planted windbreaks are central to the ability of surface soils to retain their integrity, both with respect to erosive forces and chemical change from nutrient depletion. Crop rotation is simply the conventional alternation of crops on a given field, so that nutrient depletion is avoided from repetitive chemical uptake/deposition of single crop growth.

Water Conservation

Water conservation encompasses the policies, strategies and activities to manage fresh water as a sustainable resource to protect the water environment and to meet current and future human demand. Population, household size and growth and affluence all affect how much water is used. Factors such as climate change will increase pressures on natural water resources especially in manufacturing and agricultural irrigation.

Soil Erosion

Soil erosion is the phenomena of wearing away of the land surface by the action of natural agencies such as water and wind.

Types of Soil Erosion

Basically soil erosion is of two kind (i) Normal or geologic erosion, and (ii) Accelerated erosion. Normal or geologic erosion is an extremely slow natural process by which the surface of the land tends level off to ultimately from a plain land called pene-plains. This process is so slow that the removal of surface soil is balanced by the formation of soil from the weathering of rocks and minerals contained in them. Accelerated erosion means the quick removal of surface soil is balanced by the formation of soil from the weathering of rocks and minerals contained in them. Accelerated erosion means the quick removal of soil from the land surface due to mismanagement of the land, which includes excessive grazing and deforestation of lands and cultivation of soil, exposing crops without adopting proper soil conservation measures. Accelerated erosion includes wind erosion and water erosion.

Wind Erosion

The wind is responsible for the removal of soil particles by the following three kinds of erosion is semi arid and arid region:

1. **Saltation:** The soil particle of size 0.1 to 0.5 mm is pushed along the surface of the land by the wind. They collide with other soil particle and leap vertically upwards. This phenomenon is called Saltation. Some soil particles of a 0.5 mm size rise only a little distance upwards. Others may move 30 cm upwards.
2. **Suspension**: very fine soil particles, of less than 0.1 mm are kicked upwards by the action of soil particles in Saltation to from suspension of very fine soil particles in air which are carried away.
3. **Surface creep:** Soil particles of size between 0.5 to 1 mm are pushed along the surface by the impact of soil particles in Saltation.

About 90 percent of the soil particles move within 30 cm about 50 percent of the soil particles move within 5 cm from the ground surface, by the action of the wind. The control of wind erosion is based on reduced or elimination of particles in Saltation.

Types of Soil Erosion Caused by Water

Soil erosion caused by water may be of the following kinds.

1. **Splash erosion**: the raindrops which fall at an approximate speed of 75cms per second on ground strike it with a force of about 14 times its own weight. The impact of this great force causes the soils particles to detach each other to from flowing mud. This mud is then splashed as much as 30 cms high and 12 cms down the land slope. Fine sandy soil and salty soils are dislodged easily. Such a removal of the soil by the impact of the fast falling raindrops is known as splash erosion.
2. **Sheet erosion**: This uniform layer of soils are removed from the surface of the land by rain water flowing over the land during the initial stage of soil erosion called sheet erosion when muddy water flows over the land.
3. **Rill erosion:** if sheet erosion is not controlled immediately, the downward flow of muddy rain water concentrates to from minute finger shaped channels called rills over the entire field during the later stage of soil erosion called rill erosion.
4. **Gully erosion**: if rill erosion is not controlled in time, then rills are deepened by the downward flow of water. Ultimately rills are converted to deep channels called gullies, which may be "U" or "V" shaped "U" shaped gullies are formed if the subsoil has a coarse texture whereas "V" gullies are formed if the sub- soil has a fine texture. Gullies become deeper and wider during heavy rains. Large fields are gradually fragmented and ultimately destroyed.
5. **Slip erosion:** Large masses of rocks and soil materials are detached from the sides of mountains during the rainy season and are carried down by the action of gravity. This phenomenon is known as slip erosion.
6. **Stream bank erosion**: River *e.g.,* Kosi in Bihar frequently changes its course when one bank is cut and the soil materials are carried downstream. The finer soil articles are deposited along the other bank. This phenomenon is known as stream bank erosion.

Agronomic Practices for Soil and Water Conservation

By following different agronomic practices we can reduce soil erosion, increase moisture-holding capacity of soil and can minimize problems like water logging, soil salinization etc.

Following agronomic practices are performed to achieve the above-mentioned objectives.

1. Contour-Farming

Generally, as the rain falls, a lot of runoff is generated which generally leads to soils erosion on its way downward. This removes the top fertile soil along with soil nutrients and plant seeds thus leading to scanty and uneven growth of crop.

To avoid this, a simple practice of farming is done across the slope so that there are no steep slopes on the field. The ridges and furrows thus formed act as continuous barrier to the free movement of water downwards thus provides more infiltration time. Hence, the removal of soil along with nutrients is checked to a great extent leading to increment in soil fertility and crop yield.

2. Mulching Practice

Mulching is one of the simplest and beneficial practices for soil and water conservation. Mulch is simply a protective layer of material that is spread on top of the soil to prevent it from blowing and being washed away. Mulch can either be organic-such as grass clippings, straw, bark chips and similar materials or inorganic such as stones, brick chips and plastic. Conservation tillage is a common practice that creates mulch on the soil surface. It leaves the crop residue on the top of the soil as mulch. The mulching practice yields following benefits:

I. Protects the soil from erosion.

II. Conserve moisture in soil thus saving the need for frequent irrigation.

III. Reduce compaction of soil thus saving the need for frequent irrigation.

IV. Maintains a more even soil temperature.

V. Prevents weed growth to check loss soil nutrients.

3. Enhancing the Growth of Specific Crops

Enhancing the growth of specific crops which provide the maximum cover, reduce runoff and soil loss *e.g.* legume crops in general furnish a better cover and hence better protection to cultivated land against erosion than ordinary cultivated crops. These may vary from region to region depending upon topographical and climate conditions.

4. Strip Cropping

It is a combination of contouring and crop rotation in which alternate strips of row crops and soil conserving crops (sods) are grown either at right angles to the direction of the prevailing wind, or following the natural contours of the terrain to prevent soil erosion of the soil. When soil is detached from the row crops by the forces of wind or water, the dense soil conserving crops traps some of the soil particles and reduces wind translation and/or runoff.

5. Mixed Cropping

In this practice two or more crops are grown in the same field at a particular time. Some of the benefits of mixed cropping are a better and continuous cover of the land, good protection against the beating action of the rain. The different crops grown in mixed cropping have their roots at different depths holding the soil more firmly thus preventing soil erosion.

Mechanical Measures for Soil Water Conservation

These measures play an important role in soil and water conservation. These are used in conjugation with agronomic practices when they alone are not much effective. The main principles of mechanical measures are:

(i) To facilitate infiltration by increasing the time of concentration.

(ii) To break up a long slope into several short ones to decrease velocity of runoff.

Major mechanical measures to control soil and water conservation are given as under:

1. Contour-Bunding

In this practice small bunds are constructed at regular intervals across the slope of the land. This practice is very useful in arid and semi-arid areas with high infiltration and permeability rates.

2. Sub-Soiling

It is basically a primary tillage operation, which consists of break opening the soil structure up to a depth of 30 to 60 cm. This practice facilitates greater infiltration rates and moisture holding capacity of the soil.

3. Basin Listing

In this method of soil and water conservation basins are constructed using a special implement called basin-lister. These basins are constructed across the slope. Basin listing provides maximum time to rain water for infiltration into the soil.

4. Bench Terracing

In this practice a series of platforms are constructed having suitable vertical drops. The range of vertical drop may vary from 2 to 6 feets depending upon prevailing conditions. The capital cost of bench- terracing is more than that of bunding initially but in longer run it proves economical.

By above-mentioned agronomic and mechanical measures, we can have efficient soil and water conservation.

5.4. Soil Micro-organisms, their Types and Role in Plant Nutrition

Soil Micro-organism

The soil is considered as the land surface of the earth which provides the substratum for plant and animal life. The soil represents a favourable habitat for microorganisms and is inhabited by a wide range of microorganisms, including bacteria, fungi, algae, viruses and protozoa. The physical structure, aeration, water holding capacity and availability of nutrients are determined by the mineral constituents of soil, which are formed by the weathering of rock and the degradative metabolic activities of the soil microorganisms. Cultivated soil has relatively more population of microorganisms than the fallow land, and the soils rich in organic matter contain much more population than sandy and eroded soils. Microbes in the soil are important to us in maintaining soil fertility, cycling of nutrient elements in the biosphere and sources of industrial products such as enzymes, antibiotics, vitamins, hormones, organic acids etc. But certain microbes in the soil are the causal agents of various human and plant diseases.

The plant and animal remains deposited in the soil contribute organic substances. Soil microorganisms breakdown a variety of organic materials and use a portion of these breakdown products to generate or synthesize a series of compounds that make up humus, a dark coloured amorphous substance composed of residual organic matter not readily decomposed by microorganisms. The three major fractions of humus are humic substances, poly-saccharides and other non-humic substances, and humin. These materials impact on the physical, chemical and bio-chemical properties of soil in many ways. Humus improves the texture and structure of the soil, contributes to its buffering capacity and increase the water holding capacity of the soil.

Types of Microorganisms in Soil

There are several types of microorganisms in soil that benefit plants. Together they make up an immense population of living organisms. One teaspoon of soil may contain millions of various types. Below is a list of common soil microorganisms found throughout the world.

Bacteria

Small, single cell organisms that make up the single most abundant type of microbe. They have a very wide range of conditions that they live in from the artic wastelands to the steaming waters of volcanic hot springs. In soils, they multiply rapidly under the proper conditions. When conditions are wrong for one species, it is right for another. This is not always a good thing since a balance is what is required.

Fungi

The largest microbe group in terms of mass. Some fungi are beneficial, called mycorrhizas that form a symbiotic relationship with plant roots, either externally or internally. Within the fungi group are pathogen fungi. These are disease causing fungi, some of which can be quite devastating to plants.

Protozoa's

Small single cell microbes that feed on bacteria.

Actinomycetes

Necessary for the breakdown of certain components in organic matter.

Algae

Beneficial groups such as blue-green algae, yellow-green algae and diatoms. Some of these can produce their own energy through photosynthesis.

Soil microorganisms are living, breathing organisms and, therefore, need to eat. They compete with plants for nutrients including Nitrogen, Phosphorus, Potassium and micronutrients as well. They also consume amino acids, vitamins, and other soil compounds. Their nutrients are primarily derived from the organic matter they feed upon. The benefit is that they also give back or perform other functions that benefit higher plant life.

Categories and Characteristics of Soil Organisms

Category	*Characteristics*	*Organisms*
Permanent	Whole life cycle in the soil	Mites, collembola, earthworms
Temporal	Part of life cycle in soil	Insect larvae
Periodical	Frequently enter into the soil	Some insect larvae
Transitory	An inactive phase in the oil (*e.g.*, eggs, pupa, hibernation) but the active period not in the soil	Some insects
Accidental	Organisms fall down or they are drawn along	Insect larvae

The easiest and most widely used system for classifying soil organisms is by using body size and dividing them into three main groups: macrobiota, mesobiota and microbiota (Wallwork, 1970; Swift, Heal and Anderson, 1979). The ranges that determine each size group are not exact for all members of each group.

Role of Soil Micro-organism in Plant Nutrition

Micro-organisms

These are the smallest organisms (<0.1 mm in diameter) and are extremely abundant and diverse. They include algae, bacteria, cyanobacteria, fungi, yeasts, myxomycetes and actinomycetes that are able to decompose almost any existing natural material. Micro-organisms transform organic matter into plant nutrients that are assimilated by plants. Two main groups are normally found in agricultural soils: bacteria and mycorrhizal fungi.

Bacteria

Bacteria are very small, one-celled organisms that can only be seen with a powerful light (1 000×) or electron microscope. They constitute the highest biomass of soil organisms. They are adjacent and more abundant near roots, one of their food resources. There are many types of bacteria but the focus here is on those that are important for agriculture, *e.g.* Rhizobium and actinomycetes.

Bacteria are important in agricultural soils because they contribute to the carbon cycle by fixation (photosynthesis) and decomposition. Some bacteria are important decomposers and others such as actinomycetes are particularly effective at breaking down tough substances such as cellulose (which makes up the cell walls of plants) and chitin (which makes up the cell walls of fungi). Land management has an influence on the structure of bacterial communities as it affects nutrient levels and hence can shift the dominance of decomposers from bacterial to fungal.

One group of bacteria is particularly important in nitrogen cycling. Free-living bacteria fix atmospheric N, adding it to the soil nitrogen pool; this is called biological nitrogen fixation and it is a natural process highly beneficial in agriculture. Other N fixing bacteria form associations (in the form of nodules) with the roots of leguminous plants.

The nodule is the place where the atmospheric N is fixed by bacteria and converted into ammonium that can be readily assimilated by the plant. The process is rather complicated but, in general, the bacteria multiply near the root and then adhere

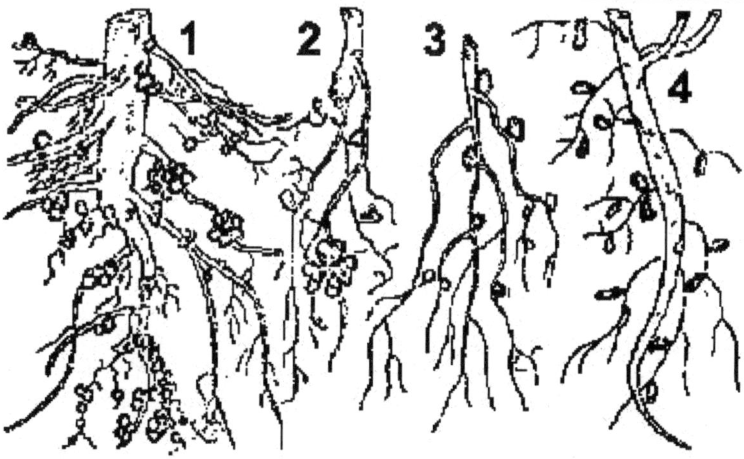

1. Soyabean 2. Alfalfa 3.Pea 4. White clover

Different types of nodules on leguminous roots

(Soltner, 1978)

Rhizobium and the Nodulation Process

to it. Next, small hairs on the root surface curl around the bacteria and they enter the root. Alternatively, the bacteria may enter directly through points on the root surface. Once inside the root, the bacteria multiply within thin threads. Signals stimulate cell multiplication of both the plant cells and the bacteria. This repeated division results in a mass of root cells containing many bacterial cells. Some of these bacteria then change into a form that is able to convert gaseous N into ammonium nitrogen (they can "fix" N). These bacteria are then called bacteroids and present different properties from those of free cells. Most plants need very specific kinds of rhizobia to form nodules. A specific Rhizobium species will form a nodule on a specific plant root, and not on others. The shapes that the nodules form are controlled by the plant and nodules can vary considerably in size and shape.

The nodulation process is a series of events in which rhizobia interact with the roots of legume plants to form a specialized structure called a root nodule.

Actinomycetes are a broad group of bacteria that form thread-like filaments in the soil. The distinctive scent of freshly exposed, moist soil is attributed to these organisms, especially to the nutrients they release as a result of their metabolic processes. Actinomycetes form associations with some non-leguminous plants and fix N, which is then available to both the host and other plants in the near vicinity.

Bacteria produce (exude) a sticky substance in the form of polysaccharides (a type of sugar) that helps bind soil particles into small aggregates, conferring structural stability to soils. Thus, bacteria are important as they help improve soil aggregate stability, water infiltration, and water holding capacity. However, in general their effect is less marked than that originated by large invertebrates such as earthworms.

Fungi

These organisms are responsible for the important process of decomposition in terrestrial ecosystems as they degrade and assimilate cellulose, the component of plant cell walls. Fungi are constituted by microscopic cells that usually grow as long threads or strands called hyphae of only a few micrometres in diameter but with the ability to span a length from a few cells to many metres. Soil fungi can be grouped into three general functional groups based on how they source their energy:

1. Decomposers - saprophytic fungi - convert dead organic material into fungal biomass, CO_2, and small molecules, such as organic acids. These fungi generally use complex substrates, such as the cellulose and lignin, in wood. They are essential for decomposing the carbon ring structures in some pollutants. Like bacteria, fungi are important for immobilizing or retaining nutrients in the soil.
2. Mutualists - mycorrhizal fungi - colonize plant roots through a symbiotic relationship. The definition of symbiosis is a close, prolonged association between two or more different organisms of different species that may benefit each member. Mycorrhizae increase the surface area associated with the plant root, which allows the plant to reach nutrients and water that otherwise might not be available. Mycorrhizae essentially extend plant reach to water and nutrients, allowing plants to utilize more of the resources

available in the soil. Mycorrhizae source their carbohydrates (energy) from the plant root they are living in/on and they usually help the plants by transferring phosphorus (P) from the soil into the root. Two major groups are identified: (i) ectomycorrhizae, that grow on the surface layers of the roots and are commonly associated with trees; and (ii) endomycorrhizae, such as arbuscular mycorrhizal fungi and vesicular mycorrhizal fungi, that grow within the root cells and are commonly associated with grasses, row crops, vegetables and shrubs. Arbuscular mycorrhizal fungi can also benefit the physical characteristics of the soil because their hyphae form a mesh to help stabilize soil aggregates. Vesicular-arbuscular mycorrhizae are the most widespread mycorrhizal fungi. Mycorrhizae are particularly important for phosphate uptake because P does not move towards plant roots easily. These organisms do not harm the plant, and in return, the plant provides energy to the fungus in the form of sugars. The fungus is actually a network of filaments that grows in and around the plant root cells, forming a mass that extends considerably beyond the root system of the plant.

3. Pathogens or parasites cause reduced production or death when they colonize roots and other organisms. Root-pathogenic fungi, such as *Verticillium*, *Pythium* and *Rhizoctonia*, cause major economic losses in agriculture each year. Many fungi help control diseases, *e.g.* nematode-trapping fungi that parasitize disease-causing nematodes, and fungi that feed on insects may be useful as bio control agents.

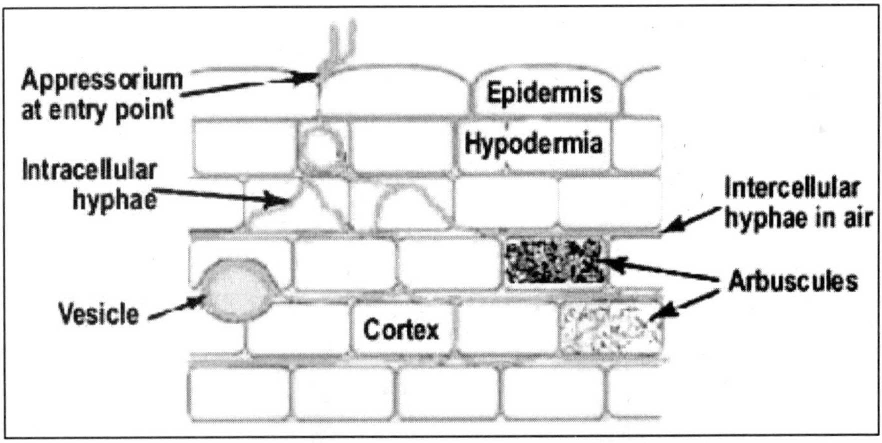

Mycorrhizal Roots and the Associated Networks of Hyphae are a Major Component of most Soils

Microfauna

The microfauna (<0.1 mm in diameter) includes *inter alia* small collembola and mites, nematodes and protozoa that generally live in the soil water films and feed on microflora, plant roots, other microfauna and sometimes larger organisms (*e.g.*

entomopathogenic nematodes feed on insects and other larger invertebrates). They are important to release nutrients immobilized by soil microorganisms.

Nematodes

Nematodes are tiny filiform roundworms that are common in soils everywhere. They may be free-living in soil water films; beneficial for agriculture or phytoparasitic and live at the surface or within the living roots (parasites). Free-living nematodes graze on bacteria and fungi, thus they control the populations of harmful micro-organisms. These nematodes are 0.15-5 mm long and 2-100 ìm wide; an exception are Mermithidae nematodes, which may be 20 cm long and are very common in tropical soils, being parasites of some arthropods such as locusts. Nematodes can only move through the soil where a film of moisture surrounds the soil particles. They live in the water (they are hydrobionts) that fills spaces between soil particles and covers roots. In hot and dry conditions, they enter into a dormant stage, and as soon as water becomes available, they spring back to activity.

Nematodes are recognized as a major consumer group in soils, generally grouped into four to five trophic categories based on the nature of their food, the structure of the stoma (mouth) and oesophagus, and the method of feeding (Yeates and Coleman,

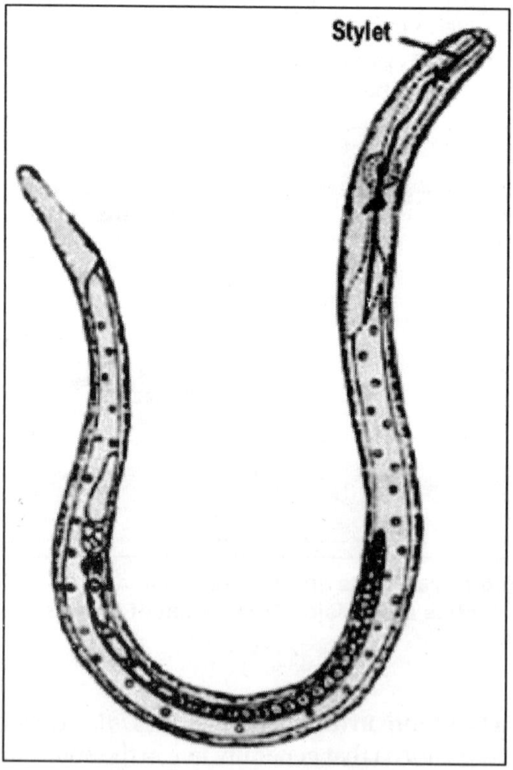

Drawing of a Plant-Parasitic Nematode Showing the Stylet Used to Penetrate Plant Roots

1982): bacterial feeders, fungal feeders, predatory feeders, omnivores, and plant feeders. The bacterial feeders prey on bacteria (bacterivores) and may ingest up to 5 000 cells/minute, or 6.5 times their own weight daily. This helps disperse both the organic matter and the decomposers in the soil. Bacterial- and fungal-feeding nematodes release a large percent of N when feeding on their prey groups and are thus responsible for much of the plant available N in the majority of soils (Ingham *et al.*, 1985). The annual overall consumption may be as much as 800 kg of bacteria per hectare and the amount of N turned over in the range of 20-130 kg (Coleman *et al.*, 1984).

Phytophages or plant-feeding nematodes damage plant roots, with important economic consequences for farmers. They possess stylets with a wide diversity of size and structure, and they are the most extensively studied group of soil nematodes because of their ability to cause plant disease and reduce crop yield.

Macrofauna

Members of species classed as macro fauna are visible to the naked eye (generally- 2 mm in diameter). Macro fauna includes vertebrates (snakes, lizards, mice, rabbits, moles, etc.) that primarily dig within the soil for food or shelter, and invertebrates (snails, earthworms and soil arthropods such as ants, termites, millipedes, centipedes, caterpillars, beetle larvae and adults, fly and wasp larvae, spiders, scorpions, crickets and cockroaches) that live in and feed in or upon the soil, the surface litter and their components. In both natural and agricultural systems, soil macro fauna are important regulators of decomposition, nutrient cycling, soil organic matter dynamics, and pathways of water movement as a consequence of their feeding and burrowing activities. Here the focus is on soil invertebrates.

Earthworms

The effects of earthworms in the soil differ according to the ecological category of the species (Bouché, 1977; Lavelle, 1981) involved:

- ☆ **Epigeic:** They live in the litter layers, a very changing environment, subject to drought, high temperatures and predator presence. These earthworms are generally small and pigmented (green or reddish) with rapid movements.
- ☆ **Endogeic**: These are unpigmented (with no colour) worms that live and feed in the soil. This group is further divided into three subgroups: oligohumic, mesohumic and polyhumic, depending on the organic matter content of the soil ingested.
- ☆ **Anecic**: These earthworms feed on the surface litter that they generally mix with soil, but they spend most of their time in the soil. They are large, with dark antero-dorsal pigmentation, and they dig sub-vertical burrows.

As a result of this wide range of adaptations, earthworms have diverse functions in the soil. Epigeic worms can be used as compost makers with no impact on soil structure. Anecics and endogeics do have an impact on soil structure owing to their mixing and burrowing activities, and on soil organic matter.

Earthworms generally exert beneficial effects on plant growth. However, negative effects may be induced under particular situations. The effect on grain yields is also proportional to the earthworm biomass; significant effects start to appear at biomass values> 30 g fresh weight (Brown *et al.*, 1999), although very high biomasses of single species of earthworms, (*e.g.*, *Pontoscolex corethrurus*) may inhibit production under particular situations. Many mechanisms are involved in the growth stimulation. These vary from large-scale effects on soil structure and nutrient availability, to the enhancement of mycorrhizal infection or control of plant-parasitic nematodes. Once the earthworms are established, a dynamic cropping system - involving crop rotations with long cycle crops or perennials with good organic matter additions - contributes to securing long-lasting benefits from earthworm activities.

Termites

Termites are important members of soil macro fauna in various regions of the world. They are social insects, living in organized colonies with a number of castes (different individuals) with a set of morphological and physiological specializations. The main castes are: queen (the termite that founds the colony), worker and soldier.

Neither individual termites nor colonies normally travel long distances as they are constrained to live within their territorial border or within their food materials. A number of species feed on living plants and some may become serious pests in agricultural systems where dead residues are scarce (Wood, 1996). Most species feed on dead-plant materials above and below the soil surface. Their food sources include plant-decaying materials, dead foliage, woody materials, roots, seeds and the faeces of higher animals (Lavelle and Spain, 2001). There are also soil-wood feeders and soil feeders, which means that they ingest a high proportion of mineral material. Their nutrition derives mainly from well-decayed wood and partly humified soil organic matter. Another group of termites grow fungi in their nests (fungus-growing termites).

Termites may be classified by their feeding habits:

- ☆ Grass harvesters,
- ☆ Surface litter feeders,
- ☆ Wood feeders,
- ☆ Soil-wood feeders,
- ☆ Soil feeders (humivores).

The nests formed by termites may occur in different locations, *e.g.* within the wood of living or dead trees, in subterranean locations, in other nests formed by other termite species, and by forming epigeal nests (above the soil surface) and arboreal nests.

Ants

Ants build a large variety of structures in the soil. However, because of their feeding habits, they are of less importance in regulating processes in the soil than termites or earthworms.

Beetles

Beetles (Coleoptera) are diverse taxonomically and differ widely in size and in the ecological role they perform in soil and litter. They are either saprophagous, phytophagous or predators. Two groups are of particular relevance in agricultural soils: larvae from the family Scarabeidae (dung-beetles), crucial to burying cowdung in natural savannahs and grasslands used for cattle grazing (*e.g.*, in Africa); and Melolonthinae beetles, whose larvae may be abundant in grasslands and affect crop production by feeding on living roots (Villalobos and Lavelle, 1990).

Dung beetles dig sub-vertical galleries 10-15 mm wide down to a depth of 50-70 cm with a variable number of chambers, which are further filled with large pellets of dung. The adult beetle lays one egg in each chamber and then the larva feeds on the pellet to complete the cycle (Lavelle and Spain, 2001). They generally give rise to small mounds a few centimetres high on the soil surface (Hurpin, 1962).

Biogenic Structures

Biogenic structures are those structures created biologically by a living organism. Three main groups of biogenic structures are commonly found in agricultural systems: earthworm casts and burrows, termite mounds and ant heaps. The biogenic structures can be deposited in the soil surface and in the soil, and generally they have different physical and chemical properties from the surrounding soil. The colour, size, shape and general aspect of the structures produced by large soil organisms can be described for each species that produces it. The form of the biogenic structure can be likened to simple geometric forms in order to facilitate evaluation of the volume of soil moved through each type of structure on the soil surface.

5.5. Soil Population and Waste Management

Definition

Soil pollution is defined as the build-up in soils of persistent toxic compounds, chemicals, salts, radioactive materials, or disease causing agents, which have adverse effects on plant growth and animal health.

Soil is the thin layer of organic and inorganic materials that covers the Earth's rocky surface.

The organic portion, which is derived from the decayed remains of plants and animals, is concentrated in the dark uppermost topsoil. The inorganic portion made up of rock fragments, was formed over thousands of years by physical and chemical weathering of bedrock. Productive soils are necessary for agriculture to supply the world with sufficient food.

There are many different ways that soil can become polluted, such as:

- Seepage from a landfill
- Discharge of industrial waste into the soil
- Percolation of contaminated water into the soil
- Rupture of underground storage tanks

- ☆ Excess application of pesticides, herbicides or fertilizer
- ☆ Solid waste seepage

The most common chemicals involved in causing soil pollution are:

- ☆ Petroleum hydrocarbons
- ☆ Heavy metals
- ☆ Pesticides
- ☆ Solvents

Types of Soil Pollution

- ☆ Agricultural Soil Pollution
  1. Pollution of surface soil
  2. Pollution of underground soil

Soil Pollution by Industrial Effluents and Solid Wastes

1. Pollution of surface soil
2. Disturbances in soil profile

Pollution due to Urban Activities

1. Pollution of surface soil
2. Pollution of underground soil

Causes of Soil Pollution

Soil pollution is caused by the presence of man-made chemicals or other alteration in the natural soil environment. This type of contamination typically arises from the rupture of underground storage links, application of pesticides, percolation of contaminated surface water to subsurface strata, oil and fuel dumping, leaching of wastes from landfills or direct discharge of industrial wastes to the soil. The most common chemicals involved are petroleum hydrocarbons, solvents, pesticides, lead and other heavy metals. This occurrence of this phenomenon is correlated with the degree of industrialization and intensities of chemical usage.

A soil pollutant is any factor which deteriorates the quality, texture and mineral content of the soil or which disturbs the biological balance of the organisms in the soil. Pollution in soil has adverse effect on plant growth.

Pollution in soil is associated with:

- ☆ Indiscriminate use of fertilizers
- ☆ Indiscriminate use of pesticides, insecticides and herbicides
- ☆ Dumping of large quantities of solid waste
- ☆ Deforestation and soil erosion

Indiscriminate Use of Fertilizers

Nutrients are important for plant growth and development. Plants obtain carbon, hydrogen and oxygen from air and water. But other necessary nutrients like nitrogen, phosphorus, potassium, calcium, magnesium, sulphur and more must be obtained from the soil. Farmers generally use fertilizers to correct soil deficiencies. Fertilizers contaminate the soil with impurities, which come from the raw materials used for their manufacture. Mixed fertilizers often contain ammonium nitrate (NH_4NO_3), phosphorus as P_2O_5, and potassium as K_2O. For instance, As, Pb and Cd present in traces in rock

Phosphate mineral gets transferred to super phosphate fertilizer. Since the metals are not degradable, their accumulation in the soil above their toxic levels due to excessive use of phosphate fertilizers becomes an indestructible poison for crops.

The over use of NPK fertilizers reduce quantity of vegetables and crops grown on soil over the years. It also reduces the protein content of wheat, maize, grams, etc., grown on that soil. The carbohydrate quality of such crops also gets degraded. Excess potassium content in soil decreases Vitamin C and carotene content in vegetables and fruits. The vegetables and fruits grown on over fertilized soil are more prone to attacks by insects and disease.

Indiscriminate Use of Pesticides, Insecticides and Herbicides

Plants on which we depend for food are under attack from insects, fungi, bacteria, viruses, rodents and other animals, and must compete with weeds for nutrients. To kill unwanted populations living in or on their crops, farmers use pesticides. The first widespread insecticide use began at the end of World War II and included DDT (dichlorodiphenyltrichloroethane) and gammaxene. Insects soon became resistant to DDT and as the chemical did not decompose readily, it persisted in the environment. Since it was soluble in fat rather than water, it biomagnified up the food chain and disrupted calcium metabolism in birds, causing eggshells to be thin and fragile. As a result, large birds of prey such as the brown pelican, ospreys, falcons and eagles became endangered. DDT has been now been banned in most western countries. Ironically many of them including USA still produce DDT for export to other developing nations whose needs outweigh the problems caused by it.

The most important pesticides are DDT, BHC, chlorinated hydrocarbons, organophosphates, aldrin, Malathion, dieldrin, furodan, etc. The remnants of such pesticides used on pests may get adsorbed by the soil particles, which then contaminate root crops grown in that soil. The consumption of such crops causes the pesticides remnants to enter human biological systems, affecting them adversely.

An infamous herbicide used as a defoliant in the Vietnam War called Agent Orange (dioxin), was eventually banned. Soldiers' cancer cases, skin conditions and infertility have been linked to exposure to Agent Orange.

Pesticides not only bring toxic effect on human and animals but also decrease the fertility of the soil. Some of the pesticides are quite stable and their bio- degradation may take weeks and even months.

Pesticide problems such as resistance, resurgence, and health effects have caused scientists to seek alternatives. Pheromones and hormones to attract or repel insects and using natural enemies or sterilization by radiation have been suggested.

Dumping of Solid Wastes

In general, solid waste includes garbage, domestic refuse and discarded solid materials such as those from commercial, industrial and agricultural operations. They contain increasing amounts of paper, cardboards, plastics, glass, old construction material, packaging material and toxic or otherwise hazardous substances. Since a significant amount of urban solid waste tends to be paper and food waste, the majority is recyclable or biodegradable in landfills. Similarly, most agricultural waste is recycled and mining waste is left on site. The portion of solid waste that is hazardous such as oils, battery metals, heavy metals from Smelting industries and organic solvents are the ones we have to pay particular attention to. These can in the long run, get deposited to the soils of the surrounding area and pollute them by altering their chemical and biological properties. They also contaminate drinking water aquifer sources. More than 90 per cent of hazardous waste is produced by chemical, petroleum and metal-related industries and small businesses such as dry cleaners and gas stations contribute as well.

Solid Waste disposal was brought to the forefront of public attention by the notorious Love Canal case in USA in 1978. Toxic chemicals leached from oozing storage drums into the soil underneath homes, causing an unusually large number of birth defects, cancers and respiratory, nervous and kidney diseases.

Deforestation

Soil Erosion occurs when the weathered soil particles are dislodged and carried away by wind or water. Deforestation, agricultural development, temperature extremes, precipitation including acid rain, and human activities contribute to this erosion. Humans speed up this process by construction, mining, cutting of timber, over cropping and overgrazing. It results in floods and cause soil erosion.

Forests and grasslands are an excellent binding material that keeps the soil intact and healthy. They support many habitats and ecosystems, which provide innumerable feeding pathways or food chains to all species. Their loss would threaten food chains and the survival of many species. During the past few years quite a lot of vast green land has been converted into deserts. The precious rain forest habitats of

South America, tropical Asia and Africa are coming under pressure of population growth and development (especially timber, construction and agriculture). Many scientists believe that a wealth of medicinal substances including a cure for cancer and aids, lie in these forests. Deforestation is slowly destroying the most productive flora and fauna areas in the world, which also form vast tracts of a very valuable sink for CO_2.

Effects of Soil Pollution

Agricultural

- ☆ Reduced soil fertility
- ☆ Reduced nitrogen fixation
- ☆ Increased erodibility
- ☆ Larger loss of soil and nutrients
- ☆ Deposition of silt in tanks and reservoirs
- ☆ Reduced crop yield
- ☆ Imbalance in soil fauna and flora

Industrial

- ☆ Dangerous chemicals entering underground water
- ☆ Ecological imbalance
- ☆ Release of pollutant gases
- ☆ Release of radioactive rays causing health problems
- ☆ Increased salinity
- ☆ Reduced vegetation

Urban

- ☆ Clogging of drains
- ☆ Inundation of areas
- ☆ Public health problems
- ☆ Pollution of drinking water sources
- ☆ Foul smell and release of gases
- ☆ Waste management problems

Control of Soil Pollution

The following steps have been suggested to control soil pollution. To help prevent soil erosion, we can limit construction in sensitive area. In general we would need less fertilizer and fewer pesticides if we could all adopt the three R's: Reduce, Reuse, and Recycle. This would give us less solid waste.

Reducing Chemical Fertilizer and Pesticide Use

Applying bio-fertilizers and manures can reduce chemical fertilizer and pesticide use. Biological methods of pest control can also reduce the use of pesticides and thereby minimize soil pollution.

Reusing of Materials

Materials such as glass containers, plastic bags, paper, cloth etc. can be reused at domestic levels rather than being disposed, reducing solid waste pollution.

Recycling and Recovery of Materials

This is a reasonable solution for reducing soil pollution. Materials such as paper, some kinds of plastics and glass can and are being recycled. This decreases the volume of refuse and helps in the conservation of natural resources. For example, recovery of one tonne of paper can save 17 trees.

Reforesting

Control of land loss and soil erosion can be attempted through restoring forest and grass cover to check wastelands, soil erosion and floods. Crop rotation or mixed cropping can improve the fertility of the land.

Solid Waste Treatment

Proper methods should be adopted for management of solid waste disposal. Industrial wastes can be treated physically, chemically and biologically until they are less hazardous. Acidic and alkaline wastes should be first neutralized; the insoluble material if biodegradable should be allowed to degrade under controlled conditions before being disposed.

As a last resort, new areas for storage of hazardous waste should be investigated such as deep well injection and more secure landfills. Burying the waste in locations situated away from residential areas is the simplest and most widely used technique of solid waste management.

Environmental and aesthetic considerations must be taken into consideration before selecting the dumping sites. Incineration of other wastes is expensive and leaves a huge residue and adds to air pollution. Pyrolysis is a process of combustion in absence of oxygen or the material burnt under controlled atmosphere of oxygen. It is an alternative to incineration. The gas and liquid thus obtained can be used as fuels. Pyrolysis of carbonaceous wastes like firewood, coconut, palm waste, corn combs, cashew shell, rice husk paddy straw and saw dust, yields charcoal along with products like tar, methyl alcohol, acetic acid, acetone and a fuel gas.

Natural Land Pollution

Land pollution occurs massively during earth quakes, landslides, hurricanes and floods. All cause hard to clean mess, which is expensive to clean, and may sometimes take years to restore the affected area. These kinds of natural disasters are not only a problem in that they cause pollution but also because they leave many victims homeless.

Waste Management

Waste management is the collection, transport, processing or disposal, managing and monitoring of waste materials. The term usually relates to materials produced by human activity, and the process is generally undertaken to reduce their effect on health, the environment or aesthetics. Waste management is a distinct practice from resource recovery which focuses on delaying the rate of consumption of natural resources. All wastes materials, whether they are solid, liquid, gaseous or radioactive fall within the remit of waste management

Waste management practices can differ for developed and developing nations, for urban and rural areas, and for residential and industrial producers. Management of non-hazardous waste residential and institutional waste in metropolitan areas is usually the responsibility of local government authorities, while management for non-hazardous commercial and industrial waste is usually the responsibility of the generator subject to local, national or international controls.

Method of Disposal

Landfill

Disposal of waste in a landfill involves burying the waste, and this remains a common practice in most countries. Landfills were often established in abandoned or unused quarries, mining voids or borrow pits. A properly designed and well-managed landfill can be a hygienic and relatively inexpensive method of disposing of waste materials. Older, poorly designed or poorly managed landfills can create a number of adverse environmental impacts such as wind-blown litter, attraction of vermin, and generation of liquid leachate. Another common product of landfills is gas (mostly composed of methane and carbon dioxide), which is produced as organic waste breaks down anaerobically. This gas can create odour problems, kill surface vegetation, and is a greenhouse gas.

Design characteristics of a modern landfill include methods to contain leachate such as clay or plastic lining material. Deposited waste is normally compacted to increase its density and stability, and covered to prevent attracting vermin (such as mice or rats). Many landfills also have landfill gas extraction systems installed to extract the landfill gas. Gas is pumped out of the landfill using perforated pipes and flared off or burnt in a gas engine to generate electricity.

Incineration

Incineration is a disposal method in which solid organic wastes are subjected to combustion so as to convert them into residue and gaseous products. This method is useful for disposal of residue of both solid waste management and solid residue from waste water management. This process reduces the volumes of solid waste to 20 to 30 percent of the original volume. Incineration and other high temperature waste treatment systems are sometimes described as "thermal treatment". Incinerators convert waste materials into heat, gas, steam and ash.

Incineration is carried out both on a small scale by individuals and on a large scale by industry. It is used to dispose of solid, liquid and gaseous waste. It is recognized as a practical method of disposing of certain hazardous waste materials (such as biological medical waste). Incineration is a controversial method of waste disposal, due to issues such as emission of gaseous pollutants.

Incineration is common in countries such as Japan where land is more scarce, as these facilities generally do not require as much area as landfills. Waste-to-energy (WtE) or energy-from-waste (EfW) are broad terms for facilities that burn waste in a furnace or boiler to generate heat, steam or electricity. Combustion in an incinerator is not always perfect and there have been concerns about pollutants in gaseous emissions from incinerator stacks. Particular concern has focused on some very persistent organics such as dioxins, furans, PAHs which may be created which may have serious environmental consequences.

Recycling

Recycling is a resource recovery practice that refers to the collection and reuse of waste materials such as empty beverage containers. The materials from which the items are made can be reprocessed into new products. Material for recycling may be collected separately from general waste using dedicated bins and collection vehicles are sorted directly from mixed waste streams and are known as kerb-side recycling, it requires the owner of the waste to separate it into various different bins (typically wheelie bins) prior to its collection.

The most common consumer products recycled include aluminium such as beverage cans, copper such as wire, steel food and aerosol cans, old steel furnishings or equipment, polyethylene and PET bottles, glass bottles and jars, paperboard cartons, newspapers, magazines and light paper and corrugated fibre board boxes.

PVC, LDPE, PP, and PS are also recyclable. These items are usually composed of a single type of material, making them relatively easy to recycle into new products. The recycling of complex products (such as computers and electronic equipment) is more difficult, due to the additional dismantling and separation required.

The type of material accepted for recycling varies by city and country. Each city and country have different recycling programs in place that can handle the various types of recyclable materials. However, certain variation in acceptance is reflected in the resale value of the material once it is reprocessed.

Sustainability

The management of waste is a key component in a business' ability to maintaining ISO14001 accreditation. Companies are encouraged to improve their environmental efficiencies each year by eliminating waste through resource recovery practices, which are sustainability-related activities. One way to do this is by shifting away from waste management to resource recovery practices like recycling materials such as glass, food scraps, paper and cardboard, plastic bottles and metal.

Waste Management Concepts

There are a number of concepts about waste management which vary in their usage between countries or regions. Some of the most general, widely used concepts include:

- ☆ Waste hierarchy - The waste hierarchy refers to the "3 Rs" reduce, reuse and recycle, which classify waste management strategies according to their desirability in terms of waste minimization. The waste hierarchy remains the cornerstone of most waste minimization strategies. The aim of the waste hierarchy is to extract the maximum practical benefits from products and to generate the minimum amount of waste.

- ☆ Polluter pays principle - the Polluter Pays Principle is a principle where the polluting party pays for the impact caused to the environment. With respect to waste management, this generally refers to the requirement for a waste generator to pay for appropriate disposal of the unrecoverable material.

— PAPER-B —

Biology of Mulberry and Biology of Silkworm and Rearing Technology

Unit-I

Dr. Ravinder Sharma

1.1. Taxonomy of Mulberry and Popular Mulberry Cultivators, Morphology and Anatomy of Mulberry Stem, Root and Leaf. An outline and floral biology of mulberry flower, fruit and seed development. Mulberry the "Kalpa Vrikasha" the economical importance. Different agro climates of mulberry

Taxonomy of the Mulberry (*Morus alba L.*)

Kingdom:	Plantae- plants
Subkingdom:	Tracheobionta – Vascular plants
Superdivision:	Spermatophyta- Seed plants
Division:	Magnoliophyta- Flowering plants
Class:	Magnoliopsida- Dicotyledons
Subclass:	Hamamelididae
Order:	Urticales
Family:	Moraceae- Mulberry family
Genus:	*Morus* L. – mulberry

Importance of Mulberry Cultivation for Sericulture

Mulberry silkworm, *Bombyx mori*, is a stenophagous (feeding on a narrow range of food items) insect that has been reported to feed on the plants listed in Table in addition to mulberry, its principal host plant(Anonymous 1975; Ganga and Chetty, 1997; Minamizawa, 1997).

Family	Name of the Species
Moraceae	*Cudrantia triloba, C.javensis, Maculura aurantiaca*, Ficus pumilla, F. nipponia, F. carica, F. erecta* and *F. hirata*
Ulmaceae	*Ulmus pumilla, U. parvifolia, U. lactuca*
Compositae	*Lactuca sativa, L. lanceolata, L. debilis*
Companulaceae	*Adenophora* sp.
Cruciferae	*Brassica oleracea*
Rosaceae	*Rosa multiflora, Duchesnea chrysantha*
Utricaceae	*Urtica thunbergiana*
Papaveraceae	*Papaver somniferum*
Umbelliferae	*Oenanthe javanica*
Aceraceae	*Acer caesium*
Elaeagnaceae	*Elaeagnus multiflora*

* The leaves of Maculura aurantiaca have been tried in the preparation of artificial diets.

Unfortunately, none of the plant listed in Table has been able to replace mulberry for commercial rearing because life of larvae reared on these plant was prolonged, the cocoons spun were small and sometimes the life cycle was not completed and metamorphosis failed to occur. Hence, for practical commercial purposes, B.mori is a monophagous (feeding on one type of food) feeder, consuming only mulberry. Cultivation, maintenance and harvesting of mulberry plants is indispensable for silkworm rearing. These activities account for more than 50 per cent of the cost of cocoon production. Further, the quality and quantity of the yield is largely dependent upon the quality and amount of mulberry leaves provided during the larval period.

Mulberry leaf is not available throughout the year in temperate regions and cannot be stored for very long as its quality varies with the variety of mulberry, season, type of pruning, dosage and schedule of fertilising and irrigation, and growth stage of the leaf. To ensure uniform quality of food and to reduce the cost of labour involved in harvesting, sorting and feeding of mulberry leaves, artificial diet- both with and without mulberry leaf powder- have been developed in Japan. But even there an artificial diet has costly and can only be used up to the third instar; it cannot be used for the fourth instars, which account for more than 80 per cent of the total consumption of the larval period. Hence, throughout the world an important and indispensable requirement for silkworm rearing in the cultivation and management for mulberry plantations.

History of Mulberry Cultivation

The mulberry plant is believed to be a native of the lower ranges of the Himalayas. It occurs in the wild in many countries but its deliberate cultivation carried out only in countries where Silkworm rearing is practised. In other countries, it is put to other uses. The earliest record of its cultivation is in 2800 B.C. in China, where Ching Nong, one of the successors of Emperor Fo-Hi, is credited with the initiation of the technique. Mulberry cultivation, along with silkworm rearing, must have spread from China to the rest of the world by various routes- travellers, prisoners of war, traders their country. One legend holds that a princess carried mulberry seeds in her headgear and another legend that a monk carried them in his walking stick.

Morphology of Mulberry Plant

Mulberry grows in tropical and temperate regions. It is a fruit plant and food plant of mulberry silkworm. Mulberry is largely cultivated in Tamil Naidu, Karnataka, Orissa, West Bengal, Jammu and Kashmir and other part of India. Mulberry is a perennial tree or woody shrub plant, living for a number of years either cultivated or in wild state, mulberry having vegetative organs that have well developed root system, woody stem, leaves and reproductive organs *i.e.,* monocious or diocious flower and fruit.

General Features of Mulberry

Mulberry is the basic food material for silkworms, Morus is the Latin word for mulberry in French: muries, Italian:gelso, Japanese: lewwa etc. Mulberry plant is exploited in different ways for commercial production of silk. The leaf protein morin is main source for the silkworm to bio-synthesize the silk, which is made up of two proteins, fibrion and sericin. Nearly 70 per cent of the silk proteins produced by a silkworm are directly derived from the proteins of the mulberry leaves. Mulberry is grown as from bush in tropical countries and as middlings and tree in temperate countries. Breeding of mulberry has resulted in evolving over 200 varieties of mulberry. Studies on the ecological factors and adaptability of these varieties have helped in selecting varieties suitable to different agro-climatic tracts. The soils grow to mulberry are mostly alluvial soil and volcanic types. Mulberry being highly responsive to fertilizer applications, agronomical studies in India have shown that 30,000 kg of quality leaf can be harvested/hectare/annum under tropical conditions.

2800 B.C. Ching-Nong, one of the successors of Emperors Fo-Hi taught cultivation of mulberry in China. Silk industry took its origin in the province of Chang-tong. According to Western historians mulberry culture spread to India from China through kotan (Tibet) by about 140 B.C. origin of Mulberry is believed to be a native either of India or China and it is believed to have originated on the lower slopes of the Himalayas.

In India the land area under mulberry in 1971 was 104885 ha. together with about four million scattered mulberry trees grow in the northern parts of India (i.S. CSB, Vol. XII, No.3, July 1973, page 15). A survey of sericulture industry reveals that there are at least 29 countries where mulberry is cultivated and they are: (1) Japan, (2) China, (3) the Republic of Korea, (4) the U.S.S.R. (5) India (6) Brazil, (7) Italy, (8) France, (9) Spain, (10) Greece, (11) Yogosalavia, (12) Turkey, (13) Sri Lanka, (14) Hungary, (15) Egypt, (16) Syria,(17) Poland, (18) Bulgaria, (19) Iran, (20) Lebanon, (21) Thailand, (22) Burma, (23) Bangladesh, (24) Afghanistan, (25) Cyprus, (26) The Republic of South Vietnam, (27) Indonesia, (28) Rumania, (29) Cambodia. The geographical position, *i.e.*, the latitude and longitude of the mulberry growing countries lie north of the equator, except Brazil that lies south of the equator (14° to 23° S) and countries, that lie in the belt of high range of latitude, *i.e.*, 28° N to 55° N are Japan 30° N-41° N, China, U.S.S.R., the Republic of Korea, India, Yogosaliva, France, Spain Italy, Greece,Afganistan and Rumana are food for mulberry growth. The principal mulberry growing states of India are Karnataka, West Bengal, Jammu and Kashmir, Tamil Naidu etc.

Mulberry can be grown under various types of climatic conditions, ranging from temperate and tropics. In the temperate climate, mulberry does not sport during the winter season, while in the tropic the growth is continuous. In temperate climate, mulberry sprouts in April and continues to grow up to October. From October to March the plant remains dormant due to sever winter. Thus temperature varies from 26.0 to 34°C the mean minimum temperature varies from 13.9 to 20.5°C. The climatic conditions in India are favorable for luxuriant growth of mulberry and rearing of silkworms throughout the year. The temperature in Karnataka state, the major silk producing state in India, ranges from 21° C to 30° C, while extremes of temperature are observed in West Bengal, the temperature falls below 15.5° C in winter and reaches as high as 37°C in summer. Climatic conditions in Kashmir are favorable to rear silkworms rearing during May to October.

For the optimum growth of mulberry and good sprouting of the buds the mean atmospheric temperature should not fall below 13° C and if the temperature falls below this limit, mulberry remain in the dormant condition. The mean maximum temperature should not be the above 37.7° C. thus for best mulberry growth, 24 to 26.6° C are found to be optimum temperature.

The range of temperature fluctuations prevalent in the mulberry

1. Average temperature 13.8°C
2. Average daily highest temperature 13.7 to 21.5°C.
3. Annual daily lowest temperature 4.5 to 13.6°C.
4. Maximum highest temperature 34 to 41°C.
5. Minimum lowest temperature 6.4 to 25.5°C.

The suitability of the climatic condition for mulberry cultivation alone cannot sustain continued culture of silkworms on industrial scale in a country. The deciding factor is the economy of the industry, *i.e.* the cost of production, which in turn reflects the efficiency of leaf production, utilization of the leaf by the silkworm race and the spinning quality of the silk, etc. The availability and cost of labour are also important factors contributing to the cost of production; various scientific methods of mulberry cultivation have been adopted to maximize production in unit area of land and the cost analysis of input- output ratio have been worked out. The new researches have been reported not only to increase the leaf production but also to reduce the cost of production of unit weight of leaf. Another interesting feature is the net profit earned from unit land through sericulture is more than any other agricultural for commercial crop, especially in developing and under developed countries where the average income is low. The product of the land is mulberry leaf, which is converted into raw silk by rearing silkworms and the extraction of silk, both of which require large labour force. The quantity of silk produced varies from 20 to 120 kg/hectare.

The area needed to produce one ton of raw silk depends on the intensity of mulberry cultivation and the quality of silkworm that is reared. With rain fed mulberry cultivation without the application of artificial fertilizers, and rearing in inferior quality of silkworm, 20 kg of raw silk is produced from one hectare of mulberry plantation. For a country intending to start silk production, assuming that from the very beginning the most suitable variety of mulberry is cultivated and high quality silkworm races are reared, a yield of 40 to 60 kg of raw silk could easily be produced.

General Description

Mulberry belongs to the genus Morus. Hooker (1885) has given the botanical description of the genus Morus that is trees or shrubs. Leaves alternate, entire toothed or three lobed. In the base three to five nerved stipules small lateral and caduceus. Flower mono or dioecious spikate in nature, male flower; imbricate four sepals, stamens four inflexed in bud. In female flower four sepals, decussate, imbricate, accrecent and succulent in fruit. Ovary straight one called, style central, two partile; ovule pendulous, fruiting spikes or hea many, achene's enclosed in the succulent perianth, Seed; sub- globose, aluminous, freshly, embryo incurved, cotyledons oblong equal, radical ascending incumbent are found.

The plant is a perennial one, living for a number of years either cultivated or in wild state depending upon the type of cultivation, the plant is grown as a bush, tree or a middling. The plant is of branching type and the branching character varies considerably due to the influence of different factors, such as the type of cultivation, fertility of the soil, rainfall etc. In a field crop, profuse branching is preferred, as the production of leaves will be more. The plants when allowed to grow as tree attain a height of 20-25 m. with a girth of the trunk about 8 meter in the case of Morus serrata. In India, multivoltine areas like Karnataka and West Bengal, the plants are grown as bushes by pruning the plants once a year or after every crop.

In the univoltine area of Jammu and Kashmir, the plants are grown as tree mostly wildly in nature. In some areas the plants are allowed to grow as middling, *i.e.*, they are pruned at a height of 45 to 90 cm from the ground level, every year. The bush and the middling usually attain a maximum height of 1.5 to 1.8m. and hence make it easy for the harvesting of leaf.

Stem Colour

Mulberry plants show a number of stem colour depending upon their species, climate and origin. The Mysore local, Kanva2 and Berhampore varieties of *Morus indica* are white to greyish white colour.

Bud

In mulberry, generally one bud is found in the axil of a leaf, sometimes two more independent buds on either side of the main bud are also found and these are called accessory buds. Some of the axillary buds of the scale leave of the main bud peep out of the bud they are the accessory buds. They are generally called "scale buds". The covering of young leaves, which are in turn covered by older and oldest leaves to protect buds. The growing point emerges as a shoot under favorable climatic conditions. Generally, mulberry varieties growing in tropical climatic conditions sprout throughout the year. The rate of sprouting of vegetative buds is of primary consideration in introducing a variety or species in an area. The size, shape and position of the axillary bud vary from variety to variety.

Low temperature, nitrogen deficiency, inactivation of enzymes due to excessive accumulation of carbohydrate, photoperiodism etc. might be responsible for dormancy in bud. Recently, evidences show that dormancy is mainly due to auxin that the lateral buds during dormancy. It is not established as yet whether the lateral bud dormancy is due to excess of hormone they receive or loss of hormone. Yahira and Hayashi (1971) analyzed the auxin content of the dormant buds and suggested that there are at least three growth factors responsible for dormancy.

Methods of Breaking Dormancy in Buds

Mechanical

Under tropical climate, during winter period, the buds do not sprout quickly. In order to hasten the sprouting in such buds, the plant shoots after leaf harvest are bent in such a way to from an arch. Due to this certain amount of stress an strain is exerted on the scale leaves of the buds and they drop off. Then buds start emerging.

Chilling Treatment

Gururajan (1962) reported the success of braking dormancy in buds of *Morus nigra* by subjecting them to a low temperature of 0 to 6° C.

Chemical Treatment

Iwata (1970) reported the effect of chemicals such as methyl caprate on the sprouting of mulberry buds and retardation of growth of mulberry plants. Mulberry plants grow were sprayed by aqueous emulsion of methyl caprate in summer with varying concentrations ranging from 0.01M to 0.2M. The tender portion of the plants were retarded with the sprays at the concentrations of 0.01M and the terminal buds were injured severely at concentration higher than 0.25 M. Axillary buds of mulberry treated with higher concentrations than 0.2 M were forced to sprout earlier with vigorous recurrent shoots within 50 to 60 days after treatment.

Anatomy of Root, Stem and Leaf

Mulberry is a deep-rooted perennial plant. Its root system is very well developed in growth and spread of the root depends upon the texture of the soil. The root tip shows the same structure as in other dicotyledonous plants. There is a clear differentiation of root cap that protects is growing meristamatic tissue from desiccation and injury by the various soil organisms. The root hairs that are ephemeral serve the function of absorption of water and salt from the soil.

Internal Structure of Root

There is a singled layered epidermis that consists of tubular shaped cells, closely arranged without inter-cellular space. Its outer walls are not cutinized and a few of the epidermal cells enlarge into hairs. Below the epidermis there is a large cortex that consists parenchyma cells. There is a clear single layered endodermis enclosing the pericycle and vascular bundles. The vascular bundles are diarch, sometimes triach, radial and without cambium. The pericyle is many layered which later forms the cork cambium. Some of the cells of parenchyma outside the protoxylex convert themselves into a small strip of cambium. These cambial strips divide and redivide to produce a sinuous (cambium layer, which later becomes circular). Pericycle also converts themselves into meristematic cells to from cork cambium. The cork cambium cuts off cells towards outside and inside, more cells towards inside then outside, more of secondary phloem is produced the primary xylem strand remains undistributed as main medullary ray.

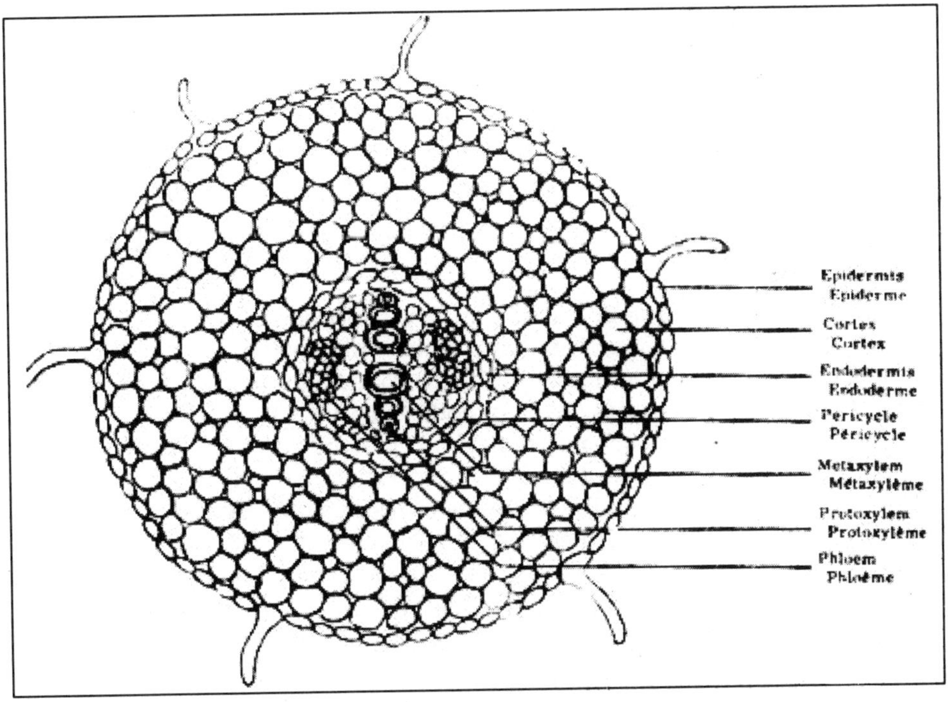

Structure of a Primary Root of *Morus indica*

Thus in the secondary root, there is a thick bark including the primary cortex. The cork consists of rectangular cells whose contents are absorbed below the cork is the secondary phloem and secondary xylem are formed from the activity of the cambium. The roots with two or three layers of cambium are preferred for purposes of grafting or cutting.

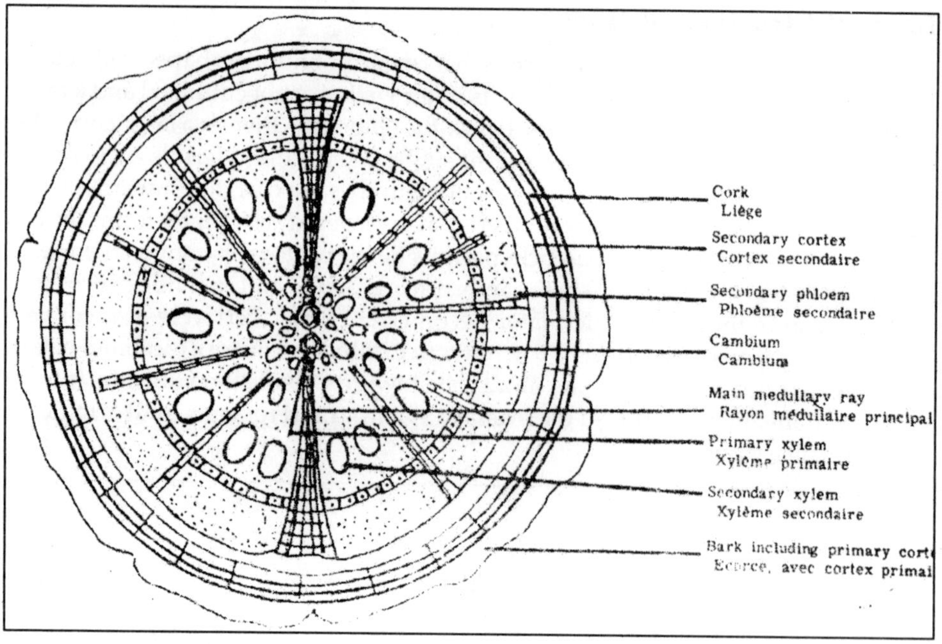

Transverse Section of the Root of *Morus indica* (Secondary)

Anatomy of Stem

The anatomy of the stem is similar to any dicotyledonous stem. The primary stem consists of a single-layered epidermis with tubular shaped cells closely arranged without inter- layered epidermis with tubular shaped cells closely arranged without inter-cellular space. The outer cells of the epderminal cells are cutinised. Some of the epderminal cells are draw into unicellular hairs that protect the plant from injurious insects and minimize the rate of transpiration. These epidermal hairs are coarse and profuse in polyploidy species. Below the epidermis is a multi- layered cortex. Some of the cells contain chloroplasts; there are many laticiferous cells in the cortex that are the storehouses of organic excretory products. The pericycle is many layered. The vascular bundles are few, collateral, conjoined, open and endarch. There is a conspicuous medulla.

The secondary stem with the union of the cambial strips of the vascular bundles a continuous ring of cambium is developed which cuts off secondary xylem inside and secondary phloem towards outside. Due to increase in the girth of stem, the continuity of the epidermis is broken at various places. The function of protecting the inner tissues is taken up by some of the cells of collenchymas, converting themselves into cork cambium or phellogem, which cuts off more cells towards outside and a few cells towards inside. Those cells that are formed towards outside from the cork or phellum and those that are formed towards inside from the secondary cortex or phelloderm.

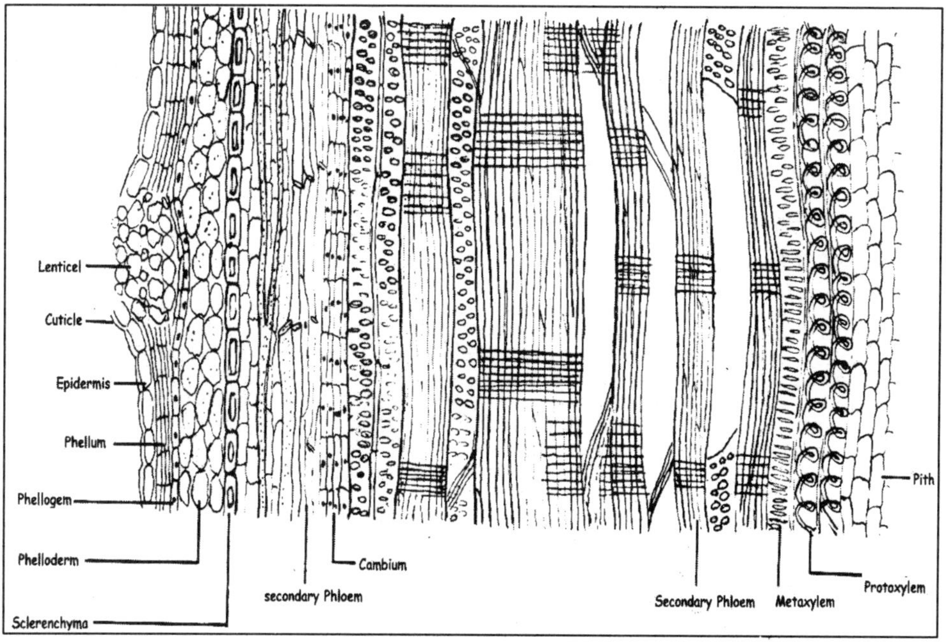

Longitudinal Section of the Stem of *Morus indica* (Secondary)

The phellogen with phellem and phelloderm is the periderm. The removal of the periderm with the bud is the main operation of bud grafting. The cork cambium at some places, where the epidermis is broken, does not form the cork cells; a group of powdery cells known as complimentary cells are formed. The structure is called, the lenticels that facilities exchange processes. The secondary cortex consists of parenchyma cells, traversed by many laticiferous cells. The secondary phloem consists of well- developed sieve tubes to conduct the food material. The cambium in between the phloem and the xylem cuts cells regularly, adding more of secondary tissues year by year.

Due to increase in the girth of the stem, the primary xylem is pushed to the centre, which is ultimately crushed to from the hard wood. Depending upon the requirement of the water in different seasons, the cambium cuts off xylem cells of high and narrow calibre.

The amount of wood–produced in one year is the annual ring. The winter and autumn seasons, the plants under temperate climate, shed their leaves and practically there will be dormant condition. During this period the xylem cells of narrow calibre are formed. But during spring, as the plants put forth a large number of branches and leaves, it requires more water to be absorbed from the soil. Therefore, the xylem of high calibre is produced. The shoots with active cambium are selected for propagation through cuttings of scions in grafting.

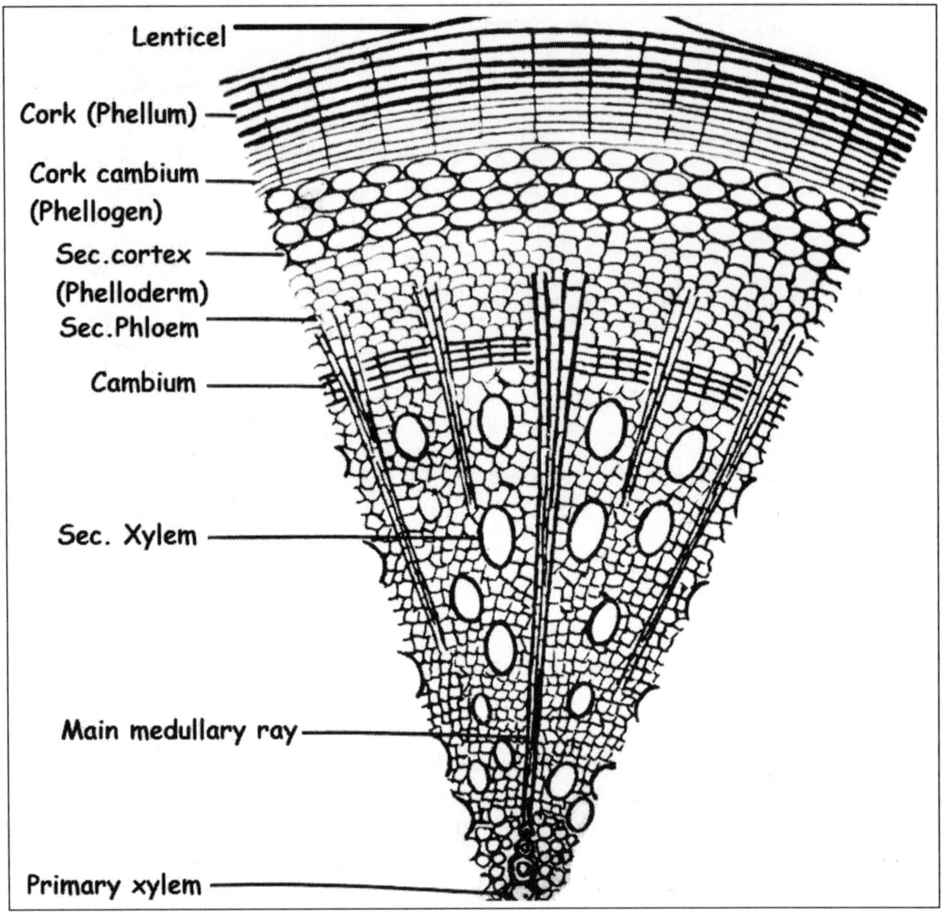

Transverse Section of the Stem of *Morus indica* (Secondary)

Anatomy of Leaf Blade

The leaves are dorsiventral with recticulate vention. The upper epidermis consists of a single layer of tabular shaped cells closely arranged without intercellular space. However, the continuity is broken at certain places, due to enlargement of the cells in the form of idioblasts. The outer walls are cutinized and a layer of cuticle is found. The thickness of the cuticle varies with mulberry variety. The thickness of the cuticle, number of idioblasts and thickness of the blade have a significant role in determining the feeding quality of leaf. Those with thinner cuticle, thinner leaf blade and less number of cystoliths are more palatable to silkworms. The palisade parenchyma is usually a single layer of closely packed, elongate prismatic shaped cells with their long axes at right angles to the upper epidermis, with numerous chloroplasts along the inner sides. The cells are loosely packed leaving large inter cellular space and respiratory cavities near the stoma.

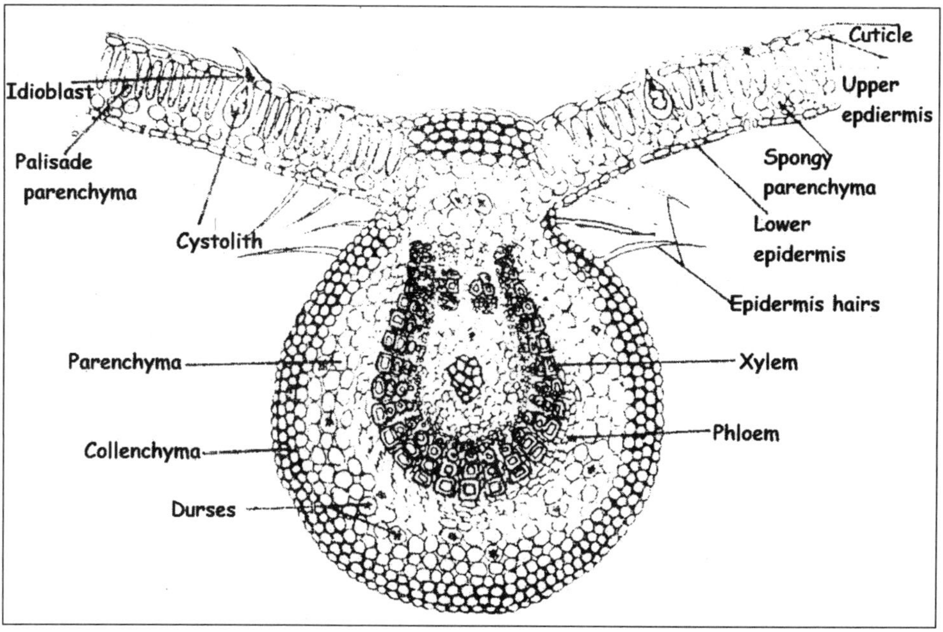

Transverse Section of the Leaf Blade of *Morus indica*

Vascular bundle consists of xylem and phloem. Xylem is arranged towards the upper epidermis and phloem towards the lower epidermis with a bundle sheath of a single layer of compactly arranged colourless parenchymatous cells extending on one or other side of the bundle towards epidermis in almost all the prominent veins. The bigger vascular bundles found to have a sclerenchyma sheath within the bundle sheath, covering completely the vascular bundle or as patches on one or both of the sides.

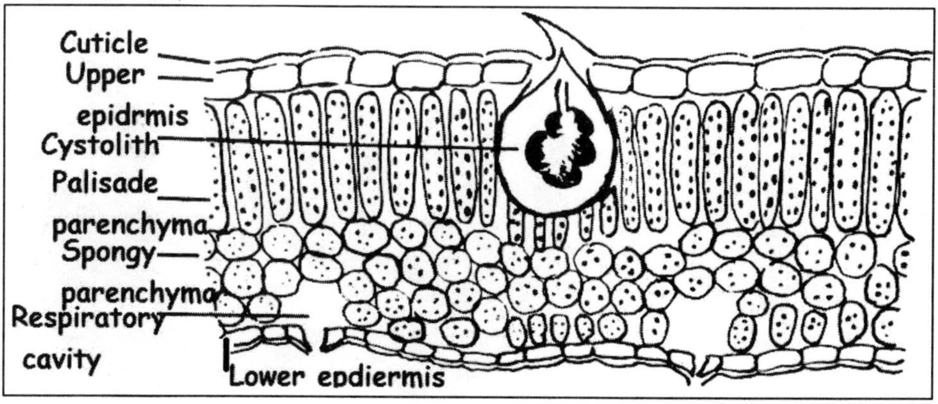

A Portion Enlarged

Floral Biology of Mulberry Flower, Fruit and Seed Development

Flowers

The flowers of mulberry are small, usually sessile or infrequently shortly pedicillate, regular and unisexual. The male flower consists of four perianth leaves, arranged in two whorals with imbricate aestivation. The interior –posterior perianth leaves are outside and the perianth leaves in the transverse plane are inside. They are green, homochlamydous, sometimes the margins of the perianth leaves and the outer surface are provided with hairs. The androecium consists of four stamens arranged oppostive to perianth leaves. The filaments of the stamens are bent inward in bud condition. Each stamen has a broad filament and a narrow top on which two anther lobes are fixed in versatile condition. Anthers are dithecems with icuous, longitudinal dehiscence; the pollen grains are round, dry, light and dust like smooth exine. The female flower has 4 perianth as in male due to fertilization the perianth leaves of female flower stimulated and become thick, contains a juicy material, which helps in the formation of the fruit. Ovary is made up of a bicapellary syncarpous, superior and unilocular containing a single pendulous ovule attached to the margin of the ovary. There is a single. The length of the style is an important character in distinguishing various species of mulberry which have longer tyles are grouped under Dolichostylae (*Morus bombycis, M. Kagayamae*) and those with shorter styles are grouped under Macromorus (*M. formosensis, M. tiliaefolia*). Stigma bifid, trigid stigma has also been reported.

Flowers of mulberry are unisexual, only cross pollination take place. The chief pollinating agent in mulberry is wind. The flowers of mulberry are well adapted to suit their pollinating agent. Some of the anemophilous characters seen in mulberry

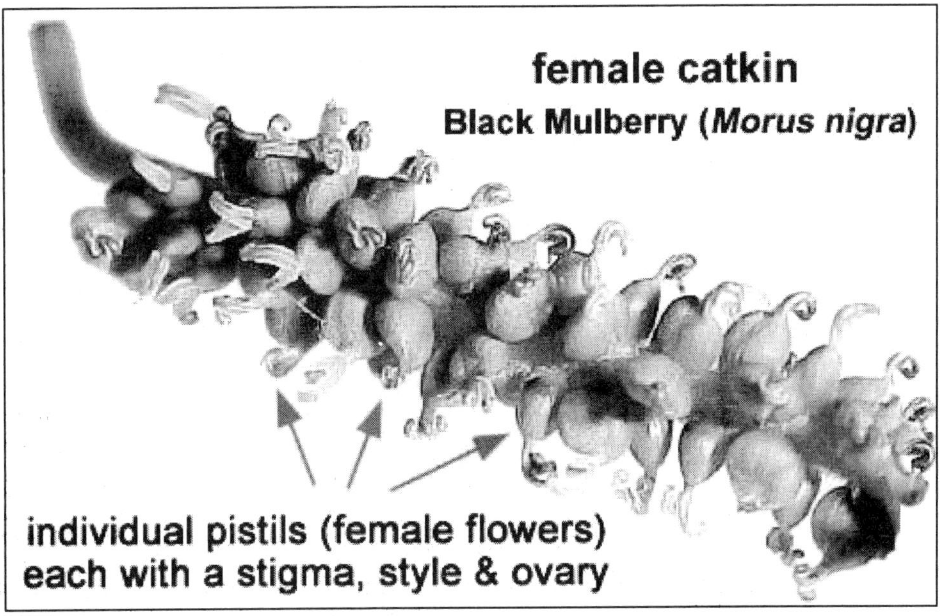

flowers *i.e.*, in male catkin of mulberry, the flowers are loosely attached to the peduncle; as they are flexible, they can be easily shaken off by wind and for every gust of wind a large quantity of pollen is spread. Flowers are small and inconspicuous, they posses neither honey, colour, nor emit any smell. Perianth leaves are very much reduced. Anderoecium and gynoecium are well exposed to wind currents. Anthers are versatile and situated on long slender filaments that peep out of flowers. The filaments are long and bent inward in bud condition. The pollen grains are dry, dust like, small and light coast and never stick to one another. The stigma is very much pronounced exposing a large surface to the wind currents and this increases the chances of receiving pollen.

Seed

Mulberry seed is oval in shape, flat surface at the micropylar region. On one edge it is found an elongated streak the hilum. At one end of the hilum is found a mall pore of micropile through which the seed absorbs water when soaked. The seed coat consists of two layers, the outer hard and brittle layer testa and the inner thin papery and slightly brownish layer tegmen. If seed coat is removed the kernel is disclosed. This consists of an endosperm in which the material is stored. The seeds contain 25-35 percent 0f a yellow drying oil with the following characteristics: sp. Gr.0.924-0.926, saponification value 190-192, iodine value 140-144 and R.M. value 0.10 to 0.35. Liquid fatty acids constitute the major part (80-90 percent) of the total fatty acids of the oil.

The embryo consists of a primary axis plumule and radical and two cotyledons. On germination, the plumule gives rise to the shoot system and the radical to the root system. The size and weight of the seed varies with the variety. The seeds of polyploidy species weight more than those of diploids.

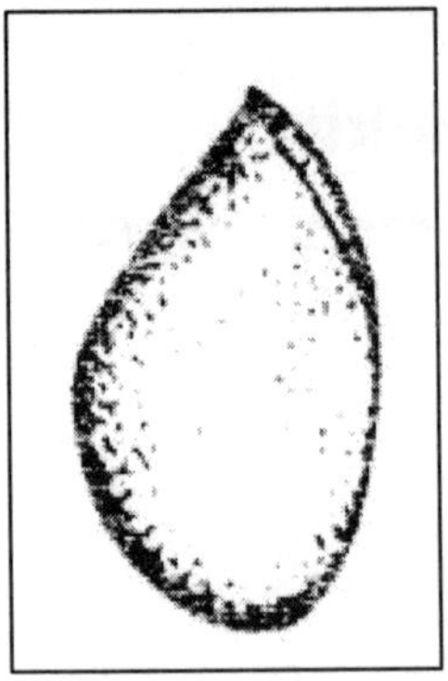

Seed

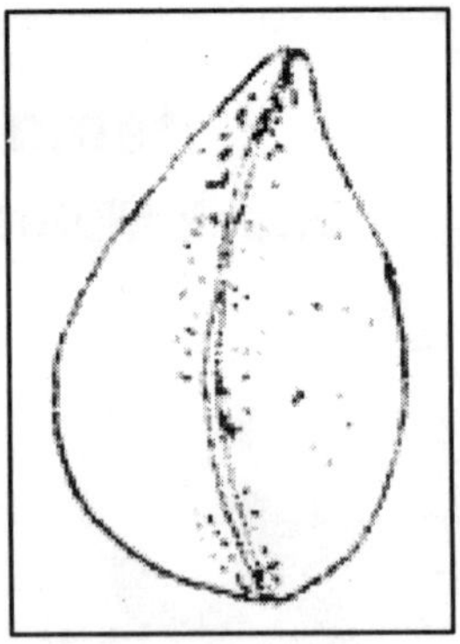

Seed, Side View

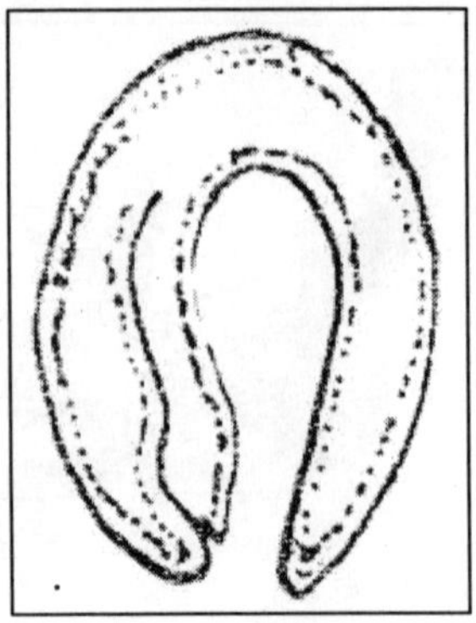

Longitudinal Section of Seed

Fruit

The fruit of mulberry is a multiple one, as all the flowers of the inflorescence give rise to a single fruit. The inflorescence axis and the perianth parts become persistent and fleshy. As the individual fruitless fuse together with the fleshy peduncle, it is described as sorosis. Due to the act of fertilization the perianth leaves of female flowers also get stimulated, become succulent with a large quantity of juicy material and contribute to the formation of fruit. Thus, the individual berries of the sorosis of mulberry are described as pseudo-carps or false fruit. The fruit contain seed but this is not invariably true. Seedless fruits are also of common occurrence in certain polyploids species like *M.nigra* and *M. Latifolia.* This condition of seedlessness is called parthenocarpy. Even if there are seed in such parthenocarpic fruits, they are without embryos. Parthenocarpy may be of natural occurrence or may be induced by artificial means by spraying certain types of hormones called auxins.

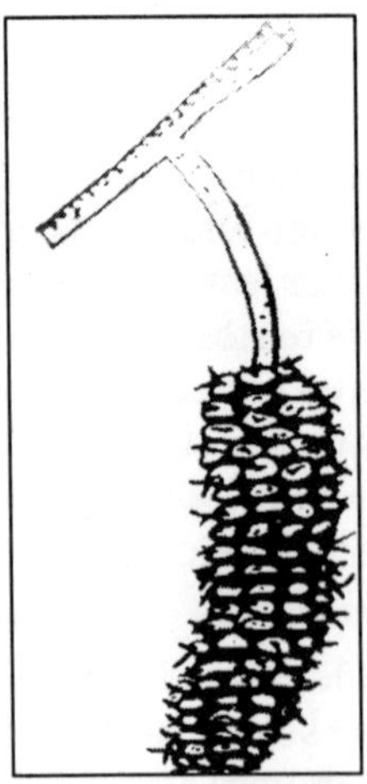

Fruit of a Diploid

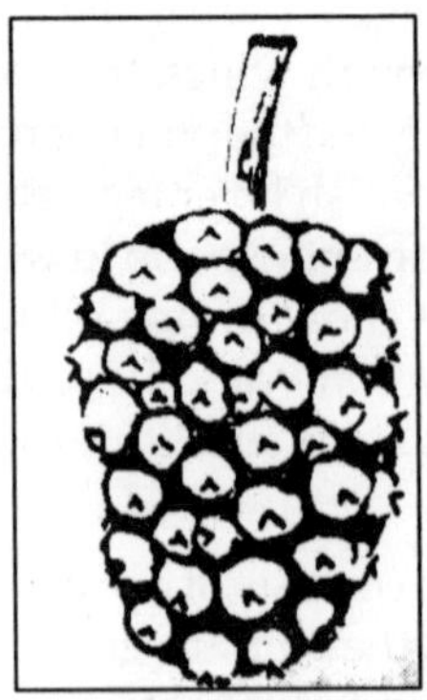

Fruit of a Polyploid

Economical Importance of Mulberry

More than hundred species of *Morus* exist. In taxonomy, species generally are identified not by the color of the fruits (berries) but by the color of flower buds and leaves. So, a morus plant can exhibit different color berries (black, purple, red, white, etc.) in the same plant.

Three species have been recognized for their economic importance.

- ☆ The white mulberry (Morus alba) is native to eastern and central China.
- ☆ The red or American mulberry (Morus rubra) is native to eastern United States.
- ☆ Black mulberry (Morus nigra) is native to western Asia.

Mulberries are large, deciduous trees native to warm, temperate, and subtropical regions of Asia, Africa, and the Americas. Technically, the mulberry fruit is an aggregation of small fruits arranged longitudinally around the central axis as in blackberry or loganberries. Each fruit measures 2-5 cm long. In most species, these berries are purple-red when ripen; however, they can be white, red, purple or multiple colors in the same fruit.

Health Benefits of Mulberry

- ☆ Delicious, fleshy, succulent mulberries are low in calories (just 43 calories per 100 g). They contain health promoting phyto-nutrient compounds like polyphenol pigment antioxidants, minerals and vitamins that are essential for optimum health.
- ☆ Mulberries have significantly high amounts of phenolic flavonoid phytochemicals called **anthocyanins.**Scientific studies have shown that consumption of berries have potential health effects against cancer, aging and neurological diseases, inflammation, diabetes, and bacterial infections.
- ☆ The berries contain **resveratrol,** another polyphenol flavonoid antioxidant. Resveratrol protects against stroke risk by altering molecular mechanisms in the blood vessels; reducing their susceptibility to damage through decreased activity of angiotensin (a systemic hormone causing blood vessel constriction that would elevate blood pressure) and increased production of the vasodilator hormone,*nitric oxide.*
- ☆ In addition, these berries are an excellent source of vitamin-C (36.4 mg per 100, about 61 per cent of RDI), which is also a powerful natural antioxidant. Consumption of foods rich in vitamin-C helps the body develop resistance against infectious agents, counter inflammation and scavenge harmful free radicals.
- ☆ Further, the berries also contain small amounts of vitamin A, vitamin E and in addition to the above-mentioned antioxidants. Consumption of mulberry provides another group of health promoting flavonoid polyphenolic antioxidants such as *lutein, zea-xanthin, ß-carotene and dinna-carotene* in small but notably significant amounts. Altogether, these compounds help act as

protect from harmful effects of oxygen-derived free radicals and reactive oxygen species (ROS) that play a role in aging and various disease processes.

☆ **Zea-xanthin,** an important dietary carotenoid selectively concentrates into the retinal macula lutea, where it thought to provide antioxidant functions and protects the retina from the harmful ultraviolet rays through light-filtering actions.

Mulberry (*Morus nigra* L), Fresh Raw, Nutrition Value per 100 g.

Principle	*Nutrient Value*	*Percentage of RDA*
Energy	43 Kcal	2 per cent
Carbohydrates	9.80 g	7.5 per cent
Protein	1.44 g	2.5 per cent
Total Fat	0.39 g	2 per cent
Cholesterol	0 mg	0 per cent
Dietary Fiber	1.7 g	4.5 per cent
Vitamins		
Folates	6 µg	1.5 per cent
Niacin	0.620 mg	4 per cent
Pyridoxine	0.050 mg	4 per cent
Riboflavin	0.101 mg	8 per cent
Vitamin A	25 IU	1 per cent
Vitamin C	36.4 mg	61 per cent
Vitamin E	0.87 mg	6 per cent
Vitamin K	7.8 µg	6.5 per cent
Electrolytes		
Sodium	10 mg	0.75 per cent
Potassium	194 mg	4 per cent
Minerals		
Calcium	39 mg	4 per cent
Copper	60 µg	6.5 per cent
Iron	1.85 mg	23 per cent
Magnesium	18 mg	4.5 per cent
Selenium	0.6 µg	1 per cent
Zinc	0.12 mg	1 per cent
Phyto-nutrients		
Carotene–ß	9 µg	–
Carotene, dinna	12 µg	–
Lutein-zeaxanthin	136 µg	–

Source: USDA National Nutrient data base.

- Mulberries are an excellent source of iron, which is a rare feature among berries, contain 1.85 mg/100 g of fruits (about 23 per cent of RDI). Iron, being a component of hemoglobin inside the red blood cells, determines the oxygen-carrying capacity of the blood.
- They also good source of minerals like potassium, manganese, and magnesium. Potassium is an important component of cell and body fluids that helps controlling heart rate and blood pressure. Manganese is used by the body as a co-factor for the antioxidant enzyme, *superoxide dismutase.*
- They are rich in B-complex group of vitamins and vitamin K. Contain very good amounts of vitamin B-6, niacin, riboflavin and folic acid. These vitamins are function as co-factors and help body in the metabolism of carbohydrates, proteins and fats.

1.2. Propagation of Mulberry; Seedling Methods of Raising Viable Seeds, Saplings; Preparation and Selection of Cuttings Grafting Stem Root and Bud Grafting Techniques, Layering, Raising of Nursery, its Maintenance and Care, Use of Growth Regulators in Mulberry Propagation

Propagation of Mulberry

Seedling Propagation

Seedling propagation is rarely practices by commercial rearers because the quality of the variety cannot be maintained, as mulberry is normally a wind – pollinated plant.

- Seedling used as stock in grafting method.
- To carry out research in breeding method like selection and hybridization. Some exotic varieties of mulberry can be propagated only by seedling propagation.

Propagation of Bed

The nursery for seedling is selected in a shady area to protect the seedling from direct sunlight and avoid excessive temperature. The soil is prepared to a fine fit by ploughing and breading the clumps. Basal application of fertilizer (for 1m 5kg of compost 150 kg charcoal ash and 50-100 kg of mixed fertilizer) is scattered on the entire sowing bed and mixed by ploughing, convenient sized seed bed normally 0.9 m. square are made the bed is kept moist by irrigation.

Collection of Seeds

The seed are extracted from ripe fruits available in march- April in tropical region and May-June in temperate region.

As there is no dormancy period for the seeds, freshly collected seed have a high germination percentage. The germination ability is gradually lost if seeds are stored for more than three months. If the seeds are to be preserved for a longer period, they should be stored in a sealed, airtight container and keep is a cool place.

Sowing of Seed

Seeds are soaked in water for 24 hours of soften the testa and at the same time to eliminate unviable seeds, insects infected seed, unfertilized seed etc, which float on the water. This is a called the floatation test of testing seed viability.

The viable seeds are either broadcast in the field or sown individually in holes in a line with the help of a rope at a depth of less than 25mm. If sown in deeper layers, the seed fail to germinate due to oxygen. The bed in then irrigated with sufficient water.

Factors Affecting Germination

Germination is also affected by environmental temperature and light. The minimum, optimum and maximum temperature ranges for germination are 18-21°C, 33-36°C and 36-39°C respectively. The time taken for germination is ten days at 27°C, eight days at 30°C and six days at 33-36°Cin dark condition. After sowing at the time of the seed germination water is sprinkled once or twice every day. After germination, depending upon the requirement water supplied.

Mats mode of bamboo strips, coconut leaves is placed on the seedbeds to protect the germinating seeds from excessive sunlight. Seeds germinated in 10 days. After three months, the first transplanting is done to give a wide space of 22.5cm between them. After two years, they are once again transplanted to their final location or used to prepare. Cutting or as stocks for grafting method.

Preparation and Selection of Cuttings Grafting Stem Root and Bud Grafting Techniques, Layering

Mulberry is mostly propagated by asexual method. Among the asexual methods, vegetative propagation is easy and mostly used in South India. Let us learn the various procedures for vegetative propagation through stem cuttings, grafting, layering and raising of saplings.

Stem Cutting

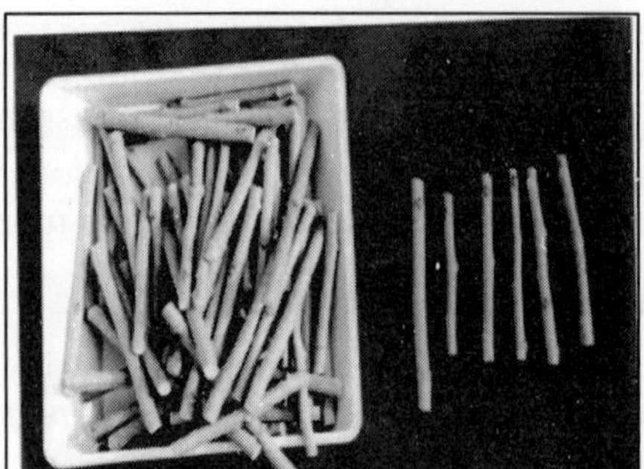

The varieties having high rooting ability can easily multiplied through stem cutting. The process starts with harvesting of shoots from a matured mulberry garden (seed plot) meant for this purpose. Precautions are taken to keep the garden free from disease and pests. We must keep in mind that stem cuttings should be selected from at least 6 months old shoots free from disease and pests. Cuttings of 15-

18cm length and 10-15 mm diameter with 3-4 healthy buds are prepared using sharp Bill-hook or Secateurs without any damage to the bark. While preparing the cuttings, upper immature and lower thick portion of the shoots should be rejected. The cuttings can also be prepared with the help of a shoot cutting machine developed at CSR and TI, Mysore which can make the job of preparation of cuttings easier and economic. Care must be taken not to dry the cutting. The drying of the cuttings can be avoided by putting the cuttings in shade covered with wet gunny cloth. Before planting cuttings in the nursery, the cuttings are treated with 0.1 per cent Dithane M – 45 solution for 20-30 minutes for avoiding fungal disease. The cuttings are planted immediately after treatment. Atmospheric temperature is a very important factor for the propagation. Suitable temperature can facilitate multiplication. Hence temperature of 20–25°C is considered as ideal for cutting propagation. Similarly, soil temperature in the range of 15-20°C is desirable in raising the cuttings. High humidity can be an added advantage in the process of multiplication. Cuttings are planted in the nursery bed in a vertically straight position exposing only one bud above the soil. The distance between the row to row should be 20 cm and cutting to cutting 10 cm. Besides this, soil is pressed around the cuttings firmly to ensure contact of cuttings with the soil to develop roots. During the process of development of roots, the cutting should not be disturbed. Weeds can be removed 45 days after planting cuttings with the help of a sharp weeding sickle without disturbing the cuttings. After one month of planting, urea at the rate of 10 g/sq. meter is applied to the nursery and irrigated immediately. Subsequently the irrigation is done once in every 4 days to get uniform size saplings with good vigor. The saplings are transplanted for plantation after 4 months.

Grafting

There are various methods, depending upon the part used as the stock, the grafting can be classified into root, shoot and bud grafting.

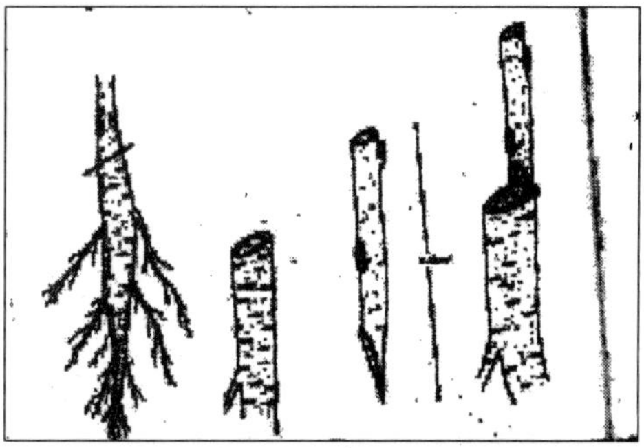

a. Root Grafting

Root grafting practiced with mulberry varieties which cannot be propagated through stem cuttings usually adopted with temperate mulberry varieties. The procedure involves inserting a small branch of a plant into a rooted plant. The branch that is inserted is called as scion and to which the scion is inserted is known as stock. It is important to choose the right variety of mulberry as scion. The stocks can be raised by sowing the seeds uniformly in a nursery bed. The seeds should be covered with soil to avoid drying. The seeds are sown and allowed to grow with 3cm. distance in between. This can be done by thinning the seedlings. Besides this, water is sprinkled to help in germination. The seedlings are used for grafting. However, it can be indicated here that root grafting is expensive but unavoidable in mulberry propagation, where response for multiplication through stem cuttings is poor.

b. Bud Grafting

Bud grafting involves removal of only one bud and bark and grafting it on the other plant. Following types of bud grafting can be used.

i. Patch Budding

A portion of the bark with an active bud is removed from the stem as scion and correspondingly a portion of the bark along with bud is removed from another stem (stock) to which bud grafting is to be made. To this required portion of stock a bud of the scion is inserted and properly tied using polythene tape.

ii. T-Budding

A "T" shaped insertion is made on the barks of the stock at the nodal region and a slit is formed by opening the cut ends. A " T " shaped bud from the selected plant as scion is inserted in this (stock) slit and properly bandaged.

c. Shoot Grafting

It is followed to renovate the old plants.

i. Wedge Grafting

This is similar to root grafting except that in this case "V" cut is given on a shoot (stock). Prior to this, the plant is pruned at a required height and the scion is inserted latter.

ii. Crown Grafting

This is similar to above, except that more than one scion is inserted into the stock.

Layering

It is important to know that if the layering is done with the shoots, it is known as air layering. In this case roots are allowed to develop at the nodes of the stem while it is attached to the parent plant. The bark and some portion of wood is removed all around a shoot. Besides this, mosses are wrapped around the shoot at the point of cut. Subsequently a polythene sheet is wrapped around the shoot. The two cut ends of the polythene are closed with a tag. It is to be kept in mind that shoots on which layering has been done should not be disturbed for 4-6 weeks. The rooted shoots are then removed from the parent plant and planted in nursery beds. A comparison of this method with propagation through stem cutting shows that this method is expensive and cumbersome. However this method has been identified for those varieties which don't respond to rooting through stem cutting. A close look of the above methods shows that in practice, propagation through stem cuttings or sapling is popular method and extensively used in South India.

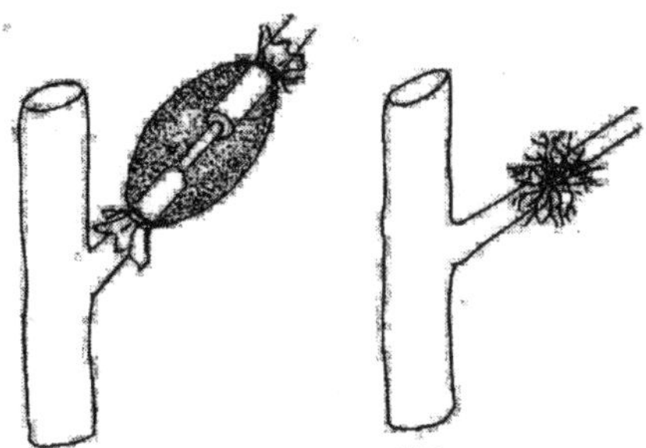

(1) (2)

The Major Advantage of Layering

1. It us simplicity.
2. No fear of the root getting dried as an in cutting or grafting.
3. Safer than the other method or vegetative propagation
4. To obtain a large sized plant in a short time

Disadvantages

Unsuitability for large-scale multiplication

Types of Layering

1. Simple Layering

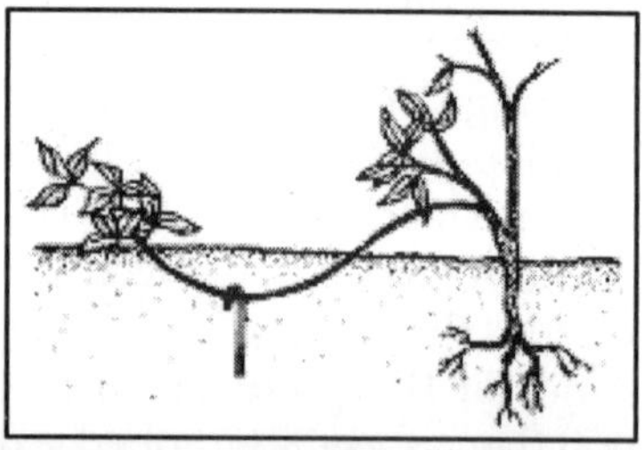

From a lower branch of bush mulberry the bark is removed from a 2.5 to 3 cm. portion in middle of branch the branch is hart in such a way that this portion comes in contact with the soil root developed in the covered region and the branch is cut from the parent plant to lead an independent existence

2. Trench Layering

A variant on simple layering, this technique involves burying the actual stem tips, and awaiting the growth of a new plant. In late summer, bend stem tips toward the ground, and bury them vertically some 3-4" into good, well-draining soil. New plantlets will develop, and are removed and replanted the next spring, including the distal tip of the original plant. Place the new plantlets in 6" holes and fill half way, gradually filling it completely over the growing season, or simply replant even with soil surface.

3. Air Layering

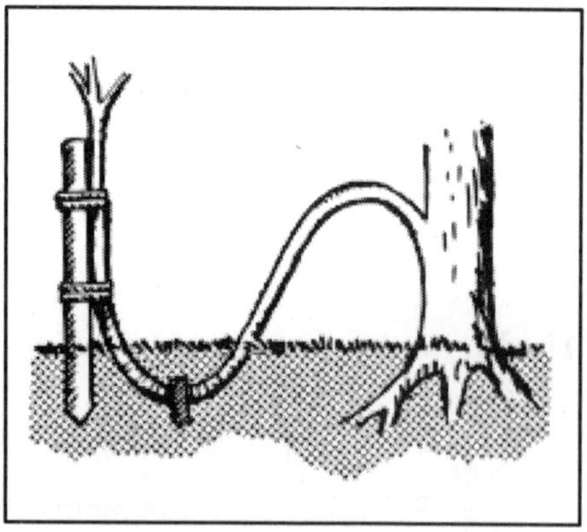

Air layering involves the same principles as simple layering: surrounding the stem with a rooting medium and encouraging root growth while the stem is still attached to the parent plant. The difference is that this technique is used on woody stems or stems that are not as flexible.

This technique involves first creating a wound on the stem. The wound should be a 1 or 2 inch cut about 1/3 through the stem for monocot plants. This slit should be wedged open with something small like a twig, small pebble, or a toothpick. If the plant is a dicot, remove a 1 inch wide strip of bark and cambium all the way around the stem. Cambium is the layer of stem just beneath the bark. Next, take some rooting medium such as unmilled sphagnum moss, moisten it, but do not soak it, and press it around the stem over the wound. Use plastic or foil to keep this rooting medium in place. Make sure that none of the rooting medium is not protruding out of the plastic or foil, as this would cause the medium to dry out. If you use plastic, you will need to tie a knot at each end, or use tape to keep the plastic in place. If plastic is used, and it will be in the sun, you will need to cover it so that the newly developed roots do not get burned.

Raising of Nursery, its Maintenance and Care

Land Preparation for Nursery

Immediately after the selection of the land for nursery, get it ploughed with tractor for two times minimum. Spread 10-20 MT/acre of decomposed farm manure to the entire land followed by ploughing with country plough. You have to level the land for easy irrigation. You have to make the raised beds and also irrigation channel all round the beds. Do not forget to irrigate the beds 15 days prior to planting of cuttings so that all weed seeds will germinate and you can get them removed by light hoeing just before plantation of the cuttings.

Seed Cuttings

How to Select the Material for Seed Cuttings

You should be very careful in selecting the source of seed cuttings. The source material from which the cutting material is obtained should be free from diseases and pests. The seed material should have an ample supply of stored food to nourish the developing roots and shoots until new plants become self-sustaining. Hence collect the seed cuttings from exclusive seed gardens of 6-8 months growth after pruning.

"Transport the seed cuttings during cooler hours to avoid driage."

Preparation of Cuttings

After collection of the shoots for seed cuttings, prepare cuttings of 10-15 cm. length with 3-4 healthy buds using a secateur or sharp bill hook. Nowadays cutting

Mulberry cutting

Manual

Mechanized

preparation machine is also available. Do not take over matured basal portion and immature green portion of the shoots at top. Cut the shoots on both the sides cleanly without splitting the stem or peeling of the bark.

Soak the cuttings in 0.1 per cent Diathane M-45 solution for 30 minutes before plantation to prevent any fungal disease.

Plantation

Plantation in the Nursery Bed

Plant the cuttings as early as possible to avoid driage. Preserve the cuttings under the shade covered with wet gunny bags or green leaves if you cannot plant immediately.

Plant the cuttings in the nursery bed in a straight position exposing only one bud above the surface of the soil. Leave 20 cms distance in between rows and 10 cms. in between cuttings.

After planting do not forget to press the soil around the cuttings to ensure firm fixing and give the irrigation immediately.

Please note–irrigate once in 4-6 days depending on the soil texture and weather conditions."

Nursery

Maintenance of Nursery

Weeding

Manual weeding first after 25-30 days and second after 55-60 days of planting. While weeding, sprouted cutting should not disturbing.

Sprouting

Small shoots starts coming out after 10-12 days of planting from the buds. From each cutting allow only one shoot to develop by removing smaller shoots using secateur.

Fertilizer Application

When saplings attain 20-25 cm. height in about 55 to 60 days after planting, apply chemical fertilizer. Do you want to boost the growth of sapling? Then apply urea at the rate of 20g/sq. m. after second weeding *i.e.*, 60 g/bed.

Disease Control

How do you control diseases and pests in the nursery beds?

Follow this schedule

After 30-40 days

Spray 0.1 per cent Bavistine to prevent foliar disease

Spray 0.1 per cent D.D.V.P. to prevent pest infestation

Transplantation

Uprooting and Transportation

After 4 months of planting, the saplings will attain about 90 cm – 100 cm height ready for transplantation. Uproot the saplings very carefully without damaging the bark of main roots. Two days before uprooting, irrigate the beds for easy uprooting.

"Plant the saplings as quickly as possible for high rate of survival and Transport the saplings during cooler hours."

Check for any root borne diseases like root knot and root rot before taking up the plantation. Burn the infected saplings and discard.

Economics

By following standard nursery technique 1.28 lakhs good saplings can be raised in one acre of nursery with the cost of production of Rs.0.48 per saplings. A net profit of approx. Rs.34, 250.00 by raising saplings in one acre in four months if sell the sapling for 75 paisa per sapling.

Use of Growth Regulators in Mulberry Propagation

The naturally occurring (endogenous) growth substances are commonly known as plant hormones, while the synthetic ones are called growth regulators. A plant hormonc (synonym: phytochrome) is an or-ganic compound synthesized in one part of a plant and translocated to another part, where at very low con-centrations it causes a physiological response. Plant hormones are identified as promoters (auxin, gib- berellin, and cytokinin), inhibitors (abscisic acid, xanthoxin, and violaxanthin), and ethylene and other hypothetical growth substances (florigen, death hormone, etc.). They usually exist in plants and crops at a concentration lower than 1 ^M; above this, they are generally considered supraoptimal.

Mulberry is propagated either through seeds or vegetatively. The latter is the more common method of propagation because of such advantages as maintenance of particular properties of the plant, relative speed in raising saplings in large numbers for plantation, adaptability to a particular habitat, and abilities to develop resistance to pests and diseases and to modify the growth of plants. Propagation through seeds has reached certain limitations. For example, triploid plants, which do not produce viable seeds, cannot be propagated. It is not possible to reproduce true to the type from a seed of biparental origin.

In India, the most common method of propagating mulberry is through cuttings in multivoltine re-gions (*e.g.*, Karnataka and West Bengal). Exotic varieties that are not established by cuttings are propa-gated through root grafts. Many of the indigenous varieties and well-acclimatized exotic varieties are propagated through cuttings. Bud grafting (budding) is used only when scion material is scarce. When-ever a large number of mulberry plants must be obtained in a shorter time than would be possible if they were started as a cutting, the method of layering is used. Layering allows the grower to fill in the gaps formed as a result of the failure to sprout of certain cuttings planted in pits of established plantations.

In univoltine areas (*e.g.*, Kashmir), the mulberry is propagated through seedlings and the exotic va-rieties through root grafts. In India, the field-scale propagation through cuttings of Japanese varieties of mulberry is still a problem.

Propagation through seeds is used mainly to bring about a varied population for the purpose of se-lection and hybridization. Because mulberry flowers are open for cross-pollination, the seeds thus col-lected serve mainly as sources of stock material for grafting.

In general, a deficiency of hormone must be created experimentally (as by removing young leaves or using a hormone-deficient mutant) to show that adding a hormone has an effect. In this respect, the Mitscherlich law of diminishing return can be modified as follows: the increase in plant response pro-duced by a unit increment of a deficient (limiting) hormone is proportional to the decrement of that hor-mone from the maximum.

Mulberry varieties that do not ordinarily produce roots from a cutting are induced to root with ap-plication of the requisite quantity of root hormones. The following chemicals are generally used, but their efficiency varies from species to species and from variety to variety: (1) IAA, (2) IBA, and (3) NAA.

The objective of using growth regulators is to increase the percentage of cuttings that form roots, has-ten root initiation, and increase the number of roots per cutting. IBA and NAA have proved to be better in producing roots than other growth regulators.

Effect of Different Concentrations of IAA and NAA on Bud Sprouting (BS), Initiation of Leaves (L), and Inflorescences (I) on Stem Cuttings of *M. alba* (Cultivated Variety 92)

Concen-tration (ppm)	*Total Buds on cuttings*		*Jan. 25*		*Feb. 01*		*Feb. 03*		*Feb.11*	
BS	L I	BS	LI	BS	L I	BS	L	I		
Control	5	1		2	1	3	13	3	4	6
IAA										
10	5	3		4	1	4	2	5	5	7
20	8	4		5	1	5	1	5	3	4
NAA										
10	7	2		5		5		5	3	2
20	9			3		3		3	4	3

Development of the root primordium depends on the relative amount of natural auxin present in the plant. Varieties that do not root apparently contain less auxin. The growth regulators act like auxins when applied in small quantities and move upward in mass translocation through the xylem when the bases of the cuttings are soaked in their solutions. The objective of treatment is to increase the percentage of cut-tings that form roots, hasten root initiation, and increase the number of roots per cutting. Indole butyric acid and naphthalene acetic acid appear to be better at producing roots than other agents. The chem-icals may be applied by various methods, including direct application of a powder, soaking the cuttings in dilute solutions, dipping the cuttings in concentrated solutions, and application as a paste in lanolin.

The action of many gibberellic acids (GAs) is similar to that of IAA, including elongation, promo-tion of cambial activity, induction of parthenocarpy, and stimulation of nucleic acid and protein synthe-sis. The GA3s vary greatly in their biological activity, and GA5 and GA7 are considered to have the widest range. In ferns, algae, and fungi, GA3s have also been shown to influence growth and development.

1.3. Establishment of Mulberry Garden, Strategies for Long Term Basis-Intensive Cultivation for High Leaf Productivity and Quality, Mulberry Farm, Bush, Middlings and Low Trees

Mulberry is a hardy plant capable of thriving under a variety of agro climatic conditions. At the same time, it is also sensitive responding extremely well to optimum agricultural inputs but showing practically no growth when plant nutrients and moisture begin to operate as limiting factors. This is evident from the fact that under the poor rainfall conditions of (625-750 mm) prevailing in South India, the current leaf yield is of the order of only 3,000-3,500 kgs per hectare whereas under assured irrigation and appropriate fertilizer application, it can be stepped up to 30,000 kgs or so, or nearly ten times. Further, mulberry under South Indian conditions, unlike in temperate regions like Japan, Korea and USSR, gives continuous growth almost throughout the year, because of optimum temperature conditions and good sunshine available. It is these aspects that should be properly appreciated and accordingly, every effort made to step up the leaf yield as indicated in this paper.

Soil and Climatic Conditions

Mulberry can grow practically on any type of land except on very steep lands. Good growths, however, are obtained when it is raised on either flat land or gently sloping or undulating lands. On more sloppy or steep lands, necessary attention to proper soil conservation methods as contour drains, contour planting or even bench terracing should be given.

Mulberry grows in a wide range of soils, but best growth is obtained in loamy to clayey loam soils. The mulberry plant can tolerate slightly acidic conditions in the soil. In the case of too acidic soils with pH below 5, necessary corrective measures through application of Dolomite or Lime should be adopted. In case of alkaline soils, application of Gypsum should be resorted to for correction of the soil alkalinity.

Since, mulberry is a deep rooted plant; the soil should be sufficiently deep upto about two feet in depth. In respect of elevation, mulberry thrives well up to about 4,000 feet, above growth will be retarded because of the cooler temperature.

Establishment of the Mulberry Gardens during the First Year

Mulberry falls under the category of perennial crops and once it is properly raised during the first year, it can come to full yielding capacity during the second year and lasts for over 15 years in the field without any significant deterioration in the yield of leaf. It is therefore, very important that the initial planting and establishment of the crop is carried out according to scientific methods for obtaining best yield results in the subsequent years.

Land Preparation

Land should be prepared by deeply ploughing with heavy mould board plough up to depth of (30-35 cm) in order to loosen the soil before planting, taking advantage of the pre-monsoon showers during April-May. Thereafter, the land may be ploughed once or twice with a light plough or country plough to bring the soil to a fine tilth. Afterwards, a basal dose of organic manure like compost or cattle manure should be applied at the rate of at least 10 tonnes per hectare for rain fed mulberry and 20 tonnes per hectare for irrigated mulberry. Finally, the manure should be properly incorporated into the soil by ploughing, and the land leveled and made ready for planting during the monsoon rains of June-July. It must be stressed here that application of basal dose of organic manure like compost or cattle manure is essential for successful initial establishment of the plantation. Under very exceptional circumstances, where these are not at all available, an alternative may be resorted to by growing nursery raised plants and transplanting them into the main field.

Generally, pit system of planting with wider spacing should be adopted for rainfed mulberry while row system with closer spacing can be adopted for irrigated mulberry. Therefore, for planting mulberry under rainfed conditions pits should be dug at a spacing of (0.9 m x 0.9 m). The pits should be of the size (35 cm x 35 cm) and at least (35 cm) deep. These pits are filled with soil, preferably mixed with some cattle manure, and in the pits the cuttings or rooted saplings are planted.

In the case of irrigated gardens, the prepared land is throwing into ridges and furrows (by using a ridge former or working with manual labour)

It may be noted that there is only one irrigation channel for every two rows of mulberry plants. This helps in both saying and more effective use of the irrigation water.

Planting Material and Planting

In tropical conditions as in South India, mulberry can root easily and, therefore, can be easily propagated through cuttings with minimum of time and expenditure. The cuttings should be prepared from 4-8 months old hard wood branches which are brown in colour and atleast (10-12 mm) in diameter. The cuttings should be atleast (18-20 cms) long with a minimum of three buds. The ends of the cuttings should be clean cut with a sharp knife, without splits or bark peeling off.

It is in the selection of planting material that mistakes are often made which result in poor establishment of the plants with lots of failures and resultant gaps. Cuttings either thin in diameter or green in colour should be avoided as the chances of their success are poor. Therefore, for successful rooting of the cuttings, every care should be taken to see that the cuttings of the desired maturity, thickness and length alone, as indicated above, are selected for planting. Because, only such cuttings provide necessary nutrients for the buds to sprout and grow till such time adequate root formation takes place.

It is also to be remembered that the soil should be very fertile containing adequate quantities of organic matter. It is, therefore, absolutely necessary that whenever straight planting of cuttings is resorted to, the soil should receive a basal dose of manure like compost or organic manure at the rate indicated already. The manure should be thoroughly mixed with the soil before planting is undertaken.

At the time of planting, it is important to see that the cuttings are placed deep and the soil around well compacted, leaving just one inch alone of the cutting exposed. This ensures the cuttings being planted sufficiently deep in the soil resulting in the formation of roots below the ground level. Further, this will prevent the cuttings from drying up. While planting, the cuttings should be planted either upright or with only a very slight tilt.

In places where compost or cattle manure is not available, it is highly risky to resort to direct planting of cuttings. Under such conditions, it will be found necessary to raise rooted plants, in nurseries and transplant 2 to 3 months old rooted plants with about growth and a stem thickness of about 10 mm in the main field. While transplanting nursery raised plants, it is important to see that the original cutting from which the plants have grown are buried deep in the soil at least one to two inch below ground level and the soil around pressed hard as in the case of planting cuttings. This ensures better anchoring of the plants.

In all the new planting with either cuttings or nursery raised plants, it should be so timed that there is 1-2 months of rainfall following the planting operation, particularly in the case of rainfed mulberry

Spacing

In the case of rainfed mulberry gardens, the aim should be to raise mulberry plant with a sturdier frame so that it is able to withstand prevailing drought conditions, better. Therefore, the spacing should be at least 3 x 3 (0.9 m x 0.9 m) as is being currently practiced. When cuttings are planted in the pits prepared for the purpose, they should be planted in threes at a spacing of 6 (15 cm) from each other, forming an equilateral triangle. When nursery raised rooted plants are transplanted, they may be planted as single plants.

In the case of irrigated qualitative mulberry, the overall advantage in raising mulberry for both quantitative and qualitative harvest is in favour of planting mulberry with a spacing of 2 (0.6 m)d between the rows and 9-10 (23-25 cm) within the row. This slightly wider spacing as compared to the existing Kolar system of row cultivation helps to produce better quality leaves from the point of view of silkworm rearing. In the case of irrigated gardens, where the practice of leaf picking instead of whole shoot harvest is followed, it would be found necessary to adopt a wider spacing namely 2 x 2 (0.6 m x 0.6 m). Upto 3 x 3 (0.9 m x 0.9 m) is also practiced sometimes, but in this case, the plants tend to become almost small trees and present problems of harvest.

Variety of Mulberry

An improved selection namely K2, also referred to as M5 is a superior variety evolved by the Institute, which is a vigorous strain responding well to manuring and capable of giving about 25 per cent more leaf yield. This variety thrives well both under dry as well as irrigated conditions. Quality wise also, it is superior to the local variety of mulberry and, therefore, could be used with great advantage.

Manuring

As pointed out earlier, application of a basal dose of organic manure like compost or cattle manure is necessary for successful establishment of the garden. Thereafter, the young growing plants should be assisted to put forth vigourous and maximum growth through periodical fertilizer application.

In the case of the rainfed garden, which is planted in June-July during the South-West monsoon season, the mulberry will receive sufficient rains from both the monsoons and this fact should be taken full advantage of, to achieve maximum growth and build up a huge sturdy frame so that the plant may stand the following drought months, from January to April, very well. This is achieved by applying two doses of nitrogenous fertilizers such as Ammonium sulphate or Urea at the rate of 25 kg of N/ha for the first application after 2 to 3 months of growth and again, another 40 kg of N/ha as the second dose after an interval of another three months. This should enable the plants to reach a growth of about 6 (2 m) in about 6 to 8 months time.

In the case of irrigated mulberry, where the plants will grow vigorously due to assured irrigation, the first dose of nitrogenous fertilizer should be given after 2 months of planting at the rate of about 40 kg N/ha. In another 2 to 2 months the plants would be ready for first harvest of leaves. Thereafter, the normal fertilizer application programme (described later) could be resorted to.

Weeding and Inter-Cultivation

During the initial stage of plant establishment in the field, weed growth should be kept to the minimum, so that the growing young plants are not smothered by the weeds. At least two weeding should be carried out during the first six months after planting of cuttings, once after two months of planting and again after an interval of 2 to 3 months. The weeding operation should be thorough and the soil should be dug deep to remove the weeds with roots. This deep digging is carried out as part of the weeding operation and results in necessary loosening of the soil and a stimulation to the plants to grow vigorously. Thus special care should be taken to reduce the weed growth as much as possible in the first year of planting. Thereafter, the shade effect of the fully grown mulberry will tend to keep the weeds down. Similarly, periodical inter-cultivation should be resorted to particularly in the case of dry mulberry gardens during the first year so that soil loosening results in better aeration and stimulation of plant growth. This also helps in catching the rain water and its deep penetration for better retention of soil moisture.

Maintenance of the Mulberry Gardens after the Initial Establishment

During the first year, all attention should be concentrated on establishing the mulberry field properly as indicated above. One should not be in a haste to take early leaf harvests before the plants attain full growth. In the case of mulberry under rainfed conditions, it will take ten to twelve months before first pruning is resorted to and systematic cultivation is taken up. On the other hand, in about six months time, the plants will reach full growth under the irrigated conditions and thereafter, systematic cultivation can be taken up. These are described below:

Rainfed Mulberry

As mentioned earlier, mulberry planted in June-July will be ready for first pruning in June of the following year. Prior to that, two small harvests may be taken, once sometime in November-December and again in April-May. The harvest should be light and made by picking only mature leaves, leaving major part of the growing branch covered with leaves.

Pruning

Rainfed mulberry should receive one annual bottom pruning in June coinciding with the receipt of the South-West monsoon rains. It is carried out by cutting the plants at height of 3 to 4 (8-10 cm) above the ground level with a sharp pruning knife or saw, in such a way that clean cuts are made without splitting the stem or branches. The system of guddali pruning currently practiced is too drastic and cuts into the root zone which leads to reduced branching and gradually to even ultimate mortality of plants. Therefore, such a practice should be given up and pruning carried out as indicated above.

Weeding and Inter-Cultivations

Normally within a week of pruning, weeding and inter-cultivation should be carried out by ploughing or using a harrow. The weeds around the plants which are not generally removed by ploughing or harrowing are removed by weeding manually. This operation stimulates growth of plants and also assists in providing necessary tilth and deep penetration of rain water in the soil, resulting in better conservation and utilization of the soil moisture. In all, upto four weeding and inter-cultivation operations should be carried out in June, October, January and April.

Manuring

The present low yields of leafy under rainfed mulberry are mainly due to poor rainfall and lack of or inadequate application of manures or fertilizers. Even under the limitations of scanty rainfall prevalent in South India, scope exists to improve leaf yields through optimum manuring of the fields. Therefore, manure should be applied in the form of both bulk organic manure like compost or cattle manure and chemical fertilizers.

Organic manure should be applied at the rate of ten tonnes per hectare, immediately after pruning and inter-cultivation, and thoroughly incorporated in the soil. This should be carried out systematically once in the year so that the organic content in the soil is improved and as a result, the fertilizer application is more effectively utilized. Alternatively, where organic manure is not available, a green manure crop like sun hemp can be raised annually during the rainy seasons and incorporated into the soil to serve the same purpose.

In addition to bulk organic manure, chemical fertilizers should also be applied at the rate of 100 kg N, 50 kg P and 50 kg K per hectare per annum, which may be applied in two equal split doses. The first dose should be applied sometime in late August, *i.e.*, 6-8 weeks after the application of the organic manure and the second dose sometime in late November during the North-East monsoon rains. The first dose may be in the form of complex manure like 15:5:15 or 17:17:17. About 300 kg or 6 bags of 17:17:17 will be required to meet the requirements of the first dose of 50 kg N, 50 kg P and 50 kg K. The second dose maybe given as 50 kg N only which is available in 250 kg or 5 bags of Ammonium sulphate or about 100 kg or 2 bags of Urea.

While applying the fertilizers, it should be spread close to the plant in either sides along the row. After application the fertilizer should be incorporated well into the soil by digging with spade of forking in with a digging fork for good results. This is very important operation as otherwise the fertilizer would be wasted and would not be effectively utilized by the plant.

Harvesting of Leaves

Leaf harvest commences after about ten weeks from the time of pruning in June and upto six harvests can be taken during the year at an interval of roughly 7-8 weeks in between harvests. The quantum of harvests will depend on the precipitation received in the different seasons, being more during rainy seasons (more than 2/3rd of the total harvest) from August to December during the first three harvests and comparatively poorer during the drought months from January to May, except the Mungaru season when pre-monsoon showers are received resulting in a slightly improved harvest.

Picking of leaves should be carried out in time, that is to say, when the leaves are at the correct stage of maturity for harvest. Otherwise, part of the leaves will become over mature coarse and suffer in quality from the point of view of nutritive value for the silkworms. Also part of the leaves may turn yellow, shed and be lost. Therefore, timely harvest, as the leaves reach the required stage of maturity, will lead to fuller harvest of the available leaves without wastage, and realization of maximum yield.

It is also important to stress here that while harvesting, the terminal buds of branches should not be picked but allowed to grow till the plant reaches its full frame of growth upto about 6 or so. Thereafter, the tips of the branches may be picked so as to encourage the formation of secondary branches. Unfortunately, the current practice is to strip the entire branch from top to bottom at every harvest which results in serious setback to the growing plant. This is also one of the main factors responsible for reduced harvests in the case of rainfed mulberry at present.

Mulberry Farm, Bush, Middlings and Low Trees

The methods of plantation and how the plant can be shaped to get higher leaf yield for many years. Briefly it can be said that the desired shape of the plant is an essential aspect in mulberry cultivation as mulberry is a woody plant and produces number of branches. Therefore, it needs training, to keep the plant in good shape. In fact the training to the plant is done to suit the management practices. Classification of the types of plantation is based on the height at which the plant is pruned or cut. Moreover, once the pruning is done a crown develops on the plant from where shoots (branches) develop. Formation of the crown is an essential aspect in the establishment of a garden. It has a significant role to play for the shape of the plant and leaf yield.

On the basis of the stump height from which the crown is developed the pruning is classified in to following types

Low cut (bush): Crown height is restricted to 20-25 cm.

Medium cut (dwarf): Crown height 60-70 cm.

High cut (tree) : Crown height 150- 175 cm.

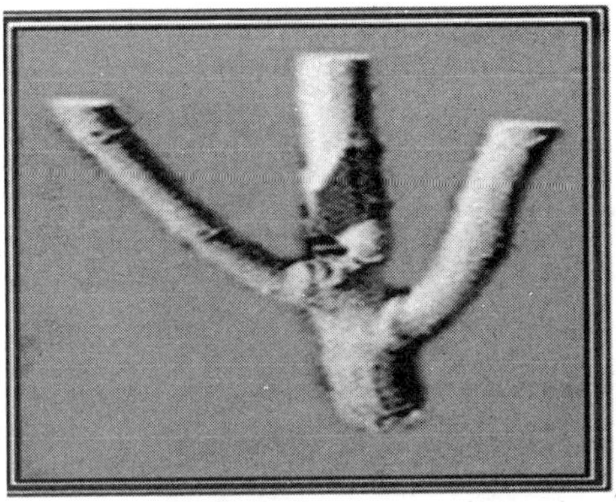

Formation of Crown

Bush type

Dwarf Type

Tree Type

In low cut (mostly referred as bush) one main stump is allowed to develop and 3-4 well developed shoots per plant are allowed to grow and the remaining shoots are removed for the development of proper crown. By this way three to four shoots are allowed to develop from each main shoot. It takes a year or so for the development of good stump after plantation. For the proper development of plants, leaf is not harvested for six months after plantation. Similarly we may note that medium and high cut mulberry is also trained similarly except that the crown height is maintained as mentioned above. In South India mostly bush type of plantation is being followed. Bush type of plantation yields significantly more leaf in an unit area than dwarf and tree type of plantation.

1.4. Cropping Pattern, Mono Crop and Mixed Crop, Selection and Preparation of Site Soil Testing and Soil Improvement Methods, Plot Size, Orientation and Layout, Selection of Varieties for Cultivation, Planting System, Row System and Pit System, Advantages and Disadvantage and Recommended System, Spacing for Mulberry and its Significance in Leaf Productivity and Quality Under Various Field Conditions

Cropping Pattern; Mono Crop and Mixed Crop

Cropping Pattern

The selection of crops and their varieties is to be made depending on the soil and rain fail situation in the rained areas. The photo insensitive crops and varieties with shorter duration should be chosen to escape drought of different intensities. There are wide variations, location to location in water availability periods in dry land areas. Thus depending upon water availability following are the different crops and cropping patterns to suit different climatic situations.

Mixed cropping is growing of two or more crops simultaneously on the same piece of land. It is also known as multiple cropping. This type of cropping leads to an improvement in the fertility of the soil and increases in crop yield. The products and refuse from one crop plant help in the growth of the other crop plant and vice-versa. Mixed cropping is an insurance against crop failure in abnormal weather conditions.

By planting one line of one crop, then a line of another crop, both crops can get better. In one line a legume and in another line the main crop. So, if the main crop takes the nitrogen from the soil, the legume fixes the soil. The nitrogen is fixed in the root nodules of the leguminous plants in the form of nitrates (soluble form of nitrogen) and keeps the soil fertile. This helps the farmers to produce more and more crops without the nitrogen being depleted from the soil.

Mixed cropping is not the same as crop rotation. In crop rotation you plant different crops in the same field in different years. Some plants add nitrogen to the soil, some take it out. If you would plant the same crop year after year, you wear out your soil.

Multiple-cropping patterns are described by the number of crops per year and the intensity of crop overlap. Double cropping or triple cropping signifies systems with two or three crops planted sequentially with no overlap in growth cycle. Intercropping indicates that two or more crops are planted at the same time, or at least planted so that significant parts of their growth cycles overlap. Relay cropping describes the planting of a second crop after the first crop has flowered; in this system there still may be some competition for water or nutrients. When a crop is harvested and allowed to regrow from the crowns or root systems, the term ratoon cropping is used. Sugarcane, alfalfa, and sudan grass are commonly produced in this way, while the potential exists for such tropical cereals as sorghum and rice. Mixed cropping, strip cropping, associated cropping, and alternative cropping represent variations of these systems.

Monocropping

Monocropping is an agricultural practice in which the same crop is planted year after year, without practicing crop rotation or resting the soil. While there are some distinct advantages to this technique, it is environmentally questionable and can potentially lead to serious economic problems for farmers, as well. Many environmental advocates would like to see a shift away from this type of farming, as would people who work in the developing world.

The obvious advantage to monocropping is that it allows a farmer to specialize in a particular crop, which means that he or she can invest in machinery designed specifically for that crop, along with high-yield seeds that will generate a large volume of the crop at harvest. With staple crops like wheat, corn, and soy, farmers can also be confident that the crop will produce a high income, although this scheme can backfire; if demand declines radically, a farmer's monocrop may become a liability.

From an environmental perspective, farming in this way is harmful for a number of reasons. For one thing, it severely depletes the soil, as the plant will strip the soil of the nutrients it needs. This forces farmers to use fertilizers, which can disturb the natural balance of the soil and contribute to a host of environmental problems, from pollution to desertification. The practice can also contribute to the proliferation of crop pests and diseases, which can be a serious liability when a farmer's land is planted exclusively with one crop.

Selection and preparation of site. Soil testing and soil improvement methods, plot size, orientation and layout, selection of varieties for cultivation, planting system, row system and pit system Advantages and Disadvantages and recommended system.

Soils and climate comprise important components for the growth of mulberry. In first instance let us outline that mulberry is a deep rooted perennial plant. Therefore, the soil on which the mulberry garden is established should be able to supply air, water and nutrients to the plants even from deeper layers. Preferably soils for mulberry should be deep and fertile to support the proper growth of the plants. Mulberry is a hardy plant and accordingly it can be grown in a wide range of soils.

The soils are classified as sand, silt and clay. On the basis of which the soils are formed as alluvial, red loam, black cotton, loam and clayey loam. Though mulberry can be grown in different types of soils, the clayey loam to loam soils are much preferred. Again, on the basis of pH (chemical reaction), soils can be classified into acidic or alkaline. For normal growth of mulberry, soil having a pH ranging from 6.2 to 6.8 (slightly acidic) is very ideal. However, if a soil is alkaline (more than 7.4 pH) and highly acidic (less than 6 pH) should be reclaimed by the application of recommended quantity of gypsum and lime respectively depending upon the range of pH as shown below.

In Karnataka, soils are mostly red loamy which are poor in organic matter. A comparative account of soils in other regions shows that in West Bengal and Kashmir mulberry is grown in alluvial soils. Mulberry is grown in black cotton soils also. These soils are low in organic matter but high in water holding capacity. The availability of moisture is governed by the water holding capacity of soils to a very great extent.

So far the soils have been discussed and it is important to learn about the land on which the plantation is established. For mulberry, the land should be either flat or slightly sloppy. If the land is having a steep slope it can be made into rows and terraces depending upon the degree of slopes for plantation.

Climate is classified broadly as follows;

Temperate: A temperate climate can have very changeable weather. One day it may be raining, the next it may be sunny. This changeable weather occurs in summer as well as in winter.

Sub-tropical: The places adjacent to the tropics, usually roughly defined as the ranges 23.5-40° N and 23.5-40° S latitude. These areas typically have very warm to hot summers, but non-tropical winters.

Tropical: Places close to the equator where the Sun is hot all the year round.

The temperature of a place also governs the physiological activities of living organisms. Thus, temperature has a specific role to play in the growth of the plant. Studies indicated that the temperature range from 20-30 °C suits the growth of mulberry plants. However, temperature below 13 °C and above 40° C affects the growth of the plant adversely.

An altitude of a place speaks about the height and climate of the particular place. Mulberry is known to grow between 200 m to 1200 m altitude above mean sea level (MSL). However, an altitude of 700 m above mean sea level is suitable for good growth of mulberry.

Since mulberry requires a good irrigation for its normal growth, it is highly important to know the pattern of rainfall of the place for its proper growth. The rainfall of a place may vary from 300 mm to 2000 mm. Thus optimum rainfall (1000 - 1500 mm) of even distribution is known to make a significant improvement in the growth of mulberry plants. However, excess rainfall may lead to water logging condition which may lead to wilting of the plants. Thus it is highly necessary that the plantation should be raised in a well drained soil.

Sun shine of a place plays a great role in any crop cultivation and mulberry is one such crop which responds positively to the sunlight and shade affects the growth of the plants adversely. For luxuriant growth of mulberry sunshine ranging from 9.0 to 13.0 hours per day is desirable. Such long hours of sunshine is available in South India due to which mulberry cultivation can be carried out very profitably throughout the year in South India.

Mulberry can be grown in all the above three climatic zones. A poor climatic condition may not allow the luxuriant growth of mulberry. We are aware among all the factors, a suitable climate ranks second for success of good cocoon crop production. Thus gathering information on the various factors required for profitable mulberry cultivation is of paramount importance for establishing a good mulberry garden.

The Quantity of Limestone/Gypsum Required for Reclamation of Soil

pH range	*Quantity(Tons/ha)*	
	Lime Stone (for Acid Soil)	*Gypsum (for alkaline soil)*
3.5	12.5	–
4.5	8.75	–
5.5	5	–
7.4–7.8	–	2
7.9–8.4	–	5
8.5–9.0	–	9
9.1 and above	–	14

Preparation of land

Preparation of land is a prerequisite for taking up mulberry plantation. In fact it can be said that preparation of land is the first step in establishing a mulberry garden. To prepare the land for mulberry plantation it should be thoroughly ploughed by a tractor or power tiller or with the help of bullock drawn plough or by manually. The process of preparation of land includes removal of stones or boulders if any from the

Land Preparation by Tractor

plantation area and leveling the land if the surface is uneven to facilitate uniform irrigation after the plantation for the uniform growth of the garden. Let us recall that mulberry is a deep rooted plant and hence deep ploughing at 30-40 cm. depth is essential. This will help loosen the soil and make soil powdery and eliminate weeds due to turning the soil. Removal of weeds in mulberry garden is very essential as it hampers the growth of the plant. They compete with mulberry plant especially during the early stages of the establishment and thereby suppress the growth of the plant. However, weeds can also be eliminated effectively manually and also by the application of suitable weedicide. Once the land is ploughed thoroughly and surface is made even for plantation, basal dose of well decomposed farmyard manure is applied at the rate of 20 MT per hectare/yr or 10 MT/yr/ha in irrigated and rainfed land respectively and mixed with the soil thoroughly. This will complete the preparation of land to take up plantation.

Mulberry has number of popular varieties which are suitable for different agro climatic conditions. These varieties are evolved from time to time by the mulberry plant breeders. Mulberry varieties have an immense role in boosting the leaf production and improving the production of silk of a country. A suitable mulberry variety can be listed as the one which has following characters in addition to leaf yield and quality.

Should be a good rooter, early sprouter, fast grower and high biomass producer.

Should respond well to the application of manure and fertilizers.

Should be able to adopt to wide climatic conditions.

Should be tolerant against diseases and pests.

Should be able to produce palatable leaf for the silkworm rearing.

Should be rich in its nutrient contents.

Availability of different mulberry varieties to grow in different climatic conditions are listed in below. The significance of the development of a high yielding mulberry variety can be demonstrated if we compare the very poor mulberry leaf yield during 1960's (Approximately 15MT/ha/year under irrigated and 3 MT/ha/year under rain fed conditions) with that of the present scenario of the high yielding varieties capable of producing leaf yield ranging from 30-70 MT/ha/yr under irrigated and 10-12 MT/ha/year under rain fed conditions. Earlier mulberry variety Kanva-2 was predominantly used for establishing a mulberry garden in South India which has the potential to yield 32-35 MT of leaf/ha/year under irrigated condition. This has been partially replaced by the development of high yielding varieties like S-36 and later by Victory-1 (V-1) which has spread in over 19,000 hectares in South India. Variety V-1 is also gaining popularity in other traditional and non-traditional sericultural states of India.

Planting System, Row System and Pit System Advantages and Disadvantages and Recommended System

Planting System

The major systems of planting followed for mulberry cultivation in India are described in below:

List of Mulberry Varieties Cultivated in South India and their Leaf Yield

Sl.No.	*Variety*	*Area of Cultivation and Salient Features*	*Leaf Yield mt/ha/yr*
1.	Kanva-2	Erect branching, high rooting (>80 per cent), leaf – entire, medium size, pale green and soft Irrigated	32-35
2.	S-36	Branches slightly spreading, medium rooting (48 per cent), leaf – entire, large, pale green, glossy, soft and thick, most suitable to young silkworm rearing	38-45
3.	RFS-175	Semi- irrrigated	32-35
4.	S-13	Erect branching, high rooting (>80 per cent), leaf – entire, medium size, dark green, thick and soft, tolerant to soil moisture stress Rain fed	10-12
5.	S-34	Errect branching, high rooting (>80 per cent), leaf – entire, medium size, dark green, thick and soft, tolerant to soil moisture stress and alkaline soils Rainfed	10-12
6.	MR-2	Erect branching, high rooting (>80 per cent), leaf – lobed and unlobed, medium dark green Irrigated	30-32
7.	V1	Errect branching, high rooting (>94 per cent), leaf – entire, large, dark green, thick and succulent, very high yielder. Irrigated	45-55
8.	AR-12	Alkaline soil	15-18
9.	DD (Viswa)	Irrigated high temp. black/red soil	35-40

In South India, mulberry is being cultivated both under irrigated and rain fed condition. Under irrigated condition supplementary irrigation is provided when there is inadequate rainfall. Whereas under rain fed condition it is entirely dependent on rainfall. Under irrigated condition mulberry is planted either in " Pit" system or with wider spacing or in " Row " system following very close spacing. Under rain fed condition only pit system of plantation is followed.

Pit/Trench system

In pit system under irrigated condition, pits of 25 x 25 x 25 cm size or trenches of 25-30 cm deep are prepared along the rows and saplings of the required variety are planted at a distance of 90 cm apart from each other. In this system of plantation it is possible to accommodate a total of **12,345** plants per hectare of land. Now-a-days, planting mulberry in paired rows following (150cm+90cm) x 60cm spacing is becoming more popular as it facilitates adoption of mechanization for intercultural operations by using tractcr/power tiller besides accommodation of more number of plants per unit area than 90cm x 90cm spacing. In this system of plantation it is possible to accommodate a total of 13,888 plants per hectare of land.

While under rain fed condition, mulberry is planted only in pits of 35 x 35 x 35 cm size each at a distance of 90 x 90 cm. Before planting, the pits are filled with FYM or well decomposed compost and sand in a ratio of 2:1. Under rain fed condition well developed saplings of recommended variety only should be used.

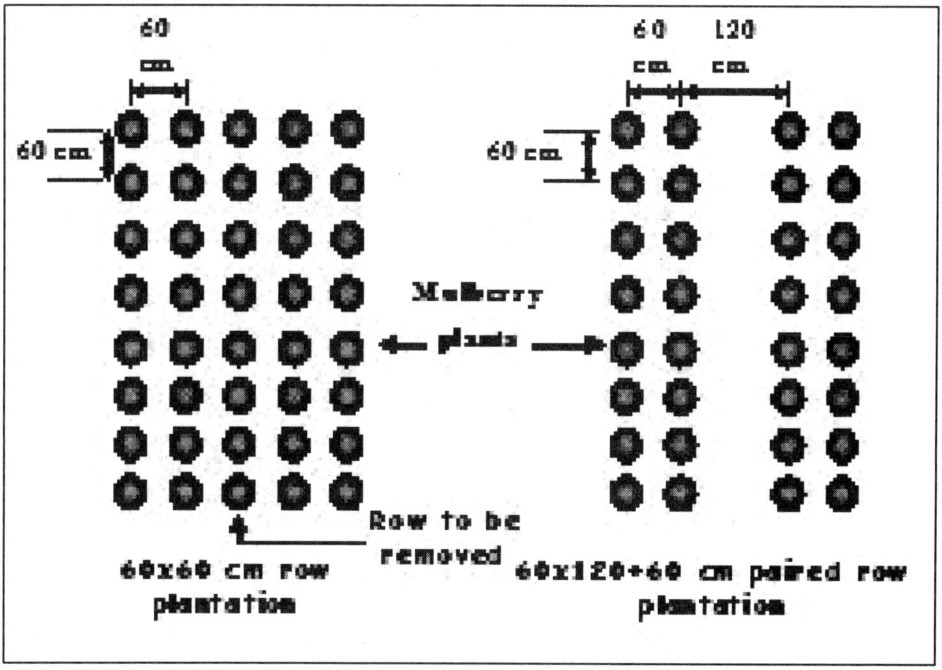
60
cm.
60 cm.
60 120
cm. cm.
60 cm.
Mulberry
plants
Row to be
removed
60x60 cm row
plantation
60x120+60 cm paired row
plantation

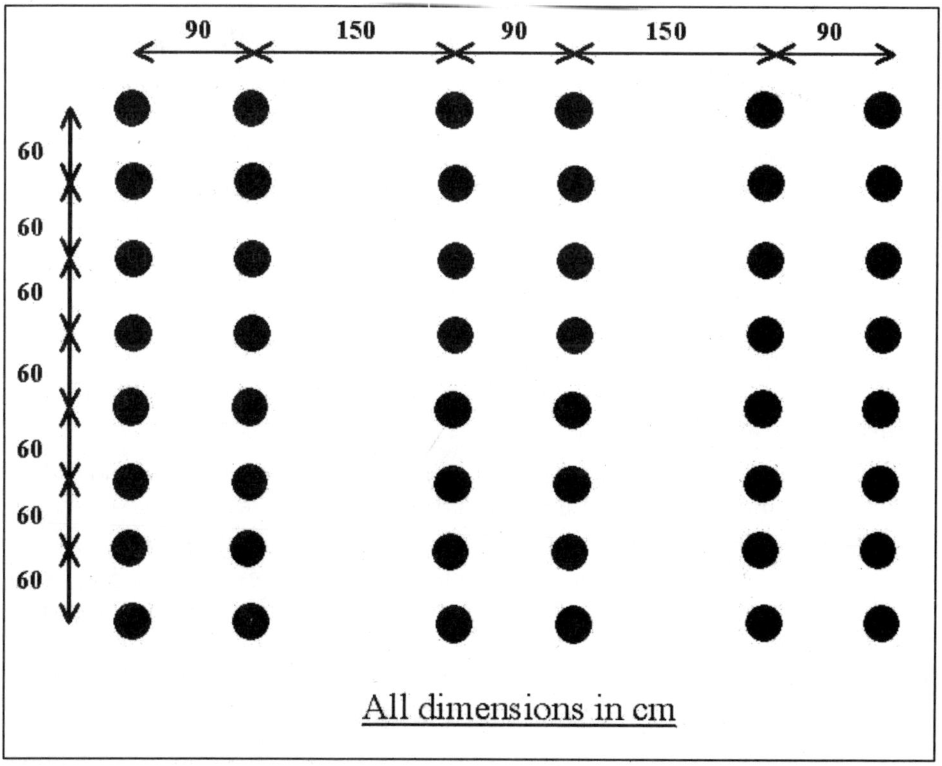
90
150
90
150
90
60
60
60
60
60
60
60
All dimensions in cm

While planting, precautions should be taken to plant the saplings upright position. This will allow the establishment of plantation vertically straight and in desired manner. Once the saplings are planted, the trenches/pits are filled with soil to cover the root system properly. Also we may note that soil is to be pressed firmly around the saplings for proper establishment of the plants. While preparing the trenches, it is logic to keep top and bottom soil separately at the time of digging out trenches. While planting top soil can be placed near the root zone. It is simple to interpret that top soil is mostly rich in nutrients and placing it near the root zone will boost the growth of the plant. This technique is simple to execute while planting. For proper survival of the plant irrigation should be given immediately. Subsequent irrigation can be given as and when required. Preferably the planting should be done during rainy season.

Row System

It is an age old practice of mulberry plantation in South India under irrigated condition. In this system of plantation, at first the ploughed land is thrown in to ridges (Rows) and furrows alternately at a distance of around 60 cm apart from each other and the cuttings are planted at a distance of around 20 cm at the edge of the ridges. All other procedures of planting for establishment should be followed as indicated in the pit/trench methods. This system accommodate about 83,000 plants per hectare of land and inter-cultivation is highly dependent on the man power although bullock plough can also be followed only in the space of 60 cm.

Advantages of Pit and Row System of Mulberry Plantation

- ☆ In pit or row system or Indo-Japanese system of plantation spacing followed in the garden (90+150cm x 60 cm as shown above is ideal for any improved mulberry varieties.
- ☆ This system of plantation can accommodate 13,888 plants/hectare in comparison to 12,345 plants in 90x90 cm spacing *i.e.,* wider spacing.
- ☆ By adopting this system, leaf quality is improved due to better sunlight and more space in between 2 paired rows.
- ☆ Parried row system of cultivation also helps in saving the cost of cultivation by adopting mechanization.

Disadvantages

- ☆ The only limitation with paired row plantation is that tractor and power tiller movement is possible only along the rows.
- ☆ Difficulties are faced in removal of weeds between the plants in a row. Hence, farmers use country plough for maintenance of garden. This make a farmers to use both tractor and bullock plough for maintenance of garden.

Spacing for Mulberry and its Significance in Leaf Productivity and Quality Under Various Field Conditions

Spacing varies in different sericultural countries of the world. The planting distance depends upon the agro-climatic conditions (sunshine, precipitation, temperature *etc.*) soil fertility level, intensity of cultivation practices adopted including the training and harvesting methods and also the variety of mulberry planted. The spacing between plants is closely related to the quaintly and quality of mulberry leaves.

When climatic conditions and agricultural inputs are not the limiting factors, maintenance of high plant density in an unit area results in creased leaf yield. To decide upon the optimum population density the variety of mulberry, training and harvesting methods to be adopted are to be determined first. Also the spacing along and between rows differs as to whether the plantation is raised as pure, mixed, companion or inter-crop. Regarding inter-plant spacing, considerations like number of branches, and branches habit of the variety. Methods of training and fertilizer practices and moisture status in the soil should be kept in view. In general, mulberry varieties which have profuse branching habit must be planted with wider spacing than those having less branches. The inter-plant spacing within the row can be made narrower in mulberry plantations adopting medium cut training. In mulberry plantations raised under rainfed dry-farming conditions, where moisture is a limiting factor wider spacing is adopted.

In the case of mulberry gardens exclusively meant for use in the rearing of young silkworms, it would be profitable to have a close planting. However, there is a limit, that is, if the plants are planted too close to one another, they will be deprived of adequate sunlight and aeration resulting in unhealthy quality of leaves.

Mulberry Cultivation Practices (Under Irrigated and Dry Land Conditions)

Unit-II

Dr. Ravinder Sharma

2.1. Irrigated Conditions: Water Requirement for Mulberry and Different Field, Situations and Seasons, Over Irrigation and its effects. Sewage water irrigation its effects. Dry land conditions: Land leveling, Budding, Moisture conservation practices and rain H_2O recycling; Mulching its purpose and methods

Irrigated Conditions; Water Requirement for Mulberry and Different Field Situations and Seasons, Over Irrigation and its Effects, Sewage Water Irrigation and its Effects

Being a perennial plant, mulberry requires high inputs of water and fertilizers. Productivity and quality of leaves, both in the tropics and in temperate regions, largely depends upon on the availability of soil water. Only in areas where there is uniform rainfall at the rate of 100-150 mm per month throughout the year, is leaf production of mulberry not limited by availability of soil water (Rangaswami *et al.*, 1987). Such an ideal condition does not exist in the major sericultural countries in the world, except perhaps in some area of Japan. Excesses or deficiencies of precipitation often occur in the major mulberry-producing countries of the world. Hence proper facilities for drainage to deal with excess water or for supplemental irrigation in cases of rainfall deficiency are essential for maintaining soil conditions for optimum leaf yield.

Water Requirement for Mulberry

To produce just one gram of dry matter of mulberry tissues, about 280-400 ml water is required (Rangaswami *et al.*, 1987). The amount of water supplied by way of irrigation should enable the plant to meet this requirement after taking into consideration the amount of rainfall received in the area. The root distribution pattern of the plant, climatic conditions and soil type are important factors that influence the quantity of water to be supplied at every irrigation. Further, the method of irrigate must make the water available to the root zone of the plant and avoid loss by surface evaporation. At least 1.5-2 acre inches of water should be given as irrigation at one time. The annual water requirement of irrigated mulberry is roughly about 40-45 acre inches or 125-150 cm (Krishnaswami, 1994).

Quality of Water

The quality of water supplied during irrigation is an important as its quantity. Normally, irrigation water for mulberry should contain less than1000ppm total soluble salts. It should not be contaminated with pesticides and effluents from factories. It should not come after irrigating a tobacco plantation, as nicotine is poisonous to silkworm.

Maintenance Under Rainfed Conditions

Recommended inputs (per ha per year) for gardens maintained under rainfed conditions at spacing of 90 cm x 90 cm:

- ☆ FYM or compost, 10 tonnes in a single dose at the onset of monsoon
- ☆ Azotobacter biofertilizer, 4 kg/crop, twice a year (during rainy season)
- ☆ VAM inoculums, 1 000 kg, once in mulberry lifespan (inoculation through maize rootlets)
- ☆ Suphala, 167 kg, first crop
- ☆ Single super phosphate, 156 kg, first crop
- ☆ Muriate of potash, 42 kg, first crop
- ☆ Urea (55 kg) or cam (100 kg), third crop
- ☆ Green manuring, 15 kg

Crops such as horse gram, cowpea, sun hemp and *dhaincha* should be incorporated into the soil by ploughing before flowering and cessation of the monsoon.

Leaf harvest: Individual leaf harvesting should be carried out. The expected yield (tonnes/ha/year) for different varieties is: Kanva-2, 10-12; S-13, 14-15; S-34, 14-15.

Maintenance Under Irrigation

Spacing. 90 x 90 cm or (90 + 150) cm x 60 cm

Recommended inputs:

- ☆ FYM (20 tonnes) in two equal doses with one tonne of vermicompost

- ☆ Azotobacter (20 kg) in five equal doses
- ☆ N-triacontanol (250 ml) in two equal doses (sprays): first between 10-15 days after pruning, second, ten days after the first spray
- ☆ VAM inoculums (1 000 kg) One dose in plantation of lifespan (inoculation through maize as the host the plant). Not required for plantations established with saplings inoculated with mycorrhiza
- ☆ Ammonium sulphate (750 kg), urea (325 kg) or calcium ammonium nitrate (600 kg) in five equal doses
- ☆ Single super phosphate (375 kg) in two equal split doses (crops 1 and 3)
- ☆ Muriate of potash (200 kg) in two equal split doses crops 1 and 3 days after first spray

Leaf harvest. Leaves are harvested either by individual leaf harvest or shoot harvesting. The latter is more economical and used for the shoot method of silkworm rearing. The expected yield (tonnes/ha/year) of varieties is Kanva-2, 32-35; S-36, 38-45; and Victoria-1, 60-70.

Over Irrigation and its Effects

Irrigation is the artificial application of water to the land or soil. It is used to assist in the growing of agricultural crops, maintenance of landscapes, and revegetation of disturbed soils in dry areas and during periods of inadequate rainfall. Additionally, irrigation also has a few other uses in crop production, which include protecting plants against frost,suppressing weed growing in grain fields and helping in preventing soil consolidation. In contrast, agriculture that relies only on direct rainfall is referred to as rain-fed or dry lànd farming. Irrigation systems are also used for dust suppression, disposal of sewage, and in mining. Irrigation is often studied together with drainage, which is the natural or artificial removal of surface and sub-surface water from a given area.

In mulberry cultivation it may causes damage, if irrigation is done out any decision and proper management. If excess water is applied, it will be lost from the root zone by downward percolation or evaporation. The water layer of soil *i.e.,* ground water layer gradually increase due to the over irrigation and soluble salts more than 1000PPM that cannot uptake by the plants may rise up with the ground water and stored in field. The soil salinity may increases sometime due to the evaporation, if irrigated water raised in the field. The soil salinity is very harmful both the plans *i.e.,* crop and soil. if over irrigation is done the crop fields become water logged and in this condition on the mulberry plants will under severe tension resulting poor respiration and for this the roots of the plants may rooted. Hence, over irrigation is very harmful for crop as well as in mulberry. Irrigation is very important for the growth of plants but excessive irrigation of field leads to water logging of soil. Too much irrigation is harmful for crop production as discussed under:

- ☆ Too much water is the soil inhibits the process of germination of seeds. It due to the reason that under these conditions the seeds do not get sufficient air to respire. Is due to the reason that under these conditions the seeds do not get sufficient air to respire.our might have observed that the seeds fail to germinate, if it rains soon after sowing. This is due to excessive water in the field, which affects the soil aeration.

- ☆ Roots do not grow properly in a waterlogged field. You must have seen that potted plants do not grow well if they are given excess water. This is due to the reason that excess water affects soil aeration and hence plants roots do not grow properly.
- ☆ Excessive water in the field increases the amount of salt on the surface of soil due to evaporation. The accumulation of salts damages the soil fertility, except rice; almost all crops receive as ever set back in their growth when excess water stagnates. Damage caused by excess water and consequent development of salt problem can be minimized by removing standing water from the fields through proper drainage system.
- ☆ The excessive irrigation may lead to lodging of the crop, may fall on the ground under the effect of strong winds. Due to excess water the roots of the plant may not be able to provide necessary anchorage in the wet soil.

Thus, excessive watering may damage the crop and reduce the quantity and quality of the produce. This also results in wasting of expensive water.

Sewage Water Irrigation and its Effects

Sewage is a water-carried waste, in solution or suspension that is intended to be removed from a community. Mulberry is a hardy and fast growing perennial crop grown on a wide range of soils and climatic conditions. It is cultivated on alluvial. Red loam and black cotton soil with a pH range of 5.5-8.5. The quality and quantity of mulberry leaves is directly proportional to the cocoon production which in turn depends on different factor like environmental conditions, mulberry varieties, soil fertility, fertilizers applied, irrigation. Sewage water is an important source of nutrients and can be sued for irrigation of different crops without affecting the plant growth and production (Angin *et al.*, 2005). However, the waste water is likely to contain high levels of bacteria, parasitic organism and other pathogens as well as heavy metals (Srikanth *et al.*, 1994). The use of untreated waste water and water supplies contaminated with sewage for irrigation has been implicated as one of important resources of pathogenic micro-organism contaminating crops. Sewage water has a high nutrient load, suspended solids, dissolved nitrates, pesticides, heavy metals and many other toxic materials/chemicals which may be hazardous and it may affect the soil micro-flora, soil texture, quality and also the plant growth and development. The agronomic and economic benefits and adverse effects of waste water or sewage water irrigation for different agricultural and horticultural crops categorically states increase in plant growth and productivity, probably due to high nutrient content in the sewage water used for irrigation (Lal *et al.*, 2003; Rija *et al.*, 2005). The increase in productivity will also have limitations and it may not be a permanent feature as the cumulative of heavy metals can affect adversely the growth and development of mulberry which in turn may affect the silkworm rearing.

Dry Land Conditions

- ✰ Soils under no-till production systems store more water than soils on conventional stubble mulch systems and allow conversion to more intense crop rotations.
- ✰ Conversion to no-till systems using a three- to four-year rotation such as wheat-corn-fallow, wheat-millet-fallow, or wheat-corn-millet-fallow, results in more profitability.
- ✰ Conversion to no-till, three- to four-year rotations results in greater risk and requires greater management input.

Water savings in no-till systems can be converted to profit only by switching to more intense cropping systems where fallow time is decreased and summer Crops, like corn, grain sorghum, proso millet and annual forages are added to the rotation.

Maximizing water storage, which permits more intensive rotations, requires residue maintenance on the soil surface to trap snow, absorb raindrop impact, slow runoff and minimize evaporation, as well as complete weed control at critical times in the production system.

Producers can use the following recommendations to improve precipitation use efficiency in eastern Colorado dry land farming systems, and improve soil, water and air quality while increasing net income. These steps are built around rotations where winter wheat is the starting point in the system.

How to Intensify Dryland

1. **Weed control:** Weed control in growing wheat is the goal of this step. If controlled in the wheat, the stubble at harvest is essentially weed free. Weeds include winter annuals such as mustard, kochia and Russian thistle. If weeds are present at harvest, apply the appropriate herbicide for that species. Apply residual herbicides in late July to mid-August to control volunteer wheat, downy brome and jointed goat grass. Various combinations of herbicides with small amounts of atrazine are effective for this purpose.
2. **Spring Crop Choices and Cultural Practices:** Possible summer Crops to follow wheat in the rotation are corn, sorghum, proso millet, sudex or sunflowers. Plant corn in areas north of Cheyenne Wells and grain sorghum in southern areas. Proso millet is a good option in the northern area, but not in the southern areas where yields and markets are poor. Annual forages, like sudex and hay millet, are excellent choices for livestock producers.

   Whatever the summer crop, plant it into the wheat stubble or other residue base with minimal disturbance. A minimum till or slot planter is recommended. Apply an appropriate herbicide according to the label and use for weed control during the summer period. Avoid cultivation of row Crops unless the herbicide fails. Choose crop varieties that adapt to your elevation, latitude and longitude.

3. **Rotation Choice:** Specific rotation choices include: wheat-corn-fallow; wheat-sorghum-fallow; wheat-proso millet-fallow; wheat-corn-proso millet-fallow; etc. More intensive rotations (wheat-corn-proso millet-forage) are possible where no fallow is used. Consider any combination of Crops that adapt to your environment and fit your equipment, budget, and overall livestock feed requirements. **Do not follow** a particular crop with itself. There are too many insect, disease and volunteer problems when you repeat a species in a rotation.

   Research suggests that corn follow wheat and proso millet, or annual forage follow corn or grain sorghum. If you intend to keep winter wheat in your rotation, some fallow prior to planting winter wheat probably will be necessary. Another way to get back to winter wheat is to plant a short-season annual forage in the spring and harvest the forage prior to August 1. If regrowth occurs, kill immediately with a contact (no residual) herbicide so that all precipitation received after August 1 is stored for wheat planting. Wheat should be planted no-till into the forage stubble. If it was a dry summer and no stored soil moisture is present, you may have to wait until spring and go back to another summer crop.

4. **Fertilization:** Nitrogen, phosphorus and zinc are the nutrients of concern when making fertilizer decisions. Zinc deficiency on wheat has never been observed in Colorado, but it is common for corn and sorghum. Wheat is the crop most likely to respond to phosphorus fertilization.

   Base the amount of fertilizer to apply, if any, on soil test results. Ideally, collect separate samples from various soils on your farm. Sample eroded hillsides separately from summits and separately from lower-lying areas. Soil colour is a good way to judge whether soils should be sampled separately.

   Apply fertilizer according to each soil test if possible. This will result in the least-cost fertilizer program.

5. **Over Considerations:** All of the suggestions for intensifying cropping under dry land conditions are contingent upon maximum water capture and minimum losses to weeds, runoff and evaporation. No-till practices are required in certain phases of each system to be reasonably sure of conserving enough water to be successful. No-till is essential, for example, when going from wheat to corn or from corn to proso millet. It is feasible and most profitable, however, to substitute some tillage for herbicides in a summer fallow phase preceding wheat planting. An exception is a short fallow period from harvest of a summer forage crop in August to a September planting. No-till is the only feasible means of weed control in that situation.

Land levelling

Land levelling or levelling is the process of flattening land. This process is often undertaken for some of the following reasons:

- ☆ Creating larger drainage areas

- Altering flow of surface water.
- Stabilizing the ground for other construction projects.
- Increasing arable land.

Methods

Land levelling can be undertaken by adding, removing or moving mass, or by using special constructions like terraces, tunnels, bridges, channels or aqueducts. The process for most simple forms of land levelling would be to first, take a topographic survey of the land to determine the high points and low points of the ground. Once these points are determined the ground should be ploughed, then the ground from the high points should be dragged and brought to the low points.

Advantages

There can be various advantages for land levelling including:

- Providing faster transportation.
- Enabling construction of taller buildings.
- Leading water to or away from an area (*i.e.* irrigation, sewage systems, or avoiding erosion)
- Creating better growing conditions.

Disadvantages

Some of the many disadvantages for land levelling are:

1. Many environmental issues could arise due to the levelling of land.
2. Many animals may lose their homes due to the construction.
3. The plants and trees in the area can be affected due to the large earth movement.
4. The flow of storm water over the land can change affecting any bodies of water in the area.

The land may have to be re-levelled frequently due to erosion.

Procedure

The procedure for land levelling is as follows:

- First a topographic map/survey should be taken and the elevations of the ground should be obtained.
- The land should then be marked with either marking paint, or stakes.
- A contractor should then come in with a tractor and the land levelling should be started by moving land.
- If it is too far to drag the dirt from the low places to the high places, it could be brought to the middle. Then it can be taken from the middle and spread out evenly so that the land will be flat.
- After this is done, the procedure of land levelling is completed.

Mulching

The inter row spaces are covered with cut-straw mats or mulberry twigs as a protective materials. This is called mulching. Its purposes include conservation of soil moisture, maintenance of soil in a loose and friable condition, protection of plants from winter injury and suppression of weed population. Paddy straw, leaf moulds, autumn leaves, stubbles etc. serves as mulches under natural conditions. These, by gradual decomposition, also used. Using black sheets is encouraged in temperate regions as they also help to improve soil temperature.

Benefits of Proper Mulching

- ✰ Helps maintain soil moisture. Evaporation is reduced, and the need for watering can be minimized.
- ✰ Helps control weeds. A 2- to 4-inch layer of mulch will reduce the germination and growth of weeds.
- ✰ Mulch serves as nature's insulating blanket. Mulch keeps soils warmer in the winter and cooler in the summer.
- ✰ Many types of mulch can improve soil aeration, structure (aggregation of soil particles), and drainage over time.
- ✰ Some mulches can improve soil fertility.
- ✰ A layer of mulch can inhibit certain plant diseases.
- ✰ Mulching around trees helps facilitate maintenance and can reduce the likelihood of damage from "weed whackers" or the dreaded "lawn mower blight."
- ✰ Mulch can give planting beds a uniform, well-cared-for look.

Trees growing in a natural forest environment have their roots anchored in a rich, well-aerated soil full of essential nutrients. The soil is blanketed by leaves and organic materials that replenish nutrients and provide an optimal environment for root growth and mineral uptake. Urban landscapes, however, are typically a much harsher environment with poor soils, little organic matter, and large fluctuations in temperature and moisture. Applying a 2- to 4-inch layer of organic mulch can mimic a more natural environment and improve plant health.

The root system of a tree is not a mirror image of the top. The roots of most trees can extend out a significant distance from the tree trunk. Although the guideline for many maintenance practices is the drip line–the outermost extension of the canopy–the roots can grow many times that distance. In addition, most of the fine, absorbing roots is located within inches of the soil surface. These roots, which are essential for taking up water and minerals, require oxygen to survive. A thin layer of mulch, applied as broadly as practical, can improve the soil structure, oxygen levels, temperature, and moisture availability where these roots grow.

Types of Mulch

Mulches are available commercially in many forms. The two major types of mulch are inorganic and organic. Inorganic mulches include various types of stone, lava rock, pulverized rubber, geotextile fabrics, and other materials. Inorganic mulches do not decompose and do not need to be replenished often. On the other hand, they do not improve soil structure, add organic materials, or provide nutrients. For these reasons, most horticulturists and arborists prefer organic mulches.

Organic mulches include wood chips, pine needles, hardwood and softwood bark, cocoa hulls, leaves, compost mixes, and a variety of other products usually derived from plants. Organic mulches decompose in the landscape at different rates depending on the material and climate. Those that decompose faster must be replenished more often. Because the decomposition process improves soil quality and fertility, many arborists and other landscape professionals consider that characteristic a positive one, despite the added maintenance.

As beneficial as mulch is, too much can be harmful. The generally recommended mulching depth is 2 to 4 inches. Unfortunately, many landscapes are falling victim to a plague of over mulching. A new term, "mulch volcanoes," has emerged to describe mulch that has been piled up around the base of trees. Most organic mulches must be replenished, but the rate of decomposition varies. Some mulches, such as cypress mulch, remain intact for many years. Top dressing with new mulch annually (often

"Mulch volcanoes" cause many problems for trees.

for the sake of refreshing the color) creates a build-up to depths that can be unhealthy. Deep mulch can be effective in suppressing weeds and reducing maintenance, but it often causes additional problems.

Problems Associated with Improper Mulching

- ☆ Deep mulch can lead to excess moisture in the root zone, which can stress the plant and cause root rot.
- ☆ Piling mulch against the trunk or stems of plants can stress stem tissues and may lead to insect and disease problems.
- ☆ Some mulches, especially those containing cut grass, can affect soil pH. Continued use of certain mulches over long periods can lead to micronutrient deficiencies or toxicities.
- ☆ Mulch piled high against the trunks of young trees may create habitats for rodents that chew the bark and can girdle the trees.
- ☆ Thick blankets of fine mulch can become matted and may prevent the penetration of water and air. In addition, a thick layer of fine mulch can become like potting soil and may support weed growth.
- ☆ Anaerobic "sour" mulch may give off pungent odours, and the alcohols and organic acids that build up may be toxic to young plants.

Proper Mulching

It is clear that the choice of mulch and the method of application can be important to the health of landscape plants. The following are some guidelines to use when applying mulch.

- ☆ Inspect plants and soil in the area to be mulched. Determine whether drainage is adequate. Determine whether there are plants that may be affected by the choice of mulch. Most commonly available mulches work well in most landscapes. Some plants may benefit from the use of slightly acidifying mulch such as pine bark.
- ☆ If mulch is already present, check the depth. Do not add mulch if there is a sufficient layer in place. Rake the old mulch to break up any matted layers and to refresh the appearance. Some landscape maintenance companies spray mulch with a water-soluble, vegetable-based dye to improve the appearance.
- ☆ If mulch is piled against the stems or tree trunks, pull it back several inches so that the base of the trunk and the root crown are exposed.
- ☆ Organic mulches usually are preferred to inorganic materials due to their soil-enhancing properties. If organic mulch is used, it should be well aerated and, preferably, composted. Avoid sour-smelling mulch.
- ☆ Composted wood chips can make good mulch, especially when they contain a blend of leaves, bark, and wood. Fresh wood chips also may be used around established trees and shrubs. Avoid using non-composted wood chips that have been piled deeply without exposure to oxygen.

For well-drained sites, apply a 2- to 4-inch layer of mulch. If there are drainage problems, a thinner layer should be used. Avoid placing mulch against the tree trunks. Place mulch out to the tree's drip line or beyond.

2.2. Manures and their Applications; Basic Approaches in Mulberry Cultivation High Soil Productivity and its Significance in Sericulture, Natural Farming and Vermiculture, Organic Manures Type (FYM and Compost) Methods of Compost Preparation and its Use in Mulberry Fields, Advantages and Constraints, Fertilizers, Types, Importance, Application Methods and Limitations

Manures and their Applications

Manure is both a natural by-product of livestock production and an excellent source of nutrients for crop production. The use of manure as a fertilizer is a beneficial way to recycle manure nutrients within an agricultural system. Most livestock operations are on, or surrounded by, large areas of productive agricultural land where manure can be applied in a sustainable manner. In many instances, manure can be a substitute for commercial, inorganic fertilizers. Manure not only acts as a source of plant nutrients but, through the addition of organic matter, it also helps to improve soil tilth, structure, aeration and water holding capacity.

Manure as a Fertilizer

Manure contains both macro- and micro-nutrients needed for crop production in organic and inorganic forms. Inorganic nutrients are readily available to the growing crop, while the organic nutrients become available gradually overtime. A crop responds to inorganic nutrients in soil, whether they originate from manure or commercial fertilizer. The manure nutrients of primary interest for crop production are nitrogen (N) and phosphorus (P).

There are many factors that affect the nutrient composition of manure including the type of housing system, whether or not bedding is used, the type of bedding, the age of the animals, the feeds and feed supplements that are being used and the type of manure storage and handling system.

Nitrogen in Manure

The nitrogen (N) content of manure is highly variable. A manure analysis is required to determine how much N is in the manure and in what forms. A proper manure analysis contains three N measurements:

- ☆ Total nitrogen
- ☆ Ammonia (or ammonium) nitrogen
- ☆ Organic nitrogen

As the term suggests, total nitrogen is an estimate of all the N contained in the manure. It includes ammonium N, organic N and any nitrate N that may be present.

Not all of this N will be available to the crop following application. Ammonium N (NH_4-N) is the predominant inorganic form of N in manure and it is immediately available to the crop following application. It may be expressed as either ammonium or ammonia on the manure analysis and it is the same form of N as is in ammonium based commercial fertilizers. Nitrate N (NO3-N) is another inorganic form of N. Although soil can contain significant quantities of nitrate N, it is typically present in manure in very low or insignificant amounts.

Organic nitrogen is determined indirectly by calculating the difference between total N and ammonium N. Organic N is slowly released to the crop and can have a significant impact on the N-supplying power of the soil if it is allowed to build up after several years of manure applications.

Organic N = Total N – Ammonium N

Phosphorus in Manure The phosphorus (P) content of the manure is also highly variable. Although manure is a mixture of organic and inorganic P, manure analyses routinely measure only total P.

Manure Application to Soil

When manure is applied to soil, the nutrients can undergo a number of transformations that may accelerate or delay their availability for crop uptake. The availability of the N in manure is highly variable and is influenced by the forms of N in the manure, application techniques and timing, along with weather conditions. The availability of the P in manure depends on the forms of the P and its placement relative to the plant root system.

Nitrogen Behaviour in Soil

Mineralization

The organic N in manure must go through a decomposition process known as mineralization the conversion of organic N to ammonium N. In Manitoba, it is estimated that about 25 per cent of the organic N in manure is mineralized and available to the next crop. The remainder becomes available during subsequent years at significantly decreased rates.

Nitrification

Although nitrate is present at low concentrations in manure, manured soils can contain significant amounts. This is because the ammonium from the manure is converted to nitrate by soil microorganisms through the nitrification process.

Volatilization

The ammonium N in manure can be lost to the atmosphere as ammonia gas through the chemical process of volatilization. The amount of N lost through volatilization during application of manure depends on the amount of ammonium in the manure, exposure of the manure to the atmosphere and weather conditions. The actual amount of ammonium available to the crop is calculated by subtracting the amount of ammonia estimated to be lost by volatilization during application from the amount of ammonium in the manure.

Available Ammonium N = Total

Ammonium N x (100 per cent - per cent Volatilization loss)

Management practices that minimize N losses due to volatilization include:

- Injection of manure
- Surface application of manure with immediate incorporation;
- Cool conditions;
- Humid conditions (note: manure should not be applied in wet or rainy conditions that increase the risk of surface runoff).

Immobilization

Immobilization is the conversion of inorganic N to organic N (*i.e.* the opposite of mineralization).

Denitrification

Nitrogen can be lost to the atmosphere as N_2 and N_2O through a microbial process called denitrification. N_2O is a potent greenhouse gas. Management practices that minimize N losses due to denitrification include:

- Avoiding nutrient applications to areas of the field that are wet such as poorly drained soils and depressional areas
- Late fall (when soil temperatures are below 4°C), spring or in-season applications of N containing fertilizers including manure, whenever possible.

Nitrate Leaching

Nitrate is highly soluble in water. As water moves down through the soil, such as after snowmelt or heavy rainfall, it can carry nitrate with it. Nitrate contamination of groundwater is a concern, particularly if the groundwater is a source of drinking water. The guideline maximum acceptable concentration of nitrate in drinking water, set by Health Canada, is 10 milligrams per litre (mg/L) nitrate N (or 45 mg/L nitrate).

Management practices and conditions that minimize the risk of nitrate leaching and nitrate

Contamination of groundwater includes:

- N applications that target crop N requirements
- Annual soil testing for residual N at a depth of 0-24 inches
- Residual soil nitrate N is the concentration of nitrate in the soil after harvest when the crop is not actively growing
- Adjustment of N application rates to maintain low concentrations of residual soil nitrate N

- Medium to fine textured soils
- Coarse textured soils such as sands are at the highest risk of nitrate leaching
- Crops with dense or deep rooting systems such as grass and alfalfa that are efficient at intercepting and withdrawing soil nitrate N
- Judicious irrigation to avoid excess moisture levels
- Deep groundwater that is protected by fine textured materials such as clay.

Phosphorus Behaviour in Soil

Although P is less dynamic in soil than N, its management in manure is challenging. Most Manitoba soils are naturally deficient in plant available P. Crops growing on low P soils require fertilization to reach optimal yields and will benefit from a buildup in soil P until agronomic requirements are met. However, repeated applications of manure can result in soil P levels well above agronomic requirements. In addition to being a valuable crop nutrient, P is a serious contaminant at elevated levels in surface water. For this reason, loss of P from agricultural lands is of particular concern to surface water quality.

Mineralization

As with N, mineralization of organic P to inorganic P takes place in the soil and contributes to the supply of plant available P.

Retention

Inorganic P tends to bind readily in both alkaline and acidic soils to organic matter, calcium (Ca), magnesium (Mg), iron (Fe) and aluminum (Al). Fine textured soils (*i.e.* clays) are able to bind considerably more P than coarse textured soils (*i.e.* sands).

Manure Analysis

Testing manure for each livestock operation and each application event is the best way to estimate the nutrient content of manure. A manure analysis should be based on a well-mixed, representative sample. Manure is very heterogeneous and obtaining a representative sample can be very difficult. Sometimes, more than one sample is required to estimate the nutrient concentration because the characteristics of the manure change (for example, during pump-out of a liquid manure storage structure).

It is ideal to know the nutrient content of the manure before application so that application rates can be set to meet crop nutrient requirements or removals. Receiving test results prior to manure application can be challenging, particularly for liquid manure. This is because the manure in storage is not typically agitated until just before and during pump-out for application.

One way to address this concern is to have a database of historical manure test results for a given operation to use until recent test results can confirm nutrient contents.

Manure samples should be analyzed by an accredited laboratory on at least an annual basis. More frequent manure analyses may be required if the manure is applied at multiple times during the year (such as spring and fall) or if management practices are likely to create a change in the nutrient content of the manure. Rapid field test kits for liquid manure exist for estimating the readily available portion of N, however, the result of a field test should be verified by comparing it to a laboratory analysis of the same manure sample.

Historical laboratory test results for a given operation can be used to assess the accuracy of recent laboratory and field test results. A basic manure analysis package should include total nitrogen, ammonium N, total P, total K and dry matter content. The cost of a basic manure analysis package will vary depending on the laboratory and the type of analyses conducted. Field test kits allow for immediate estimation of the ammonium N content of liquid manure.

Approaches in Mulberry Cultivation, High Soil Productivity and its Significance in Sericulture

MULBERRY (*MORUS*) is a woody tree. Mulberry leaf protein is the only source for silkworm to biosynthesise the silk, which is made up of two proteins namely fibroin and sericin. It has been cultivated widely in India for sericulture. Mulberry is cultivated in upland areas where water availability is less. Now a day's drought and saline prone soils are also targeted for its cultivation.

No two soils are similar in respect to their physical and chemical properties. This necessitates testing the soil periodically for its fertility status to take suitable corrective measures to maintain consistent high leaf yield and its quality. Mulberry leaf yield is primarily influenced by the system of cultivation, soil fertility and manurial practices. The nutrient demand in case of mulberry is high due to intensive cultivation, repeated harvesting of the leaves and periodic pruning of the branches causes loss of nutrients from the soil. Therefore, it is very essential to replenish the deficient nutrients after assessing the soil fertility status. Soil test should be undertaken at least once in two years. The following information will give an idea about soil fertility rating for important soil nutrients to take suitable corrective measures.

Fertility Rating of the Soil

Sl.No.	*Nutrient*	*Fertility Rating*		
		Low (Below)	*Medium*	*High (Above)*
1.	Organic carbon (per cent)	0.5	0.5-0.75	0.75
2.	Total Nitrogen (kg/ha)	250.0	250-500	500.00
3.	Available phosphorous (kg/ha)	20.0	20-50	50.00
4.	Available potassium (kg/ha)	125.0	125-300	300.0

Natural Farming and Vermiculture

The present level of use of chemical fertilizers and pesticides is harmful to ecological balance and sustainable use of natural resources. So, on realizing the utility of earthworms in agriculture, a beginning has been made in our country in vermiculture which aims at natural farming. Vermiculture is the culturing of earthworms. They are beneficial to agriculture as they continuously plough the soil, makes the soil porous and adds nutrient rich vermin castings to soil. Hence, they are rightly called as "friends of the farmers". This booklet deals with entire vermiculture biotechnology.

The growth in agricultural production has to be consistent. This becomes possible when soil is maintained in good health. The prime factor that influences the soil health is its organic matter content. The organic fraction of cultivated soil is under constant threat of depletion due to inadequate replenishment. Organic matter is the soul of the soil which on decom-position releases nutrients. The nutrients can also be added by fertilizer application. But due to their residual effects continuous application of fertilizers alone is not recommended. The alternative method is to go for organic farming. As organic manures contain low nutrient contents and slow in releasing the same, an integrated nutrient system is recommended. At the same time, other factors of ecological farming such as green manuring, bioinoculants or bio-fertilizers, vermiculture are also recommended.

For all the inhabitants of soil like micro-organisms, fungi, bacteria, algae, earthworms, lichens, nitrogen fixers etc. organic feed or organic component is essential for their growth and multiplication. Among the living organisms in soil, earthworm is such an organisms which not only improves the soil condition but also reduces the fertilizer requirement. Vermiculture is a science dealing with earthworms. This booklet mainly focuses and describes the functions of earthworms, vermin-composting and advantages of vermiculture from small and marginal points of view.

Earthworms and Soil Improvement

Earthworms have a special importance in soil improvement processes. They participate and involve in the soil-forming processes by influencing the pH, physical decomposition, humus formation, thus in the improvement of soil structure. Their activity is mostly in the upper layers of the soil, *i.e.* 15-35 cms of surface soil. The activities of earthworms which help in soil improvement are their locomotion and digestion processes.

While in locomotion, earthworm makes burrows by pushing the soil particles. If no suitable space is available to push the head into, it swallows the soil and makes the space. The soil that is taken in by the worm passes through the digestive system and is excreted as vermi castings. These castings contain excreta. Earthworm cocoons and undigested soil. As they involve in the digestion process, they come out with enriched nutrient content that improve the soil fertility and the soil productivity. Thus, the earthworms not only helps in improving the soil fertility but also mixes the soil thoroughly while in movement which adds pore space also. The vermicastings contains 2.5 per cent N, 2.9 per cent P and 1.4 per cent Potash. There are several evidences of extensive earthworm activities.

When it excretes, the intestinal contents of these worms also comes out which are neutral to slightly alkaline in pH or soil reaction. At this pH, bacterial activity is enhanced. If the bacterial activity is more, the more complex organic compounds can be converted to humus. Thus, the presence of earthworms creates neutral to slightly alkaline pH in the soil and this favors the bacteria, than soil fungi which survives in an acidic pH.

The physical decomposition of soils will be resulted in the gut of earthworms result in the pulverization of soil. This pulverization of the soil particles in the gut of the digestive system creates more surface area on the soil particles. Increased surface area is beneficial to micro-organisms for further decomposition and soil forming process.

Another characteristic feature is the presence of enzyme 'cellulose' in the intestine of earthworms. The very process of humus formation involves breakdown of celluloses into simple sugars like glucose, galactose, mannose etc. and various organic acids, amino acids etc. So, the enzyme cellulose can play a very active role in humus formation and hence the earth- worms have a significant role in the humus formation.

The physical pulverization of organic particles, the amelioration of soil pH and enhancement of microbial decomposition activity are the resultant of earthworm activity in the soil. All these processes are carried out by earthworms contributing to soil fertility. The process of burrowing helps in the ingestion of organic and mineral particles and formation of organic- mineral complexes. Thus, they create electrostatic bonds between negatively charged organic particles and positively charged cations such as calcium. Organo-mineral crumbs thus formed are stable and are resistant to leaching. This improves the soil structure.

Structural improvement is further enhanced by the creation of burrow systems. While burrowing they mixes the soil and the casts on the surface will be taken to the deeper parts of the profile and vice-versa. Deep burrowing species of earth-worms makes this process easy. Even the organic crumbs will be drawn into their burrows of mineral soil from the soil surface. This process also prevents the surface accumulation of acid humus. It will promotes the dispersion of finely decomposed humus down the profile enriching the deeper layers of soil. Thus, thorough mixing of soil is done by these species. The amount of soil brought by an earthworm biomass of one tonne per hectare to the surface by casting is about 100 tonnes per ha per year. The soil that passes through the earthworm gut is six to ten times richer in nitrogen, phosphorus and other micro-nutrients.

A comparison of various characteristics of the soils rich in vermicastings and the normal soil are given in table

Comparative Characteristics of Earthworm Casts and Normal Soils

Sl.No.	*Characteristics*	*Earthworm Cast*	*Normal Soil*
1.	Soil and clay (per cent)	38.80	22.20
2.	Bulk density (Mg/m^3)	1.11	1.28
3.	Structural stability (a)	849.00	65.00
4.	Cation Exchange capacity (cmols/kg)	13.80	3.50

Contd...

Table–*Contd...*

Sl.No.	*Characteristics*	*Earthworm Cast*	*Normal Soil*
5.	Exchangeable calcium (cmols/kg)	8.90	2.00
6.	Exchangeable Potassium (cmols/kg)	0.60	0.20
7.	Soluble phosphorus (ppm)	17.80	6.10
8.	Total nitrogen (per cent)	0.33	0.12

Mg/m³: Mega grams per meter cube; **a**: Number of raindrops required to destroy structural aggregates; **cmoles/kg**: Centimoles per kilogram; **ppm**: parts per million.

In acid forests, an average of one to few earthworms is found per square metre while in rich grassland soils; more than 500 per square meter are recorded. In arable soils, they range from 30-300 per sq. mt. which is equal to a live-weight or biomass of 1.0-1100 kg per hectare.

Soil Enrichment

Soil enrichment is achieved by speeding up of several soil formation processes.

The mechanisms or processes that lead to soil enrichment are mostly lead by earthworms which are as follows:

1. The physical mixing of the soil and mineralisation of organic matter will be spread by earthworms. The decomposition of organic matter will speed up at least 2-5 times by these animals.
2. When organic wastes pulverizes in the gut of these worms the surface area is increased.
3. Ingestion removes inactive (senescent) bacterial colonies and stimulates new bacterial growth.
4. The excreta of the worms contains nitrogenous matter which enriches the soil.
5. The locomotion or burrowing activity of earthworms enhances the oxygen penetration.
6. Enhanced microbial mineralisation releases plant mineral nutrients.
7. By the earthworm -micro floral interaction, it was found out that several important compounds like vitamin B12 and plant growth hormones (gibberllins) could be produced.

Organic Manures Type (FYM and Compost) Methods of Compost Preparation and its Use in Mulberry Fields, Advantages and Constraints, Fertilizers, Types, Importance, Application Methods and Limitations

Organic Manure

Organic manure plays an important role in building up of soil fertility, increasing moisture holding capacity, growth of microorganism and intern enriches micro

Vermicompost

nutrient levels and physical condition of the soil. Hence application of adequate quantity of organic manure to maintain the fertility status of the soil is very essential. The common organic manure used for mulberry is farmyard manure, however use of compost or vermicompost are very useful in enhancing the nutrient availability to the plants. Normally one third of the requirement of nutrients is provided in the form of organic sources. Mulberry garden maintained under irrigated condition is provided with 20 tonnes of farmyard manure per hectare annually in 2-3 splits. Whereas mulberry gardens maintained under rainfed condition is provided with 10 tonnes of farm yard manure per hectare during the onset of monsoon after annual bottom pruning. As the availability of good quality farm yard manure is very difficult, it is highly beneficial to use compost or vermicompost prepared out of sericultural farm residues.

Farmyard Manure (FYM)

Good quality farm yard manure is the most valuable organic matter applied to soil to enhance fertility and to increase micronutrients, which are essential for growth of plant. Generally, in sericulture farms, the leaf over mulberry leaves form rearing bed and field and other waste including silkworm litter are not properly utilized in preparing compost of high nutrient value. The traditional method of preparation of compost is generally not effective. The loose heaps lie exposed to the sun, with the result the raw organic matter dries up quickly an does not decompose properly.

Hence, it is essential to convert the sericultural farm wastes into valuable compost, adopting suitable technology.

FYM is a decomposed mixture of cattle dung and urine with straw and litter use as bedding material and residues from the fodder fed to cattle.

Method of FYM Preparation

Make a pit of size of 4.5 m (l) x 1.5 m (b) x 1 m (h).

- ☆ Fill all wastes such as excretory material, unused leaf, weeds and green leaves in the pit layer by layer.
- ☆ Pour the slurry over these in thin layers.
- ☆ Add 20 g. phosphorous, 100-150 g. lime and potash to enrich the compost.
- ☆ After filling fully, cover with mud and slurry.
- ☆ Then cover with palm leaves and grass.

In 3-4 months you will get 4 tons of compost.

Compost

A moss of rotted organic matter made from waste is called as compost. About 800 thousand tons of rearing bed refuse including silkworm litter is produced annually in India. Large quantities of waste material are available as vegetables refuse, sugarcane trash, farm litter such as weeds, stubble bhusa, sewage slugs and animal waste in houses and areas like human and industrial refuse, town refuse, sericulture wastes and silkworm litter can be converted into useful compost manure by conserving and subjecting them to a controlled process of anaerobic decomposition.

Preparation of Compost

- ☆ First fill the waste materials in a pit and allow for decomposing for 10-15 days.
- ☆ Mix slurry to it.
- ☆ Shift this half decomposed materials to another tank or pit and leave earthworms in the tanks or pits.

- ☆ Protect earthworms from ants and predators.
- ☆ Maintain the moisture in the pit by spraying water.
- ☆ After 40-50 days vermicompost is ready.
- ☆ Remove the manure from pit and separate the earthworms from manure.

Advantages

- ☆ It is an eco-friendly technology and involves earthworm's s composting agents and the composting of the wastes can be performed quickly.
- ☆ Composting is completed by 50-60 days after introducing earthworms in waste while anaerobic composting in pits takes 120-150 days.
- ☆ The material is fully digested and the final product is free from bad smell and pathogens. It contains useful microorganism and is rich in plant nutrient including micronutrients.

Fertilizers

Fertilizers are industrially manufactured chemicals containing plant nutrients. Nutrients content is higher in fertilizer than in organic manure and nutrients are reduced almost immediately.

Classification of Fertilizer

Fertilizers are classified into straight, complex and mixed fertilizer.

Straight fertilizer

Straight fertilizer are those which supply only one primary plant nutrient namely nitrogen or phosphorus or potassium. For example- urea ammonium sulphate and potassium chloride are some of the straight fertilizers.

Complex Fertilizer

Complex fertilizers contain 2 or 3 primary plant nutrients of which two primary nutrients are in chemical combination. These fertilizers are usually produced in granular farm. Diammonium phosphate, nitro-phosphate are complex fertilizer.

Mixed Fertilizer

Mixed fertilizers are physical mixtures of straight fertilizer. Mixed fertilizers are made by thoroughly mixing the ingredients either mechanically or manually. Fertilizers are grouped based on the nutrient present in the fertilizers namely - nitrogenous, phosphate potassium fertilizer, and boron fertilizer.

Nitrogenous fertilizer

According to the form of nitrogen they contain

Nitrate Fertilizer- Fertilizer containing nitrogen as nitrates $N0_3$. They are Alkaline in their residual effect in soil.

1. Sodium nitrate – 16.1 per cent N
2. Calcium nitrate – 15.5 per cent N

Ammonium fertilizer - fertilizer containing Ammonium NH_4+ they are acidic in their residual effect in soil.

1. Ammonium sulphate – 20.6 per cent N
2. Ammonium chloride – 25 per cent N
3. Ammonium phosphate – 20 per cent N
4. Anhydrous Ammonia – 82 per cent N
5. Ammonia Solution- NH_3 in water – 20.25 per cent N

Nitrate and Ammonium fertilizer- fertilizer containing nitrogen both as NO_3 and NH_4. They are acidic In Its residual effect in soil.

1. Ammonium nitrate – 33 to 34 per cent N
2. Calcium ammonium nitrate (CAN) – 26 per cent N
3. Ammonium sulphate nitrate (AHN) – 20 per cent N

Amide fertilizer- Fertilizers containing nitrogen as amine, NH_2 or Amide CN_2

1. Urea – 46 per cent N
2. Calcium Cyanamid – 21 per cent N

Slow Release Nitrogenous Fertilizer

1. Urea formaldehyde – 38 per cent N
2. Sulphur coated urea – 36 per cent–40 per cent N
3. Oxamide – 31.8 per cent N
4. N-limn (Ammoniated lignin) – 18 per cent
5. Gauzy Urea – 37 per cent N

Phosphatic fertilizer-According to the Solubility the phosphoric fertilizer are divided In following group.

The water Soluble Phasphatic fertilizer- In Alkaline and calcareous soil water-soluble phosphorus is covered into insoluble calcium phosphate

1. Single Super Phosphate (SSP) – 16–18 per cent P_2O_5
2. Double Super phosphate – 32 per cent P_2O_5
3. Triple Super phosphate – 46–48 per cent P_2O_5
4. Ammonimn phosphate – 20.1 per cent P_2O_5

Citric acid and soluble phosphatic fertilizer- they are suitable in acidic soil

1. Di-calcium phosphate – 14.1 per cent P_2O_5 extract soluble
2. Basic slag – 17- 20 per cent P_2O_5 extract soluble
3. calcium meta phosphate – 60-64 per cent P_2O_5 extract soluble

Water and citric acid insoluble phosphatic fertilizer - They are suitable in strongly acid soil or organic soil.

1. Rock phosphate – 20–30 per cent P_2O_5
2. Bone meal – 21–25 per cent P_2O_5

Other phosphatic Fertilizer

1. Kotak Phosphate – 26 per cent P_20S
2. Rhenmia Phosphate – 26–28 per cent P_20S
3. Themo phosphate – 18.3 per cent P20S

Potassic Fertilizer

1. Potaasimn chloride or muriat of potash – 48–62 per cent K_20
2. Potassiurn sulphate or sulphate of potash – 48–52 per cent K_20
3. Potassium magnesium sulphate – 22 per cent K_20
4. Potassium schoenite – 22–24 per cent K_20

Complex Fertilizers

Ammonium Phosphate	***NPK***
1. Mono ammonimn phosphate	1-48-0
2. Ammonium phosphate Sulphate	16 20 - 0 or 20-20-0
3. Urea Ammonium phosphate	24 - 24 - 0 or 28-28-0
4. Diammonium phosphate	18 - 46 - 0

Nitrophosphate

1. Nitrophosphate	16-14 -0
2. Sulphonitric nitrophosphate	12.9 -12.9 - 0

N, P, K Complex Fertilizer

N: P: K -18: 18: 9,15: 15: 15, 19: 19: 19, 17: 17:17

Mixed Fertilizer

1. From made fertilizer mixtures - some fertilizer mixtures prepared by the cultivators (former) on form.
2. Factory made fertilizer mixtures-
   i. All straight fertilizer are mixed.
   ii. Rock phosphate is mixed with sulphuric acid. But basic slag should not be mixed with ammonium sulphate, calcium ammonium nitrate and sulphar phosphate; calcium carbonate should not be mixed with Ammonium sulphate, super phosphate.

Materials Supplying secondary nutrients and micronutrient - The secondary nutrients are supplied to the soil through some commercials fertilizers.

Calcium and Magnesium

By liming material, gypsum, basic slag pyrite.

Sulphar

By ammonium sulphates, gypsum, pyrite

Micronutrients

1. Copper sulphate – 25–35 per cent Cu
2. Zinc sulphate – 22–35 per cent Zn
3. Borax – 10.6 per cent B
4. Manganese sulphate – 23 per cent Mn
5. Ammonium molybdat – 54 per cent ¥o
6. Ferrous Sulphate – 20 per cent Fe

Principals of Fertilizer Application

It is an attempt to increase the yield per unit area and time, and to reduce the cost of production. Fertilizer application is practiced based on following principles so as ensure maximum utilization of the nutrient.

1. Application at right time
2. Application at right place
3. Application by right methods
4. Application in the right form
5. Application in the right quantity
6. Minimizing the fertilizer loss

Time of Application

Fertilizer applied to the soil undergoes a number of reactions in the soil before, during and after their absorption by the plant.

Rate of nutrient uptake by mulberry is peak during 30-40 days from sprouting of buds. It declines gradually for the next 20-30 days of leaf maturation and finally riches the low peak levels till the next stage of sprouting.

Rain fed-(Tropical)-First and second dose are applied during mid or late August and October-Nov. well before assassin of monsoons respectively. Irrigated (Tropical) Each of the 5 to 6 doses is applied after four weeks after the previous harvest by pruning or after three week after leaf picking.

Rain fed (Sub- tropical)-Fertilizer is applied in 3-4 split doses each dosed is given after about 3-4 week after previous harvest.

Others-30-40 days prior to the expected date of bulk leaf harvest. Fertilizes are not applied during the period of heavy rainfall.

Site of Application

The place of fertilizer application influences its availability at the active absorption zone of the root system. In row system with closer spacing, it is supplied at about 6-8 inches away from the plants while in the tree, plantation it can be applied at about 20-24 inches around the plant. Since phosphates and potassium are immobile they may be placed deep in soil so as to facilitate its contact with active root zone.

Method of Application

Efficiency of utilization also convenience and economics determine among different methods *viz.* Broad casting, drilling, placement and foliar etc.

I. Broadcasting is not suitable in Mulberry.

II. Drilling method is recommended for tree Mulberry.

III. Placement in between the plant row in irrigation channels and around the trees is most efficient method for mulberry.

Foliar Application

Micronutrient and growth promoters are applied under low soil fertility condition.

Quality of Fertilizer

Determination of the quantity to be applied is the important aspect of fertilizer application. It assumes greater importance in case of mulberry cultivation mainly for the following two reasons:

1. It is high biomes producing plant they requiring very high doses particularly of nitrogen.
2. Mostly small formers of low-income group grow it

Fertilizer Schedule for Irrigated Mulberry Under Tropical Condition

System Plantation	*Crop Harvest*	*FYM. MT/ halY.*	*N.P.K Dose kQ/ha.*	*Timing in. Five Split Dose*
RowSystem		20	300:120: 120	
	1s crop	20	60:60:60	Within a month after pruning (early July)
	2nu crop		60:0:0	Within the month of previous nearest (mid-September)
	3m crop		60:0:0	Within the month of previous nearest (early - December)
	4" crop		60:60:60	Within the month of previous nearest (mid-February)
	5'" crop		60:0:0	Within the month of previous nearest (late April)

The following aspect is essentially considered while determining the quantity of fertilizer.

1. Nutrient requirement of the crop.
2. Nutrient removed by a crop from the soil 10,000 kg leaf Iheltare-100-125kg nitrogen
3. Soil nutrient status.
4. Soil moisture availability.
5. Effect of the quality and quantity of the crop
6. Economic cast benefits.

Loss of Fertilizer

Fertilizer gets redistribute in the soil after application. During this of redistribution they get fixed in the soil or in the soil solution. Depending upon the condition prevailing at a given time significant portion may be last either by volatilization or by latching. This loss cannot be totally eliminated it can a leads minimizes by Principe of fertilizer application.

2.3. Chemical Fertilizers; Role of Major Nutrients and Trace Elements in Plant Growth. Types (Straight, Complex and Complete Fertilizers) Important Chemical Fertilizers in Mulberry Cultivation, Chemical Composition of Different Fertilizers, Fertilizers Doses and Schedule of Application for Irrigation Rainfed Gardens, Calculation of Required Doses for Given Unit Area. Foliar Nutrition; Foliar Nutrient and Commercial Formations, Scope Limitations, Common Weeds of Mulberry, their Effects Mulberry Productivity and Quality and Control Measures

Chemical Fertilizers

Mulberry is a very nutrient hungry plant. The requirement of major nutrients especially nitrogen is very high compared to other crops as it is fast growing and grown for its leaf which is harvested at least five times in a year. Hence application of recommended dose of chemical fertilizer is essential to maintain high yield of good quality leaf consistently. Chemical fertilizers are applied to the soil in the form of straight or complex fertilizers from time to time to improve the availability of major plant nutrients, *i.e.*, Nitrogen, Phosphorus and Potash. The quantity of fertilizers and the schedule of application mainly depend upon the system of cultivation. The recommended dose of chemical fertilizers and schedule of application for irrigated and rainfed mulberry in South India is as follows.

Recommended Dose and Schedule of Chemical Fertilizer for Mulberry Garden Maintained Under Irrigated and Rainfed Condition

Sl.No.	*(NPK : kg/ha/year)*	*Schedule*	
		Crop No.	*Quantity kg/ha/crop*
1.	Irrigated garden with high yielding mulberry variety and shoot harvest NPK @ 350:140:140 in 5 equal splits	I II III IV V	NPK @ 70: 28: 28 –Do– –Do– –Do– –Do–
2.	Irrigated garden with medium yielding mulberry variety and shoot harvest/leaf picking NPK @ 300:120:120 in 5 splits	I II III IV V	NPK @ 60: 60: 60 60: - - 60: 60: 60 60: - - 60: - -
3.	Rainfed garden with and leaf picking method of harvest NPK @ 100:50:50 in 2 splits	I II III	NPK @ 50 : 50 : 50 – 50: - -

From second year onwards high yielding mulberry varieties like V-1 and S-36 maintained under irrigated condition is provided with chemical fertilizer at the rate of 350:140:140 kg NPK/hectare/year in 5 equal splits corresponding to five harvests at the rate of 70:28:28 kg NPK/ha/crop. Whereas medium yielding varieties like K-2 is provided with fertilizer at the rate of 300:120:120 kg NPK/ha/year. The first and third dose of fertilizer is applied at the rate 60:60:60 kg NPK/ha/crop in the form straight or complex fertilizer while second, fourth and fifth dose of fertilizer is applied in the form of Nitrogen only.

Under rain fed condition, NPK is applied at the rate of 100:50:50 kg/hectare/ year in two doses. The first dose of 50:50:50 kg NPK/hectare is applied after annual bottom pruning invariably during June-July months. The second dose of 50 kg nitrogen alone is applied 2-3 weeks after second leaf harvest.

Chemical fertilizers should be applied only after 20-25 days after pruning or harvest of leaf. The most commonly used straight fertilizers are urea (46 per cent N) and Ammonium sulphate (20 per cent N) for nitrogen, Single Super Phosphate (16 per cent P_2O_5) for Phosphorus and Muriate of potash (60 per cent K_2O) for Potassium. Use of complex fertilizers like 15:15:15 (Suphala), 17:17:17 (Vijay complex) and 19:19:19 (Sampurna), as Nitrogen, Phosphorus and Potassium source is also very common.

Method and Time of Application

Fertilizers are applied by opening a furrow of about 5-8 cm deep by the sides of the plants after 25 days of shoot harvest/leaf picking using bullock drawn plough and covering it after the application. Fertilizers can also be applied around the plants and mixed in the soil by ploughing. Irrigation should be provided immediately after the application of fertilizer for better uptake of nutrients by the plants. However, to reduce the cost of cultivation and supplement the chemical fertilizers one can also use biofertilizer.

Recommended Dose and Concentration Under Tree Plantation

Age Group of Trees	Expected Leaf Yield/Plant (kg)	Requirement of Fertilizer/Plant (g)				Requirement of Farm-Compost/FYM per Plant (kg) Jul/Dec
		First Dose			Second Dose	
		Nitrogen	Phosphorus	Potassium	Nitrogen	
Upto 2 years	Upto 1	5	5	5	5	4-6
	1-2	10	10	10	10	4-6
	2-3	15	15	15	15	4-6
2-5 years	2-3	15	15	15	15	4-6
	3-4	20	20	20	20	5-10
	4-5	25	25	25	25	5-10
	5-10	50	50	50	50	10-20
5-10 years	4-5	25	25	25	25	5-10
	5-10	50	50	50	50	10-20
	10-15	75	75	75	75	10-20
	15-20	100	100	100	100	10-20
	20-25	125	125	125	125	10-20
Above 10 years	15-20	100	100	100	100	10-20
	20-25	125	125	125	125	10-20
	25-30	150	150	150	150	10-20
	30-35	175	175	175	175	10-20
	35-40	200	200	200	200	10-20
	>40	250	250	250	250	10-20

Bio-fertilizer

Bio-fertilizers are made up of live or latent cells of microorganisms like bacteria and fungi capable of helping plants to get nitrogen and phosphorus in available form. Bio-fertilizers are used as a cost effective supplement to fertilizers. In mulberry

cultivation, *Azotobacter* biofertilizer called Seri-Azo has been recommended to supplement nitrogenous fertilizers through biological nitrogen fixation. While Seri-Phos biofertilizer has been recommended to supplement phosphatic fertilizer by solubilizing unavailable phosphorus from the soil. Biofertilizers also help in avoiding pollution of soil and environment from chemical fertilizers. In mulberry cultivation 20 kg Seri-Azo/ha/year and 5 kg Seri-Phos/ha/year has been recommended. Seri-Azo and Seri-Phos should be applied in 5 split doses @ 4 kg and 1 kg/crop respectively by mixing with 200 kg of powdered farm yard manure. By the application of biofertilizer, reduction of 50 per cent nitrogen and 25 per cent phosphorus fertilizers can be achieved. Similarly in rainfed mulberry Seri-Azo and Seri-phos can be applied @ 10 kg and 1 kg/ha/year in two equal splits by mixing with 200 kg of powdered farm yard manure.

Green Manuring

Soil fertility can also be improved by growing green manure plants like Sun hemp, Dhaincha, Cowpea, etc. These leguminous plants have the capacity of fixing nitrogen by root nodule bacteria (*Rhizobium*). In a year green manure plants can be grown once or twice during rainy season. About 25-30 kg seeds/ha/crop of green manure crop are broadcasted between the rows of mulberry plants after pruning. After 35-40 days of sowing or before flowering the green manure plants are cut in to small bits and incorporated into the soil by ploughing. This can supply additional nitrogen through the incorporation of green biomass, besides improving soil structure and water holding capacity of the soil by increasing soil organic matter.

Role of Fertilizers in Mulberry

Mulberry cultivation, which is an important activity in sericulture require plantation of mulberry plant. It is the primary food plant of *Bombyx* mori silkworm. Mulberry plant grows in tropical and temperate regions. The status of sericulture industry, when viewed from stable rearing of silkworm cannot be merely judged on the basis of a massive leaf crop. Besides, from the point of view of the nutrition of silkworm larvae, the mulberry leaf should also be excellent qualitatively. Particularly in the case of mulberry used for young larvae, the quality of mulberry leaf should be extremely good. In other words along with a large crop the quality is strongly required. For that the mulberry plant requires some or other farm fertilizers (that have important growth' element) that support growth, other physiological and metabolic activities. Application of fertilizer plays a significant role in the development of *Morus* spp. and leaf quality that in turn has great bearing on the rearing of silkworm, B. *mori.* From the point of view of fertilizer effect, the growth of mulberry plants can be considered at three levels:

1. The development period
2. The assimilation period
3. The strong period

The developing period is initial period of growth during this period, the leaves and branches are produced with the stored nutritional contents. It is at this stage that the nutritional contents of fertilizer are absorbed from the roots. However; the relationship with the formation of branches and leaves is relatively thin.

Assimilation Period

The period when the branches and leaves are produced actively, and the nutrients absorbed from the roots are the actively utilized. Next is the storing period, where the growth is slow and primarily mainly the nutrients assimilated in the leaves are transferred to the shoots and roots where they are stored.

Quality of yield of silkworm cocoons are greatly influenced by the quality of nutrient present in the leaf *i.e.* primary food of silkworm B. mori. But the continuous use the chemical fertilizer often effect soil fertility and cause environmental pollution. In recent days replace of the chemical fertilizer with organic ones, for reason of better soil management. Fertilizer constitutes the costly, but indispensable input for getting optimum mulberry leaf yield under intensive cultivation practices. The common organic manure used for mulberry is farmyard manure and compost. Growing of green manure crops in between mulberry rows and incorporating the same is also practices. Green manure crops like sun hemp, Soya been and cowpeas are grown for this purpose.

Role in the Growth of Plants

Both for mulberry as well as silkworm larvae, it is better to use a large amount of well-decomposed mature manure and compost in the mulberry garden. The application of such manure will make the ground of mulberry gardens healthier. Again, it is also desirable to carry out catch crop of green manure vegetation. When the compost is applied in the mulberry garden, the decomposition is accelerated. Hence it is better to add calcium and then cover it with soil.

To overcome the ill effects of chemical fertilizers, organic farming will be of use. It is a mixture of carbon, nitrogen and trace elements prepared by optimal blending of rich materials *viz.*, carbon, nitrogen and phosphate.

Beneficial aspects of organic manure are:

1. It provides sufficient nutrients and ameliorates soil texture by providing proper aeration.
2. Increase water retention capacity of soil and provide favorable condition to flourish multiplication of microbes and carries forward vital organic transformation.
3. Maintains dynamic equilibrium in soil, air and water. It also regulates mutual harmony.
4. Develops regenerative capacity of the soil to make it resilient to absorb the effect of climatic inclemency and occasional agronomic management and improves physical, chemical and biological properties of soil.
5. Minimize attack of pest and outbreak of plant diseases through antagonism and antibiosis initiated by the introduction of organic matter in to the soil.
6. Improves soil quality by increasing granulation. water infiltration and activity of the soil microorganisms, which in turn improves soil fertility.

Concentration of Different Micronutrients for Growth of Mulberry

In recent year, micronutrient deficiencies in soils have been observed due to intensive cultivation. The quality and quantity in mulberry too have got affected owing to deficiency of micronutrients. The concentration of different micronutrients for higher plants including mulberry has been reported as under.

Micronutrients Concentration (ppm)

Mo	0.10
Cu	0.60
Zn	20.00
Bo	20.00
Mg	50.00
I	100.00
Cl	100.0

Common Weeds of Mulberry, their Effects Mulberry Productivity and Quality and Control Measures

A weed is an unwanted plant or a plant that grows in an undesired place, in our case the tree plantations. Weeds have the ability to grow fast and dominate an area very quickly: they thus compete against our desired (planted) crop. Weeds are the menace in cultivated land and mulberry is not exception to it. Primarily weeds compete with mulberry plants for water and nutrients and reduce the yield considerably. Weeds also act as host for many harmful pests and diseases of mulberry. Therefore it is very much essential to keep the plantation free from weeds. Among the weeds *Cynodon* and *Cyperus* (nut grass) which are perennial and very common in mulberry field. These weeds cause maximum damage to the mulberry plantation and also very difficult to control.

The weeds in mulberry plantation retards growth, leaf yield and make the host susceptible to various diseases. Weeds growing in mulberry fields pose a serious problem for mulberry plantation; reducing the leaf yield significantly (Sikdar *et al.*, 1981; Srinivasan *et al.*, 1987; Shivakumar *et al.*, 1994).The Weed is considered as a plant where it is not desired (Bernchey, 1920; Bailey and Bailey, 1941). So from ecological and sericultural point of view, these plants are to be controlled. The Weed is considered as a plant where it is not desired and unwanted plants grown in wanted area (Brenchley, 1920; Bailey and Bailey, 1941). The growing of weeds in mulberry garden leads the competition to mulberry plant for uptake of nutrients which causes to reduce the yield and quality of mulberry leaf (Muniyppa *et al.* (2000); Jaiswal *et al.* (2006). From the economic point of view, the growing of weeds in mulberry plantation pose a serious problem, which affects to reduce the yield of leaf and automatically which affects on the production of cocoon and silk (Isaiarasu *et al.*, 2005; Setua *et al.*, 2008). So weeding is very essential every year, whereby their effect can be minimized in mulberry garden.

Identified weed species in mulberry garden have been presented in below Table. The occurrence of 58 weeds species belonging to 16 families names belongs: Acanthaceae (1), Amaranthaceae (4), Asteraceae (9), Caesalpinaceae (2), Commelinaceae (3), Convolvulaceae (5), Cyperaceae (1), Euphorbiaceae (4), Fabaceae (10), Lamiaceae (1), Malvaceae (2), Mimosaceae (2), Nyctaginaceae (1), Oxalidaceae (1), Poaceae (11), Tiliaceae (1). The highest numbers of weed species were observed in the family Poaceae, followed by the family Fabaceae and Asteraceae.

The Impact of Weeds on Tree Growth

Weeds, just like any other crops, require water, soil nutrients and other resources for growth. They therefore compete with the trees for these necessities of life. Weeds have the following negative impacts on tree growth:

- ✰ They take up the nutrients that would have been used by the mulberry to enhance growth, thereby retarding mulberry growth.
- ✰ Weeds once taller than the trees, shade them from sunlight: they thus impair tree photosynthesis and upward growth.
- ✰ Weeds provide fuel for forest fires; hence they constitute a fire hazard.
- ✰ Weeds may attract grazing animals into the plantation, which in turn may damage the trees.
- ✰ Weeds around the trees attract rodents and termites, which may then feed on the trees.

Weed Infestation along with their Respective Families in Mulberry Garden

Sl.No	Name of Weeds	Family
1.	*Justicia vahlii* Roth.	Acanthaceae
2.	*Achyranthus aspera* L.	Amaranthaceae
3.	*Alternanthera sessalis* L.	Amaranthaceae
4.	*Amaranthus hybridus* L.	Amaranthaceae
5.	*Amarnathus viridis* L.	Amaranthaceae
6.	*Agerantum conzyoides* L.	Asteraceae
7.	*Bidens biternata* (Lour.) Merr.	Asteraceae
8.	*Cat harm us tinctorius* L.	Asteraceae
9.	*Eclipta alba* (L.) Hassk.	Asteraceae
10.	*Lagascea moilis* Cay.	Asteraceae
11.	*Parthenium hysterophorus* L.	Asteraceae
12.	*Synedralla nudUlora* L.	Asteraceae
13.	*Tridax procumbens* L.	Asteraceae
14.	*Vernonica cinerea* (L.) Less.	Asteraceae
15	*Cassia obtusifolia* L.	Caesalpinaceae
16.	*CassiatoraL.*	Caesalpinaceae
17.	*Commelia communis* L.	Commelinaceae
1 8.	*Commelia eracta* L.	Commelianceae
19.	*Commelina bengnalensis* JRA.	Commelianceae
20.	*Convolvulus arvensis* L.	Convolvulaceae
21.	*Ipomoea indica* (Berm.) Merr.	Convolvulaceae
22.	*Ipomoea maxima* L	Convolvulaceae
23.	*Ipomoea postigridis* L.	Convolvulaceae
24.	*Ipomoea sinensis* (Ders.) Choicy.	Convolvulaceae
25.	*Cyperus strigosus* L.	Cyperaceae
26.	*Acalypha indica* L.	Euphorbiacae
27.	*Euphorbia hirta* L.	Euphorbiacae
28.	*Euphorbiaprunfolia* Jaca.	Euphorbiacae
29.	*Phyllamthus niruri* Auct.	Euphorbiacae
30.	*Alysicarpus ovalifolius* Leonard	Fabaceae
31.	*Crotalariajuncea* L.	Fabaceae
32.	*Crotairia medicaginea* Lamk.	Fabaceae
33.	*Crotalaria notonhi* Wt. and Ar	Fabaceae

Contd...

Table–*Contd...*

Sl.No	*Name of Weeds*	*Family*
34.	*Goniogyna hirta* (Wilid) Au	Fabaceae
35.	*Indigofera cordifolia* Heyne ex Roth.	Fabaceae
36.	*Indigofera duthiei* Drum ex Naik	Fabaceae
37.	*Indigofera glandulosa* Wendi.	Fabaceae
38.	*Indigofera linfolia* L.	Fabaceae
39.	*Tephrosiapurpurea* L.	Fabaceae
40.	*Lavandula bipinata* (L.) 0. Ktze	Lamiaceae
41.	*Sida acuta* Burm.	Malvaceae
42.	*Sida cordfolia* L.	Malvaceae
43.	*Mimosa pudica* L.	Minosaceae
44.	*Neptunia triguetra* (Wilid) Benth.	Minosaceae
45.	*Boerharia repens* L.	Nyctaginaceae
46.	*Oxalis corniculata* L.	Oxalidaceae
47.	*Brachiaria erucjformis* L.	Poaceae
48.	*Cynodon doctylon* L.	Poaceae
49.	*Dactyloctenium sindicum* Boiss.	Poaceae
50.	*Digitaria stricta* Roth.	Poaceae
51.	*Dimeria connivens* L.	Poaceae
52.	*Eragrostis bjfaria* (Vahl.) Bot.	Poaceae
53.	*Eragrostis ciliaris* Staff.	Poaceae
54.	*Eragrostispoacides* D. Beaul.	Poaceae
55.	*Heteropogon contortus* (L.) D. beau!	Poaceae
56.	*Iseilema laxum* Hack.	Poaceae
57.	*Melanocenchrisjacguenmonti* Jaub.	Poaceae
58.	*Triumfettapentendra* A.Rich.	Tiliaceae

Source: Bhalerao *et al.* (2011). *Bangladesh Journal of Agriculture Research.* 36(1):183-188.

Generally weeds are removed manually by using weeding implement like weeding sickle and by ploughing. However, these practices are not very effective while controlling perennial weeds. In such situation it is advisable to go for chemical method by spraying herbicide, Glyphosate (Glycel).

Spraying of 0.71 per cent of Glycel @ 1.36 kg active ingredients/hectare (7.1ml Glycel in one litre of water) is found to be very effective in controlling the perennial weeds. Spraying of weedicide two times in a year after bottom pruning (before I crop and after II crop) is found very effective. Care should be taken to remove all the leaves from the mulberry plants before spraying the weedicide. About 600 litres of solution is required for one hectare in every spray.

2.4. Pruning and Training; Objectives, Types and Methods of Pruning and Importance Utility of Mulberry Pruning in Sericulture Management Practices. Harvesting: Effects of Harvest on Mulberry Plant, Harvesting Methods (Leaf and Shoot Harvest), Transportation and Preservation Methods

Pruning

Pruning is one of the most important activities of mulberry cultivation. It is a process of removing certain branches systematically to give the mulberry plants a convenient shape and size and also to stimulate the buds to sprout and produce new branches. Pruning is done mainly to improve the yield and quality of the leaf. It is also followed to harvest the shoots for silkworm rearing and to carry out different intercultural operations like ploughing, weeding, application of manure and fertilizers and to synchronize the silkworm rearing. Pruning is done using sharp secateurs, pruning saw or sickle without damaging the bark or stem.

Under rain fed conditions, the plants are pruned only once in a year at 10-20 cm above the ground level during June-July at the onset of monsoon. Then the plants are allowed to grow as bush, with many branches until next year. Harvest of leaf is done by leaf picking method only.

Types of Pruning

Pruning is classified on the basis of height of stem at which it is cut. When the main stem is cut at ground level at every harvest without allowing for the formation of stump is called bottom pruning. In case of low-cut pruning the plants are cut about 10-30cm above ground level for the development of the main stump. Medium cut and high cut pruning is followed at around 60cm and 100cm above ground to develop medium to small sized trees.

There are mainly two types of pruning *i.e.*,

Fist form of training

1. **Fist form**–where the branches are cut at the base at the same height (. Since no new branches are allowed to develop into new stump it enlarges in width giving a shape of a fist to the plant.
2. **Non-fist form** -the branches are cut leaving 2-3 buds at the bottom of the shoot. Due to this, the height of the plants increases after every harvest of shoot. Non-fist form of pruning helps to produce more number of shoots.

Non-fist Form

Thinning of Branches

When mulberry plants are pruned, many bud sprouts. However, after few days, we can observe that only few branches develop into healthy shoots while other sprouted buds remain stunted and weak. Such weak shoots are not suitable for silkworm rearing. In addition, the competition among many growing shoots causes improper development of shoots. Hence, it is very essential to restrict the number of branches per plant. For better growth it is advisable to maintain about 8-10 good branches per plant by removing excess branches after 30-35 days of pruning. This results in better development of retained branches and production of quality leaves.

Methods of Harvesting of Leaves

Harvesting of leaves is an important activity for successful silkworm rearing. There are mainly two methods of harvesting of leaves *viz.* (i) leaf picking and (ii) whole shoot harvest depending on the type of rearing practice.

Leaf Picking

In this method the leaves are harvested by picking the leaves individually. In southern states, after the harvest of leaves from the main branches the terminal buds are removed and the auxiliary buds are allowed to develop into many lateral branches. Subsequently the leaves from the lateral branches are harvested by picking. This

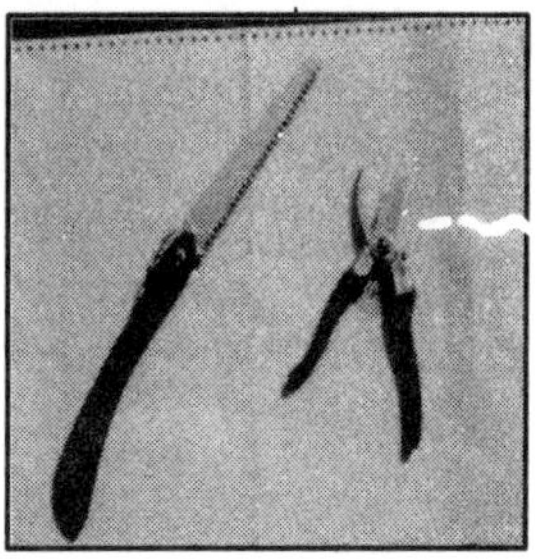

method has the advantage of harvesting the leaf according to the growth stage of the silkworm. Tender leaves are harvested to feed the young age silkworm and matured leaves for late age silkworm rearing. The disadvantage of this method is that it is highly labour intensive and therefore, becomes expensive. In leaf picking method, 6 harvests can be made in a year at an interval of 55-60 days per crop. Normally after annual bottom pruning, first leaf plucking starts after 8-10 weeks and for subsequent harvests picking of leaf is followed at an interval of 6-8 weeks.

Shoot Harvest

In this method of harvest, whole shoot is cut at the stump height of 20-25 cm from ground level and the entire shoot is used for feeding the silkworm. The crop cycle is maintained at 70 days from pruning to harvest of shoots to complete the rearing and thus 5 shoot harvests per year can be made at an interval of 70 days. Harvesting of leaf and pruning are followed simultaneously in this method.

Transportation and Preservation of Leaf

In mulberry cultivation with the primary objective to produce nutritious, succulent and palatable leaf to feed the silkworm. When the leaf/shoot is transported to the rearing house after harvesting, it starts loosing moisture very fast particularly when the atmospheric temperature is high and the humidity is low. This makes leaf unfit to feed the silkworm. Therefore it is very essential to transport the leaf from the field to the rearing house with great care to avoid moisture loss. This is more important when the leaves are harvested for young age silkworm rearing.

In order preserve the leaf moisture it is desirable to construct the rearing house/ shed near the mulberry field for easy and quick transportation of leaf/shoot. This will ensure the supply of fresh leaves for silkworm rearing and also reduces the cost of transportation. Harvest of leaf/shoot should preferably done during cooler hours and transported to the rearing house in baskets covered with wet gunny cloth. When large quantity of leaf/shoot is required to be transported it must be covered with wet gunny cloth or polythene sheets to reduce the loss of moisture.

As the silkworms are fed 2-3 times in a day, it is very important to preserve the leaf/shoot in a cool, moist and clean place. Leaf should be preserved in leaf chamber

covered with wet gunny cloth while the shoots are preserved by covering with wet gunny cloth.

2.5. Mulberry Management; Significance of Leaf Cocoon Ratio Concept, Exclusively Mulberry Garden for Chawki Rearing, Concept and Methods, Maintenance of Mulberry Plants and their Relation to Rearing Schedules

The silkworms consumes leaves of different mulberry varieties but the success of cocoon production depends on the efficient utilization and conversion of food to silk. Nutritional efficiency of the food ingested by silkworms is usually evaluated in terms of the proportion of cocoon shell weight to the amount of food ingested, *i.e.*, production efficiency of cocoon shell.

Concept of Chawki Mulbery Garden

The concept behind the chawki mulberry garden is to develop a completely separate mulberry garden as a continous source of production of quality leaf suitable for young silkworm. You cannot produce such speciifc quality of leaves in sufficient quality from a geenral mulberry garden meant for late age silwkorm rearing. Because

A chawki mulberry garden in different

the leaves of general mulberry garden contain very less moisture (60-70 per cent) and poor in other nutritional contents, a separate mulberry gardien is required to develop healthy and robust silkworm so that the worms can produce better quality cocoons and you can get increased silk production. Furtehr, hygienic and proper chawki rearing with good quality leaf will increase disease tolerance in silkworm and reamin healthly till spinning of cocoo. Suppose if you want to take up sericulture as a livelihood this concept will be of very much useful. You can also reduce the expenditure in rearing by obtaining chawki reared worm from commercial chawki rearig centre (CRC's) and you can engage yourself in other household works till you get the chawki reared worms. The concept of a chawki mulberry garden is thus very appropriate for a chawki rearing centre.

Mulberry Varieties

To develop a chawki mulberry garden exclusively for young age silkworm rearing, a high yielding mulberry varieties with superior leaf quality is requried. In south India S36 or V1 mulberry varieties are found to be most suitable for young age silkworm rearing. These produce high quality leaf rich in moisture, sugar and protein, besides various other nutrients required for good growth of silkworm. The characteristic features of the two varieties are described below.

Variety S_{36}

- ☆ Branch type: Spreading
- ☆ Leaf: Large, entire, pale green, smooth and glossy
- ☆ Leaf yield from late age garden: 40-50 metric ton per hectare per year (Tender, medium and mature leaves)
- ☆ Leaves yield from chawki garden: 30-35 metric tons per hectare per year (only tender chawki leaves)

Variety V_1

- ☆ Branch type: Errect
- ☆ Leaf: Large, entire, dark green, thick and glossy
- ☆ Leaf yield from late age garden: 50-60 metric ton per hectare per year (Tender, medium and mature leaves)
- ☆ Leaves yield from chawki garden: 30-40 metric tons per hectare per year (only tender chawki leaves)

Plantation

This part of the lessson is very important, as you will be able to learn how to take up a mulberry plantation to raise a chawki garden. Once the plantation is completed, it is now the time to take up establishment care of the plantation. Weeding should be done manually after two mo

Establishment of Plantation

Mulberry plantation gets established generally by 8-10 months time. Thus during the establishment period of the plantation we should take much care to support the plants grow properly. Irrigation should be provided at regular intervals of 7-10 days depending on the soil condition. Weeding should be done manually after two months of planting. When the plantation is of three months old, we have to apply first dose of chemical fertilizer @50 kg nitrogen (250 kg of ammonium sulphate) 50 kg phosphorous (300 kg single super phosphate0 per hectare as first dose and the plants should be allowed to grow for six months withou pruning or leaf harvest. The second weeding should be done after four months of plantation and we should apply another dose of nirogen @ 50 kg per hectare as ammonium sulphate (250 kg). When the plants are 6-8 months old it is suitable for first pruning. The plants should be pruned with the help of a secatuer at the height of 20-25cm above the ground level to build a well developed crown. Only 10-12 well developed shoots should be allowed to grow from each plant and al the exces side branches including weak branches should be removed. If we follow al the procedures mentioned above, we can get a very well established chawki mulbery garden. Afterwards the chawki mulberry garden has to be maintained following the package of practices.

Established Chawki Mulberry Garden

Maintenance of Chawki Mulberry Garden (Second Year Onwards)

Package of practices for the maintenance of chawki mulberry garden from the second year onwards involves pruning, ploughing of land, weeding, application of manure and chemical fertilizers in time, irrigation at regular intervals as well as harvest of eight crops per year as leaf and shootlet alternately. Since from a particular chawki mulberry eight crops will be harvested in a year. It is highly necessary to follow the recommend package of practices without any deviation to make a sucessful chawki garden as stated below.

Pruning

Once the garden is established, first pruning has to be done at 20-25 cm above the ground level. First crop of chawki leaf is harvested after 40-45 days of pruning and the plants are top clipped. After 35 days of top clipping the second crop is harvested in the form of shootlets and then the plants are once again pruned at 20-25cm above the ground level. Thus in a span of 90 days two crops are harvested. However, the pruning should be done with secateur soas to maintian proper stump height and without any injury to the plants.

Chawki Mulberry Garden Pruned at Height 20-25 cm

Ploughing of Land

Ploughing of land is very essential to maintian the health of soil. It helps the soil to absorbs rain water or irrigation water effectively. It also increases the soil areation and helps to remove weeds along the roots so that the plants can grow properly. Ploughing has tobe done after every pruning to remove the weeds. You can get the land ploughed by a tractor or power tiller or by a country plough. The land should be ploughed along the mulberry rows as well as acrooss the rows. The space (150 cm width) between paired rows of plantation can be maintained by a tractor or a power tiller through ploughing along the rows of mulberry while it is not possible to plough across the rows due to narrow space (60 cm x 60cm) between the plants. Hence, one country plough is also necessary plough the land and to remove all the weeds specially grasses. It is better to provide one irrigation at least 5-6 days before each ploughing.

Weeding

Weeds in mulberry garden especialy grasses take out a good quantity of soil moisture and plant nutreints, as a result reduce the leaf production and leaf quality. Hence, removal of weeds from mulberry garden is very essential to maintain muberry growth and yield. Weeds can be easily removed from mulberry garden manually after ploughing. Ploughing will uproot weeds along with the roots and will be easy to remove with the help of garden implement. Thus ploughing is very important for weed control. You can also check the weed incidence in mulberry by spraying 0.71 per cent glycel, a chemical for killing the weeds. The spraying of weedicide should be done preferably in the morning hours on a sunny day within 2-3 days after prunning. All the left leaves in the mulberry plat should be removed prior to the spraying. This practice can save mannual weeding operation and money.

Application of Organic Manure

Once a chawki mulberry garden is established it can produce leaf continously for a period of 15-20 years without any decrease in leaf yield and quality provided manure and fertilizers are applied timely along with irrigation and weeding. Since the plants are pruned four times and the leaves are harvested eight times in a year, a large quantity of leaves and branches are removed by the process. These in turn remove good quantity of nutrients from the soil, which needs to be added from the time to time to maintian the soil health. Thus farm yard manure or compost should be applied @ 40 metric tons per hectare per year in four equal split does (10 metric tones per split) after every pruning. This helps in maintaining soil health and improves leaf yield and quality. Apply farm yard manure after every pruning and weeding. The manure should be applied and mixed the soil by ploughing. Irrigate the garden after manure application.

Application of Chemical Fertilizers

Since chemical fertilizer is very important input for the supply of nitrogen, phosphorous and potash to the mulberry plants, its application is must for the production of good quality of leaf in the mulberry chawki garden. Apply chemical fertilizer in the chawki garden @260 kg nitrogen, 140 kg phosphorous and 140 kg potash per hectare per year in eight egual split doses corresponding to the eight crop harvest. For this you can apply 1300 kg ammonium sulphate. 875 kg single super phosphate and 23 kg muriate of potash annually in one hectare of chawki garden. If you divide this in eight equal split does then you have to aply 163 kg ammonium suplhate, 109 kg single super phosphate and 30 kg muriate of potash in every crop in one hectare garden. You should apply chemical fertilizer in chawki gaden within 10-15 days of every crop harvest. Before fertilizer application you should be very sure that the garden is made weed free and arranged for irrigation. This will help the mulberry plants to get proper nutrition.

Apply fertilizer in 5-8 cm deep furrows made by ploughing and cover the furrows with soil after fertilizer application. This will minimize the loss of nutrients applied through fertilizer by direct exposure to rain and sunlight. Irrigate the garden in furrows immediately after fertilizer application.

Irrigation

Irrigation is an important aspect in mujlberry cultivation as it helps in dissolving the nutrients for its proepr use by the plans. Provide irrigation to a chawki mulberry garden once in every 4-5 days so that the soil remains wet and the leaf gets more water content. Since chawki mulberry leaf should contain more than 70 per cent moisture it is very essential to provide sufficient irrigation without fail.

Irrigate the garden by nmaking furrows at least 15cm deep in between every paired row or mulberry and fill it with irrigation water. This will be sufficient to keep the leaf afresh up to 4-5 days. During rainy season the frequency of irrigation can be reduced as per the need.

Harvest Schedule

After the establishment of the chawki mulberry garden, the first pruning of the plants should be done at 20-25 cm above the ground level. This is done preferably in rainy season (July-August). After 45 days of bottom pruning, first harvest is done by leaf picking for 5 days for the first batch of chawki rearing of silkworm up to second moult. At the end of the chawki rearing, the top terminal buds of each shoot of the plants are clipped on 5th day. Other practices like ploughing, weeding, fertilizer application and irrrigation are to be followed as detailed above. Thirty five days afte top clipping, second harvest in the form of shoot let (branches) is done for another 5 days for second batch chawki rearing. Thereafter the plants once again bottom pruned at 20-25 cm above the ground level. This completes cycle of ninety days and harvest of two crops. The similar cycle has to be repeated four times to get eight crops in a year.

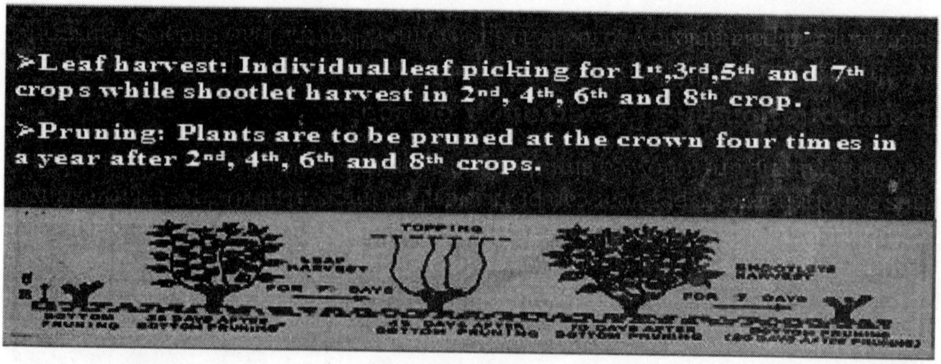

Yield and Qualities of Chawki Leaf

Following the package of practice as mentioned above, it is possible to obtain 30-35 and 35-40 metric tons of chawki leaf/hectare/year from S36 and V1 mulberry varieties respectivley. Further, it is also possible to achieve 78 per cent moisture, 3.75 per cent nitrogen and 23.43 per cent of crude protein in chawki leaf of S36 and 79 per cent leaf moisture, 3.8 per cent nitrogen and 23.75 per cent crude proteins in chawki leaf of V1.

Capacity of Chawki Silkworm Rearing

From the above mentioend quantity of leaf it is possible to rear approximately 1.66 to 1.94 lakhs of chawki silkworm per hectare per year or 20,000-24,000 DFls per crop with the chawki leaf of S36 variety. Similarly it is possible to rear 1.94 to 2.20 DFls per hectare per year or 24,000-27,000 Dfls per crop with the chawki leaf of V1 variety.

Biology of Silkworm

Unit-III

Dr. Amardev Singh

3.1. Systematic Position of Silkworm and Salient Features of Order Lepidoptera Silkworm Races and Geographical Distribution

Systematic Position of Silkworm and Salient Features of Order Lepidoptera

From prehistoric days, Indian aborigines used to reel silk fibre from wild silkworm cocoons. However, there is record of the introduction of mulberry silk culture, around 140 B.C., in India from China, through Khotan. Based on the type of the silk insect, used for producing, four kinds of commercially important silks are found.

- ☆ **Mulberry silk:** produced by *Bombyx mori* L. which is monophagous on the mulberry plant?
- ☆ **Tasar silk**: produced by either *Antherae pernyi* G. or *A.mylita* D. or *A.yamamai* G. These insects feed on leaves of arjun, sal or oak plants.
- ☆ **Muga silk:** produced by *Antheraea assamensis* Ww. They feed on the leaves of som, soalu etc., plants.
- ☆ **Eri silk**: produced by *Phylosomaia ricini* Bsd. They feed on the leaves of the *Ricinus communis* or rari plant.

Among these four silk insects, *Bombyx mori* belongs to the family Bombycidae and all the rest belong to the family Saturnidae. However, the mulberry silk production excels over all other types of silk production.

The systematic position and important characters of the silkworm are:

Systematic Position of Silkworm

Phylum	Arthopoda
Class	Insecta
Subclass	Pterygota
Division	Endopterygota
Order	Lepidoptera
Super family	Bombycoidea
Family	A) Bombycidae B) Saturniidae
Genus	*Bombyx*
Species	*mori*

Salient Features of Order Lepidoptera

The characters on which the classification is based are:

Phylum-Arthropoda

☆ Segmented body with externally jointed limbs.

☆ Chitinous exoskeleton.

Subphylum-Mandibulata

☆ Mandibles and antennae present.

☆ Body divisible into head, thorax and abdomen.

Class-Insecta

☆ Thorax 3-segmented and each segment bear a pair of legs.

☆ Respiration by trachae.

☆ Wings may be present or absent.

Sublass-Pterygota

☆ Wing present.

Division-Endopterygota

☆ Wings develop internally.

☆ Metamorphosis complex.

Order-Lepidoptera

☆ Two pairs of membranous wings.

☆ Mouth biting type in larval stage.

☆ Pupa always enclosed in cocoon.

Superfamily-Bombycoidae

- ☆ Proboscis rarely developed.
- ☆ Maxillary palpi and tympanal organs absent.
- ☆ Antennae pectinated.

Family-Bombycidae

- ☆ Antennae pectinate.
- ☆ Comparatively small.
- ☆ Eye spot absent.

Family-Saturniidae

- ☆ Antennae bipectinate.
- ☆ Comparatively large and stout.
- ☆ Presence of transparent eye spot near the centre of each wing.

Silkworm Races and Geographical Distribution

Classification based on moulting

Trimoulters

Trimoulters are characterized by three moults, shorter larval duration, small body and cocoon and fine silk filaments.

Tetra Moulters

Tetra moulters are characterized by four moults, with normal larval duration. They are reared for commercial exploitation.

Penta Moulters

Penta moulters are characterized by five moults, longer larval duration and large filament size.

Classification Based on Voltinism

Mulberry silkworms can be divided into three groups:

Univoltine (One Generation per Year)

Univoltine breed is usually found in Europe. Because of the cold climate, the eggs are dormant in winter and they are hatched only in spring. Therefore, they generate the silkworms once in a year.

Bivoltine (Two Generations per Year)

Bivoltine breed is normally found in Japan, Chain and Korea. The life cycle of the breed starts twice within the same year because the climate is suitable for developing two life cycles per year.

Polyvoltine (Up to Eight Generations per Year)

Polyvoltine breed is customarily found in tropical zone. After eggs are laid by female butterflies, the eggs will be hatched after between nine and twelve days.

Classification Based on Distribution

Broadly the silkworm races are classified into two categories *viz.*, temperate and tropical. Based on the geographical distribution the silkworms races are grouped into:

- ☆ **Japanese races:** are univoltine producing white dumbbell/spindle shape cocoon. The larval duration is usually larger. The larvae are slow in their early habits. The occurrence of double cocoon is high.
- ☆ **Chinese races:** are in general uni/bi and polyvoltie. The larvae are fast growing and the larval duration is short. They produce golden, yellow, pink or white cocoons. The shape of the cocoon varies elliptical/oval and occasionally spindle in some exceptional aces.
- ☆ **European races:** are in general univoltine and produce white or cream color cocoon. they produce large eggs and larvae that eat voraciously. the larval duration, especially in the 5th instar stage is long. The ratio of the double cocoon in the breed is low.
- ☆ **Tropical races:** These are polyvoltine having a short larval duration, except in the case of the some Mysore breed. They produce spindle/shaped cocoons (Indian races).

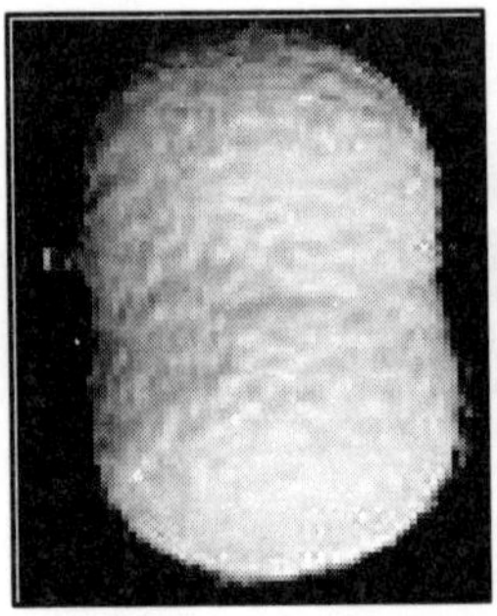

Dumbell Shape (Japanese Races)

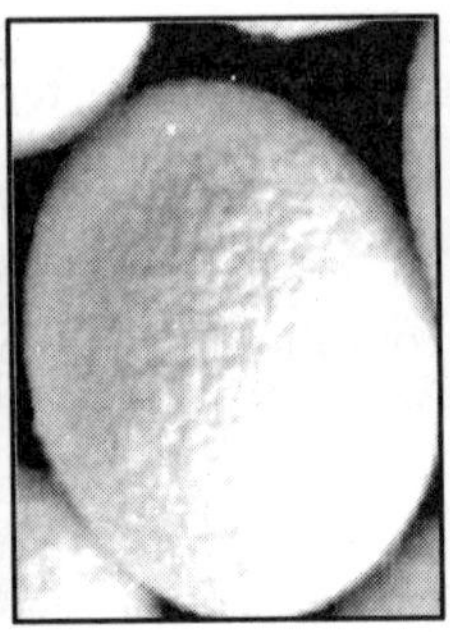

Oval Shape (Chinese Races)

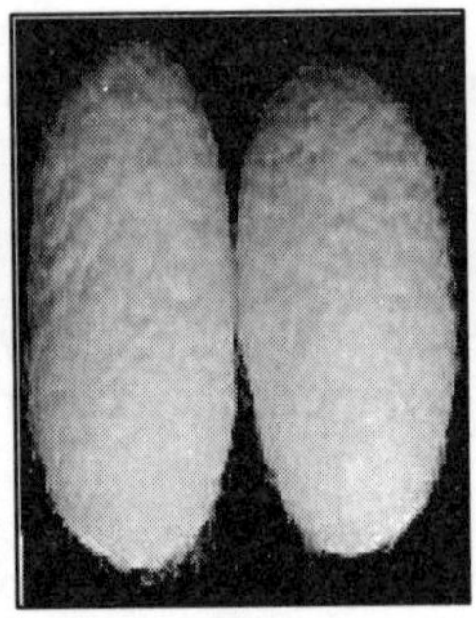

Normal Shape (European Races)

Pointed shape (Tropical Races)

3.2. Life History of *Bombyx mori*; Morphology of Egg, Larva, Pupa and Adult, Morphology and Anatomy of Organ System in Silkworm, Mouth Parts, Digestive System and Reproductive System, Silk Gland-Divisions, Spinneret Silk Proteins and their Synthesis, Moulting: Formation and Shedding of Cuticle, Hormonal Control

Life History of *Bombyx mori*

The silkworm is one of the insects that repeat a typical, four-stage cycle of transformation, namely from egg-larva-pupa-moth and back to egg again. The silkworm whose life returns, in natural environments, only one a year is called a "univoltine" one: twice yearly, a "bivoltine" one; and three times or more per year, a

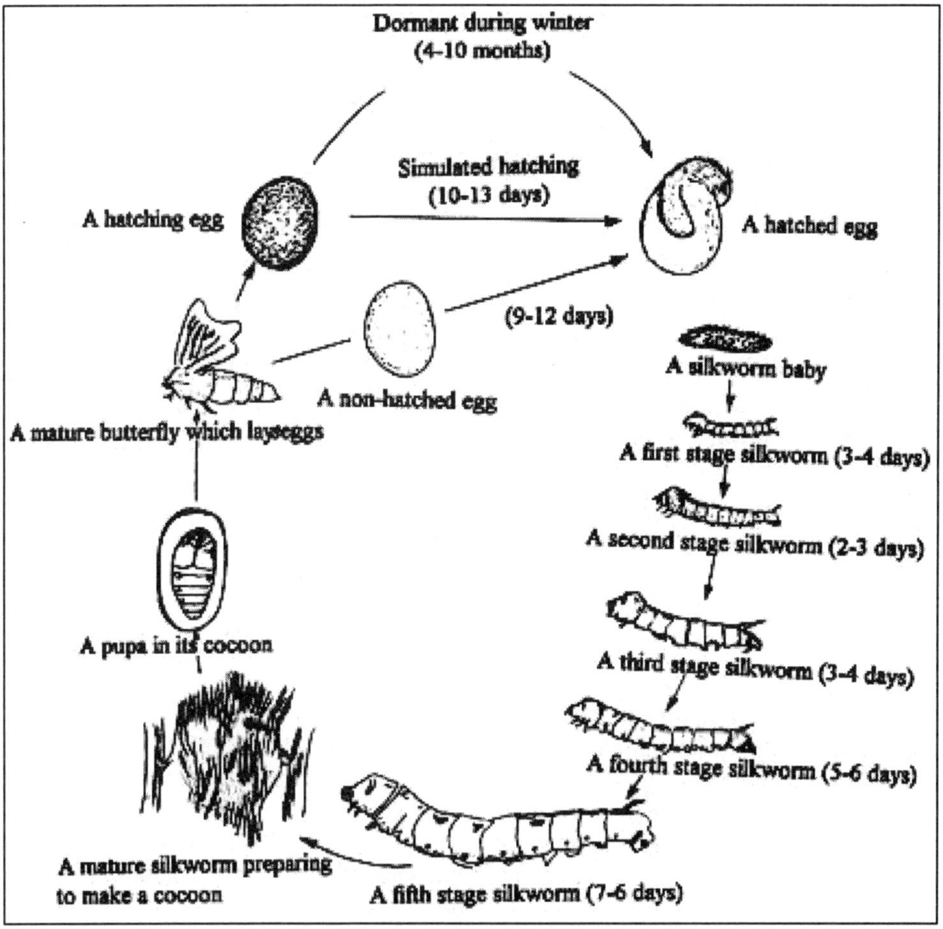

Life History of Silkworm, *Bombyx mori* L.

"polyvoltine" one. However, it is made possible that out of the eggs laid by a univoltine moth are artificially hatched larvae that have two life returns a year. Likewise, bivoltine or polyvoltine silkworms can be changed to univoltine ones by exercising an environmental control while are in the egg or larval stage.

Out of the eggs passing winter or an artificial hatching method applied to will, when incubated at a temperature of 25°C, be hatched larvae in about 11 to 14 days. Te newly hatched larvae look like ants, and that is why they are called "kego" ants in Japan.

The larva usually goes to sleep four times during its life. These four sleeps are called the first, the second, the third, and the fourth sleeps. After each sleep of the larva comes its ecdysis. The part of the larva's life between its hatching and the first ecdysis is called the first age; that between the first ecdysis and the second, the second age; and thus coming through the third and the fourth age, the larva's fourth ecdysis comes and the fifth age follows. Towards the end of its fifth age, the larva gets matured and spins a cocoon. It is transformed to a pupa within the cocoon, the pupa in turn to a moth, and the moth pushes up an end of the cocoon and comes out of it.

The larva age lasts some 25 days. At the end of its fifth age, a matured larva is over ten thousand times heavy a "kego" or ant, and starts spinning a cocoon. The larval stage is split into 3 or 4 days of the first age, 2 or 3 days of the second age, 3 or 4 days o the third age, 5 or 6 days of the fourth age, and finally 7 or 8 days of the fifth.

In each of the first to the fourth ages, the silkworm larva is sufficiently fed on mulberry leaves, and when it becomes quite a grownup it ceases to eat mulberry leaves and bids itself to a mulberry leaf with the silk thread it sends forth from the mouth part. Then it is ready for ecdysis. This stage in which the silkworm larva has fallen is described here in Japan as "sleeping". A silkworm larva in this stage is called a "sleeping silkworm"

In 15 to 30 hours after its going to sleep, the larva casts its skin off ready to enter its next age. The wording "to take" is for this state the larvae is in, and a "waken silkworm is for the larva that has just cast off its skin.

After being fed mulberry leaves for 7 to 8 days, the fifth age larva finally stops feeding, the fore half of its body turn transparent, and it begins to move around. A larva falling in this stage is termed a matured larva. This action of larva's in search of a place where to spin a cocoon is called that the silkworm "mounts". To mount also means to provide a matured larva with a cocooning frame.

After mounting, the matured larva completes its work of spinning a cocoon in 3 days or so. With the lapse of another 2 or 3days time, the larva gets transferred to a pupa within its cocoon. In 10 to 1 days the pupa transforms to a moth. The moth secretes alkaline saliva from the mouth, with which to moisten one end of the cocoon thereby from to loosen the cocoon's fibrous tissue, and forcing its way with the head it bores an opening and comes out of it. Moths soon copulate and the females lay egg.

Beside the usual four-time sleeping silkworm, there are three-time and five-time sleeping ones. It sometimes happens that the four-time sleeping silkworms are turned to three-time sleeping of five-time sleeping ones in accordance with the environmental and feeding conditions.

Morphology of Egg

The silkworm egg is a small ellipsoid, covered by hard chorion. The shape and size vary a little with races and individuals. There are also hereditarily deformed ones. The color of egg just laid is milky white or deep yellow, which is a compound color of the chorion and the yolk seen through the former.

The egg is not an exact ellipsoid. Looking it down from above, the egg, as it is laid down, is not bisymmetrical as shown in next page figure.

The swollen side (at the left) is called the ventral side; the other side (right the dorsal side). The top of egg (upper end) is called the anterior pole; the opposite end, the posterior pole. It is not fixed whether the ventral side is at the left or at the right. The probability is about 50 per cent. The micropyle and the respiratory canal pass through the chorion. There is only one micropyle at the anterior pole. The micropyle

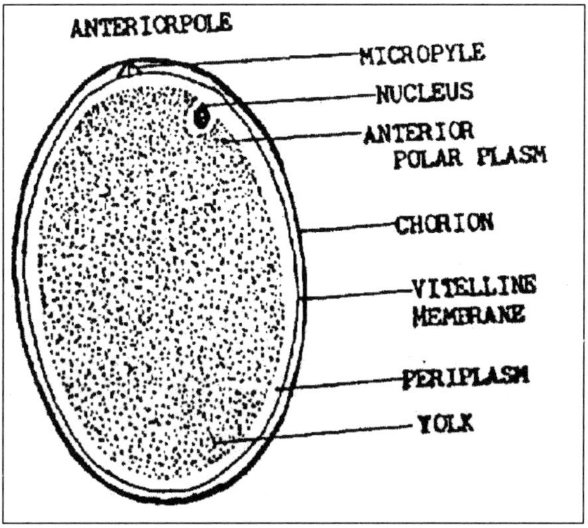

Structure of Silkworm Egg

usally branches out into three small tubes, which reach the inside of chorion. Through this micropyle, sperm gets in. the respiratory canal is a funnel-shaped tube which becomes smaller as it goes inward. They, totaling 5,000 to 10,000 spread over the surface of the egg expect around the micropyle. Through the respiratory canal, enters the air necessary for respiration, and CO_2 gas is exhausted.

Adjacent to the inside of chorion, there is a thin vitelline membrane that covers the protoplasm and the yolk. Not that the yolk is present throughout the egg-there is, just below the vitelline membrane, a thin layer, of cytoplasm that does not contain the yolk. This is called periplasm, which becomes especially thick around the micropyle. This part is called anterior polarplasm, where the egg nucleus exists.

Morphology of Larva

The newly hatched larva is about 3mm long, black in colour and is covered with bristles so that it looks like a hairy caterpillar. As the larva grows, it becomes smoother and lighter in color due to the rapid stretching of the cuticular skin, during different instars of the larval stage.

Larval life may last from 20 to 24 days in the case of the multivoltine species in tropical areas or 24 to 28 days in the case of univoltine and bivoltine races in temperate areas. During the larval life, the worm moults or casts off skin four times to be able to grow. In view of the four intervening moults, the larval life is divided into five distinct stages or instars which are popularly referred to as 5-different stages. The first three instars are referred to as young ages, and the 4th and the 5th instars as late stages.

Description of a Mature Larva

The larva possesses a head, distinctly segmented thorax, and elongated abdomen. The head is formed by the fusion of six segments, thorax has three segments and the abdomen has eleven segments.

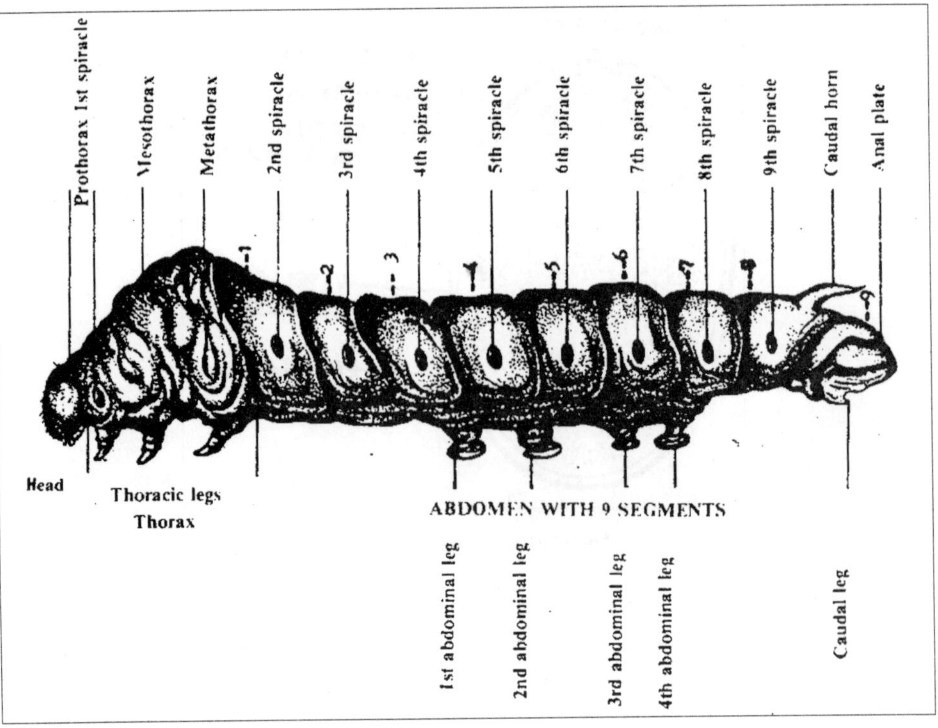

Structure of Silkworm Larva, *Bombyx mori* L.

☆ **Head:** The head is small, hypognathous (*i.e.*, mouth ventral in position), heavily chitinised and brown in colour; it bears sense organs (ocelli) and mouth parts. The mouth parts include a pair of strong mandibles, a pair of lips (upper labrum and lower labium), and a pair of maxillary and labial palps. It also bears a pair of antennae. A distinct hook-like structure, the spinneret, is present for the extrusion of silk from the inner silk gland.

☆ **Thorax**: The thorax consists of three body segments called pro- meso- and metathorax. Each thoracic segment bears a pair of legs, having three articulations. These are true legs. The lip of each leg has a curved-hook like claw. These claws are used for holding mulberry leaves while feeding. All the silkworm larvae, that show body markings, carry the so-called eye spot on the dorsal side of the meso-and metathorax.

☆ **Abdomen:** The abdomen is comprised of eleven body segments, although only nine can be distinguished as the last three are fused together to form the apparent ninth segment, the anal plate and the caudal legs. The third to sixth and the last abdominal segments bear a pair of abdominal legs or prologs. On the dorsal side of the eight abdominal segments, the larva carries the caudal horn. There are in all nine pairs of spiracles, placed laterally on either side of the body. They are found on the first thoracic segment and the first eight abdominal segments. These are the breathing or respiratory pores. The larva has number of projections or nodules all over the body and markings on the skins. The number and distribution of the nodules as well as the nature of markings are racial and mutant characters.

Sex-Differences in the Larva

The two sexes can be distinguished from each other by sex-markings developed when the female larva pupates, and transforms into an adult, the anterior, Ishiwata's glands become part of "bursa copulatrix", "receptaculum" and its duct/At the same time, the posterior Ishiwata glands are modified to form the posterior part of oviduct and necessary gland.

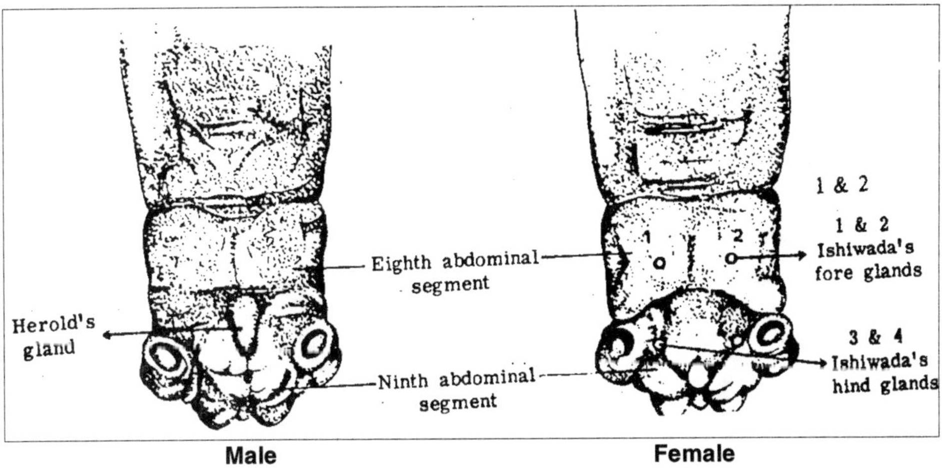

Larval Sexual Marking

Similarly, as the male larva transforms into a mature adult male, the Herold's gland changes into seminal vesicle and ejaculatory duct.

Female	*Male*
Female larva has a pair of sex-marks on the ventral side of the 8th and 9th abdominal segments, called Ishiwata's fore gland and Ishiwata's hind glands, respectively.	The male larva has a single median bud at the junction of the 8th and the 9th segments, called Herold's gland.

However, these can be seen clearly only in the freshly moulted larva. This is why special races, with sex markings, are used in silkworm breeding stations to separate the sexes in the larval stages.

After the silkworm passes through 4-moults, it reaches the 5th and the final instars when it attains its maximum weight, a day prior to maturity and before it stops feeding. When the worm is fully matured for mounting, it loses appetite, stops feeding and excretes soft faeces with high moisture content. At this stage, the silk gland is visible through the body integument and, therefore, the thorax, the thorax and body segments of the mature larva appear translucent. In fact, the silk gland is so enlarged as to account for nearly 40 per cent of the body itself. The mature worms become very restless and raise their heads in search of support so as to be able to start spinning.

Spinning of Cocoon

The spinning of the cocoon starts almost immediately after artificial mounting and, in 48 to 72 hours, the spinning is completed by the mature worm. In another day or two, the worm transforms itself into the pupa, within the cocoon.

Morphology of Pupa

The pupal period may last from 8 to 14 days, after which the adult mouth emerges, slitting through the pupal skin and piercing the fibrous cocoon shell, with the aid of the alkaline salivary secretion that softens the tough cocoon shell.

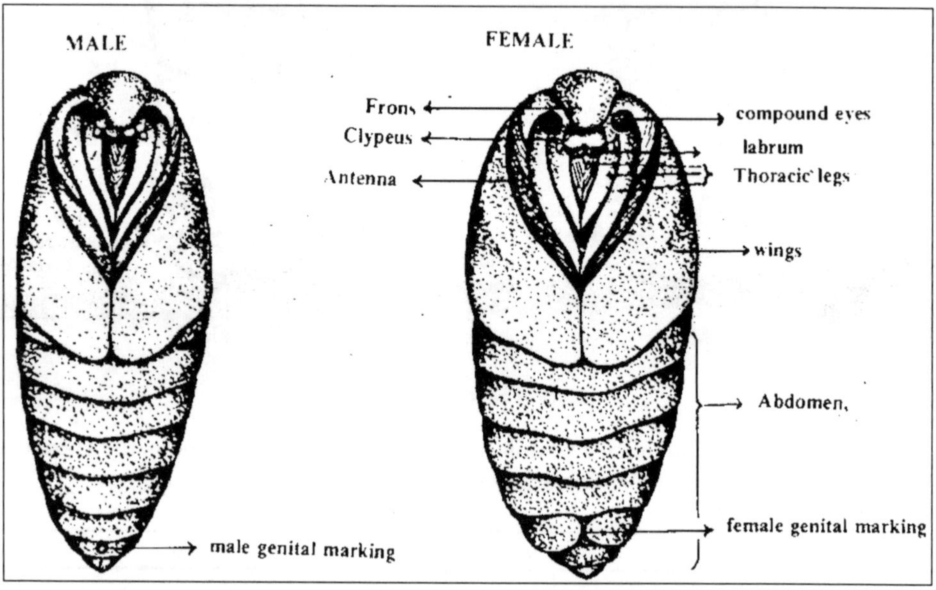

External Morphology of Female and Male Pupa

The pupa is a non-motile and non-feeding stage. The larval organs are destroyed and the adult organs are differentiated during this stage. These are differentiated into three regions-head, thorax and abdomen.

- ☆ **Head:** The head is small and situated on the ventral side of thorax. It has a pair of compound eyes, a pair of large antennae, and vestigial mouth parts.
- ☆ **Thorax:** The thorax is large and prominent. Two pairs of wings and three pairs of legs are immovably pressed against the body on the ventral side and enclosed in a chitinous case.
- ☆ **Abdomen:** The abdomen is composed of eleven segments but only nine are visible dorsally. Ten pairs are represented in the first seven segments of the abdomen, and, of these, the last pair is non-functional.

Sex-Differences in the Pupa

The sex markings are more clearly visible than in the larva

Female	Male
i. The pupa is larger with a broader abdomen	i. The pupa is thinly built narrow abdomen.
ii. A vertical line is present in the centre of the 8th abdominal segment on the ventral side.	ii. The vertical line is absent.
iii. The "x" marking in between 8th and 9th segment.	iii. The "dot" like marking on 9th segment.

Morphology of Adult

The adult mouth, emerging from the pupa, is incapable of flight as a result of domestication. It does not feed during its short adult life. The entire body and the wings are covered with epidermal scales. The body is divisible into head, thorax and abdomen.

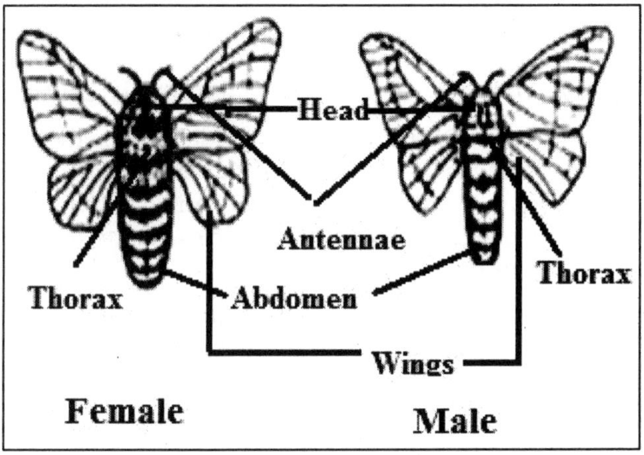

Female and Male Moth

- **Head:** The head is small. The paired compound eyes are prominent on the sides of the head. On the inner side of the eyes, arise a pair of bipectinate antennae. The coiled proboscis is non-functional.
- **Thorax:** Each of the mesothoracic and metathoracic segments bears a pair of wings. The forewings overlap the hind wings.
- **Abdomen:** Eight abdominal segments are visible in the abdomen in the male and only seven in the female. There are six pairs of spiracles in the abdomen.

Sex-Differences in the Adult

Female	Male
i. Colour paler.	i. Colour darker.
ii. Less active.	ii. More active.
iii. Body size relatively large.	iii. Large antennae.
iv. Abdomen large and flat with seven visible segments.	iv. Body size relatively small.
v. Female moth has a knob like projection with sensory hairs at the caudal end.	v. Abdomen long, narrow with eight visible segments.
	vi. The caudel end of the moth has a pair of hooks known as harpes.

Fertilization is internal, preceded by copulation. Just after emergence, the male moths copulate with females for about 2 to 3 hours and, if not separated, they may die after a few hours of copulation with females.

Morphology and Anatomy of Organ System in Silkworm, Mouth Parts, Digestive System and Reproductive System

Morphology and Anatomy of Organ System in Silkworm

Silkworms do not have bones. Therefore, the skin protects the body and also acts as an exoskeleton. The inside the silkworm is tightly packed with the digestive organs, like silk gland, malpighian tubules which are concerned with excretion, the dorsal vessel (heart) which circulates the blood, the spiracles that carry respiration, nerves, sexual organs, muscles, fatty acids *etc.*

The anatomy of the larva is different from that of the adult. The anatomical changes required for the formation of the adult anatomy are brought about in the pupal stages. The following account pertains to the anatomy of the 5th instars silkworm larvae.

Viscerea

When the larva is cut open mid-dorsally or laterally, the organs which are exposed in the body cavity constitute the viscerea.

Longitudinal sectional view from the side (5th instar silkworm larva)

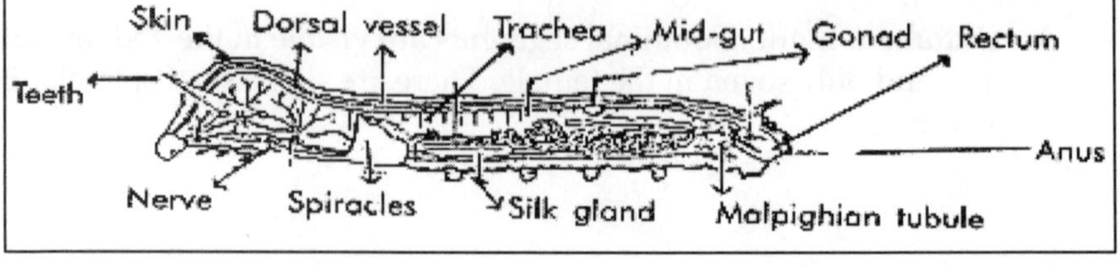

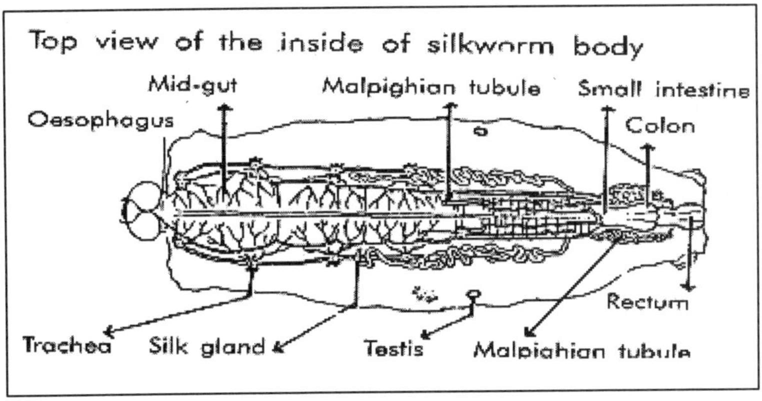

Larva

The visceral organs revealed in the larva above are:

i. **Dorsal vessel:** This is the tubular blood vessel attached to the tergum by eight pairs of alary muscles. This is the dorsal most organ. It can be seen only if the larval skin is cut on one side and deflected on the other. If the larva is opened mid dorsally, the heart is also cut.

ii. **Alimentary canal:** This is the straight tube that can be easily identified from the green colour of the food inside. It extends from the mouth to the anus.

iii. **Malpighian tubules:** Three pairs if pale-yellow malpighian tubules which have an inverted U-shape can be seen arising from the junction of the midgut and hindgut. It extends up to the fourth or fifth abdominal segments. Of the three tubules on one side, one is dorsal, one dorso-lateral and one ventral in position. They are found closely applied to the alimentary canal and do not float in the haemocoel.

iv. **Tracheal bushes:** From the spiracles, on either side, arise a bunch of tracheal tubes called tracheal bushes. These are connected to longitudinal trachea on each side and the two longitudinal trachea are connected by ventral transverse trachea. The tracheal bushes, the longitudinal tracheal trunk and the trachea attached to the alimentary canal and silk glands can be clearly seen on either side of the gut.

v. **Silk glands:** The middle part of the silk gland is prominently visible and fills up most of the body cavity ventral to the alimentary canal. The posterior part and anterior part of the silk gland are entangled within dermo-visceral muscles; trachea and fat body are visible only partially.

vi. **Ventral nerve cord:** This can be seen by cutting the tracheal and muscular attachment of the alimentary canal and pushing the gut to one side. The ventral nerve cord and its ganglia lie on the mid-ventral line and are attached to the sternum.

vii. **Fat body:** Fat body is arranged as a loose mesh of cells invested by delicate membranous connective tissue and joined by strand-type connective tissue.

The fat body is the storage organ for reserve materials such as glycogen, proteins and fat. It is also the site of intermediary metabolism.

Mouth Parts of Silkworm Larva

The mouth parts of silkworm include:

i. **Labrum:** This is an unsegmented projection of the ante-clypeus which forms the upper lip.

ii. **Mandibles:** These are the paired appendages of the fourth cephalic segment. They are toothed and chitinised. They lie in the mouth cavity and serve to cut the mulberry leaves by a side to side action like the blades of a scissors. The duct of the salivary glands opens at the base of the mandibles.

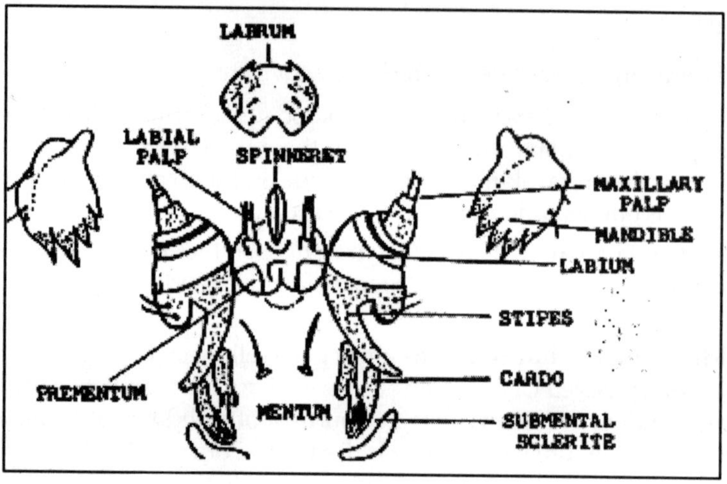

Mouth Parts of Silkworm

iii. **Maxillae:** These are the short paired appendages of the 5th segment. Each maxilla has a basal portion made of two segments the proximal cardo and the distal stipes. A maxillary lobe and a three segmented maxillary palp are present on the stipes. Taste sensillae are located on this appendage. They help in the discrimination of the taste of the food.

iv. **Labium:** This median organ forms the lower lip. It is formed by the fusion of the appendages of the last or sixth cephalic segment. The cardo and the stipes of the appendages of the two sides are fused to form two median structures, the lower, lightly chitinised, mentum and the upper, heavily chitinised, black colored, prementum. There is a median process in the distal end of the prementum called the spinneret. The silk gland open through this opening and silk exudes through the spinneret during the spinning of the cocoon. The labial palps are short and separate and lie on either side of the spinneret. They are sensory in function.

Digestive System of Silkworm Larva

The alimentary canal is a straight tube extending from the mouth to the anus as depicted in below. The wall of the alimentary canal is made up of three layers:

i. **Tunica intima:** a chitinous layer secreted by the underlying ectodermal cells. This layer is thick in the foregut and hindgut but thin in the midgut.

ii. **Epithelial layer**: which has gland cells interspersed in between columnar cells. This layer serves digestive and absorptive functions.

iii. **Muscle layer:** composed of longitudinal and circular muscle layers which aid in the movements of food through the alimentary canal.

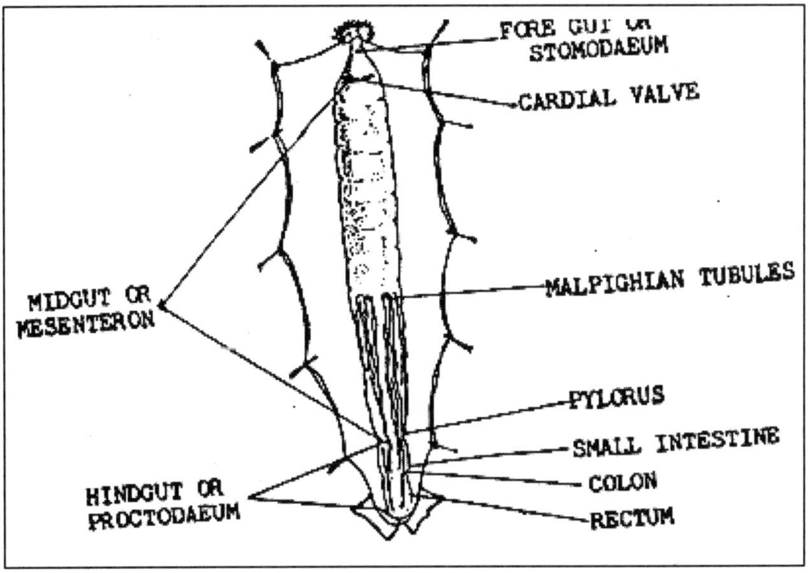

Alimentary Canal or Digestive System of Silkworm Larva

Structurally and functionally, the alimentary canal is divided into three regions- the foregut or stomodaeum, the midgut or mesenteron and hindgut or proctodaeum. The foregut and the hindgut are derived from the ectoderm and the midgut from the endoderm. The tunica intima is shed at each moult in the foregut and hindgut. Functionally, the foregut is the region of the reception and storage of food, the midgut is the region of digestion and absorption and the hindgut is the region of water reabsorption

Foregut

This part of the gut receives and stores the food. It includes:

i. **Mouth cavity:** The funnel-shaped cavity enclosed by the mouth parts and opening posteriorly into the pharynx.

ii. **Pharynx:** The narrow cylindrical part which connects the mouth cavity with the oesophagus. It has two pairs of muscles which help in swallowing.

iii. **Oesophagus**: This is the main part of the foregut which is narrow in front and enlarges posteriorly to form a funnel-shaped structure. It is the organ of storage of food.

iv. **Cardiac valve or fore sphincter:** It is the projection of the posterior part of the oesophagus into the midgut as a fold. It regulates the passage of food from fore to the midgut and prevents regurgitation. It allows the retention of food in the foregut for a longer duration. It is also involved in the formation of the peritrophic membrane found in the midgut.

Midgut

It is straight and long tube occupying eight out of the thirteen segments of the body. It has a number of wrinkles which increase its surface area. The tunica intima is thin but the muscle layers are well developed. The epithelial layer contains:

i. **Columnar cells or cylindrical cells:** which have a brush border and, considered to be absorptive in function.

ii. **Glandular or goblet cells:** which are secretory in function.

iii. **Regenerative cells:** which help in replacing the cells lost by wear and tear, and

iv. **Basement membrane:** on which the other cells lie. The midgut is composed to the body wall by ten pairs of muscles. The cytoplasmic. Midgut polyhedrosis virus affects only the columnar cells.

Internally, the midgut has the peritrophic membrane, a chitinous structure which has a dual origin. The peritrophic membrane is supposed to be formed by the secretory activity of the cardiac valve as well as by a delamination from the midgut epithelium. The periotrophic membrane isolates the gut contents from direct contact with gut wall.

The midgut serves functions other than digestion and absorption. It acts as a storage organ of glycogen, which is stored in the epithelial cell of the posterior half of the midgut. It also has a synthetic function. Proteins functioning as antibodies and as yolk proteins are supposed to be synthesized in the midgut.

Hindgut

This develops as an invagination of the outer ectoderm. The tunica intima layer has thorny projections and is shed at each moult. The epithelial and muscle layers are also well developed. At the junction of the hind and midgut is a pyloric valve or hind sphincter which regulates the passage of food from the midgut to the hindgut.

The hindgut is differentiated into three regions-**Ileum or Small intestine, Colon and Rectum.** The ileum is the short tube between the midgut and the colon. At the junction of the midgut and the hindgut arise three pairs of cryptonephric malpighian tubules. The distal ends of the malpighian tubules penetrate into the muscular wall of the rectum. The next region is the colon. The tunica intima and epithelial layers have longitudinal folds in the colon. Dermo-visceral muscles connect the colon with the body wall. The rectum is swollen at the anterior end and narrows towards the anus. Thorny projections are present in the tunica intima in this part of the alimentary canal. The circular muscles of this layer are continuous as in other regions but the longitudinal muscles are arranged in six bundles which press the faecal matters into hexagonal pellets. The time taken for food to travel through the entire alimentary canal varies from 2-3 hours to 4-5 hours.

Digestive Gland

The salivary glands are small tubular glands situated on either side of the oesophagus and open at the base of the mandibles. The saliva is an alkaline fluid and contains the enzyme amylase. Some races of *Bombyx mori* lack amylase and others have little activity. The major digestive glands are the unicellular gland cells lining the midgut. The gastric juice is a yellow, alkaline fluid. It contains proteinase, peptidases, glucosidases, nucleases, lipase etc., which digest all the organic constituents of the food. The digestive juice dissolves the protein of the polyhedral inclusion bodies and the spore wall of the perbrine spores. It is also reported to contain a red fluorescent anti-ciral protein. There are two digestive glands in the walls of either foregut or hindgut.

Reproductive System of Silkworm

Larva

The rudiment of the reproductive system of the adult is represented s the genital imaginal disc in the larva. It is clearly visible in the 5th instar larva. It consists of the gonad (ovary in the female and testis in the male) and the band or duct in a rudimentary condition. Besides, the female has a pair of Ishiwata's gland in the 8th and 9th segments and the male has a pair of Herold's gland in the 9th segment.

Adult

Female

The female reproductive system consists of a pair of ovaries with four ovarioles occupying the entire abdominal cavity. The ovarioles are covered by a sheath which has muscle fibers. The ovarioles are polytrophic. In each ovariole there is a succession of nutritive cells surrounding an egg cell which they nourish. The ovarioles of a side unite to form an oviduct. The oviducts join to form the common oviduct which opens to exterior by the female genital pore. Arising from the junction of the two oviducts is a sac-like structure called bursa copulatrix. This opens to the exterior by the opening called ostium bursae. The male transfers the spermatophores through the ostium bursae to the bursa copulatrix from where they are transferred to the common oviduct by a seminal duct. A sac like spermatheca opening into the common oviduct serves to store the sperms received during copulation. A pair of accessory glands lies dorsal to the common oviduct and they secrete the adhesive glue by which the eggs are attached to the substratum.

A female lays all her eggs within twenty-four hours of mating whereas a virgin female retains most of the eggs for some days. *Bombyx mori* normally lay eggs in a single layer close together. If the trichoid mechanoreceptors on the anal papillae are

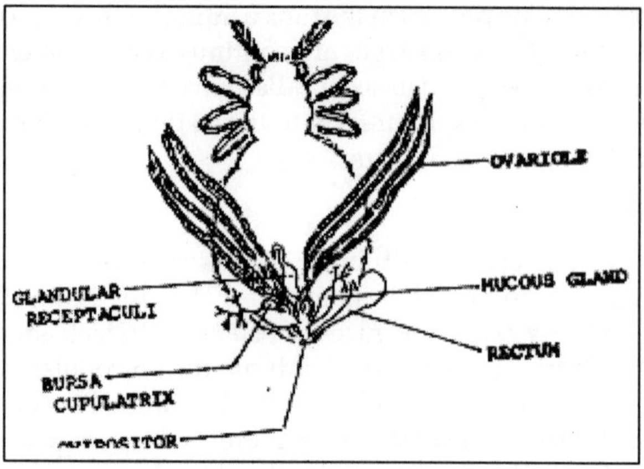

Reproductive Organ of Female *Bombyx mori*

destroyed, the eggs are laid in clusters. Tendency for sporadic parthenogenesis varies in the different races. In certain strains there is an inherited tendency to lay binucleate ova and this is associated with gynandromorphism.

Male

A pair of testis is present on the 5th abdominal segment on either side of the ventral nerve cord. Each testis is formed by a number of seminiferous tubules. The vasa efferentia of each side unite to form the vas deferens. The two vasa deferentia have each an enlarged ampulla at the distal end and open into the enlarged seminal vesicle situated in the middle. From the seminal vesicle arises the ejaculatory duct opening into the male genitalia the aedagus.

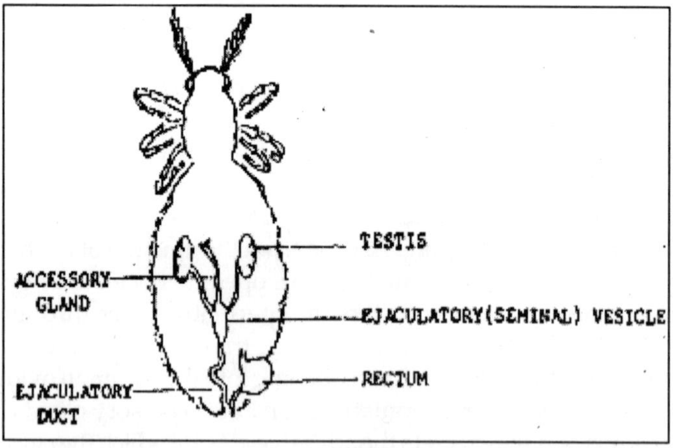

Reproductive Organ of Male *Bombyx mori*

A pair of accessory glands opens by a common duct into the seminal vesicle. The secretion of the accessory glands serve to pack the sperms in a membranous sac to form spermatophores.

Silk Gland-Divisions, Spinneret-Silk Proteins and their Synthesis

There is a pair of silk glands modified from the labial glands, which is a special organ for the synthesis and secretion of the silk synthesis. The newly hatched larva can also secrete the silk substances. Before each molting, the larva secretes the silk substances to fix its abdominal legs. This facilitates the process of the ecdysis. However, the silk glands are not well developed before the 4th instar. From the early 5th instar on, the silk glands grow sharply, and become the largest organ in the body, especially in the late 5th instar. After matured, the larva secretes the silk substances to make the cocoon, and metamorphosis and pupates in the cocoon. The cocoon serves s the protection of the pupa. After the larva has finished cocooning, the silk glands start to blight, they are disintegrated during pupation. Only a vestige of the silk glands can be detected in adult stage.

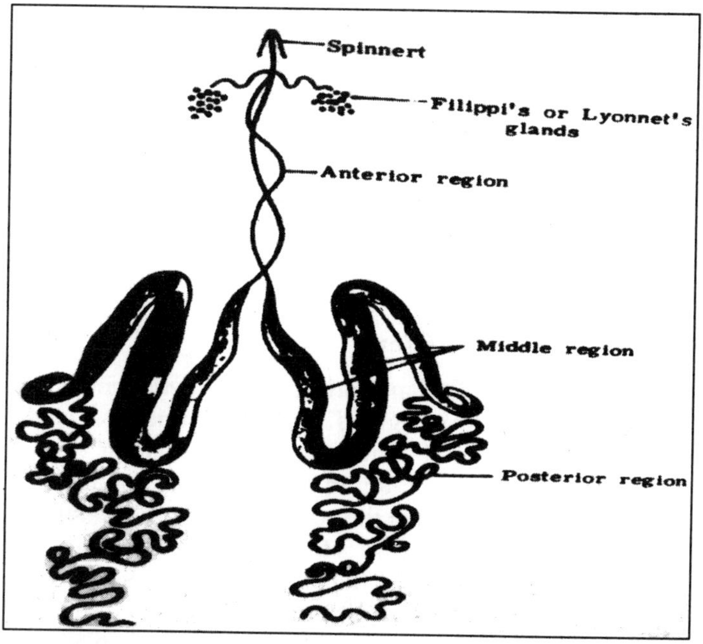

Structure of Silk Glands of Silkworm, *Bombyx mori*

Location and Form of the Silk Gland

The silk glands are located on the ventro-lateral sides of the larval digestive track, and are a pair of semitransparent curved tubular organs. Based on the form and function, the silk glands can be divided into four regions; the spinneret, anterior region, middle region and posterior region.

Spinneret

Spinneret is located in the head capsule, and is a fine tube; it can be redivided into three region: spinning portion, thread pressing portion and passage-sharing portion. The spinning portion is situated at the very anterior end and appears to be tubular, its aperture at anterior end is called spinning orifice. The pressing portion is the swollen portion and fixed on the integument by six muscles but its wall is very thick and its cavity is very thin and appears to be semilunar in cross section. The wall of the pressing region along the median dorsal line is highly sclerotized and invaginates deeply to form a longitudinal sword like black pressing pole, on the opposite side, the ventral side; there is half circular brown pressing plate. The pressing pole and the pressing plate form the pressing apparatus, which along with the musculature serves as regulator of the flow of silk substances and as a regulator of the thinness and form of the silk. The posterior portion of the spinning tube is the passage-sharing portion, which in fact, is the conjunctive portion of the two for ends of the anterior regions of the glands, its posterior dorso-lateral sides bear a pair of grape-like glands called Filippi's glands, which are composed of large gland cells, whose conducts opens into the spinning tube, some scientists thought that the glands have the secretory function.

Anterior Region of the Silk Gland

The anterior region of the silk gland links with the spinning tube or spinneret, it begins from the head and ends at the third abdominal segment, it is the thinnest region, both the anterior and the posterior portion are almost the same size in diameter, and appear to be straight linear, it does not curved until the grown larvae stage comes, no tracheae and no muscles are attached on its surface, therefore it is free in the hemocoel. It is the way that silk substance flows and it functions as fiberizing the silk substances.

Middle Region of the Silk Gland

The middle region of the silk gland connected its anterior end with the posterior end of the anterior region of the silk gland. This region thickness significantly, and prolongs from the third to the 6th abdominal segment, then folds abruptly anteriorly and prolongs p to the mesothorax, folds again abruptly backward and connects its posterior end with the anterior end of the posterior region of the silk gland at the 4th abdominal segment. The middle region is the largest one in the four regions, at the conjunction between the middle and the posterior regions, it is getting thinner. Obviously, in according the two folds, it can be divided into three portions; fore portion, middle portion and hind portion. It keeps its form changeless for almost all the larval stages. It is colorless in white cocoon varieties, while in colored cocoon varieties, it will present color similar to their cocoon normally at very beginning of the 5th instar. This region functions as the reservoirs of silk substances and as the secretor of the sericin as well.

Posterior Region of the Silk Gland

The posterior region of the silk gland prolongs backwards from the 4th to 6th abdominal segment with multiple flexes. This region is the longest region in the four region of the silk gland. There is no obvious difference in tubular diameter among the different portions. There are few flexions at the newly hatched larva, but the flexion counts increase with the growth of the larva, and may reach to more than 5o flexion at the mature larval stage. This region functions as the secretor of the fibroin, the fibroin amount secreted depends upon the length and weight of the region. In the varieties with low ratio of cocoon shell, the length of this region could merely reach to 3.7 times as many as its body length, while in the varieties with high ratio of cocoon shell, the length might reach to 4.8 times as many as its body length, absolute differences between the two kinds of varieties in the length of the posterior region may reach to about 1 times. It takes merely 9.5 percents of the total weight of the gland in the varieties with low ratio of cocoon shell, while in the varieties with high ratio of cocoon shell, it takes up to 26.2 percents of the total weight of the gland.

On all the regions but the anterior region, there are muscles on the surface, which fix the gland at its location. On the last two regions, there are tracheae on the surface, which provide the gland with adequate oxygen. If the respiration is inhibited, function for the synthesizing fibroin will be reduced greatly. In addition, the tracheae also play role in fixing the gland.

Moulting: Formation and Shedding of Cuticle, Hormonal Control

When an inset grows and develops, it must periodically shed its rigid exoskeleton in a process called moulting, in place of the old tight exoskeleton, the insect grows a new loose one that provides the insect with room to grow larger. Many insect species also transform in body structure as they moult from a juvenile to an adult form a process called metamorphosis.

Several hormones control insect moulting and development. These hormones trigger an insect to shed its exoskeleton and at the same time, progress from smaller juvenile form (*e.g.*, a young caterpillar) to larger adult form (*e.g.*, winged moth). The hormone that ceases an insect to moult is ecdysone. This hormone in combination with another hormone called juvenile hormone also determines whether the insect will undergo metamorphosis.

In addition to ecdysone Juvenile Hormone (JH) also play an important role in development. While JH is abundant, it prevents ecdysone from triggering the insect to metamorphosis after it moults instead, the larva moult into another larger larva. When the level of JH decreases, the larva moults into a pupa and metamorphosis begins.

The role of hormone, in bringing out moulting, is interesting. A flood of research papers appeared after the relationship between moulting and hormones was discovered. Research activity related to the silkworm also did not lag behind. Fukuda, as early as 1940, considered that the entre of population hormone must be located in the prothorax region. Then, from several ligation experiments, Fukuda conclude that corpus allatum produces a hormone that inhibits pupation. The prothoracic gland, on the contrary, produces a hormone that induces moulting and pupation. Thus, the roles are as given below:

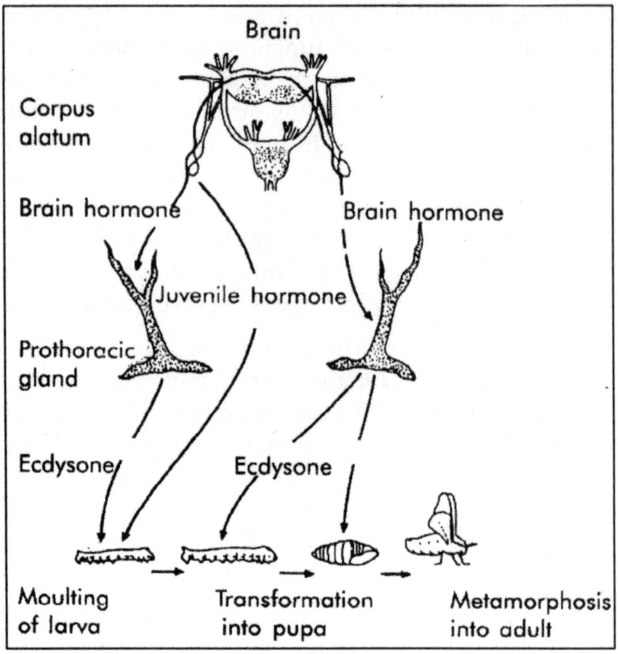

Hormones that Determines Moulting of the Larvae and Metamorphosis

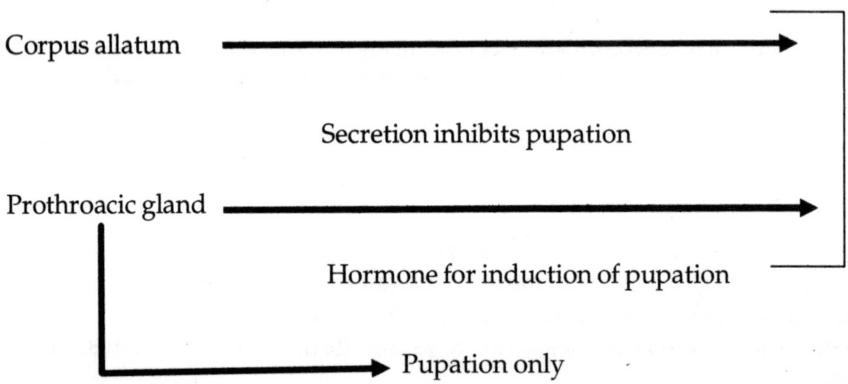

The corpus allatum hormone was named as juvenile hormone and the prothroacic gland hormone was called ecdysone. Butenqudt (1955) pioneered in extracting ecdysone in pure crystal form and characterized it; later, it was found to be a non-specific hormone. William (1950) was successful in extracting the juvenile hormone from the silkworm. Following Wigglesworth (1954), the currently held opinion is that, irrespective of the amount of moulting hormone, the larvae moult into larvae in the presence of the highest concentration of the juvenile hormone, larvae moult into pupae under intermediate concentration of the juvenile hormone and pupae moult into adults in almost absence of the juvenile hormone.

3.3. Metamorphosis and the Role of Hormones in Insect Metamorphosis

When the larva in the last instar matures, it starts spinning the cocoon. When the spinning is over the larva sheds its skin and metamorphosis into pupa. During pupation, the prothoracic glands play a very important role. The corpora allata, as referred to earlier have a role in larval moulting; if the corpora allata of a larva are removed during the third or fourth instar, the larva fails to moult any further and directly transforms into pupa. It is in this pupation process that the prothoracic glands function.

There is a pair of prothoracic glands, one each on the right and left sides of the body below the first pair of spiracles. Each gland has a central portion and anterior, middle and posterior branches. It is composed of several cells which possibly participate in its secretory activity during the development of larvae into pupae.

In the mature stage of the larvae experiments can be carried out to block the prothoracic glands on the anterior and posterior sides, whereby the flow of the secretion can be disrupted. If the larvae are blocked on the posterior side of the segment bearing the prothoracic glands, it is found that the pupation occurs only in the anterior and not in the posterior part of the larval body. In other words only the part having the prothoracic glands pupates. Hence it is clear that the material necessary for pupation is secreted by the prothoracic glands. In another experiment, when the prothoracic gland from another individual is transplanted into the posterior part of the larval body deprived of the prothoracic gland, it is found that this region also pupates. For such functioning of the prothoracic gland, air supply via spiracles is necessary. Thus the prothoracic glands play an important role in the metamorphosis of larvae into pupae. These glands also play a definite role during metamorphosis of pupae into adults.

The brain of the silkworm is also involved in the metamorphosis. Pupae, when kept at 25°C, transform into adults 11 to 15 days after pupation. If the brain of the pupa is extirpated soon after pupation, the adult does not emerge even after 40 days. However, if fresh brain from a normal pupa is transplanted into the detrained pupa, the adult emerges about 20 days after the surgery. If the surgery is somewhat delayed, and the brain is removed a few hours after pupation, the adults emerge normally.

From the above it is clear that a hormonal substance (brain hormone of activation hormone) necessary for emergence of the moth is secreted by the brain. However, it should not be assumed that the brain alone is responsible for metamorphosis. The brain functions in such a way that it activates the prothoracic glands and accelerates the secretion of the prothoracic gland hormone which indicates metamorphosis.

In the silkworm pupae, the brain secretes a hormone which activates the prothoracic glands which in turn secretes a hormone inducing the metamorphosis into the moth. From the brain of the moth also a hormone similar to that from the brain of the pupa or larva is secreted which can play a role in the metamorphosis of the pupa to a moth. The prothoracic gland hormone is also known as moulting hormone (ecdysone). This hormone can be extracted by different organic solvents and crystallized. Its molecular formula is $C_{16}H_{30}O_4$. This hormone is not species specific and is effective even in other insects, such as houseflies. The secretion of hormone from the brain can be prevented by exposing the insect to low temperature. In males the hormone secretion is inhibited at 5-15°C and in female at 2-10°C. The hormone secretion ceases at 2.5°C in females. Oenocytes also may be considered to be involved in moulting the silkworm. Aggregated of oenocytes, called subspiracles glands, ad are present in the spiracles in each segment. They are round or elliptical, and their nuclei are more or less round in the young larval stage but irregular in shape in the advanced larva. Oenocytes are present even in the adult stage and their shape and number are more or less constant as in the larval stage. Owing to a difference in the oenocytes of genetically non-moulting and normal silkworms, oenocytes are considered to be associated with moulting. Although the involvement of corpora allata in moulting larva been confirmed, that of oenocytes is still in doubt.

3.4. Structure of Egg, Development and Hatching

Soon after copulation and within 10 minutes of entry of sperm into the egg the nucleus undergoes maturation division and prepares itself for fertilization with the sperm nucleus. Within two hours of egg laying, the sperm nucleus fertilizes the egg. Soon after fertilization, the embryonic development stars by the zygote nucleus dividing

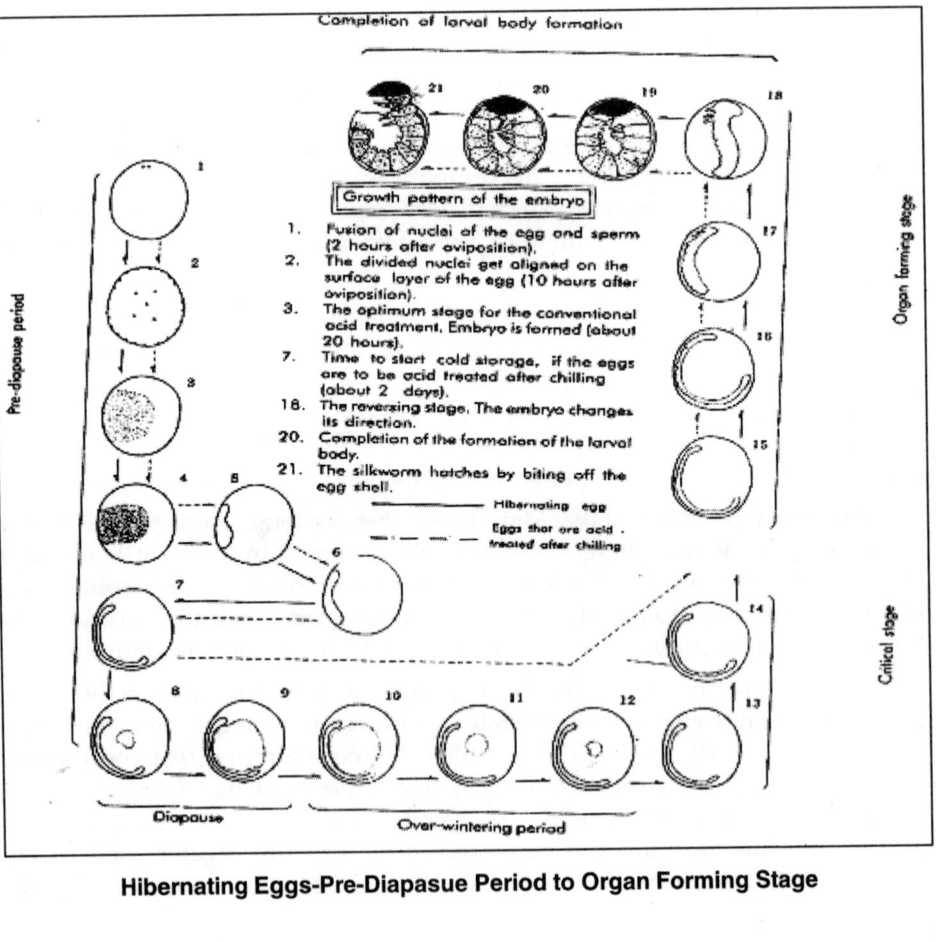

Hibernating Eggs-Pre-Diapasue Period to Organ Forming Stage

into a number of nuclei. Blastoderm is formed in about 10 hours of oviposition and the germ band in about 20 hours.

Embryonic growth in both hibernating and non-hibernating eggs continues normally till this period. The hibernating eggs start developing the brown pigment and further growth of the embryo slows down, thus ushering in hibernation. This period is ideal for acid treatment of hibernating eggs for early hatching about 30 hours of oviposition, the embryo develop the head and the tail and, by the third day, reaches the longest embryo stage and enter diapause. This stage is well suited for acid treatment after chilling. Hibernating eggs at this stage are stored in cold storage at a temperature of 2.5°C till they are released for incubation later. The diapausing substance which is secreted by the moth and which restricts the development of the egg is dissolved when eggs are stored in the cold storage.

In non-hibernating eggs there is no diapause and embryos continue to grow further to reach blastokinesis stage on the 5th day of egg laying 'eye spot" stage on the 7th day and "bluing stage" on the 9th day. Larva hatches out of the egg on the 10th day. In hibernating eggs, the embryo develop to reach the above stages of growth when they are kept in the incubation

3.5. Nutrition: Factors Influencing Silkworm Growth and Development

Silkworm nutrition, broadly speaking, refers to the mechanism which the silkworm can obtain and utilize the substance to construct/build body and sustain the life activities, including the quality and quality diet, rearing environment, physiological situation and so on, while narrowly speaking, just refers to the quality and quantity of food.

Silkworm feeds on the singular food-mulberry from which it ingests various nutrients to maintain/support physiological activities. The nutrients include protein, carbohydrates, fat, vitamin, inorganic salt and water. Besides them, air is also essential substance for silkworm growth and development.

Protein and Amino-Acids

Protein is the basic substance constituting silkworm body. It is the main component that produces tissues and organs of silkworm. Silkworm utilizes protein and amino acids present in the mulberry leaves to synthesize the proteins specific for silkworm. Variation in the protein in the mulberry leaves influence the regulation of protein quantity taken in by silkworm and consequently influences the production of cocoon fibre as well as growth of the silkworm. Essential amino-acids are Arginine, Histidine, Isolecusine, Leucine, Methionine, Phenylalanine, Threonine, Tryptophan and Valine. In addition to these amino-acids growth of larva becomes more complete when proline and either aspartic or glutamic acid are added to the diet.

Carbohydrates and Fat

They are main energy source in the life of silkworm. They are also important for store component. Highly nutritive carbohydrates are glucose, fructose, sucrose, maltose and sorbitol. Any variation in the carbohydrates and fats will influence the protein also and if they are insufficient, both growth and health will be adversely affected.

Vitamins

Vitamins contribute to the internal metabolism and in the case of silkworm, vitamin C and water soluble vitamin B, B2, B6, nicotinic acid *etc.*, are very essential.

Lipids

Lipids are not only the storage form of energy but they have highly nutritive value too. Lipids such as fatty acids, triglycerides, glycerol, phospholipids, cholesterol etc., possess high nutritive value. B-sitosterol, cholesterol and stigma sterol have good nourishing effect, promote food intake and growth in the silkworm larva.

Inorganic Salt

Inorganic salts are important as structure component of the body and they are also associated with metabolism, important inorganic salts re potassium, phosphorus, magnesium, calcium, zinc, manganese, etc. Potassium phosphate and calcium silicate increase food intake in silkworm. Depending upon the period of growth, the required amount of above mentioned components vary for silkworm. During the young larval stage, there is a large requirement for water content, carbohydrates and inorganic salts. Proteins are required in all the stages and particularly during 5th larval stage a higher quantity of protein are essential. Hence, it is very important to select mulberry, which will have an ideal composition during various stages of larval growth.

Factors Influencing Silkworm Growth and Development

Various factors affect the silkworm growth and development of the silkworm. Among the most important factors that affect are environmental factors such as temperature, humidity, intensity of light, air current etc. For the silkworm to grow healthy environmental conditions should be suitable. However, different environmental conditions are required at different stages during the growth of silkworm. Moreover environmental conditions greatly differ according to season, time and place very often the conditions are not suited for growth of silkworm. Therefore, it is necessary to make an overall adjustment to the environmental factors suitable for the growth period of silkworm.

Influence of Temperature

silkworm body temperature is higher than atmosphere temperature by about 1°C. Increase in the temperature up to 30°c increase the growth of silkworm. However, very high temperature imbalance the metabolic activities and silkworm thus become unhealthy. In case of low temperature (20°C) larval duration extends due to low metabolic activities, also leads to irregular growth.

Influence of Humidity

Atmospheric humidity influences the growth of silkworm through mulberry leaf in addition to its direct effect on the silkworm. In case of low humidity leaf withers fast, rendering it unfit for silkworm to eat as a result growth of larva slows down causing in animation (weakness) and irregular moulting. On the other hand high humidity keeps the quality of leaf better and the larva grows better because the rate of respiration increases along with the increases in humidity. Blood circulation is also rapid and quantity of mulberry leaves ingested as well as quantity of food digested also increases resulting higher metabolic activity. All these result in early development. The ideal humidity in which larva thrives best is the 70-90 per cent during which physiological activities re accelerated.

Intensity of Light

As we know that silkworm is very sensitive creature. It can neither withstand complete darkness nor can tolerate excessive brightness. They prefer dim light. Hence, the ideal intensity of light, which the silkworm prefers, ranges from 20-30lux. Therefore, 16 hours of light and 8 hours of darkness is more essential for healthy growth of the silkworm larva.

Air Current

Silkworm breathes in air through spiracle and transports it through the trachea into the cells of various parts of the body. This is how oxygen from air is supplied into the body of silkworm. The energy thus produced is utilized for growth. Thus the air current has great effect upon the physiology of silkworm. The air current affects mortality and body weight of silkworm strictly. Effect of air current upon physiology of silkworm has a relation with the speed of air flow. The minute flow of 0.1-0.3m/s is more favorable for the physiology of silkworm.

Others important factors that contribute to the healthy growth of silkworm larva are:

- ✰ Quantum of feeding
- ✰ Spacing

Quantum of Feeding

In order to make silkworm growth satisfactory enough fed must be provided but quantity of feeding differs with the stage of larva.

Optimum Feeding for Larval Growth

Recommended Amount of Mulberry Leaf/Shoot for Feeding of 100Dfls (50,000 larvae)

Larval Stages	*Quantity of Mulberry Required*	
	Bivoltine (CSR)	*Cross-breed*
1st stage	5.9 Kg (Leaf)	2.3 Kg (Leaf)
2nd stage	16Kg (Leaf)	6.7 Kg (Leaf)
3rd stage	140 Kg (Shoot)	24-30 Kg (Leaf)
4th stage	460 Kg(Shoot)	70-80 Kg (Shoot)
5th stage	2880 Kg (Shoot)	700-800 Kg (Shoot)
Total	3500 Kg	800-900 Kg

Spacing

As the larvae grows in size, they require more bed area, over crowing of the larvae leads to unnecessary competition for available food and space which weakens the silkworm to a great extent. Thus crowded condition leads to under nourishment and uneven development of silkworm. Therefore, it is necessary to follow the schedule of spacing during vapors stages of development for healthy growth of silkworm.

Standard Rearing Spacing for Growth of Larva (for 100 Dfls)

Larval Stages	*Bivoltine (CSR)*		*Cross-breed*	
	At Beginning	*At End*	*At Beginning*	*At End*
1st stage	6 sq.ft	24 sq.ft	5 sq.ft	10 sq.ft
2nd stage	24 sq.ft	5 sq.ft	10 sq.ft	30 sq.ft
3rd stage	65 sq.ft	190 sq.ft	30 sq.ft	60 sq.ft
4th stage	190 sq.ft	350 sq.ft	60 sq.ft	80 sq.ft
5th stage	350 sq.ft	700 sq.ft	180 sq.ft	360 sq.ft

Rearing Technology

Unit-IV

Dr. Amardev Singh

4.1. Rearing House Requirement for Ideal Rearing House-Selection of Suitable Site and Size of Rearing House, Orientation-Model Rearing House-CSB Model-Advantages and Disadvantages of Different Rearing Houses

Rearing House Requirement for Ideal Rearing House

The requirement of an ideal rearing house for rearing silkworms for 1 acre of mulberry garden (300Dfls about 1.45 lakh) of larvae. New improved bivoltine silkworm hybrids need more space and leaf, hence all the requirement varies accordingly. In short, for rearing 100 Dfls, 480 square feet bed area is required. Following are the requirement is as under:

Sl.No.	*Non-Recurring (General)*	*Quantity*
1.	Disinfection mask and protective gum shoes	1 set
2. .	Sprayer (Power sprayer, multipurpose pump or rocking sprayer for disinfection)	1
3.	Room heaters with thermostat 2 KV blowing type or charcoal stove	3
4.	Water air cooler 9Heavy duty)	3
5.	Kerosene blow lamp	1
6.	Wet and dry bulb thermometer	3

Contd...

Table–*Contd...*

Sl.No.	*Non-Recurring (General)*	*Quantity*
7.	Foreceps 6 long	3
8.	Plastic sieve	1

Sl.No.	*Non-Recurring (Specific)*	*Quantity*
1.	Rearing building a. Chawki rearing rooms, leaf preservation-cum-preparation room, ante room. b. Late age rearing hall, ante room, leaf preservation room.	
2.	Egg transportation box	1
3.	Egg incubation chamber	1
4.	Loose egg incubation frame	6
5.	Black box	1
6.	Chawki rearing trays (wooden, 3 × 4 ×2.5)	24
7.	Chawki rearing bottom stand	2
8.	Rearing stands (to accommodate 12 trays in a row for chawki rearing)	2
9.	Feeding stand	1
10.	Ant Wells	72
11.	Leaf chopping board	1
12.	Leaf chopping knife	1
13.	Leaf mat (4 ×6 rexin)	2
14.	Leaf chamber	1
15.	Bed cleaning nets (3 ×4 , mesh size ¼ inch × 1/4inch)	48
16.	Earthen pot	1
17.	Litter basket	2
18.	Late age rearing trays (Bamboo 3.5 dia) for leaf feeding method only	120 for CB 140 for BV
19.	Rearing stands (leaf feeding method)	12 for CB 14 for BV
20.	Feeding stands (leaf feeding method)	3
21.	Shoot rearing rack 5 ×35 ×4 tiers (for shoot feeding method)	2
22.	Mounatges (bamboo chandrike) or plastic collapsible or Rotary	120 135 40
23.	Plastic basin-18 dia 9	2
24.	Plastic bucket with lid 20 ltr cap.10 ltr cap.	22
25.	Plastic mug	2
26.	Plastic boxes of different colors	3

Contd...

Table–*Contd...*

Sl.No.	Non-Recurring (Specific)	Quantity
27.	Foam pads	50
28.	Foot rugs	2
29.	Leaf chamber for late age	2
30.	Leaf basket bambooPlastic	83
31.	Cleaning nets (4 ×4)	280
32.	Cora cloth (m)	8
33.	Gunny cloth (m)	10
Sl.No.	**Recurring**	**Quantity**
1.	Paraffin paper (20m/crop)	20m
2.	Old news papers	10 Kg
3.	Formalin	15 Kg
4.	Bleaching powder	7 Kg
5.	Lime	25 Kg
6.	Bed disinfectant	12 Kg
7.	Power and fuel	
8.	Manpower	

Up to Chawki Rearing Including Leaf Picking and after IV Instar only for Rearing

		Leaf Rearing	Shoot Rearing
1.	Cleaning	3men ×1 day	3 × 1
2.	1st age rearing	4×1	4×1
3.	2nd age rearing	2×4	2×4
4.	3rd age raring	2×4	2×4
5.	4th age rearing	4×4.5	2×4.5
6.	Bed cleaning	-	2×1
7.	5th age rearing	6×8	3×8
8.	Spinning/mounting	12	12
9.	Cocoon harvesting	12	12
10.	Marketing	2	2
11.	Leaf harvest	54	-
	Total	170	85

Selection of Suitable Site and Size of Rearing House

It should be far away from residential areas, schools, hostel *etc.* It should be far away from lime kiln, brick field, insecticides and fertilizer plant, factories and godowns that produce toxic gases, so that pollution and injury to the silkworm could be avoided.

It should be at a distance from the mulberry plantation so as to facilitate easy transportation of mulberry leaves and also to prevent infection of disease pathogen from the silkworm rearing house to the mulberry plantation. Generally, the mulberry plantation should be at least 20 mts away from the silkworm rearing house. It should be near to rich sources of water to facilitate cleaning and washing of the rearing house and appliances. The tank for disinfection of silkworm rearing tool *etc.*, should be nearby. The waste water of cleaning and disinfection should b drained through the underground pipes to the storage tank, so that the surface will not be spoiled.

Size of Rearing House

The size of the rearing house depends on the area of mulberry plantation, output of mulberry leaves and mode of leaf harvesting, number of crops per year etc. Three hundred sq.ft floor areas is required to rear 200 layings of multi × bi by shelf rearing (stand rearing) and four hundred sq.ft floor areas is required for shoot rearing. Providing single standard design is rather difficult due to vast differences in geographical regions, different climatic conditions (*e.g.*, latitudes, sea level, temperature, humidity, precipitation, wind direction *etc.*) and also due to the various methods of silkworm rearing (shelf, shoot and floor). Besides, the scales of rearing management are also different. Various types of rearing houses can be made depending upon the availability of construction materials and local needs. The floor may be simple, cow dung smeared one or cemented. The way may be of mud, brick, stone or planks. Roof may be of RCC, Mangalore tile, county tile, tin, asbestos or thatched. The cost and effectiveness of such houses for rearing depends upon the types of floor, wall and roof selected. However, the most important factor is that the design of silkworm rearing house should be in accordance with the local situations and it should be practical and economical to the sericulturists (Himantharaj *et al.*, 1994).

Orientation-Model Rearing House-CSB Model-Advantages and Disadvantages of Different Rearing Houses

Orientation of the Rearing House

Silkworm rearing house is where the silkworms live and raised. The direction to which the silkworm rearing faces, directly influence on the changes of the micro-climatic conditions indoor. The orientation of the room should be such that the interior is protected from the direct sunlight. The best direction of the building will be north-south with doors and windows on north-south walls and the sides of the building in east-west direction, avoiding the direct sunlight into the rooms. If this direction cannot be secured, the next best would be north-west face and south-east back. If there is no choice, room facing east is better than west, west would be the least convenient when room faces east to west, broad verandha should be provided or shade trees should be planted on the exposed site. But in temperate and sub-tropical regions the orientation of the rearing house should be in a north-south direction so that maximum sunlight and heat is available to warm up the rearing rooms adequately.

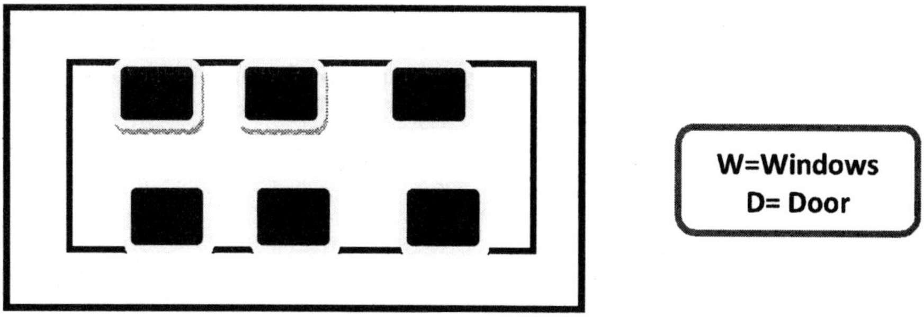

Layout/orientation for rearing house

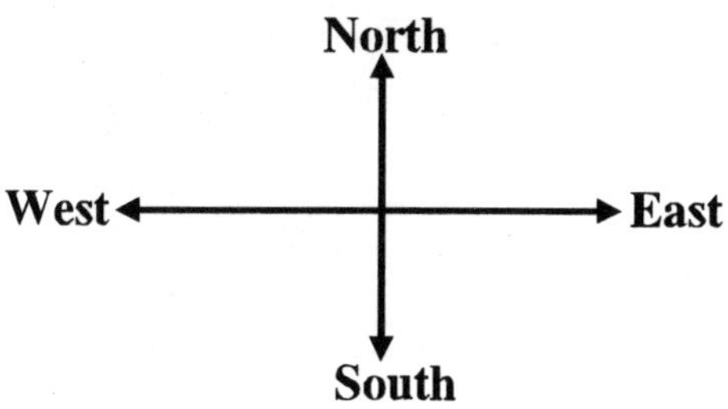

Model Rearing House-CSB Model

A model rearing house should be of convenient size. It should be rat-proof building with ledge all around to prevent rats from entering the building. The building has a verandah around and glass windows and doors to provide good ventilation and light. The ceiling of the rearing house is generally made of wood; if made of

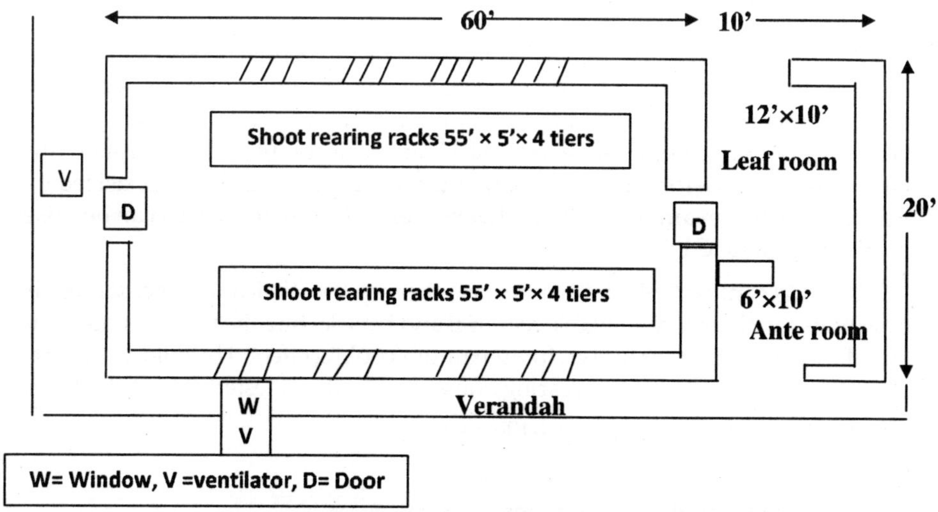

Model Shoot Rearing House (300Dfls)

concrete or tiles a false ceiling must be constructed. Ventilators must be installed to ensure free circulation of air. The rearing house should be located in such a manner as to maintain as far as possible ideal temperature and humidity conditions inside the rearing house.

Model Rearing House

Advantages and Disadvantages of Different Rearing Houses

Most of the sericulturists (farmers) especially in south India are conducting rearing in the dwelling house itself, where they face the problems for through disinfection and provision for adequate rearing atmosphere conditions; because of the above rearing the crops losses and farmers do not get better return.

Sericulture belt in India today represents varied climatic conditions, maximum temperature ranging from 46°C to 25°C and average humidity ranging from 42 to 70 per cent. But for effective management of silkworm and better cocoon crop required the temperature of 24-27°C and 70-85 per cent Relative Humidity. Thermal conditions in the convenient type of building are not satisfactory and the rooms become unbearably hot during summer months. Mechanical air conditioning is an alternative but it is too expensive for an average sericulturists. Even it may be emphasized that there is a false notion among farmers that successful silkworm crops can be raised only in high cost RCC building.

It is in this context CSRTI, Mysore has taken up the fabrication of cost effective rearing house with locally available material and by selecting the proper material for wall and roof of the rearing houses for maximum cooling effect. The following are the different models of cost effective rearing house designed and tested at CSRTI, Mysore.

- ☆ Mud wall with Mangalore tile roof.
- ☆ Mud wall with country tile roof.
- ☆ Mud wall with thatched roof.

- ☆ Planks wall with thatched roof.
- ☆ Raised platform bamboo mat wall with thatched roof.
- ☆ Kacha brick, double wall with, Mangalore tile roof.
- ☆ Split bamboo plastered with mud on either side with thatched roof.
- ☆ Wood house.

The above shown rearing houses have different advantages and disadvantages. In addition to these rearing house, RCC building type rearing house is also constructed by the sericulturists. In the state of J&K the farmers construct rearing house with the assistance provided by the Department of Sericulture, mud wall with CGI sheet roofing.

RCC Building or Pacca Type of Rearing House

Floor is made of cement concrete bed top furnished with cement mortar. Roof is made of reinforced cement concrete where in reinforced designed is governed by structure designs depending upon the span and joint/support condition. The top of roof is provided with weather proof coarse. Recommended for all regions.

RCC Building

Advantages

- ☆ More space available to carry out leaf preservation, young and late age rearing and mounting.
- ☆ Convenient to conduct cleaning and disinfection.
- ☆ It helps in getting good cocoon crops.
- ☆ With the help of optimum environmental conditions within the rearing house we can easily rear silkworms.
- ☆ Silkworm can be protected from uzi fly which is one of the harmful pest which destroy the silkworm yield.
- ☆ Adequate space is available to rear silkworms.
- ☆ Good cocoon crops can be harvested.

Disadvantages

- ☆ Rearing house requires space which may not be available to all the farmers.
- ☆ Due to high cost for construction of rearing house an average farmer cannot effort.

Mud Wall with Mangalore Tile Roof

Floor is made of hard pressed mud and stone mortar of 10 cm. thickness. Wall is made of mud. The structure is of casuarinas poles with bamboo reapers. The Mangalore tiles with intermittent ventilator tiles are used for roof. Recommended for hotter regions.

Mud Wall with Mangalore Tile Roof

Advantages

- ☆ Cost of construction is low.
- ☆ Suitable for average farmers.
- ☆ Suitable for hotter zones in the country.
- ☆ It provides excellent heat insulation, so inside a mud building is cooler in summer and hotter in winter than a building made with steel and concrete.

Disadvantage

- ☆ Rearing capacity is not so high.
- ☆ Chances of secondary contamination.

Double Brick Wall and Mangalore Tiled Roof

The floor is made of 7.5 cm thick jelly with 2.5 cm thick cement and sand mortar for a coarse finish. The wall is raised in two layers, outer layer with burnt brick and inner with kacha brick leaving an air pocket of 10 cm. in between. The two layers of brick wall are strengthened with intermittent cross-links. The inner surface of wall is plastered with lime and sand mortar. Mangalore tiles with intermittent ventilator tiles are used for roof. Recommended for hotter regions.

Brick Wall with Cement Floor and Asbestos Sheet Roof

The floor is made as per RCC model. The wall is of brick and mud or brick and cement. The roof is either asbestos sheet or tin sheet (in temperate region). Plastic sheet introduced recently is also being used. The roof structure is of casuarinas poles and reapers. Recommended for cold regions.

Brick Wall with Cement Floor and Asbestos Sheet Roof

Modification of Existing Rearing/Dwelling House

This is most common in developing countries where construction of the separate rearing house may be difficult for the farmer because of his economic condition and also when rearing is carried out as a spare time activity the construction and maintenance of rearing house may be uneconomical. Following modification can be made for the existing building where silkworm rearing is being conducted. The modifications are of two types

1. Temporary or seasonal modifications.
2. Permanent modifications.

Temporary or Seasonal Modifications

During summer season, the roof can be covered with dried coconut leaves, paddy straw, dried aquatic grass or any locally available material to reduce the temperature. Sprinkling of the water over the roof also helps in reducing the room temperature. Pendal also may be put around the building to make it cool. Wet gunny cloth may be hanged to the windows and doors to make the room cool. Mud pots filled with water can be hanged inside the rearing house to bring down the temperature of the room.

Permanent Modifications

In dwelling cum rearing houses smokeless chula should be used to avoid smoke in the rearing house. Fixing of wire mesh to the doors and windows, providing anti room and fixing of low cost automatic closing device to the doors to control the uzifly. False ceiling can be done by using thermocol, waste wooden planks, bamboo or areca nut strips, plywood sheets to avoid the fluctuation of temperature inside the rearing house. Exhaust fans can be fixed to exit the hot air from the rearing room. Floor should be plastered with lime mortor or cement to avoid the secondary contamination of the diseases and attack infestation of pests. If the rearing hall is too big, partitioned can be made so that it will be easy to maintain the temperature and humidity. Shade trees can be planted all round the building to keep the rearing house cool.

4.2. Disinfection-Importance of Disinfection, Different Disinfectants, Types of Disinfectants and their Concentrations and Formulations for Applications

Disinfection

Extermination or root out of diseases cause germs is known as disinfection. Disinfection (of room and tools) is carried out after completing the silkworm rearing and before the beginning of next one. No chemical application is made during silkworm rearing except sanitation. If diseased or dead silkworms are found, their excreta and bodies may have bacteria, viruses, fungi or other pathogens and if these contaminate the rearing room, tools, or clothes, they will cause diseases of larvae of next rearing. There are various methods of destruction of the pathogens. The simplest method is by destruction of the diseased specimens or contaminated articles by burning or burying. The most effective, simple method of disinfection is by using chemicals.

Importance of Disinfection

Rearing units, room, tools and implements are liable to infection by pathogens and these pathogens can cause serious diseases to silkworms and can lead to significant crop losses in sericulture (Kotikal *et al.*, 1989; Krishnaswamy, 1993; Pallavi and Kamble, 1997 Amardev, 2012). It is therefore paramount to disinfect the rearing room and the rearing tools. This should be done 10 days before the beginning of silkworm rearing. It is also recommended to carry out disinfection after completing the silkworm rearing. Disinfection of rearing room and units is a requirement for a successful silkworm rearing. In case of the presence of infected or dead larvae, disinfection should be carried out more thoroughly.

Disinfection: Inside and Outside of the Rearing House

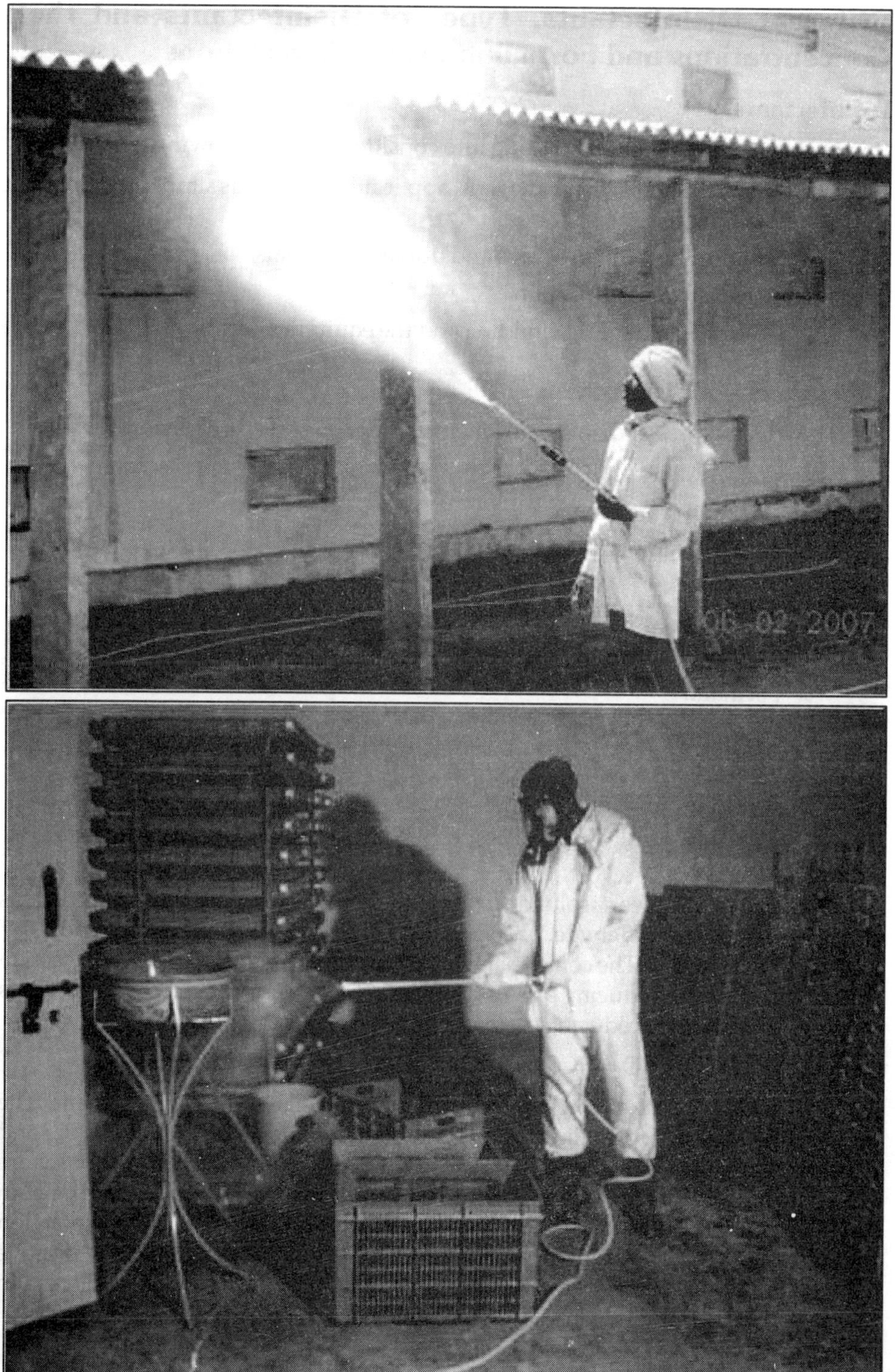

Disinfection: Inside and Outside of the Rearing House

Different Disinfectants, Types of Disinfectants and their Concentrations and Formulations for Applications

Disinfectants

Disinfectant is selected by taking into consideration of following points

- ☆ Effective against the pathogens, application method is simple and does not take long time
- ☆ Harmless to human beings and domestic animals
- ☆ Cheap and easy to obtain
- ☆ Does not damage the building and the equipments.

Effectiveness of Disinfectants

The effectiveness of disinfectant chemicals depends on three factors

- ☆ Concentration
- ☆ Duration of treatment
- ☆ Ambient temperature conditions at the time of disinfection

Common Disinfectants Used

The most commonly used disinfectants in sericulture are

- ☆ Formalin
- ☆ Bleaching powder
- ☆ Slaked lime
- ☆ Chlorine dioxide

Formalin

Formalin is an aqueous solution of formaldehyde. Commercial formalin contains 36 to 40 per cent formaldehyde. The specific gravity is 1.081 in 35 per cent and 1.087 in 40 per cent formalin. The component of formalin is HCOH. The disinfecting action of formalin is due to reducing process of formaldehyde *i.e.* formaldehyde becomes formic acid (HCOOH) reducing (deoxidizing) germ cells.

$$HCOH + O = HCOOH$$

Formaldehyde takes oxygen out of the germ cells and thus kills them. The disinfecting action of formalin is stronger at higher temperature (above 25°C) and humidity more than 70 per cent. In India, nearly 90 per cent of the rearing houses are not suitable for disinfection with formalin as they are open type and rearing cum dwelling houses. Formalin has pungent and irritating odor requiring protection against inhaling. The protective devices are not readily available. Formalin is effective at high humid (>70 per cent) condition; a constraint in tropical conditions. Formalin is reported to be a carcinogen and the uses of it need to be curtailed.

Bleaching Powder

It is white amorphous powder with a pungent smell of chlorine. For effective disinfection, a high grade bleaching powder with an active chlorine content of 30 per cent must be used. It should be stored in sealed bags, away from moisture failing which it will be rendered ineffective. The action of bleaching powder is optimal under wet and contact conditions and therefore the surface of equipment and walls should be drenched with this solution. When bleaching powder comes in contact with weak acid (CO_2 in the air), Hypochloric acid (HClO) and hydrochloric acid (HCl) are produced. Hypochloric acid reduces into HCl and Oxygen and Oxygen released is nascent oxygen. The oxygen has strong oxidizing power against germ cells. Chlorine produced has a bactericidal action. This acts upon water and produces HCl and nascent oxygen. Moreover the strong cat ion of the solution is also germicidal.

Slaked Lime

A very useful disinfectant in sericulture, especially against viruses. It absorbs moisture and can be used to regulate bed humidity and maintain hygiene. Application of lime dust in combination with bleaching powder in and around rearing houses and premises improve hygiene in the environment.

Chlorine Dioxide

Chlorine dioxide marketed as sanitech is an ideal disinfectant for sericulture. The disinfectant available at 20,000-ppm concentration is a strong oxidizing agent, effective at a broader PH range and at 2.5 per cent concentration in combination 0.5 per cent slaked lime is effective against all silkworm pathogens. It is stable and may be activated at the time of its use. It possesses tolerable odour and least corrosive at the suggested concentration.

Advantages of Sanitech Over other Disinfectants

- Sanitech is a stable product containing precursor of chlorine dioxide and forms chlorine dioxide only on activation
- Unlike chlorine it does not dissociate or react with water itself. It remains soluble in water like oxygen and exists as a gas in solution
- The disinfectant at recommended concentration is least corrosive and possess tolerable odour
- It is not known to act as a toxin to microbial pathogen and as such the microbial resistance is not expected to develop
- As it is a contact disinfectant, it is effective in all types of rearing houses
- Unlike ozone, it is also known to provide residual protection

Materials Required for Disinfection

Disinfectants, detergent, sprayer, rocking or power sprayer, buckets, measuring jars, weighing scale, gas masks, metal pans, room heaters, slaked lime, hand gloves and muslin cloth are the materials required during disinfection.

Preparation of 2.5 per cent Sanitech in 0.5 per cent slaked lime solution

A: Take 50 g activator crystals in a clean basin/bucket; B: Add 500 ml sanitech solution to 50 g activator crystals to activate the chlorine dioxide; C: Allow for 10 minutes to dissolve till colour changes to yellow; D: Add 500 ml activated yellow colored sanitech solution to 19 lit of water; E: Dissolve 100 g of slaked lime in a clean container and mix this solution with 19.5 lit of sanitech solution; F: Stir the solution thoroughly.

Measurement of Area of Rearing House

Measure the length and breadth of the rearing house including leaf preservation room, mounting room/place, etc. And calculate the floor area for disinfection.

Floor area = Length x Breadth (of the floor)

Preparation of Disinfectant

2 per cent Formalin in 0.05 per cent Detergent Solution

To prepare 2 per cent formalin + 0.05 detergent solution, mix one part of 36 per cent formalin with 17 parts of water. Then add 0.05 per cent detergent to the total formalin solution.

To prepare a known volume of 2 per cent formalin +0.05 per cent detergent solution divides the total quantity of the solution required by 18 to get the quantity of formaline required. To this formalin add water to make it up to the required quantity. Mix 0.05 per cent (0.5gm/lt) detergent to the total disinfectant.

2 per cent Bleaching Powder in 0.3 per cent Slaked Lime Solution

- ☆ Dissolve 60g of slaked lime powder in 20 lit of water (0.3 per cent)
- ☆ Dissolve 400 g of bleaching powder in 0.5 lit of slaked lime solution and make a paste
- ☆ Pour the above bleaching powder paste to rest of the slaked lime solution and shake thoroughly.

0.5 per cent Slaked Lime Solution

To prepare 1lit solution, add 5 g of slaked lime to 1lit of water.

2.5 per cent Sanitech (Chlorine Dioxide) in 0.5 per cent Slaked Lime Solution

- ☆ Add 50g of activator in a clean container
- ☆ Add 500 ml Sanitech solution to 50g activator crystals to activate the chlorine dioxide
- ☆ Leave the preparation for 5 min to allow complete dissolution of the crystals till colour changes to yellow
- ☆ Mix 500ml of yellow coloured sanitech solution with 19 lit of water
- ☆ Dissolve 100g of slaked lime in 0.5 lit of water in a clean container and mix this solution with 19.5 lit of solution
- ☆ Stir the solution thoroughly, we will get 20lit of 2.5 per cent sanitech in 0.5 per cent slaked lime solution

Estimation of the Quantity of Disinfectant Required

The disinfectant required for disinfection of rearing house is **1.5 lit/Sq m** floor area or 185 ml/sq. ft floor area. To estimate the quantity of disinfectant solution required multiply the floor area in square meter by 2.0 or the floor area in sq. ft by 0.185 which gives the actual disinfectant required in liters for disinfection of inside or rearing home. In addition, to disinfect the appliances inside the rearing house add 25 per cent and 10 per cent for outside of the rearing house to the total quantity of disinfectant solution required for disinfection of inside of rearing house.

Method of Disinfection
(After completion of silkworm rearing and cocoon disposal)

Immediately after the disposal of cocoons, collect all diseased, dead larvae, pupae, floss, left over mulberry leaves, bed refuse, silkworm faces, dust, dirt *etc.*, at one place inside the rearing house, and disinfect by sprinkling 5 per cent bleaching powder solution and dispose off by burying at 2ft depth or burning.

Preparation for Rearing

Disinfection of Rearing House and Appliances (with appliances inside the rearing house)

Power Sprayer

The required quantity of disinfectant (@2.0 lit/m floor area of the rearing house +10 per cent for outside the rearing house +25 per cent of disinfectant solution for appliances) spray using powerful jet sprayer uniformly to drench all parts of rearing house inside, outside and appliances. Keep the rearing house closed for a minimum period of 6-10 hours. Disinfect bamboo mountages with 2 per cent formalin solution. Do not spray bleaching powder solution to the mountages. After a minimum period of 18-24 hrs, shift the rearing appliances out of rearing house and sundry for 10-12 hours. Do not smear cow dung to the rearing trays and store them inside the rearing house till 5 days prior to next brushing. Rearing trays are the main source of infectious agent and most difficult and expensive to achieve disinfection. To avoid this, shoot-rearing method is recommended. This method does not require additional disinfectant for appliances as only the rack and nylon nets are used.

Disinfection Prior to Brushing

Disinfection process should start 4-5 days prior to brushing. However, the eggs may be incubated in a separate disinfected incubation room.

Disinfection of Rearing Equipments

The rearing equipments such as rearing trays, feeding stands, basins, ant wells etc; which are smaller in size and easier to handle are best disinfected by dipping them in a tank containing 5 per cent chlorinated lime for 10 minutes in the solution in a disinfection tank. A tank of 2 feet depth and 4 feet diameter is suitable for disinfection. Rearing nets, gunny cloth, towels, foam pads *etc.*, are also disinfected in the same way, thoroughly washed and dried. The bigger equipments *viz.*, stands, chandrike, leaf chamber etc;. are disinfected by spraying 2.5 per cent of sanitech in 0.5 per cent slaked lime or with 2 per cent formalin in 0.5 per cent detergent solution or with 2 per cent bleaching powder in 0.3 per cent slaked lime solution. Spray the disinfectant @35ml/sq.ft surface area. After the spray, put them together and keep completely covered with vinyl sheet for a minimum period of 6 hours. Disinfect the mountages also by following the above method. Sundry the appliances. Arrange disinfected

Disinfection of Rearing House

appliances inside the rearing house. If the prevalence of viral diseases (grasserie and flacherie) was high during the previous crop, spray 0.3 per cent slaked lime in water (3g/lit) to the rearing house and appliances @ 2lit/sq.m floor area + additional requirements.

Three days before brushing, disinfect the rearing house and appliances by spraying 2 per cent bleaching powder in 0.3 per cent slaked lime solution or 2.5 per cent sanitech in 0.5 per cent slaked lime or 2 per cent Formalin +0.5 per cent detergent solution. The quantity of disinfectant solution required is calculated and sprayed. After disinfection spray, keep the room closed preferably for 24 hrs.

Two days before brushing, dust 5 per cent bleaching powder in slaked lime powder @200 g/sq. m at the entrance of the rearing house and passage to it. Sprinkle water @ 1lt/sq. m floor area; open the windows of the rearing house and ventilate to drive off all the odour of disinfectant. Prevent the entry of unauthorized persons into the rearing room to avoid contamination of rearing house and appliances.

One day before brushing arrange appliances for chawki rearing and maintenance of hygiene. Keep the late ages rearing room and mounting hall closed and open only one day before the late age larvae are to be shifted into the rearing house.

Maintenance of Hygiene during Silkworm Rearing

- ✰ Avoid borrowing the rearing appliances. Do not use appliances without disinfection. Avoid overlapping of rearing.
- ✰ Maintain personal and rearing hygiene throughout the rearing. Special consideration for maintenance of hygiene be given during the chawki rearing. Restrict the entry of persons into the rearing house.

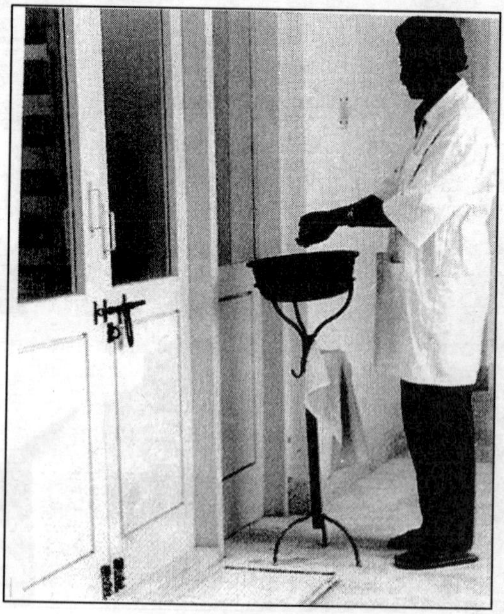

Hygiene Maintenance

- ☆ Surface disinfects the silkworm eggs before head pigmentation stage with 2 per cent formalin for 5-10 minutes and washes with water. Dry them in shade and incubate following the guidelines.
- ☆ At the passage to entrance of rearing house, sprinkle 5 per cent bleaching powder in slaked lime @18g/sq.ft. An area of 6'x8' may be covered.
- ☆ Rearer or any person entering to the rearing house must disinfect foot and hand before entry. These persons should step on to foot mat at the entrance containing a mat soaked in 2 per cent bleaching powder in 0.3 per cent slaked lime solution. Foot mat should be soaked in the disinfectant daily.
- ☆ Wash hands with 2 per cent bleaching powder in 0.3 per cent slaked lime solution and then rinse with clean water. Replace the disinfectant every day.
- ☆ Pick up diseased/unequal/suspected diseased worms and dispose into 5 per cent bleaching powder in slaked lime in a basin. Keep in basin covered with a lid and change every 3-4 days.
- ☆ Disinfect the hands after picking the diseased worms by washing in 2 per cent bleaching powder in 0.3 per cent slaked lime solution.
- ☆ Clean the rearing bed using bed cleaning net and disinfect after every use by dipping in 2 per cent formalin solution for 10 minutes. Wash hands with disinfectant.
- ☆ Spread vinyl sheet for the collection of bed refuse and shift bed refuse into manure pit. Disinfect the vinyl sheet after use. Use by dipping in 2 per cent bleaching powder in 0.3 per cent slaked lime solution.
- ☆ Rear silkworms always on rearing seat paper (news paper); change as and when soiled.
- ☆ Wipe the floor after bed cleaning with 2 per cent bleaching powder in 0.3 per cent slaked lime solution. If the floor is a mud floor, dust 5 per cent bleaching powder in slaked lime at an interval of 3-4 days.
- ☆ Dust the bed disinfectant as per the schedule, quantity and precautions. Feed the worms 30 minutes later. While extending the bed also, apply bed disinfectant to the empty tray.
- ☆ Do not store mulberry leaves inside the rearing room. Store in a separate disinfected room.
- ☆ Feed good quality and sufficient quantity mulberry leaves for robust larval growth. Provide recommended spacing sufficient ventilation for healthy growth of later instar worms.
- ☆ Avoid contamination of mulberry. Use separate baskets for collection of mulberry leaves for feeding to the worms.
- ☆ Avoid injury to silkworms while rearing and mounting for spinning cocoons. Sprinkle bleaching powder in mounting place.
- ☆ Pick diseased and non-spinning larvae from mountages and dispose them into 2 per cent bleaching powder in 0.3 per cent slaked lime solution in a basin. Wash hands and feet while coming out of rearing house/mounting hall after completion of work at every visit.

- ☆ Brushing, before the harvest of an earlier crop should be avoided.
- ☆ The rearing of chawki worms and late age worms should not be in one room.
- ☆ Paraffin paper should not be used after one rearing. After the rearing is over old paraffin paper and old newspaper should be burnt.
- ☆ The compost pit should be away from the rearing house.

4.3. Selection of Silkworms Races/Breeds for Rearing-Advantages and Disadvantages of Bivoltine, Multivoltine and their Hybrids, Estimation of Leaf Quality and Yield Appropriate Time for Estimation of Leaf Yield

Silkworm breed/race should be selected based on:

- ☆ Local environmental conditions.
- ☆ Rearing infrastructure/facilities.
- ☆ Experience and technical skill of sericulturists.
- ☆ The suitability of silkworm breed/race can be decided based on the region-wise popularity.
- ☆ Performance of different silkworm breed/race.

The following tips will be helpful to understand that breed can be regarded as good:

Hybrids are more yielding than pure races. The increase in percentage of cocoon yield in hybrids over pure race per 100 DFLs may be seen from the following table:

Name of the Silkworm Breed		*Cocoon Yield per 100 DFLs (Kgs)*
Multivoltine	Pure (PM)	30.0
	Hybrid (PM × NB_{18})	42.0
Bivoltine	Pure ($NB1_8$/NB_7)	35.0
	Hybrid (NB_{18} × NB_7)	43.0

Cocoon quality in a pure race and hybrid

Characters	*Multivoltine Pure (PM)*	*Multi x Bivoltine (PM×NB_4D_2)*	*Bivoltine Pure (NB_{18})*	*Bi × Bi (NB_{18} × NB_7)*
Cocoon yield/100 Dfls (Kg)	30.0	42.0	35.0	43.0
Cocoon shell (per cent)	15.0	18.0	22.0	23.5
Silk yield/100 Dfls (Kg)	1.75	4.20	5.00	7.16
Raw silk (per cent)	10.0	12.0	18.0	20.0
Renditta	13	10	8.5	8

(Source: Annual Report 2001-2002, DOS, Karnataka.

From the above tables, following conclusion can be drawn

- ☆ Hybrids are more yielding than pure race.
- ☆ Cocoon quality is superior in hybrids.

Multivoltine Hybrid Cocoons

Bivoltine Hybrid Cocoons

Bivoltine hybrids are superior in cocoon yield and cocoon quality. At the same time, cross breed is strong breed and it can adjust to local environment. But, the bivoltine hybrids are more productive under suitable conditions.

Therefore, selection of silkworm breeds/race for rearing based on your rearing infrastructure, skill, local environment, seasons, etc. Thus, the right choices of silkworm breed matching the season/region/condition increases stability of the crop, productivity and quality which in turn increase the profit.

Common silkworm breeds

Name of the Breed	*Cross-Breed/ Bivoltine Hybrid*	*Recommended Condition/ Zone/Season*
Pure Mysore × Bivoltine	Improved cross breed	Irrigated, throughout the year
Pure Mysore × C.Nichi	Traditional cross breed	Rainfed, throughout the year
SL-KS PM × NB_4D_2	Sex limited cross breed	Irrigated, throughout the year
MH1× NB_4D_2	White cross breed	Irrigated, throughout the year
MH1× C. Nichi	White traditional cross-breed	Rainfed, throughout the tear
NP_2 × KSO $_1$	Bivoltine hybrid	Irrigated, throughout the year
CSR_2 × $CSR_4$$CSR_2$ × CSR_5 (August–February)	Bivoltine hybrid	Irrigated during favorable season
CSR_{18} × CSR $_{19}$	Bivoltine hybrid	Unfavorable season (Mar- July)
BL_{23} × NB4D_2	Cross breed	Rainfed, throughout the year
BL_{24} × NB_4D_2	Cross breed	Irrigated, throughout the year
BL $_{67}$ × CSR $_{101}$ (Cauvery)	Cross breed	Irrigated, throughout the year

Estimation of Leaf Quality and Yield Appropriate Time for Estimation of Leaf Yield

After deciding the suitable silkworm breed, the assessment of mulberry leaf yield and quality is of prime importance for successful silkworm rearing.

Assessment of Mulberry Leaf Quality

The leaves best consumed and supporting good growth and development of silkworm larvae are the best quality leaves. They contain optimum amounts of:

- Moisture
- Protein
- Carbohydrate
- Ash
- Fiber

Good quality mulberry leaves fit for silkworm rearing can be obtained from garden by adopting optimum agronomical practices like application of manures and fertilizers, timely irrigation, inter-cultivation, plant protection measures etc.

Chemical analysis to evaluate the mulberry quality in the field is difficult. Therefore, the quality is assessed through physical characters such as the growth of the plant, size of the leaves, colour of leaves, leaf thickness etc. Estimation of moisture content, being a simple method, can be conducted wherever possible. The following aspects should be considered in leaf quality assessment:

- ☆ Mulberry variety
- ☆ Season
- ☆ Cultivation system
- ☆ Agronomical practices/inputs provided
- ☆ Leaf maturity (duration in days from last leaf harvest to assessment day) on assessment day
- ☆ Colour of leaves
- ☆ Shoot/shoot let growth
- ☆ Number of leaves per shoot/shoot let
- ☆ Size of leaves
- ☆ Fresh and dry weight of leaves
- ☆ Moisture

Assessment of Mulberry Leaf Yield

Successful silkworm rearing requires good quality leaves suitable to different instar in sufficient quantity. The assessment of these two parameters, quality and quantity of mulberry leaves is of prime importance in sericulture.

Time for Mulberry Leaf Assessment

The correct age for leaf assessment is 30-35 days from the last leaf harvest or last pruning. From the day of assessment to brushing, it is a minimum of 10 to 12 days and from brushing to peak utilization of leaf is another 18–20 days. The mulberry crop period from one harvest to another is roughly 70 days in close plantation and shoots pruning system but it is roughly 60 days in leaf feeding system. The correct time for leaf yield assessment is 30 to 35 days after pruning in shoot feeding system and 25 to 30 days in leaf feeding system.

Standard Number of Plants in Different Spacing per Acre

Before going for actual mulberry leaf yield assessment, let us know the number of plants per acre under different spacing followed in the field.

Procedure to Assess Leaf Yield

The different steps are:

- ☆ Identify the specific plot for which assessment of leaf yield is to be conducted.
- ☆ Study the cultivation system.
- ☆ Ensure that the assessment is done at the correct time.
- ☆ Follow the following steps for calculation of leaf yield.

Spacing in Feet	Area per Plant (Sq. ft)	No. of Plants
2 × 2	4.0	10890
2 × 3	6.0	7260
3 × 3	9.0	4840
3 × 4	12.0	3630
4 × 4	16.0	2722
(2 × 3) × 5	8.0	5445
(2 × 3) × 4	7.0	6223

Step 1

Expected number of plants in the plot is estimated as standard number of plants x area of the plot.

Standard number of plants per acre = 43,560 sq. ft./plant spacing.

Thus, in 3′ x 3′ system of plantation there are (43,560/9) 4840 plants per acre and if the plot size is 0.7 acre the expected number of plants are 4840 x 0.70 = 3388.

Step 2

Effective plant density is calculated based on the actual number of plants out of 200 plants in the expected area. This is calculated in percentage as Actual plant number x 100/200.

Thus, if there are only 180 plants out of 200 plants in the expected area, the effective plant density is 180 x 100/200 = 90 per cent

Step 3

Actual number of plants in a plot of 0.7 acre is thus 3388 x 90/100= 3049

Step 4

Leaf yield per plant is assessed based on actual harvest from ten plants at random. Leaf yield/plant is calculated as:

Weight of leaves harvested (Kg)/Number of plants

Say, weight of leaves harvested is 1.5 Kg from 10 plants. The leaf yield per plant is 1.5/10 = 0.150 Kg.

Step 5

Leaf yield on assessment day is calculated by multiplying leaf yield per plant and number of plants. Thus, 0.150 x 3049 = 457 Kg is the leaf yield on assessment day in a plot of 0.7 acre.

Step 6

From the period of assessment day to the peak growth stage roughly 30 to 35 days. The mulberry growth and expected increase in leaf yield should be considered to arrive at the leaf yield at the stage of matching maximum utilization for rearing purpose. Mulberry leaf yield almost doubles within one month period. Therefore, the leaf yield is assessed by doubling the estimated leaf yield on assessment day. Thus, 457 x 2 it will be 914 Kg.

Step 7

Thus, in the plot considered for calculation of leaf yield the brushing capacity ranges from 91 Dfls for PM x NB_4D_2 or 76 Dfls for NB_4D_2 x NB_7.

4.4. Incubation-Definition-Environment Conditions Required for Incubation and their Influence on Egg Development-Methods of Incubation-Conventional Method, Incubator, Low Cost Incubation Devices

Incubation-Definition-Environment Conditions Required for Incubation and their Influence on Egg Development

Silkworm eggs after receiving from grainages must be surface sterilized by dipping in 2 per cent formalin solution for about 10 minutes and dried in shade before incubation. Conditions of incubation affect the hatchability and viability of silkworms. Incubation of eggs aims at uniform development and ensures uniform hatching. The incubation temperature and humidity requirement are different for acid treated bivoltine eggs and hibernated bivoltine eggs. Incubation of silkworm eggs should be done in a room having temperature of 25°C, relative humidity of 80 per cent, air current of 0.3m per sec, and 16 hrs. light (15-20 lux), 8 hrs dark per day. The term incubation can be defined as preservation of silkworm eggs under optimal environmental conditions, which enables the embryo inside the eggs to develop normally and hatch maximum larvae on the expected day. In the incubation room it is desirable that the temperature and humidity are kept at optimum level to the best of

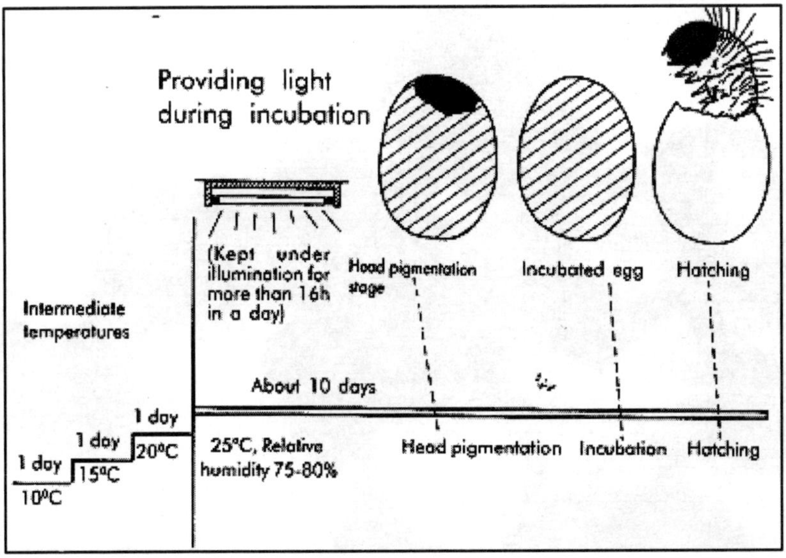

ability especially in the later period of incubation. If the humidity in the incubation room is less, it will lead to mortality of eggs, poor hatching and weak larvae.

Incubation has profound influence on the voltinism, larval health and on the yield and quality of cocoon crop. During incubation, eggs should be spread in a single layer to provide uniform humidity and temperature.

Black Boxing of Silkworm Eggs

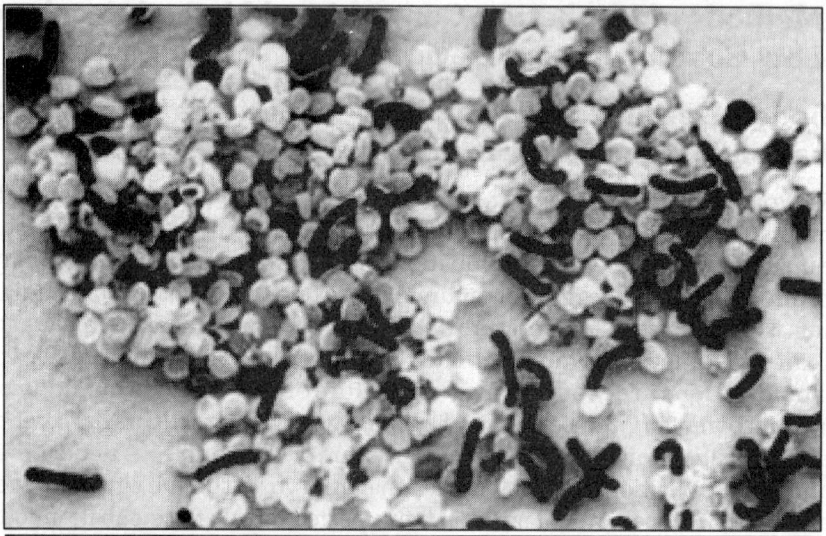

After Proper Incubation of Eggs we get Excellent Hatching

Eggs incubated as above hatch in 10-11 days after incubation has started. A day later *i.e.,* 24 hr before hatching eggs turn bluish/brownish called as blue egg or body pigmentation stage. All eggs are kept in darkness at pin head stage which is called black boxing of eggs. Darkness arrests the hatching of the fully developed eggs but facilitates the lagging embryos to develop faster. Eggs after black boxing can be stimulated to hatch by exposing them to sunlight stimulus.

Incubation is the method of protecting the silkworm eggs under ideal conditions for the natural development of embryo in it. After the eggs are released from cold storage, the environment under which they are protected has a profound influence on the development of the embryos, uniformity of hatching, robustness of the larvae and ultimately the cocoon yield (Tazima, 1978).Therefore, it is essential to provide maximum care during incubation. To get uniform, good hatching in a single day, an incubation temperature of 25-26°C, 75-80 per cent relative humidity and 16 hours light/day should be provided.

Methods of Incubation–Conventional Method, Incubator, Low Cost Incubation Devices

Methods of Incubation

Incubation is done by two methods, *viz.,* constant temperature incubation and raised temperature incubation. In constant temperature incubation, incubation is carried out till hatching at a constant temperature of 25-26°C, and this method is adopted for acid treated eggs and non-hibernating eggs. Raised temperature incubation method is used for incubating hibernating eggs. In this, soon after the release from cold storage the eggs are preserved at 10-15°C for 3 days, 18-20°C for 2 days, 23-24°C for 4 days and 25-26°C till hatching. This avoids sudden and violent shock to delicate embryo in the silkworm eggs, which are exposed from 2.5°C to 25°C and this helps in uniform development. But generally, constant temperature incubation is in practice.

Devices for Incubation

Incubation may be undertaken individually or collectively. The farmer and the latter may undertake the former by incubation centres. Incubation centres exist in China and Japan, but not in India.

(a) Incubation Chamber

This is made of an iron sheet with a double-layered wall, into which water can be poured to maintain the humidity. It has a ventilator on top and an electric heater or coal furnace at the bottom to maintain the optimum temperature. This kind of chambers is used in China. In India, an attempt has been made to design an auto controlled incubation chamber, which is a double walled metallic box with insulating materials between the walls, provided with exhaust fan and heater with thermostatic control.

(b) Incubation Room

If a large number of eggs are to be incubated, an incubation room is used. The room should be built in regions where there is large production of eggs and in places with convenient transportation. The incubation room must be built in such way to maintain a uniform temperature and humidity and should have sufficient illumination and good ventilation.

In India, to maintain the required temperature and humidity conditions, silkworm eggs are incubated in BOD incubator or spread in a wooden tray, encircled with wet foam pads and covered with paraffin paper. The former is expensive and the latter needs operation skills. Because of this disadvantage in both, Central Sericultural Research and Training Institute, Mysore has developed two incubation devices suiting to different socio economic conditions of the farmers or low cost incubation in India. They are:

1. Earthen pot for individual farmer for 250 to 300 dfl's incubation
2. Double brick wall chamber for large-scale incubation of 5000 to 6000 dfl's.

Earthen Pot

Well baked earthen pot/earthen flowerpot of wide mouth about 15" dia is chosen. This pot is filled with a layer of 2– 3" thick clean sand and made wet. This pot is provided with a row of holes about half inch dia and 2-3" above the sand level. It is covered with clean wet cloth.

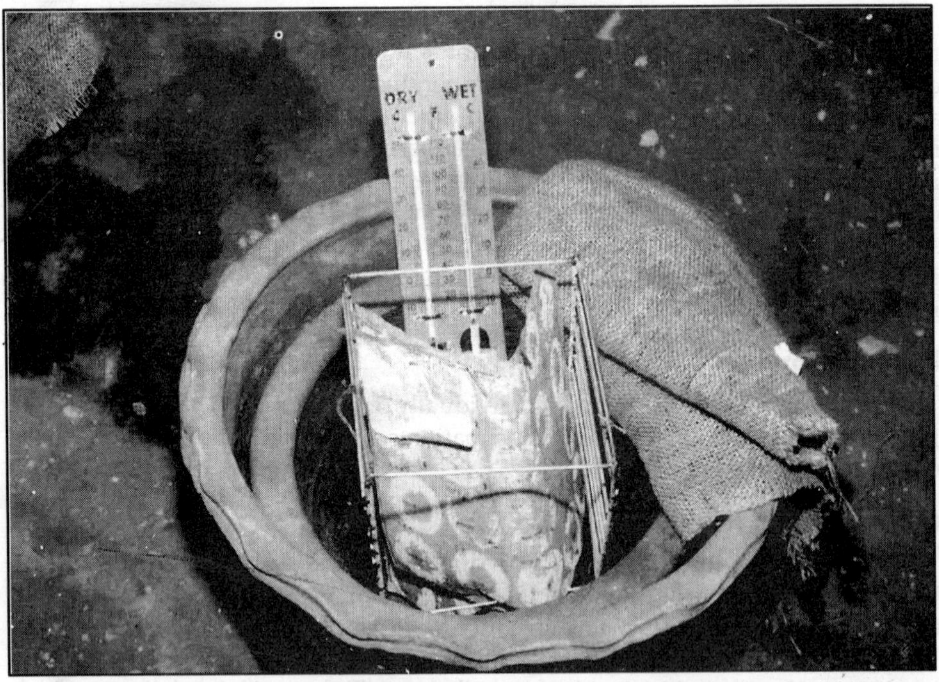

Earthen Pot Incubation

The sand is kept wet one day prior to incubation (pre-conditioning). The laying are tied to a rod and hung inside the pot and the pot is covered with a wet cloth and placed over an ant well. Monitor the wetness of the cloth/sand regularly. The temperature is reduced by 5-10 per cent. Eggs incubated by such method hatch uniformly and larvae grow better. This is suitable for individual farmers and is highly effective in dry and high temperature areas.

Double Brick Walled Chamber

It is recommended for large-scale incubation undertaken by big farmers, CRC and grainages. The chamber is constructed by using burnt bricks, sand and cement. The inner and outer walls should have about 3" gap between them throughout, that is filled with loose clean and sand. While constructing, wire mesh may be fixed to avoid rodent and predators. The standard size of the outer wall is 6′ x 4′ x 3′. The inner wall is 4′ x 2′ x 3′ with a gap of 3" between them. This accommodates 5000-6000 dfls.

Egg sheets are tied to a metal rod with sufficient gap between sheets and are hung in the chamber. The sand layer has to be soaked periodically with clean water depending upon the environmental conditions. The temperature and humidity conditions inside the chamber are on par with that of earthen pot. The same chamber can be used for loose egg incubation also.

Of the two methods, double brick wall chamber is found more useful for hotter regions where temperature is high and humidity is low and for large scale incubation, suited for farmers having large land holdings, co-operative chawki centres and chawki rearing centres under Government or private sectors also.

Double Brick Wall Chamber

4.5. Preparation of Brushing, What is Brushing, Different Brushing Methods, Loose Egg-Net and Sheet Eggs-Tapping Method-Selection of Leaf for Brushing-Advantages and Disadvantages of Different Types of Brushing

Preparation of Brushing

Before brushing, rearing facilities should be prepared according to the number of silkworms to be reared. Tender mulberry leaves should be chopped to 3-5 mm size. When the worms crawl over into the tray worm bodies should be disinfected for disease prevention by using a fine-mesh sieve to dust a fine powder of formalin (3 per cent). Bird feather or fine camel hair brush is used for brushing. On the expected day of hatching expose the eggs to light at 7 a.m. after 3hours by 10 a.m. complete hatching takes place. Sprinkle chopped mulberry leaves over the hatched larvae. The larvae crawl over the leaves transfer the larvae along with the leaves to rearing trays.If you are going to rear the loose eggs, spread two layers of mosquito net over the hatched larvae. Sprinkle the chopped leaves over the net and after 30 minutes; transfer the top net along with the larvae to the rearing tray. Lower net helps in holding back the unhatched eggs and empty egg shells.

What is Brushing

The process of transferring of newly hatched larvae from egg sheet to rearing seat is called brushing. For this, either a soft camel brush or birds feather is employed. On the expected day of hatching the eggs are exposed to light at 7:00 am. Good hatching can be obtained by 10:00 am. This is the ideal time of brushing. Delayed brushing should be avoided. If hatching is irregular, take two days brushing separately in time. Newly hatched larvae can also be refrigerated at 10 °C and 80 per cent humidity and uniform brushing can be taken up.

Brushing of Newly Hatched Larvae

Different Brushing Methods, Loose Egg-Net and Sheet Eggs-Tapping Method

Brushing Methods

Brushing method depends on the type of egg production method *i.e.*, loose eggs or sheet eggs:

In the case of eggs prepared on egg cards or sheet, the card with newly hatched worms are placed in the rearing trays or boxes and tender mulberry leaves cut into small 0.5 cm squares are sprinkled over the egg cards. The hatched silkworm crawls onto the tender leaves and start feeding. Later the cards are removed and any worms still left on the card are tapped on to the rearing bed. After some time the bed is uniformly prepared in the rearing tray and the first feeding of mulberry leaves is given.

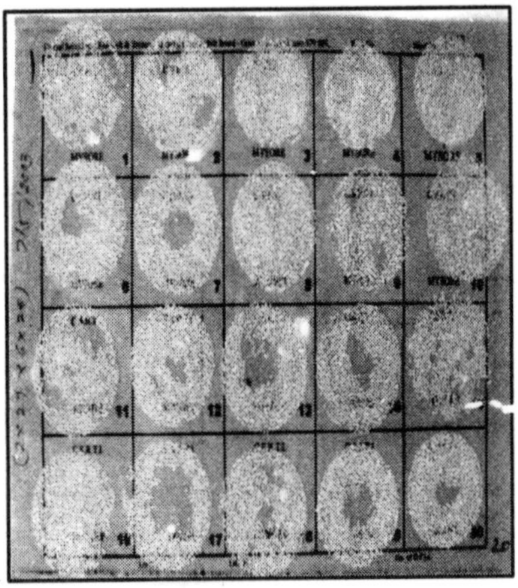

Sheet or Card Eggs

Sheet or Card Eggs

The various brushing methods are adopted in sheet eggs namely:

Feather Method

This is a popular method in India. Egg card is held vertically above the rearing bed and by gentle strokes of feathers the larvae are pulled out.

Husk Method

Powdered husk is sprinkled over the freshly hatched larvae on the egg card. Place few leaves on the centre of the husk sprinkled. The larvae crawl up the layer of husk to reach the leaves which are placed over the centre of the husk. As the larvae crawl up the layer of husk themselves and are brushed by feather along with husk, the chances of injury are less.

Cloth/Paper/Net Method

This is an adaptation from the method used for loose eggs. A cloth/paper/net with meshes is placed above the egg card and fresh chopped leaves are spread over it. After half an hour, larvae attached to the underside of net and those that have crawled on to the leaves are transferred to the bed gently.

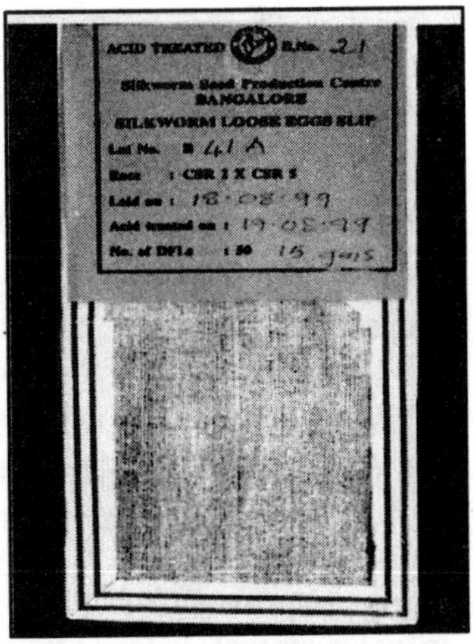

Loose Eggs

In the case of loose eggs brushing is carried out as follows: a net with small holes (mosquito netting) is spread over the box containing the hatched larvae, and mulberry leaves cut to the size indicated above

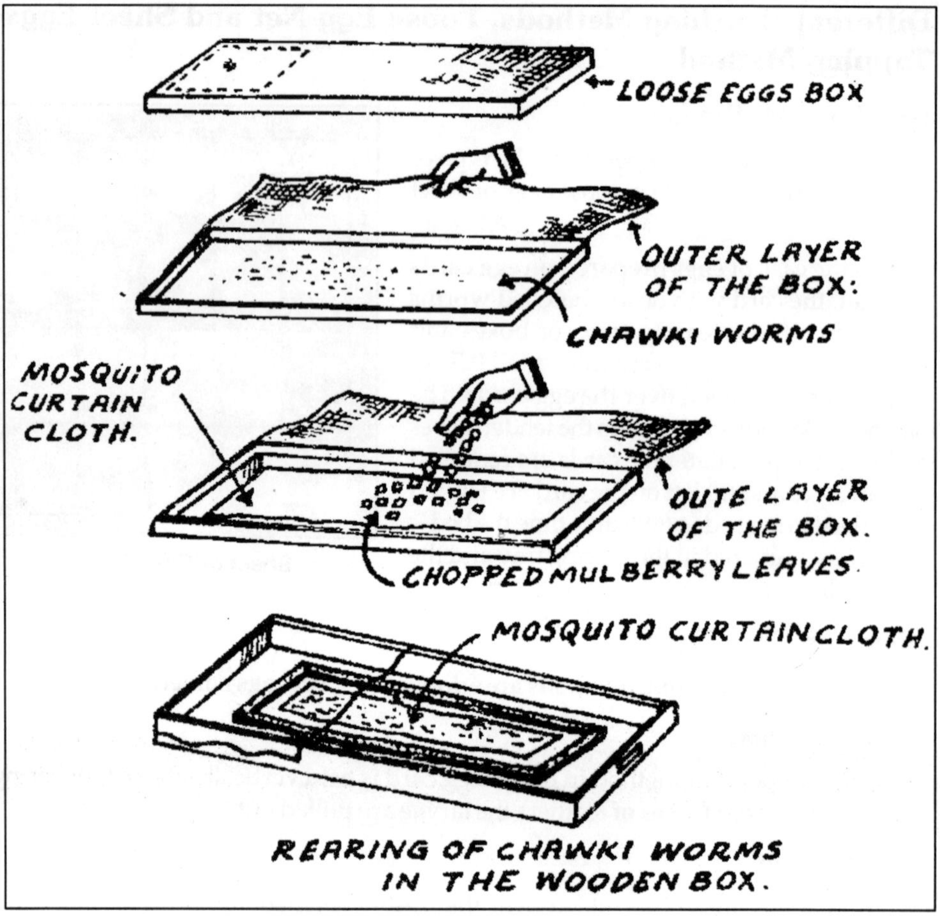

Brushing of Loose Eggs

are scattered over the net. Paper with small slotted holes or perforations can be used in place of mosquito netting. When the worms have crawled over to the leaves, the net with worms and leaves is transferred to the rearing tray.

Selection of Leaf for Brushing

The newly hatched silkworm has a low water content in the body. But, once it starts eating mulberry, the water content shows a rapid increase up to the 2nd instar. It is therefore essential to select the leaves which are soft, succulent and rich in water content *etc.*, for young age silkworms larvae.

Since silkworms do not drink water, they get moisture from leaves so they must be fresh, soft and rich in water content, protein, carbohydrates etc. Importance of leaf moisture content in relation to the performance of the silkworm has been reported by Narayanaprakash *et al.* (1985) and Paul *et al.* (1992), who observed that the decrease in water contents in feed affected different energetic parameters and they also reported

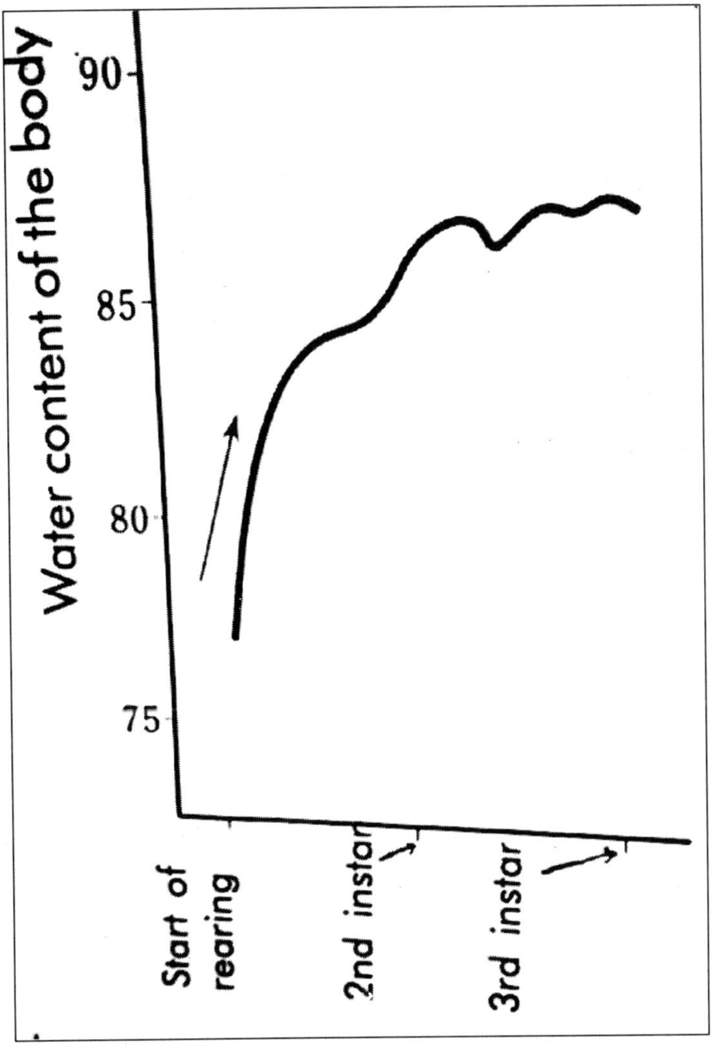

The newly hatched silkworm larvae have a low water content in the body. But once it starts eating mulberry, the water content shows a rapid increase up to 2nd instar so therefore it is necessary to feed the leaves which have more water content especially in early instars.

Changes in Water Content in the Body of Silkworm

that assimilation of food converted into body tissue decreases with decreasing moisture contents. Mulberry leaves suitable as food for silkworm must contain several chemical constituents such as, water (80 per cent), protein (27 per cent), carbohydrates (11 per cent), minerals and vitamins. It must have favorable physical features such as suitable tenderness, thickness, tightness, *etc.*, in order to render them acceptable by silkworm.

Leaves for young silkworm must be soft and succulent, rich in water content (78-80 per cent) and contain proteins (26-28 per cent), carbohydrates (11 per cent) and minerals at the desired level.

Top 3-4 full grown leaves immediately below the growing buds have relatively

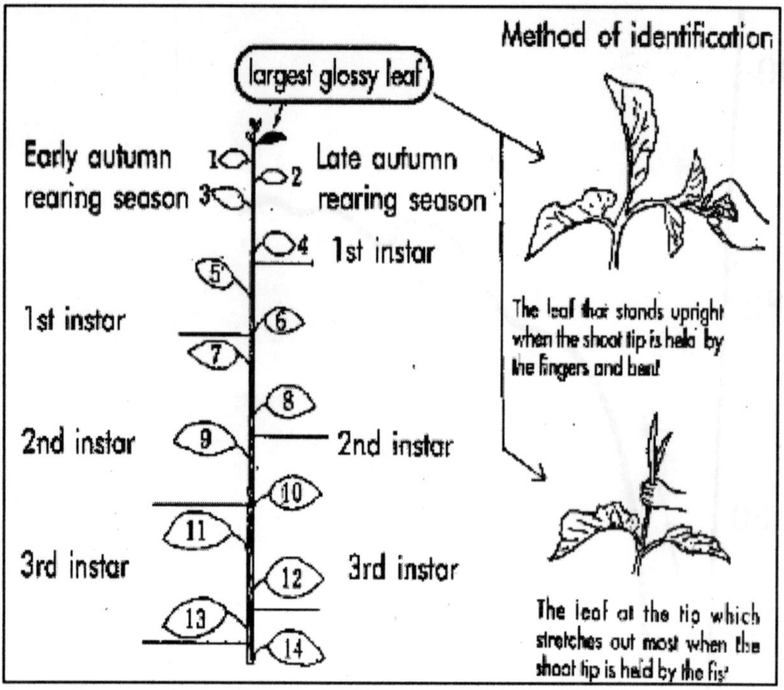

How to Identify and Select Mulberry Leaves for Early Instars Silkworm Larvae

more moisture and highly nutritious from the point of view of growth requirements of brushed or young silkworm larvae. These leaves are comparatively richer in proteins, soluble in sugar, carbohydrates and possess less fiber content.

Unit-V

Dr. Amardev Singh

5.1. Harvesting of Leaf-Methods and Time-Transportation and Storage of Leaf for Chawki and Late Age Rearing

Harvesting of Leaf-Methods

Harvesting of leaves is an important activity for successful silkworm rearing. There are mainly two methods of harvesting of leaves *viz.* (a) leaf picking and (b) whole shoot harvest depending on the type of rearing practice:

1. Leaf picking
2. Whole shoot harvest

Leaf Picking

In this method the leaves are harvested by picking the leaves individually. In southern states, after the harvest of leaves from the main branches the terminal buds are removed and the auxiliary buds are allowed to develop into many lateral branches. Subsequently the leaves from the lateral branches are harvested by picking. This method has the advantage of harvesting the leaf according to the growth stage of the silkworm. Tender leaves are harvested to feed the young age silkworm and matured leaves for late age silkworm rearing. The disadvantage of this method is that it is highly labour intensive and therefore, becomes expensive. In leaf picking method, 6 harvests can be made in a year at an interval of 55-60 days per crop. Normally after annual bottom pruning, first leaf plucking starts after 8-10 weeks and for subsequent harvests picking of leaf is followed at an interval of 6-8 weeks.

Leaf Picking

Whole Shoot Harvest

In this method of harvest, whole shoot is cut at the stump height of 20-25 cm from ground level and the entire shoot is used for feeding the silkworm. The crop cycle is maintained at 70 days from pruning to harvest of shoots to complete the rearing and thus 5 shoot harvests per year can be made at an interval of 70 days. Harvesting of leaf and pruning are followed simultaneously in this method.

Shoot Harvesting

Shoot harvest method has many advantages like,

- ☆ Reduced expenditure on labour for harvest, transportation and feeding the silkworm.
- ☆ The number of feeds per day is reduced considerably.
- ☆ Leaf moisture can be retained for longer period.
- ☆ Shoots can be easily preserved.
- ☆ It is more hygienic.

Time-transportation

The most convenient time for harvesting of mulberry leaves/shoot in the cool hours of the day-early in the morning or late in the evening as during this period retention of freshness and succulence remain in the mulberry leaves for a reasonable period. Therefore, it is advisable to harvest the leaves during these periods so that the moisture loss involved during transportation of the leaves from the mulberry field to the rearing houses is reduced to a minimum.

When the leaf/shoot is transported to the rearing house after harvesting, it starts loosing moisture very fast particularly when the atmospheric temperature is high and the humidity is low. This makes leaf unfit to feed the silkworm. Therefore it is very essential to transport the leaf from the field to the rearing house with great care to avoid moisture loss. This is more important when the leaves are harvested for young age silkworm rearing.

In order preserve the leaf moisture it is desirable to construct the rearing house/shed near the mulberry field for easy and quick transportation of leaf/shoot. This will ensure the supply of fresh leaves for silkworm rearing and also reduces the cost of transportation. Harvest of leaf/shoot should preferably done during cooler hours and transported to the rearing house in baskets covered with wet gunny cloth. When large quantity of leaf/shoot is required to be transported it must be covered with wet gunny cloth or polythene sheets to reduce the loss of moisture.

Storage of Leaf for Chawki and Late Age Rearing

It is quite clear that the success of silkworm rearing mainly depends on the quality of mulberry leaf fed. Even though the quality of the leaf is good, if it is not preserved properly, the quality of leaf deteriorates. The preservation of leaf requires low temperature and low humidity, whereas the chawki rearing requires high temperature and high humidity. The temperature and humidity inside the rearing room will alter with age of the silkworm and chances of mixing with litter is more. Hence separate place is desirable.

Leaf and Shoot Harvest and Preservation while Carrying

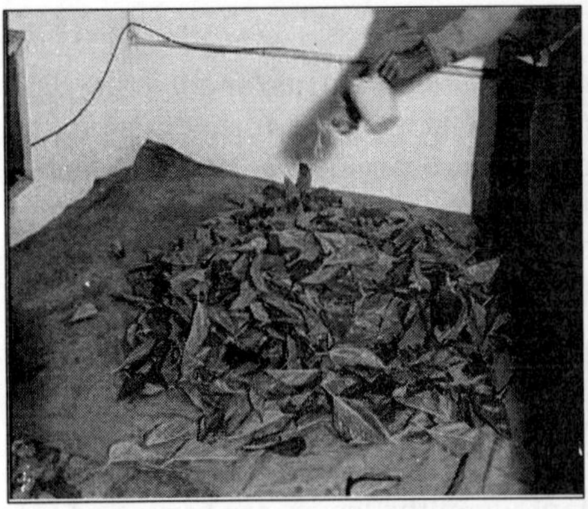

Harvested Leaf and Shoot Preservation

The ideal place for construction of leaf preservation room is north east corner of the rearing house which is the coolest place in the building. The leaf preservation room should have low temperature and high humidity in order to maintain the freshness of the leaves. The surrounding of the house should be kept cool by planting trees around the house. The room should be dark and cool to check the evaporation of water from the leaves.

Mulberry leaves in general should be preserved in a moist cool and clean place. The tender leaves meant for young age silkworm can be storage in boxes, baskets or jars covered with clean wet cloths. In tropical areas such as India, leaves for young age silkworms are usally preserved in earthen pots covered with wet cloths and placed on moist stand. Since the quantity of leaf involved is very small this method can be followed with advantage as the cool pot keeps leaves properly preserved.

Leaves meant for late age silkworms which are required in bulk quantities can be stored well if loosely packed and kept in cool room with periodical sprinkling of water to prevent withering. Leaves can also be conveniently stored by covering them under polythene sheets which prevent evaporation of water from the leaves. In tropical areas where temperature are high, leaves can be best preserved in big leaf chambers covered all sides with wet gunny cloth.

In the dry summer months when the moisture content in the leaves themselves is low and is further lost through rapid evaporation after harvesting, it is absolutely necessary to reinforce leaf moisture by constant sprinkling of water over the leaves and to preserve them under wet gunny cloth or in leaf chambers in order to have satisfactory cocoon crops. It should be borne in mind that such preserved leaves do not carry water droplets on the surface when being fed to the silkworms in the beds.

During leaf storage, high humidity and low temperature are maintained in the preservation room and periodic rotation of leaves is suggested to avoid fermentation and to release the respiratory heat.

Methods of Leaf Preservation

Various methods are followed. They are:

Conventional Method

Large quantity of leaf can be stored on a clean floor over gunny cloth, in loose layer with adequate air pockets and cover with wet gunny cloth. In summer, sprinkling of water on leaf and frequent wetting of gunny cloth is required.

Leaf Preservation Chamber Method

A convenient method is to store leaves in wooden chambers (size: 5′x3′x2′) covered with wet gunny cloth. For all practical purposes, this method is very effective.

Earthen Pot Method

This method is practiced for chawki leaf preservation. The earthen pot is buried in sand; the sand is made wet by sprinkling water. Mulberry leaves are kept in the earthen pot; the pot is covered with lid.

5.2. Chawki Rearing-Importance-Environment Conditions Required for Chawki Rearing-Leaf Requirement and Selection and Different Chawki Rearing Method Moulting; Symptoms and Moulting Care during Pre-moulting, Moulting and Post-Moulting Periods

Chawki Rearing

The rearing of first two instars of silkworm form the young age rearing. But the third instar is also closer to the young age in its nutritional and environmental requirements. Therefore, young age rearing represents growing of larvae up to second or third moult. The success of young age rearing technology depends on the perfect understanding of the requirements of silkworms, manipulation of their nutritional and environmental conditions to obtain maximum growth and robustness. Young silkworm need more care and attention as their resistance to disease is low. But they are resistant to high temperature, high humidity and bad ventilation. Cool and low humidity conditions are bad for the larvae throughout the growing stage as these conditions injure health of the larvae and lead to lower cocoon quality. Effect of pesticides, chemicals and gases are more injurious during the first instar. Of the total leaf requirement only 6.33 per cent is utilized during early three instars, but the larvae grow 400 times in body weight and 300 times in body size, during this period. Thus, maintenance of the quality of nutrient leaf supply from brushing to the end of third stage becomes very crucial to crop success.

In newly hatched larvae, the body water content remains very low, but it increases rapidly till the second instar. It requires high water content in mulberry leaves (75-80 per cent) at this initial stage. At the early instar, ingestion of mulberry leaves is slow but digestion is high. But with increases in growth ingestibility increase and digestibility decreases. The amount of ingesta and digesta per given time increases in accordance with rise in temperature. The digestibility is however, not so affected by environmental temperature; but within optimum range of temperature it increases a little with rise of temperature. The amount of ingesta and digesta is higher in the case of healthy larvae than unhealthy ones and higher in case of soft leaves than coarse leaves. Growth rate of the first instar larvae is very fast and if nutrition is poor, the larval growth gets retarded.

Importance

The importance of young age silkworm rearing to raise healthy stock has been fully appreciated. The important aspects of chawki rearing management are a suitable separate raring house, a well maintained mulberry garden with assured irrigation facility and adequate agro inputs besides well trained manpower at workers and managerial level. Practically the entire quantity of eggs used for raising cocoon crops are first reared in fully equipped young age rearing centre/co-operative centres specially organized for this purpose under expert technical supervision (Krishnaswami, 1988). In developed countries like Japan, China and Korea, about 95 per cent of the farmers receive chawki reared larvae (young age silkworms) whereas in India it is only 10–15 per cent at the most. Both nutritional and ecological requirements during young and late age of silkworm are different. Young age worms require high temperature, high humidity, tender and succulent mulberry leaves. Of the total leaf requirement only 6.33 percent is utilized during the chawki stage, where 400 times increase in silkworm body weight, 300 times in body size and 500 times in silk gland weight are achieved (Yokoyama, 1962).

The insecticides, disinfectants, injurious gases *etc.*, affect the larvae more in early instar than in late instars. The success of young age silkworms and their physiology, where manipulation of nutritional and environmental conditions suited to maximum growth and the care to raise robust and healthy batch of young age silkworm is the aim. By adopting the perfect chawki rearing procedure, maximum potential can be exploited.

Environment Conditions Required for Chawki Rearing

Environmental factors such as temperature, humidity, light and air current during rearing have a remarkable influence on the growth of the larvae and ultimately on cocoon crop quality. However, this influence is not same throughout the rearing period, but varies in different stages of growth. Hence, it is necessary to provide most favorable climatic conditions suited to the silkworms at different stages.

Temperature

Silkworms are poikilothermic animal and they do not possess a complete central nervous system to regulate the body temperature, but they have a primitive mechanism that can regulate body temperature by itself. The body temperature conforms to the surrounding temperatures. When the temperature of the surroundings increases, the body temperature of the silkworm also rises accordingly. When this occurs, the physiological activities of the silkworm are accelerated *e.g.*, ingestion, digestion, absorption, excretion, blood circulation and respiration rate. Rearing temperature directly affects the physiology of the silkworms, in nutrient absorption, digestion, blood circulation, and respiration. The first three instars of silkworms require high temperature *i.e.,* 29, 28 and 27°C respectively. However in the next two instars, the need in temperature decreases (23-24 °C).

When the temperature goes up high, the activation of enzymes is slackened or even stopped. If the temperature is very low the activation of the enzymes becomes weak and because of this the worms become sluggish, eat less, develop slowly and lose weight. At the farmer level, it might be difficult to provide optimum temperature but it is paramount that in the course of rearing the silkworms, the temperature should not fall below 20°C or rise above 30°C. This is because the temperature suitable for normal development of silkworms ranges from 20°C to 30°C. The best results, however, can be achieved if optimum temperature for each instar is maintained throughout the rearing period. In the absence of a thermometer, the feeling a person gets in a room will give guidance on how hot or cold it is. The right temperature is that which gives a feeling of comfort, neither hot nor cold. A rearer should watch closely for the withering of the leaves after a short period of feeding as this is a clear sign of high temperature. In a dry season, temperatures are usually high while in a wet season they are low. Wide fluctuations in temperature are harmful to worms and should be avoided.

Relative Humidity

Humidity influences the growth and physiology of silkworms in two ways: First, it has effect on water content and evaporation in the body of the larvae (through feeding). This parameter plays a great role in the regulation of the body temperature. Secondly, relative humidity has an effect on the preservation of mulberry leaves and therefore indirectly on the larva's appetite. The optimum relative humidity for the first 3 instars must be about 80 per cent while in the last two instars about 75 per cent. Under high humidity the body temperature of the silkworm rises, blood circulation and, respiration rate increase. Furthermore, the leaf intake by the silkworm and the digestion tend to increase accordingly. The spinning and pupating are longer in high humidity conditions. Humid air also helps to keep mulberry leaves fresh. With enough supply of fresh leaves, silkworms will be well fed, grow rapidly and healthy. However, if the humidity is high, water evaporation in the body of the silkworm will be restricted and the worm's resistance to disease weakened. It is therefore, important to maintain the recommended levels of humidity as high humidity quickens the spread of fungal diseases in rearing beds. When the air is very dry the mulberry leaves wither very fast, and this reduces silkworm's leaf intake. In dry air, water evaporation from the worm's body is high thus affecting the digestion, absorption and utilization of the nutrients by the worms. In this case, the silkworm becomes small in size.

Air and Ventilation Conditions

The rearing room should have enough fresh air to avoid accumulation of Carbon dioxide. Fresh air is necessary because the silkworms (particularly the 4th and 5th instars) have high requirements in oxygen. Excessive accumulations of Carbon dioxide will lead to vomiting of intestinal juice and result in the death of the worms. Other sources of Carbon dioxide in the rearing room other than that present in the air include workers' breath, waste matter from worms, burning of charcoal while trying to raise the temperature, etc. Carbon dioxide in the rearing room should not exceed 1 per cent and this can be achieved by proper ventilation.

Light

It is recommended a moderated intensity of lighting with duration of 15-16 hours of light and 8-9 hours of darkness. Silkworms prefer dim light during the day and darkness at night. Intense light or the direct solar radiation must be avoided in the rearing rooms. In practice, the duration of lighting is that of day, without the use of additional lighting. A simple way of finding out whether the light is enough is by holding a paper with some writing on it under the light. If one is able to see but not necessarily read the message, then that light is enough for worms during the day.

Requirement of Temperature and Humidity during early instars

Environmental Factors	*I Instar*	*II Instar*	*III Instar*
Temperature	28°C	27°C	26°C
Humidity	85-90 per cent	85 per cent	80 per cent

Besides, the environmental conditions for producing good quality cocoons following factors do influence on cocoon productivity and these are:

- ✩ Laying (eggs) eggs of a good race;
- ✩ Providing quality mulberry leaves to the silkworms;
- ✩ Proper handling of eggs during the incubation period, giving them the required conditions;
- ✩ Successful young age silkworm rearing;
- ✩ Good care of intermediate and late age worms;
- ✩ Special attention to mounting and spinning so that cocoon formation is done in a suitable environment (Amardev and Himantharaj, 2008).

Leaf Requirement and Selection

Since silkworms do not drink water, they get moisture from leaves so they must be fresh, soft and rich in water content, protein, carbohydrates *etc.* Importance of leaf moisture content in relation to the performance of the silkworm has been reported by Narayanaprakash *et al.* (1985) and Paul *et al.* (1992), who observed that the decrease in water contents in feed affected different energetic parameters and they also reported that assimilation of food converted into body tissue decreases with decreasing moisture contents. For chawki rearing, the largest glossy leaf method is adopted to pluck the correct leaves. The largest glossy leaf is the one, light green and glossy, being the largest among the first few leaves. From glossy leaf to 5 or 6 leaves below for I instar, another 4 or 5 leaves for II instar and further down up to all tender leaves for III instar are used in young age rearing.

Selection of Leaf for Young Age

Leaf Requirement and Bed Space for 100 Dfls of Bivoltine Hybrids (CSR_2 x CSR_4)

Instar	*Day*	*Leaf (Kg)*	*Space (sq.ft)*	
			At Beginning	*At End*
I	1	1.0	6 sq.ft	24 sq.ft
	2	1.8		
	3	2.5	8300 larvae/sq.ft	2100 larvae/sq.ft
	4	0.6	3	
	Total	**5.9**		
II	1	5.0	24 sq.ft	65 sq.ft
	2	8.0		
	3	3.0	2100 larvae/sq.ft	800 larvae/sq.ft
	Total	**16.0**		

Leaf Size for Young Age Silkworms

Leaf should be cut to optimum size at every stage of growth. As the worms in the young age are tiny size, chopped leaves have to be used to feed them so that leaves could be spread uniformly over the worms in the bed and the worms also can have ready and easy access to the leaves.

Chopping also helps in loosening and spreading the bed when the bed is required to be dried prior to the moulting. But, traditional practice of finely shredded leaves tend to dry too fast necessitating too many feeds and at too frequent intervals. If the leaves are chopped into big pieces or used as entire leaves without chopping, the larvae tend to get overcrowded in localized spots which are not desirable. Size of the chopped leaves at different stages should be as given below:

☆ Size to begin with – 0.5–1.00 cm^2

☆ End of first instar – 1.5–2.00 cm^2

- Second stage – 2.00 cm^2
- At the end of second instar – 3.0–4.0 cm^2

Towards the close of every instar, *i.e.,* just prior to the moult, one to two feeds are given as final cover feed and these are invariably given slightly reduced size leaves, *i.e.,* about 1 cm^2 for the first instar and about 1.5 – 2.0 cm^2 for the second instar.

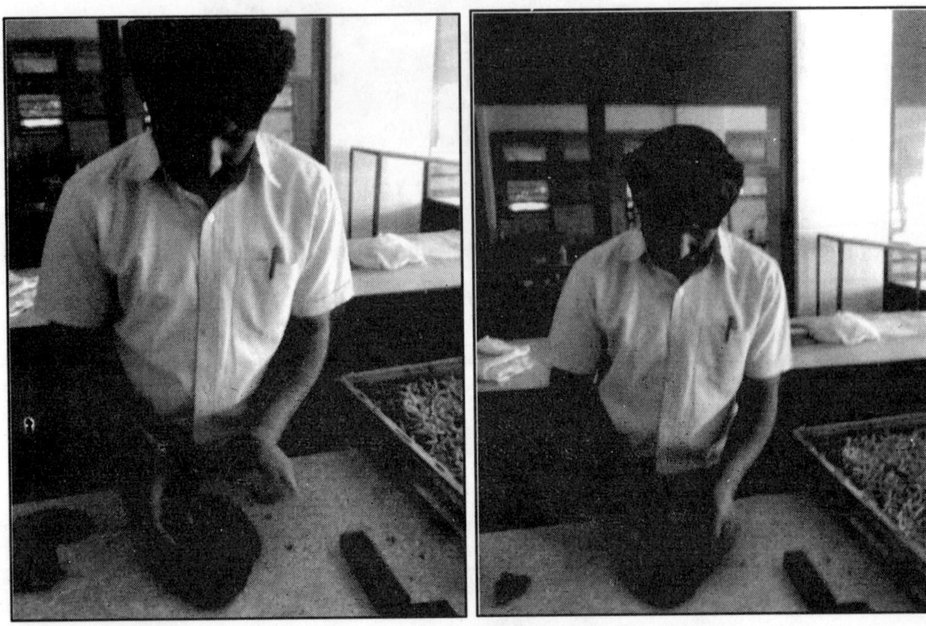

Arrangement of Leaves

Leaves Ready for Cutting

Cutting of Leaves

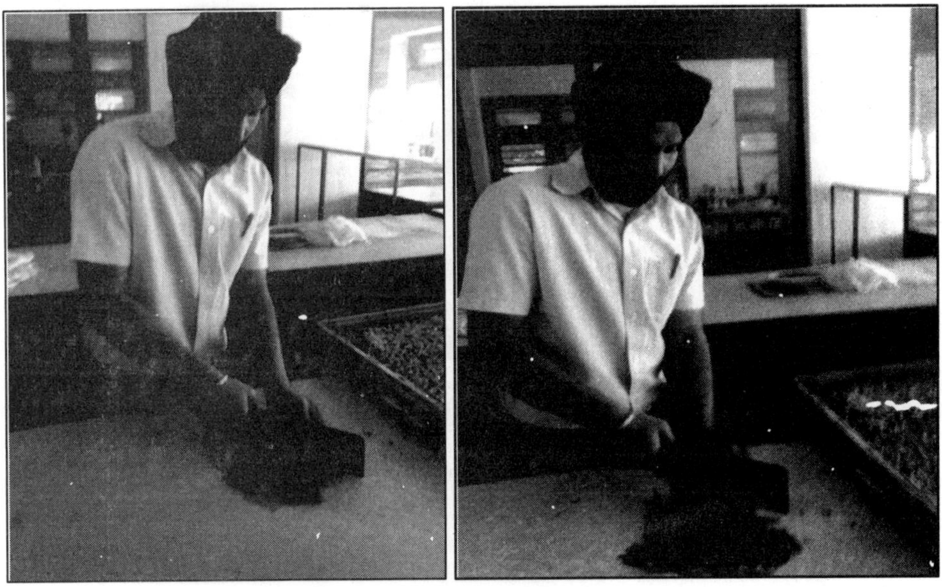

First Feeding to Newly Hatched Larvae

Selection and Cutting of Tender Leaves for Feeding to Young Age Silkworms

Different Chawki Rearing Method

There are different methods of young age silkworm rearing which are in practice. All the methods aim at preventing driage of mulberry leaves fed to the silkworms and to maintain proper temperature and humidity in the rearing bed. The most popular methods of young age rearing are box rearing, stand rearing and chamber rearing. In all the cases paraffin paper is used as both seat and cover. Wet foam pads are used all round the bed to increase the humidity. But use of foam pads without proper disinfection can lead to contamination and disease. Hence, instead of wet foam pads, use of wet folded old news paper which can be thrown away after each rearing, is more ideal when humidity is below 50 per cent.

i. Box Rearing

This method is practiced when temperature and humidity are lower. Wooden trays or plastic trays of 4' x 3' or 3' x 2' and 4" depth are used. During eating period, trays are arranged one above the other upto a convenient height on a chawki rearing stand like a box. Arranging of the trays in this method can increase the rearing bed temperature and humidity. Thirty minutes before feeding and during the moulting period, paraffin paper cover and wet old news papers are removed and the trays are arranged in a cris-cross pattern for allowing the rearing bed to dry. This method is ideal for chawki rearing centres as minimum space is required for large scale rearing.

ii. Stand Rearing

In the rearing house, optimum temperature and humidity are available or temperature is high, young age rearing is done in trays on a stand like late age

Box Rearing

Stand Rearing

rearing. Paraffin paper is used as seat and cover for young silkworms in a tray. This method is not convenient for carrying out large scale rearing, as it requires more space for rearing.

iii. Paraffin Paper or Warp Up Rearing Method

Paraffin Paper or Warp Up Rearing

In this method the rearing frames are covered with paraffin (pure paraffin paper with melting point above 55¡É should be used; perforated paraffin paper may be used if placed 10cm above bed); the larvae are spread on the paper; and a further sheet is placed over the larvae to preserve moist conditions. Normal feeding frequency is two times a day.

iv. Co-operative Rearing

It was a common practice to rear the young silkworms up to the advanced stage in the farms. But the rearing of all the larval stages involved a lot of time. Therefore, a new method was devised in which collecting rearing of only young age is carried out in different farms or Chawki Rearing Centres (CRC's) after which the larvae were distributed to the farmers for rearing up to the advanced stage. This type of co-operative rearing of the young age has many advantages. It is becoming more and more popular and is being increasingly followed. Co-operative rearing of the young age is also economical besides being profitable. For example, the labour force is reduced to 50 percent per individual rearing. Expenditure too is cut down to 40 percent.

Spacing

Requisite area in relation to its physical growth and developmental is very mush essential for proper growth of the silkworms (Krishnaswami, 1988). Many farmers go for overcrowded rearing either for want of rearing space equipments or lack of knowledge about requisite area in relation to silkworm stages or for conserving mulberry leaves. This leads to under nourishment and uneven development of the silkworms and naturally to poor harvest of cocoons. The crowded conditions also increase accumulation of gases, heat and fermentation of faecal matters in the rearing bed, particularly during high temperature and high humidity conditions (Sengupta and Yusuf, 1974). Under such unhygienic conditions, the silkworms become weak, due to inadequate mulberry leaves and results to unequal and unhealthy growth of larvae, which often leads to low cocoon crop (Ullal and Narasimhanna, 1978).

Young age rearing is often conducted in a crowded condition. Spacing required for 100 Dfls bivoltine silkworms (40,000 larvae) for chawki rearing is as follows.

Space Requirement in Early Instars

Instar	*Beginning Sq. ft.*	*End Sq. ft.*	*Larvae/sq. ft.*
I	4.00	18.00	2300
II	18.00	55.00	750
III	55.00	120.00	350

Providing Recommended Spacing to the Intermediate Silkworms Larvae

Bed Cleaning

Periodical removal of left over leaves and worms' excreta may be undertaken and is referred to as bed cleaning. It is necessary for proper growth and proper hygiene. Generally, the litter cleaning is not preferred during the first instar, as it could lead to increase in missing percentage of larvae in the first instar. Every day before the first feeding the rearing bed is extended to allow fresh air and dry the old

Bed Cleaning by Using Net

Transferring of Worms into Bed

Making the Bed by Hand

leaf and litter. This makes the larvae crawl upon the surface of the bed. Cleaning is done twice during second instar, first on the day of resumption of feeding and the next before the worms prepare for second moult. In the third instar also two cleaning is sufficient, first after second moult and second before settling for third moult. Since the young silkworms are delicate, they are not handled directly. Cleaning is done by nylon net of mesh size 1.00cm^2. Cleaning net is applied and the feeding is given above the net. At the time of next feed the net along with the larvae are transferred to another tray and fresh feed is given only after giving sufficient spacing.

Moulting; Symptoms and Moulting Care During Pre-Moulting, Moulting and Post-Moulting Periods

Silkworms settle for first moult by 3.5 days from the date of brushing if temperature (28° C) and humidity (85-90 per cent) are maintained correctly. When worms are preparing for moult, the quantum of feed and leaf size are reduced. The last feeding has to be given as late as possible in order that silkworms can eat mulberry leaves sufficiently. If the temperature in the premoulting period is high, some silkworms have a tendency to moult early without sufficient feed. If the humidity is also high the growth of the larvae becomes irregular. Settling for moult with insufficient feed is stronger in races which has high ratio of cocoon shell to cocoon weight. The moulting period of silkworm, which has set in moult in an insufficient feed is shorter than that of the silkworms which have set in moult in a sufficient feed. The time of larvae setting for the moult which is reared in humid condition is postponed than that of the larvae which are reared in a dry condition.

When larvae under moult, paraffin paper cover is removed and rearing bed is allowed to dry through free aeration by arranging the trays in a cris-cross pattern in box rearing. The first moult lasts for 20-24 hours. In case the growth of the larvae is irregular, the late moulting larvae should be picked up by chop sticks or gathered by

Dusting Vijetha on Young Age Larvae during Moult

nets if they are more. The rearing bed in moulting period is to be dusted with lime powder to dry the bed fast. In general, the first feeding is performed at the time when all the larvae have exuviated. Thirty minutes prior to feeding, bed disinfectant (RKO/ Vijetha) @ 60-120 g./100 Dfls in the first and second instar respectively) should be dusted on newly moulted larvae. The second instar generally lasts for 2-2.5 days. Litter cleaning in the second instar before moult is to be performed sufficiently early in order to reduce the missing larvae. All the premoulting care is to be followed in this instar as practicing in the first moult. The second moult lasts for 20-24 hours.

Moulting Symptoms

A) Pre-Moult Symptoms

- ☆ Shinning body.
- ☆ Small dark brown head capsule.
- ☆ Frequent raising and lowering of head and thorax.

B) At Moult-Symptoms

- ☆ Constant raising of head and thorax.
- ☆ Movement less.

C) Post-Moult Symptoms

- ☆ The mouth part is broader.
- ☆ Body is dull with loose skin.

Shinning Body

Constant Raising of Head and Thorax

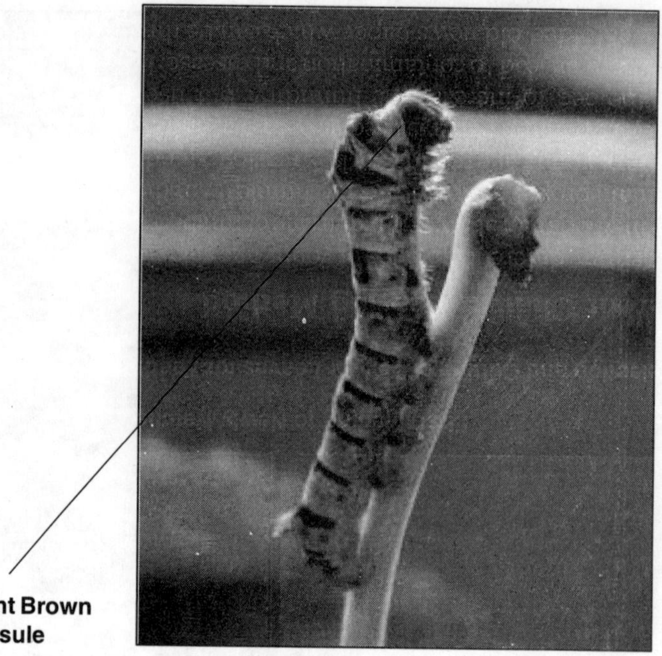

Large and Light Brown Head Capsule

- ☆ Shed off skins are easily seen on the bed.
- ☆ The worms are active and move around.

Moulting Care during Pre-Moulting, Moulting and Post-Moulting Periods

Silkworm settled for first moult in three days from the day of brushing if the temperature and humidity are maintained at optimum level. The following are symptoms of moulting larvae:

- ☆ Larval body becomes lustrous and shining.
- ☆ Prothoracic segment becomes bulged.
- ☆ Appetite weak.
- ☆ Head become narrow, pointed and black.

Pre-Moulting Car

- ☆ Reduce the leaf size and leaf quantity
- ☆ Remove top paraffin paper and wet old news paper pad.
- ☆ When 85-95 per cent of worms are settled for moult, stop feeding; apply slaked lime to dry the rearing bed.
- ☆ Maintain 24-25°C and 60-70 per cent humidity in the rearing room.

Under Moult Larva

Dusting of Slaked Lime

- ☆ Provide adequate ventilation during moulting.
- ☆ Do not disturb the worms while moulting.

Post Moulting Care

- ☆ Give the first feed after 95 per cent of the worms come out of the moult after half an hour of dusting the bed disinfectant *viz.*, Vijetha / Ankush / Resham yothi *etc.*, subjected to the availability to the farmers.

5.3. Late Age Rearing-Spacing and Leaf Requirement-Environmental Conditions Required, Frequency of Feeding Bed Cleaning Schedules, Different Rearing Methods-Shelf, Shoot and Floor Rearing-Advantages and Disadvantages

Late Age Rearing

Rearing of 4th and 5th instars silkworm is termed as late age rearing and it is easy as compared to young age rearing. However, proper care, maintenance of hygienic condition and good quality of mulberry leaves in sufficient quantity is a must to exploit the potential of a particular breed and to get good quality and quantum of cocoons. During this stage, larvae need comparatively less temperature and humidity and are a real feeding stage. The worm develops silk gland and secretes silk and keeps the energy stored for metamorphosis from the larva to pupa and moths. Late age rearing especially 5th instar needs more labour and attention to harvest good cocoons failing which all the activities get upset leading to poor yield than the anticipated. Most of developed and developing countries are facing labour problem, hence sericulture in developed country is reducing every year. Labour requirement in late age rearing especially 5th age is about 50 per cent of the total mandays required. Hence, efforts are being made to reduce the labour input and to maximize the cocoon yield. The 4th and 5th instar silkworm differ from those in earlier stages in many respects.

Spacing and Leaf Requirement

Success of silkworm crop and cocoon quality depends upon spacing given in each instar in the rearing bed and quantity of leaves provided in each instars as per the requirement, inadequate supply of mulberry leaves lead to poor growth of the silkworms as a result cocoon crops so produced will deteriorate both qualitatively and quantitatively.More or less space in rearing bed affects the economics of cocoon crop significantly, too much spacing leads to leaf wastage and higher leaf cocoon ratio while overcrowding in rearing bed leads to insufficient consumption of feed, poor growth, incidences diseases, resulting in low cocoon yield of inferior quality. To exploit growth potential of the hybrids and realizing best cocoon crop with better quality cocoons, it is paramount to provide recommended spacing and leaf to the silkworms. Everyday larvae grow in volume and accordingly space has to be increased to realize better growth. The recommended space and leaves requirement for 100 Dfls for CSR hybrids and Cross-breed is shown below.

Recommended Amount of Mulberry Leaf and Rearing Bed Space for 100 Dfls (CSR hybrids–leaf feeding)

Instar	*Day*	*Quantity of Mulberry (Kg)*	*Space (sq.ft)*	
			At Beginning	*At End*
I	1	0.8	12 sq.ft	24 sq.ft
	2	1.6		
	3	2.0		
	4	0.6		
	Total	**5.0**		
II	1	5.0	24 sq.ft	65 sq.ft
	2	7.0		
	3	2.0		
	Total	**14.0**		

Contd...

Table–*Contd...*

Instar	Day	Quantity of Mulberry (Kg)	Space (sq.ft)	
			At Beginning	At End
III	1	14	65 sq.ft	150 sq.ft
	2	22		
	3	22		
	4	7		
	Total	**65**		
IV	1	28	150 sq.ft	350 sq.ft
	2	52		
	3	62		
	4	54		
	Total	**196**		
V	1	84	350 sq.ft	650 sq.ft
	2	120		
	3	180		
	4	220		
	5	276		
	6	160		
	7	80		
	Total	**1120**		
	Grand Total	**1400**		

Recommended Amount of Mulberry Leaf and Rearing Bed Space for 100 Dfls (CSR hybrids – shoot feeding)

Instar	Day	Quantity of Mulberry (Kg)	Space (sq.ft)	
			At Beginning	At End
I	1	0.8	6.0 sq.ft	24 sq.ft
	2	1.6		
	3	2.0		
	4	0.6		
	Total	**5.0**		
II	1	5	24 sq.ft	65 sq.ft
	2	7		
	3	2		
	Total	**14**		

Contd...

Table–*Contd...*

Instar	*Day*	*Quantity of Mulberry (Kg)*	*Space (sq.ft)*	
			At Beginning	*At End*
III	1	28	65 sq.ft	150 sq.ft
	2	44		
	3	44		
	4	22		
	Total	**138**		
IV	1	55	150 sq.ft	350 sq.ft
	2	110		
	3	125		
	4	108		
	Total	**398**		
V	1	168	350 sq.ft	600 sq.ft
	2	240		
	3	360		
	4	440		
	5	552		
	6	320		
	7	160		
	Total	**2240**		
	Grand Total	**2750**		

Note: I and II instar leaf feeding and III to V instars shoot feeding.

Environmental Conditions Required

To obtain expected cocoon quality and yield, various environmental factors, quality of leaf, proper disinfection and proper hygienic conditions have to be maintained and are dealt separately below:

Temperature

Temperature plays a vital role in the life cycle of organisms and directly influences ingestion, digestion, assimilation and growth of silkworm. Silkworm rearing can be done within the temperature range of 23° C to 28°C. Optimum temperature range is 23 °C to 25 ° C and it also help in improving survival rate and cocoon characters. Standard rearing temperature recommended for 4th and 5th age instars are given below.

Optimum Temperature Required during Late Age Rearing

Instars	*IV*	*V*
Temperature (°C)	24 – 25	23 – 24

It is observed that larval duration increases by one day by lowering the temperature especially larvae exposed to 24 °C.Cocoon yield and cocoon characters are poor in the batches exposed to higher temperature. Temperature changes with the seasons (summer, rainy and winter) and within the day also, affects cocoon quality and production. Temperature beyond 36° C especially during 4th and 5th age affects the survival rate.

Humidity

Humidity also plays a very vital role like that of temperature in silkworm rearing for young and late age and for quality cocoon production. Comparatively low humidity during late age gives better results of cocoon production. It is reported that the grown larvae become weak at high humidity. As temperature and humidity are predisposing factors for various diseases, it is required to ensure that bed humidity is kept as per optimum requirement, beyond which the silkworms becomes susceptible to diseases like grasserie, muscardine etc. Humidity affects directly the physiological functions of silkworms and indirectly the driage of leaves in bed. Humidity requirement is comparatively less and requirement of humidity instar wise is given below:

Optimum Relative Humidity during Late Age Silkworm

Instars	*IV*	*V*
Relative humidity per cent	75	70

High humidity decreases growing period of silkworm, and accelerates the activity of physiological functions of silkworm. On the contrary, low humidity increases growing period of silkworm.The humidity required during feeding and moulting stages in silkworm different. Comparatively high humidity is maintained during feeding and low humidity is preferable during moulting. Care should be taken during moulting period and humidity of the bed and room has to be reduced to facilitate easy casting of skin and during eating period it has to be increased so that leaf can remain fresh for longer duration. If temperature is high as normally seen in tropical conditions, humidity has to be reduced to lower the body temperature.

Air Current

Air current has tremendous effect on silkworm rearing especially during the late age. The 4th and 5th age larvae consume 94 per cent of total consumption and at the same time water released during these instars is also very high. Fresh air which gets polluted in the rearing house by ammonia, sulphur dioxide, carbon dioxide and formalin fumes, *etc.*, through silkworm expiration, workers, mulberry leaves, fermentation of litter, burning of charcoal *etc.*, needs to be removed. This is only possible when ventilation is good. The silkworm crop may suffer in poor ventilated condition as the physiology of larvae gets affected which in turn make larvae sluggish, weak and susceptible to the various diseases. Fresh air is comparatively heavy whereas polluted air is lighter, hence enough window and ventilators should be provided in the rearing houses for better crop. Better ventilation also helps in regulation of rearing temperature and humidity. Windows and ventilators can be opened and closed when desired environmental conditions is maintained. The effect of air current during rearing in different instars and its effect on larval growth and cocoon characters are given below:

The recommended air current during late age rearing is 1.7 m/sec for 30 min before every feed. Carbon dioxide content exceeding 1 per cent in the rearing room is injurious to health. It is observed that carbon dioxide expiration from the silkworm is increased in proportion to the rearing humidity especially at higher temperature. It is also observed that rearing conducted in closed and open types of rearing house and with different types of air current 0.5m/sec especially during 5th age has also tremendously affected the ingestion and digestibility and other cocoon characters. Air current of 1.0 m/sec. during 5th age rearing reduces the larval mortality and improve ingestion, digestibility, larval weight, cocoon weight and pupation rate compared to those recorded under no ventilation condition.

Effect of Poisonous Fases inside the Rearing Bed

It is reported that less than 1-2 per cent CO_2 in the rearing room will not have any harmful effect on silkworm. Contrary to this, it is observed that more than 1 per cent CO_2 in a rearing room is harmful. However, 1 per cent of CO_2, 1 per cent of formaldehyde gas, 0.02 per cent of SO2 and 0.1 per cent NH3 in the air in rearing house is the safe limit.

Light

Silkworms are photosensitive and prefer dim light (15-30 lux) and avoid very strong light as also darkness. Though, photoperiod plays a vital role in the life cycle of silkworms it does not affect the survival rate of silkworms. If rearing is done under dark condition, the distribution of larvae becomes localized as against horizontal distribution at the surface of the rearing bed in diffused light. The rearing conducted in sufficient light 15-30 lux resulted in showed uniform growth of silkworms. The late age silkworm larvae show optimum growth at photoperiod of 16 hrs of bright light and 8hrs darkness in 4th and 5th instars.

Maintenance of Environmental Condition

To exploit the maximum potential of a breed, optimum environmental condition has to be maintained during late age rearing (23-25 °C and 60 - 70 per cent RH). To raise the temperature during winter and rainy seasons electric room heater or charcoal stove can be used whereas to increase humidity water can be sprayed on the floor or wet sand can be spread all around rearing bed. Humidifier can also be used to increase the humidity. On the contrary, when the humidity increases above 80 per cent, dusting of lime all around rearing house is recommended. Proper ventilation has to be arranged to regulate the temperature and humidity upto a considerable extent. Modification if required and proper designing of the rearing house suited to a particular agro-climatic zone also can contribute in maintaining desired environmental condition

Frequency of Feeding Bed Cleaning Schedules

India, being a tropical country different feeding schedules are followed in different agro climatic zones. If the temperature and humidity can be maintained as desired level, four feeding per day in case of leaf feeding method and 3 feedings per day in case of shoot feeding system is advocated in summer season, while 2 feeds per day in rainy and winter season. However, it is desirable to increase or decrease the feeding frequency in rainy and summer seasons after observing weather conditions without affecting the quantum of feed required at particular instars (IV and V Age) otherwise cocoon quality will be affected considerably. Recent experiments with shoot rearing indicated that if optimum quantum is given as recommended, feeding frequencies will not have any effect if desired environmental conditions are maintained.

The amount of mulberry leaves to be supplied to silkworms and the frequency of feeding are variable according to the rearing temperature, humidity, ventilation, spacing, variety of mulberry and maturity of leaves. Feeding schedule and leaf requirement for 100 Dfls is given below:

Feeding Schedule

Season	*Environmental condition/moisture Content of Leaf*	*8.00 AM*	*2.00 PM*	*8.00 PM*
Rainy season (2 feeds only)	High humidity, high moisture content in leaves	✓	--	✓
Other seasons (3 feeds only)	High temperature, low humidity and less moisture content in leaves	✓	✓	✓

Bed Cleaning Schedules

Silkworms do not consume all the mulberry leaves that are supplied to them and invariably a part of the feed is left behind on the rearing bed. At the same time, the larvae also defecate and their feaces remain on the rearing bed. If the residual mulberry leaves and the feacal matter are left on the rearing bed for long time, both start decomposing and fermenting thereby quickly increasing the dampness of the bed. This adversely affects the larval physiology. Therefore, it is essential to periodically remove the waste materials from the bed and keep it clean. The process of doing so is known as bed cleaning.

During silkworm rearing dried old leaves and litter accumulates in the rearing bed and has to be removed. In tray rearing cleaning is done every day using Nylon net. Nylon net of mesh size 2"x 2" is spread on the bed and feeding is given. After two feedings the net is lifted and the litter and old leaves below the net are removed. In shoot feeding method bed cleaning is mostly avoided except when humidity is very high. When cleaning of bed is required it is done by rope method or net method. In rope method, ropes of 8 ft length are spread parallel to one another on the rearing bed leaving a margin of one ft on both sides. After two feedings,(by providing the shoots across the ropes) when most of the larvae climb and reach the surface of the bed, both the ends of the ropes are lifted to gather the shoots with larvae in the centre, so as to make a bundle which is kept at another place. of the same rack. This helps in separating the old bed easily without damaging the larvae. In net method, nets of 5′ x 6′ size and mesh of 2"x 2" are spread over the rearing bed and after two feedings, the nets are lifted and the old leaves and litter at the bottom are removed.

Different Rearing Methods–Shelf, Shoot and Floor Rearing–Advantages and Disadvantages

The rearing of late age worms (IV and V instar) is conducted by various methods and farmers are adopting the methodology suitable to their space, infrastructure and economic condition. The silkworm rearing can be of 3 types *i.e.*

1. Shelf rearing
2. Shoot rearing
3. Floor rearing

Shelf Rearing

In this method, leaves are plucked from the bushes/tree and then fed to the worms, whole or cut as per the growth of the silkworm. The leaf rearing is done in wooden or bamboo trays in 10-12 tires stand. Tray rearing method is very much popular as it needs less space for conducting rearing. However, this method of rearing is adopted by most of the Indian farmers even though it is laborious and labour requirement is more for bed cleaning, feeding, leaf plucking etc. The stand rearing is

Shelf Rearing

carried only by research institutes for experimental purpose in Japan or by certain farmers for the preparation of parent eggs of F1 hybrid.

Advantages

- ☆ 1.5 – 2 sq.ft. floor area is required per DFL.
- ☆ In less space more number of eggs can be reared.
- ☆ Left over leaves could be used as animal feed.

Disadvantages

- ☆ Labour intensive
- ☆ Leaves dries quickly.
- ☆ Disease incidence is more

Shoot Rearing

Shoot Rearing

In this type of rearing the entire branches of mulberry are used generally after III moult. It is also evident that shoot rearing method needs less labour which constitutes major expenditure in silkworm rearing. Since, the leaf supply due to shoot feeding is distributed in three dimensions, there is better aeration in rearing bed and therefore it is possible to accommodate 50 percent more silkworm per unit area of rearing bed as compared to the leaf rearing. In tropical countries 3 tier rack method of shoot rearing is preferred than tray rearing. The beds cleaning is practiced once in 4th instar and 5th instar or only in 5th instar on second day and the yield by such practice are higher about 70 to 80 kg cocoons per 100dfls of eggs brushed. In shoot rearing, feeding is done 2 or 3 times per day according to the season. This system is popular in all sericultural countries and is getting popular in India also.

Advantages

- ☆ Labour saving up to 50 per cent
- ☆ Secondary contamination is reduced.
- ☆ More hygienic
- ☆ More organic matter will be available for compost making
- ☆ Leaf driage is reduced in rearing bed
- ☆ Cocoon yield and cocoon characters are improved.

Disadvantages

- ☆ Require more floor area (about 30 per cent extra) as compared to tray rearing. 4-5 sq. ft. floor area is required per DFL.
- ☆ Bed refusal will not be available for cattle feed.
- ☆ Planting material (cuttings) will not be available for new plantation.

Floor Rearing

In this method, rearing is conducted on the floor and silkworms are fed with individual leaves or mulberry shoots. 2-3 beds can be made with 1 to 1.5 m width and length depending upon the space available. Leaving about 1 m space between the beds to attend the feeding. This method is popular among farmers in Jammu and Kashmir states of India, Japan and northern region of China.

Floor Rearing

Advantages

- ☆ Shoot feeding is practiced in most cases as cleaning is not done in this method of feeding which is an added advantage for maintaining hygienic conditions.
- ☆ It is economical, time and labour saving method.

Disadvantage

- ☆ More floor area is required.

5.4. Preparation for Mounting-Methods of Mounting, Types of Mountages Advantages and Disadvantages of their Use, Spinning-Environmental Conditions Required for Spinning

Preparation for Mounting

On the sixth or seventh day of fifth instar the silkworms show less appetite and discharge hard dark brown colored faeces which are soon replaced by soft light brown ones, which indicate that spinning stage has set in. The skin becomes gradually transparent due to growth of silk gland which occupies almost the whole body, when the entire gut remains emptied. Silkworm discharge liquid excreta at the time of cocooning which is almost about 0.5ml. In large scale rearing if this urine is left without check, the humidity in the rearing room becomes high and spoils the quality of cocoons. Hence it is necessary that good ventilation is provided in the mounting room to drive away moisture. When maturation sets in, larvae crawl about looking for a place to make a cocoon by spitting out the liquid silk through spinneret located below the mouth. Silk material is secreted and immediately fixed and hardened when silkworm touch spinneret to any solid matter. When silkworm moves, the silk materials are drawn out from the spinneret to the point where the spinneret touches next. When silkworms are insufficiently fed the silk gland will be smaller and the spinning process is delayed and spins small cocoons. A silkworm can spin silk filament length ranging from 500 m to 1500 m depending on the breed. Preparation for transformation into pupa inside the cocoon shell begins as soon as spinning is completed.

Spinning a cocoon is the final process of silkworm rearing. The process of transferring matured larvae to a suitable frame to spin cocoon is called mounting. Building a cocoon is a necessary and indispensable activity for metamorphosis of a larva in to moth via pupal stage. It is desirable to have a separate mounting hall with good aeration for keeping the mountages. Mounting work requires the most intensive labour during a short period. After mounting, larva takes 48 hrs for complete spinning of cocoon depending on the environmental conditions. Hence protection of larvae for 3-4 days after mounting has a profound influence on quality of cocoons. If the mounting is delayed by more than a half day, the larvae stop spinning before emptying all the silk material in the body as the preparation for transformation has already initiated resulting in flimsy cocoons. Hence in a mass rearing when 40 per cent of the larvae show maturation, all the larvae can be collected and mounted at the same time. The following points to remember:

- Mounting should not be delayed when larva get matured.
- Mounting should be done in a place where it can be handled easily.
- Mounting place should be kept dry with good ventilation

Methods of Mounting

Mounting is one of the most laborious activities in silkworm rearing. If the mounting method is wrong, the quality of cocoons suffers which in turn reduce the income of the farmer (Amardev *et al.*, 2009). There are different methods of mounting depending on the type of mountage used and method of rearing. They are:

- Pick up method.
- Natural or self mounting method
- Jobarai or shoot shaking method and
- Netting method

Pick Up Method

This is a method by which the properly matured larvae are picked up by hand one by one and placed on a mountage. By this method silkworms can be mounted at the right time and is the most ideal method for getting quality cocoons. But labour requirements are very high causing economic loss. If the labour required for picking matured larvae is inadequate, larvae become over mature and will result in inferior quality cocoons.

Pick Up Method

Natural or Self Mounting Method

This method of mounting is also called self mounting as it makes use of the negative geotropic character of the matured silkworms, the tendency to climb up. When about 20 per cent of larvae get matured, mountages like plastic collapsible mountage, bottle brush mountage and dried grass/straw mountage are placed on

Self or Natural Method of Mounting

the rearing bed. After few hours when the expected number of larvae climbs over the mountage it is picked up and hanged from the roof or separated from the bed. This operation is repeated two or three times and the small number of larvae left in the bed are mounted by pick up method. By this method labour can be saved and changing of mountage becomes convenient in relation to the progress of maturation of larvae. At the time of keeping the mountage on the rearing bed, the upper surface of the bed is made even by providing leaf feeding in shoot rearing method. This help in the larvae not going inside the bed to spin cocoons.

Netting Method

When large number of larvae gets matured at a time and difficult to pick up one by one, straw rope or reed mats are placed on the rearing bed after feeding mulberry leaves. When sufficient number of larvae climbs over the net, the net is lifted up with the larvae and then shaken out to a mountage.

Jobarai or Shoot Shaking Method

It is also called shaking of the shoots to separate matured larvae from mulberry branches. Shaking can be done manually or by using machine. Jobarai method is ideal for shoot rearing method and can save up to 40 per cent labour. However this method is not suitable when there is infection.

Jobarai or Shoot Shaking Method of Mounting

Types of Mountages Advantages and Disadvantages of their Use

A mountage for good quality reelable cocoon should have the following minimum features.

- ☆ Should have sufficient cocooning space between frame works.
- ☆ Material used for mountage should favor reelability of cocoons.
- ☆ Material should be cheap, durable and easily available.
- ☆ Should be convenient for the process of mounting and harvesting.
- ☆ Should be convenient to prevent faeces and urine coming in contact with cocoons.

Different types of mountages are used by the sericulturists in India. But the most commonly used mountage for spinning cocoons of silkworms are:

- ☆ Bamboo chandrike.
- ☆ Plastic collapsible mountage.
- ☆ Rotary card board mountage.
- ☆ Bottlebrush mountage.
- ☆ Dried grass/straw/twigs mountage.

Bamboo Chandrike

It is the most commonly used mountage in India. It is made of bamboo spirals woven on a bamboo mat with two supporting bamboo sticks. The mat is of size 1.8 x 1.2 m. The spirals are made of bamboo tapes on mat base with 5-6 cm width. Small holes are made on the mat base to provide ventilation. Matured silkworms are transferred to the chandrike @40-50 worms per sq ft. After mounting the chandrike is kept at a slanting back position of 45° to allow the urine to fall on the ground and to prevent the staining of cocoons. During mounting care should be taken to prevent damage to the soft skin of larvae which may result in pupal mortality. It is mostly popular in south India and West Bengal.

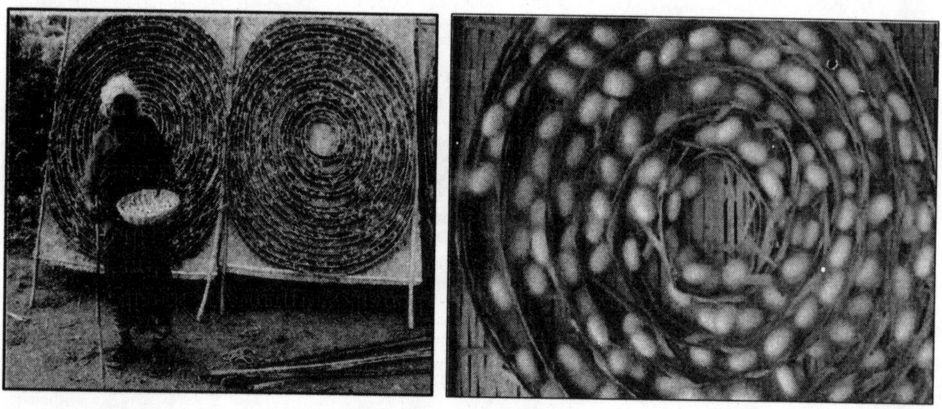

Bamboo Chandrike

Advantages

- ☆ It is cheap in cost.
- ☆ Can get locally.
- ☆ Mounting of matured silkworms are easy.
- ☆ Can mount 1200 matured silkworms in per mountage.

Disadvantages

- ☆ Need more space for storage.
- ☆ Disinfection is difficult.
- ☆ Percentage of defective cocoons is more.

- Low Reelability.
- Durability is only 3-5 years.
- Prone to damage by rodents and ants.
- High floss formation and irregular shape.

Plastic Collapsible Mountage

These are also called as Netrikes and are made of plastic mesh having 11 folds of 2.2" height and can be placed in a wooden tray of size 2′ x 3′ for mounting the larvae. It can be stored by folding. Newspaper is spread at the bottom of the mountage for

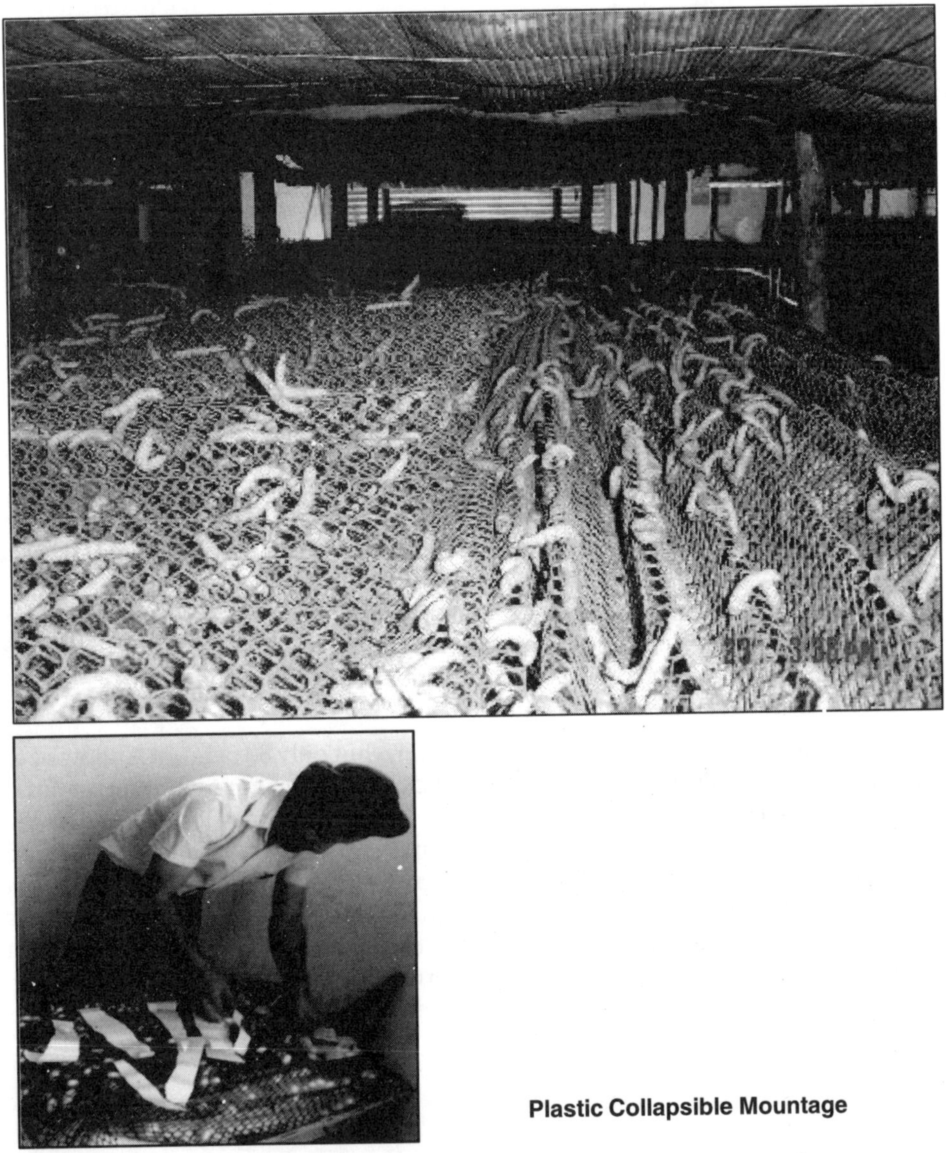

Plastic Collapsible Mountage

absorption of urine. Each mountage can hold 350-400 larvae for spinning. After mounting strips of paddy straw or pieces of old news paper are put on the mountage for providing anchorage to the spinning silkworms. Plastic collapsible mountage can also be used for self mounting. It can be directly placed on the rearing bed when the larvae start spinning by self mounting

Advantages

- ✰ Easy for handling and disinfection.
- ✰ Durability is high.
- ✰ Less space for storage.
- ✰ It can be sued for self mounting.
- ✰ Harvesting of cocoons is easy.

Disadvantages

- ✰ Destroyed by rodents while storing.
- ✰ Loss of corrugation due to frequent use resulting in uneven space for making cocoons.
- ✰ It is also noticed that reelability is not good in cocoons harvested from this type of mountage as humidity is built up in the rearing bed.

Rotary Card Board Mountage

These are made of pieces of cardboard assembled in a checkered pattern consisting of 13 rows and 12 sections each providing a total mounting space of 156 sections of size 4.5 x 3 x 3 cm.Each mountage is 55 cm long, 40 cm wide and 3 cm deep and can be folded completely when not in use. Ten such mountages are fixed on a wooden rectangular frame using ten iron clamps on each of the four sides. The frame consists of two rectangular frames of size 120 x 58 cm and 115 x 44 cm and is made of square wood of size 1 x 2 cm. Both the ends of the shorter axis are fixed by an iron screw and the whole wooden frame can be hanged horizontally. It can also revolve by the horizontal short axis. Hence, the name rotary mountage. The wooden frame can also be folded when not in use.

Each frame can hold 1560 larvae for spinning, but only 80 per cent is allowed to mount, *i.e.*, about 1300 larvae to provide sufficient spacing. For mounting matured larvae on this mountage first newspaper are spread on the floor and then the mountage is kept horizontally on the newspaper. Mature larvae are collected and transferred to the mountage. After 4-5 hrs when the larvae climb on the mountage, it is lifted from the ground and suspended from the ceiling using iron hooks. Urine is collected at the bottom on gunny cloth which can be removed. The mountage get rotated as the larvae move up and gets uniformly distributed till it starts spinning. Disinfection of rotary mountage is done by fumigation and sun drying.

Advantages

- ✰ Uniform size and shape cocoons.

Rotary Card Board Mountage

- ☆ Less defective cocoons.
- ☆ Higher Reelability.
- ☆ Harvesting of cocoons is easy.
- ☆ Need less space for storing.

Disadvantages

- ☆ Due to high cost all the farmers are not reluctant to adopt it.
- ☆ More space and separate mounting hall is required

Bottlebrush Mountage

The structure of the mountage is same as that of plastic mountage except that coir rope is used as a support and bamboo pieces or coconut broomstick of length 15

Bottle Brush Mountage

cm are inserted into a coir rope at a distance of 3 cm in groups of eight. Different types of bottlebrush mountages are available depending on the material used. Bottlebrush mountages are made of plastic, bamboo or coconut broomsticks.

Advantages

- ✰ It is cheap.
- ✰ Farmers can make themselves.
- ✰ Useful for self mounting.
- ✰ Detachable nature helps in easy storage.

Disadvantages

- ✰ Defective cocoons formation is more.
- ✰ Harvesting is difficult.

Dried Grass/Straw/Twigs Mountage

When silkworm starts maturing, a thick layer of dried grass or mango leaves or straw is spread over the rearing bed. Matured larvae crawl through the bed on the mountage and spin cocoons. For mounting 100 Dfls of larvae 80 m^2 space is required.

Advantages

ü Labour saving.

ü Ideal for shoot rearing method.

Disadvantages

ü Formation of floss and deformed cocoons are more.

Cocoon Spinning on Paddy Husk

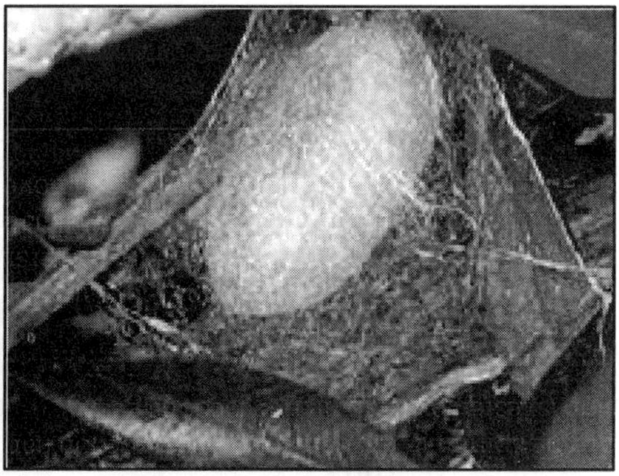

Cocoon Spinning on Mango Leaves

Spinning-Environmental Conditions Required for Spinning

Spinning (pre-pupal period) is the most sensitive stage in silkworms, as histolysis of larva organs takes place during that time. Matured silkworms larvae exhibit instinct behavior in cocooning and pupation. Several scientists reported that the environmental factors like temperature and humidity play a crucial role in determining the quality of cocoons spun and pupation (Reddy *et al.*, 2004). Further, improvement of reelability of cocoon filament and quality of silk can be affirmed by providing ideal environmental condition required for mounting. These are:

Ideal Condition for Spinning Worms

Temperature	*Relative Humidity (per cent)*
25-26º C	60-70 per cent

The temperature above the optimum makes the cocoon quality poor and below the optimum increases the pupation period. High humidity leads to formation of soft and poor quality cocoons and also increases urination in silkworms thus resulting in formation of rusted cocoons.

Good ventilation is essential for quick drying of urine and avoids stains due to urination by the silkworms. If this urine is left without check, humidity becomes higher; the moisture released by silkworm during mounting will be about 20 liters by respiration and 40 liters as contained in the spun silk material for 40,000 larvae. This moisture can raise the mounting room humidity and spoil the quality of cocoons. As to the effect of the rise of humidity upon the quality of cocoon, the effect of the rise of humidity from 60 per cent to 70 per cent upon the quality of cocoon is comparatively less, however if the humidity is raised from 70 per cent to 90 per cent the number of lower quality of cocoon is remarkably more.

Low intensity light (dim light) condition is congenial for spinning. Mature silkworms favor dim light of 15 to 30 lux. When the mounting room is lighted only

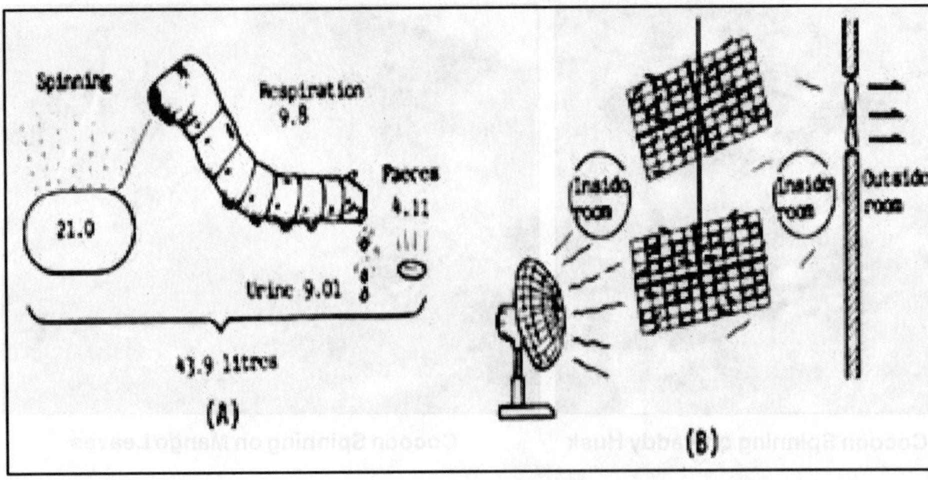

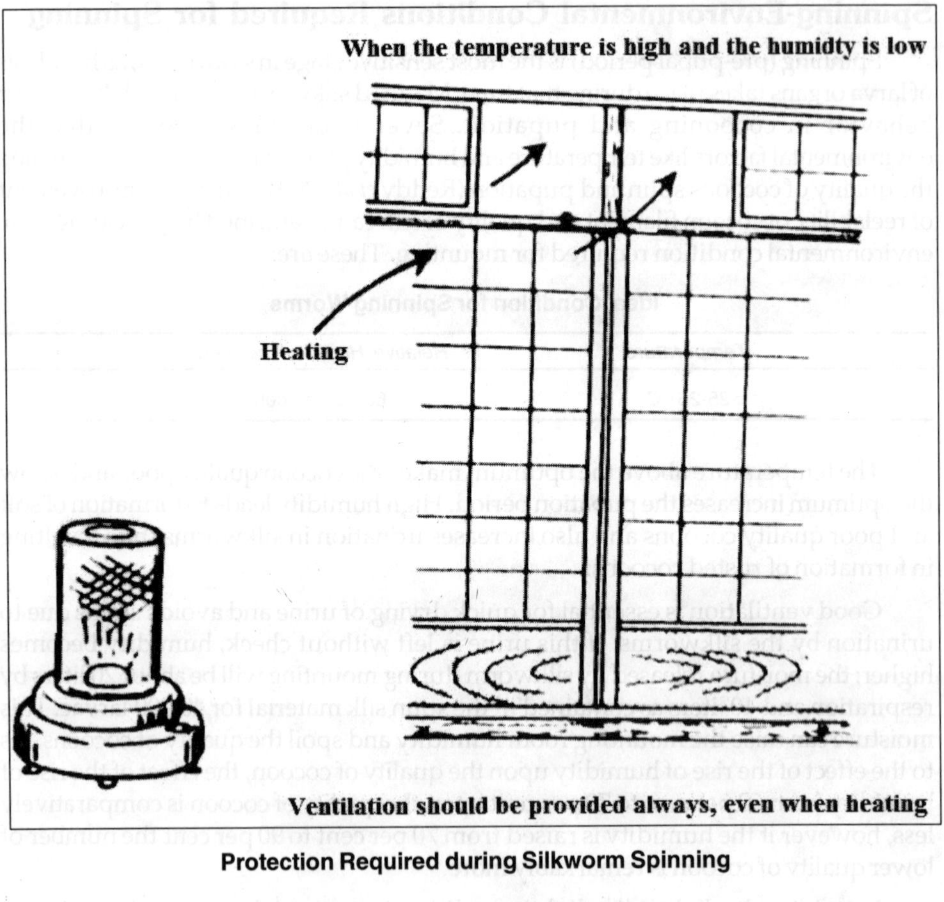

Protection Required during Silkworm Spinning

from one side of the room, mature larvae move to the opposite side and increase the percentage of double cocoons. The shell is thicker to words the direction of light.

Hence, uneven shell formation occurs. Direct sunlight affects spinning process resulting in poor spinning and decreased cocoon quality.Suffocation or insufficient fresh air leads to the formation of defective cocoons.

5.5. Harvesting of Cocoons-Time of Harvest of Seed Crop, Hybrid Crop, Sorting of Cocoons, Preservation-Transportation of Cocoons

Harvesting of Cocoons

Mounted silkworms can complete cocooning in 2-3 days. It becomes pupa in another 2-3 days. At the beginning of pupation, the skin of pupa is soft, fragile and liable to be wounded easily. If cocoons are harvested at this stage, the interior layer of cocoon shell is soiled which affects the reelability. Hence, cocoon should be harvested only on the sixth day after mounting.

Harvesting Methods

Before harvesting, all diseased and un-spun larvae and dead larvae should be removed from the mountage. Cocoon harvesting methods depends on the kind of mountage used:

Plastic Collapsible Mountages

The mountage is stretched both sides to deform the lupes and take out the cocoons by hand from the mountage.

Bottle Brush Mountages

Harvesting can be done by hand or using a short iron rake and cocoons can be collected from both the sides.

Rotary Mountage

First dismantle the rotary mountage. Then, remove the dead worms, unspun larvae, thin cocoon, etc. Harvest the cocoons using wooden cocoon harvester. Cocoons in the frame are pushed out one line after another by a cocoon pusher setting the frame in the wooden frame. Pushed out cocoons hanging with silk filament can be collected by hand.

Time of Harvest of Seed Crop, Hybrid Crop

The actual time for harvesting the seed cocoon crops is 6th after mounting the bivoltine silkworms and after 5th day in the case of multivoltine silkworms. By this time the worms has completed spinning of cocoon and transformed to pupae by casting its larval skin and has developed brown thick cuticle. This is the proper time for harvest of seed cocoon crops. If harvested earlier the skin of pupa is soft and has not yet turned brown, such pupae when distributed burst and die in the cocoons. These are called melted cocoons. Increase in melted cocoons makes the batch unfit for seed. By the time the larvae started spinning, the Extension Officer (EO) of the grainage visit the rearer's house frequently and periodically, test the larvae for disease and watch the progress of the cocooning. Before the cocoons are harvested some flimsy cocoons and early spun cocoons are examined for perbrine. It even traces of perbrine is noticed such lots are not taken for seed. The aim of the seed cocoon grower is not only to produce cocoons with high yield but also those which are free from perbrine disease. Cocoons are harvested on the 6th day; they are cleaned of faecal matter, melted cocoons and flimsy cocoons. Only good quality cocoons are separated and sent to the grainage. Seed cocoons should never be transported on lorry or on top of the bus and that too in afternoon when the temperature is high. This leads to pupal death and melted cocoons.

Time of Harvest of Hybrid Crop

Mounted silkworm can complete cocooning in about two days. It becomes pupae in another two days. At the beginning of pupation, the skin of pupae is soft and gets wounded easily. If cocoons are harvested at this stage the insides of cocoon shell is soiled and affect the reelability. It takes another 2 or 3 days after pupation for the skin to harden Hence, cocoon should be harvested only on the 6 or 7th day in the case of bivoltine hybrids and in the cross-breed harvesting to be carried out on 5th day of mounting when temperature is 25-27°C to prevent injury. But again the harvesting of cocoons is depends upon to the season and environmental conditions prevailing during spinning. It is safe to conduct cocoon harvesting after hardening of the pupal skin is tested by shaking the cocoons gently.

Sorting of Cocoons

Among the harvested cocoons there are double, flimsy, outside stained cocoon, pierced, thin end, deformed cocoons, undersize, inside stained cocoon etc. It is necessary to reject these defective cocoons. This is known as sorting of cocoons. After sorting of cocoons, it is also imperative to remove floss before marketing to get a good

Sorting of Cocoons

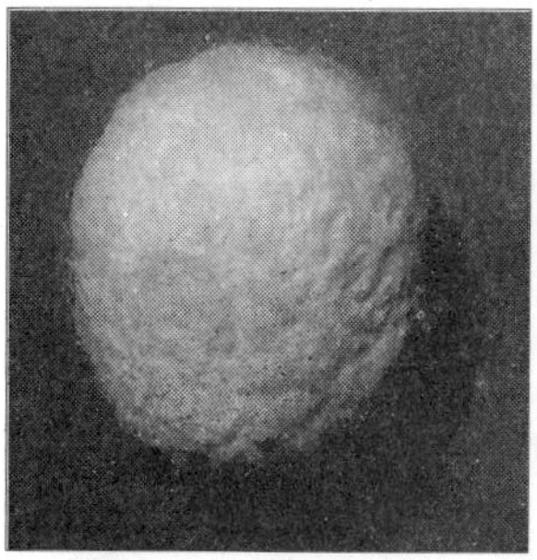

Double Cocoon

Flimsy Cocoon

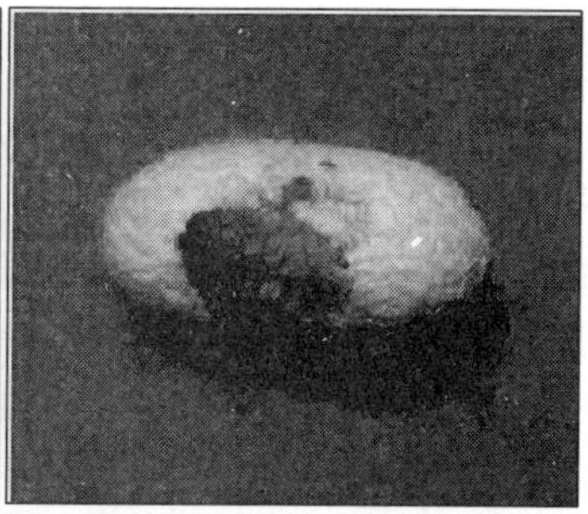

Outside Stained Cocoon

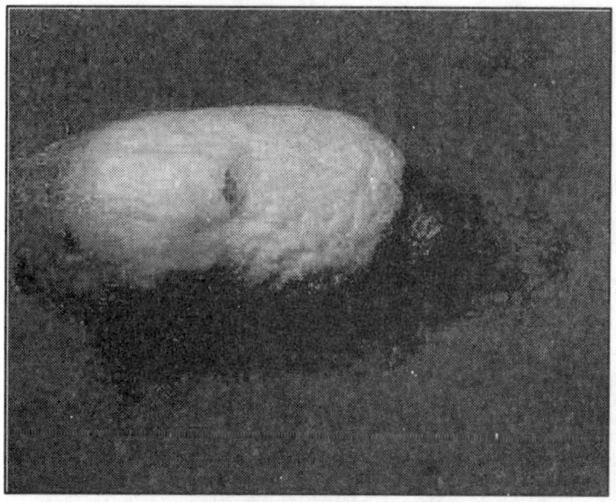

Pierced Cocoon

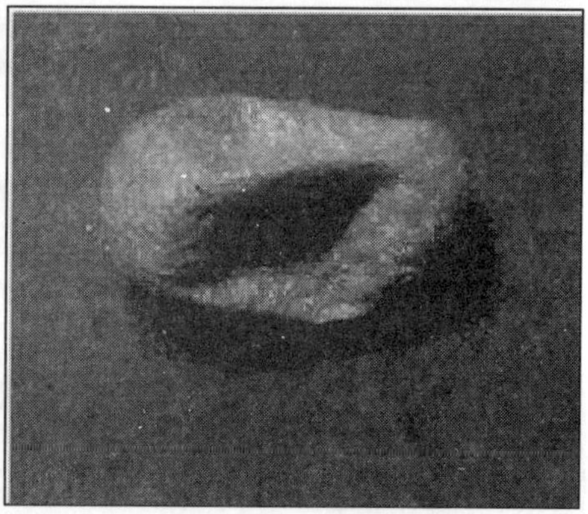

Thin Shell Cocoon

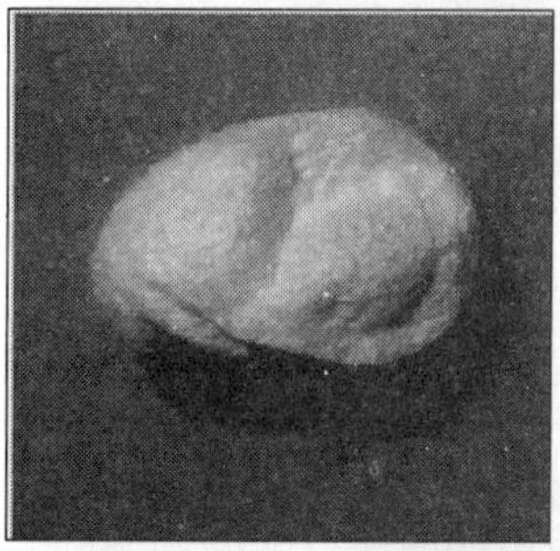

Deformed Cocoon

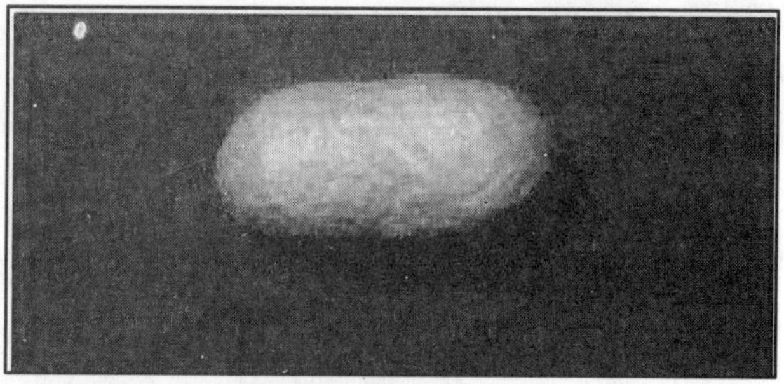

Undersize Cocoon

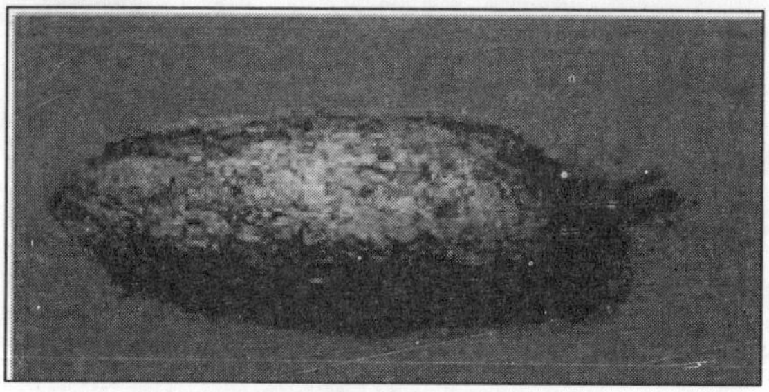

Inside Stained Cocoon

Different Types of Defective Cocoons

price for the cocoons. Floss can be removed by hand if the quantity is small. If the quantity is more, use electrically operated deflossing machine.

Preservation-Transportation of Cocoons

As far as hybrid cocoons is concerned whether it is from bivoltine or multivoltine or cross-breed reared by the farmers they sell their cocoon after harvesting immediately to the cocoon market that is green cocoon and no preservation of cocoon is needed, whereas in some northern states like J&K where farmers after harvesting dry their cocoons and preserved them in gunny bag *etc.*, as there is no immediate market take place.

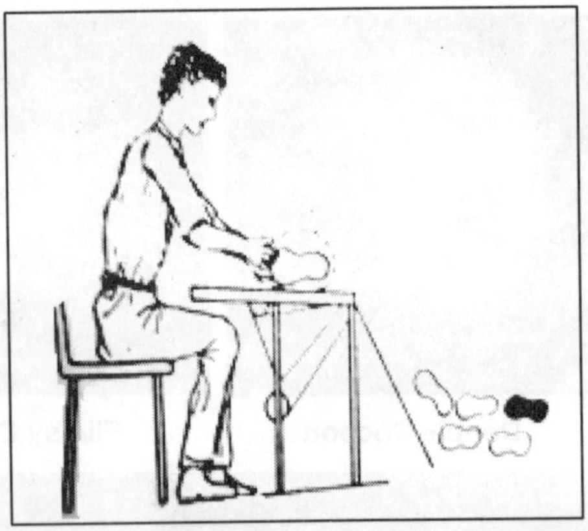

Sorting of Cocoons

For seed cocoons preservation, the temperature to which seed cocoons are exposed, that is, the high or low during the period between mounting and moth

Transportation of Cocoons

emergence has a great bearing on the percentage of unfertilized eggs among the eggs laid by the emerging moths. In the range of 15-30°C.At 20°C, the number of unfertilized eggs tends to increase and at 15°C and 30°C, the number of such eggs is found to be large.

There is also a close relationship between preservation temperature of seed cocoons and the number of eggs laid by the moths emergence there from. This relationship was studied for the Japanese, Chinese and European races in the temperature range of 15-30°c. The results indicate same trend as for the occurrence of unfertilized eggs, described above. The number of eggs is the maximum at 23-25°C followed by 20°C, and significantly low at 30°C and 15°C. Hence, it is ideal to preserve the seed cocoons to be used for eggs production at 23-25°C.

Transportation of hybrid races cocoons means carrying cocoons from farmer's house to the cocoon auction market for selling under proper care. While transportation the cocoons it is essential the cocoons should be loosely packed and most preferably in onion bag for providing good aeration. Tight packing of cocoons damage the pupae inside and pressed cocoons as a result good cocoon become defective. The cocoons should be transported in the cooler hours of the day.

Transportation of seed cocoons means, carrying seed cocoons safely from production centres to egg production centres, safe transportation of seed cocoons is necessary in order to keep the pupae and the cocoons unaffected without physical damage so that the moths emerging from such pupae are fit for the production of rich and healthy silkworm eggs.

Packing and Transportation of Cocoons

The best time for transportation of seed cocoons is the cooler hours of the day *i.e.,* early morning or late evening. Transportation of seed cocoons during the hot hours of the day damage the pupae due to heating up of the cocoons. Under such condition the pupae inside the cocoons become weak and the moths from such cocoons either die or lay poor eggs. Laying and hatching of such eggs will be irregular.

Bibliography

1. *A Guide for Construction of Silkworm Rearing House*–Published by Member Secretary, Central Silk Board, Bangalore, (1999).
2. Agarwal, S.C., Jolly, M.S., Sinha. A. K. and Banerjee. N.D. (1974). Free amino acids in healthy and diseased larvae of A. mylitta D. reared on S. robusta. *Proceeding of 1st International Seminar on Non-Mulberry Silks,* Ranchi. India. p. 142-153.
3. Agarwal. S.C., Jolly. M.S.,' Sinha. A. K. and Banerjee. N.D. (1974). Utilization of by-products in tasar industry. *Proceeding of 1st International Seminar on Non-Mulberry Silks,* Ranchi. India. p. 225-230.
4. Ahsan, M.M. (2000). Sericulture Status and Technologies for Cold and Temperate Conditions in India. *National Conference on Strategy Sericulture Research and Development* (*Souvenir*), 16-18 November 2000, CSR and TI, Mysore, pp. 41-45.
5. Ahsan, M.M. Jolly, M.S. and Khatri, R.K. (1974). Some preliminary studies, on the various aspects of grainage in tasar silkworm (A. my/itta D.). *Proceeding of 1st International Seminar on Non-Mulberry Silks,* Ranchi. India. p. 158-159.
6. Ahsan. M.M., Jolly, M.S., Banerjee, N.D. and Yishwakarma, S.R. (1976). Role of phylohormone in terminating pupal diapause of A. mylitta II. Indian Journal of Sericulture.15:21-26.
7. Akerele, L. (1970). A review of the technique of silkworm rearing and silk production Federal Institute of Industrial Research, Nigeria. p. 24.

8. Amardev Singh (2012). Effect of two different bed disinfectants on cocoon productivity in spring rearing of silkworm, *Bombyx mori* L. Green Farming. *An International Journal of Applied Agricultural and Horticultural Sciences.* Vol. 3(1): 122-124.

9. Amardev Singh and Himantharaj, M.T. (2008). A study on constraints faced in mounting practices and factors influencing the cocoon quality among farmers in three southern states. *Journal of Experimental Zoology,* Vol. 11. No.2, pp.267-271, India.

10. Amardev Singh, Himantharaj, M.T., Vindhya, G.S., Vijaya Prakash, N.B. and Kamble. C.K. (2009). Use of plant based repellents for self mounting in silkworm *Bombyx mori* L. and their effects on cocoon parameters. *Insect Pest Management and Environment Safety,* (suppl.,) 4(11): 131-139.

11. Angin, 1., Yaganohlu, A.V. and Turan, M. (2005). Effect of long term waste water irrigation on soil properties. *Journal of Sustainable Agriculture,* 26:31-42.

12. Anitha, A. (2011). Indian silk industry in the global scenario. *International Journal of Multidisciplinary Management Studies.* 1(3), pp.101-106.

13. Annual Report (2004-05). Sericulture Chapter-VIII.

14. Anonymous (1987). Proceedings of National Seminar on Micronutrients in Crop production. May 28-29, 1987 held at Institution of Agricultural Technologists. Bangalore.

15. Anonymous (1996). Cocoon and raw silk production. *Sericologia,* 35: 5.

16. Arseniev. A.F. and Bromley, N.V. (1951). The oak silkworm. Moscow. Selkozgiz.

17. Ashiru, M.D. (1975). Some aspects of work on insect pests of leaves and fruits of Triplochiton seleroxylon K. Schum. Ibadan, Federal Department of Forest Research.

18. Bailey and Bailey, E. Z. (1941). Hortaus the Second. Macmillan, New York, pp. 778.

19. Bharali, N. (1967). Som the muga food plant success in air layering. *Indian Silk,* 6: 5-7.

20. Bharali, N. (1972). Studies on the density population of muga silkworm. A. assamensis Westwood. *Indian Journal of Sericulture.* II: 1-5.

21. Bird, F.T. and Whalen, M.M. (1954). A nuclear and cytoplasmic polyhedral virus disease in the spruce bud worm. *Canadian Journal of Zoology.* 32: 82-86.

22. Bose, P.C. and Sengupta, K. (1990). Problematic soils of Tropical mulberry garden and their management - CSR and TI, Mysore.

23. Bouché, M.B. (1977). Stratégies lombriciennes. *Ecology Bulletin,* 25: 122-132.

24. Brenchley, W. E. (1920). Weeds of Farm-land, Longmans, Green, London.

25. Brij Kishore, Singhal, Mohammad Ashraf Khan, Anil Dhar, Farooq Mohammad Baqual and Bharat Bushan Bindroo (2010). Approaches to industrial exploitation

of mulberry (*Mulberry* sp.) fruits. *Journal of Fruit and Ornamental Plant Research.* 18(1): 83-99.

26. Brown, G.G., Pashanasi, B., Gilot-Villenave, C., Patrón, J.C., Senapati, B.K., Giri, S., Barois, I., Lavelle, P., Blanchart. E., Blakemore, R.J., Spain, A.V. and Boyer, J. (1999). Effects of earthworms on plant production. *In* P. Lavelle, L. Brussaard and P.F. Hendrix, eds. *Earthworm management in tropical agro ecosystems,* pp. 87-147.
27. Central Silk Board (2011). Report under 11th plan.
28. Central Silk Board (2012). *Sericulture Industry.*
29. Chandrama Goswami and Manisha Bhattacharya (2013). Contribution of Sericulture to Women's Income in Assam-A Case Study in Goalpara District of Assam, India. *International Journal of Scientific and Research Publications.* 3(3):1-6.
30. Chhabra, R. (1996). Soils Salinity and Water Quality. Oxford and IBH Publishing Co. Pvt. Ltd., New Delhi (South Asian edition) and A.A. Balkema Uitgevers BC, Rotterdam (edition elsewhere). p. 284.
31. Chikkanna, G.S., Vindhya, Amardev Singh and S. M. H. Qadri (2009). Qualitative improvement in terms of economic gained by using two different types of mountages for silkworm cocoon. *Green Farming. An International Journal of Horticultural and Allied sciences.* 2(14):1014-1016.
32. Chowdhaury, S. K. and Jolly, M.S. (1967). Spinning compartment of tasar silkworm, A. mylitta. *Indian Journal of Sericulture.* p.22
33. Chowdhaury, S. N. (1960). Genetics of tasar silkworm. *2nd International Technical Sericultural Conference,* Murcia, Spain.
34. Clark. R.B. 1982b. Iron deficiency in plants growing in the Great Plains of U.S. *Journal of Plant Nutrition,* 5: 241-268.
35. Coleman, D.C., Ingham, R.E., McClellan, J.F. and Trofymow, J.A. (1984). Soil nutrient transformations in the rhizosphere via animal-microbial interactions. *In* J.M. Anderson, A.D.M. Rayner and D.W.H. Walton, eds. *Invertebrates-microbial interactions,* pp. 35-58.
36. Dandin, S.B., Jayant Jayaswal and Giridhar, K. (2001). *Handbook of Sericulture Technologies,* Central Silk Board, Bangalore.
37. Datta, R.K. (1992). *Guidelines for Bivoltine rearing CSB* - Bangalore. Jolly, M. S. 1986 - Organization of Industrial Bivoltine Grainage for Tropics - CSR and TI-Mysore.
38. Datta, R.K. (2000). Mulberry cultivation and utilization in India. *This electronic conference.*
39. Dent, D. (1986). Acid sulphate soils: a baseline for research and development. Publ. 39, ILRI, Wageningen, The Netherlands.
40. Devlin, R.M. and Witham, F.H. (1986). Plant Physiology. CBS Publishers, New Delhi.

41. Dhar, A., Farooq, M. and Mir Nisar (2011). "Recent Trends in Development of Bivoltine Sericulture in Jammu and Kashmir". *Technical Compendium of workshop* held at SKICC, Srinagar on Oct.29, 2011.
42. Dudal, R. (1976).Inventory of the Major soils of world with special reference to mineral stress hazards" In Wright, M.J. (Ed.) Plant adaptation to mineral stress in problematic soils, Ithaca, New York, USA, Comell University of Agricultural Experiment station, PP. 3 - 13.
43. Ehow (2009). *How to make mulberry wine*. Food and Drink.www.eHow.com.
44. Emil Truog, V. (1973). Mineral Nutrition of Plants. Oxford and IBH Publishing Co., New Delhi. India.
45. Escap (1993). *Techniques of Silkworm Rearing in the Tropics*. Published by United Nations, New York.p.88.
46. Fairjuice (2008). *Super fruit mulberry juice*. Food and Beverage International. 13: 44.
47. FAO (1987). *Manual on Sericulture.* Printed by CSB, Bangalore, India.pp.84-85.
48. FAO (2000). *Guidelines and reference material on integrated soil and nutrient management and conservation for farmer field schools*. p.164
49. Govt. of India, Ministry of Textiles (2012). To be published in Part II, Section 3, Sub-section (i) of the Gazette of India. (Extraordinary), p.16.
50. Gupta, P.K. (2004). A. hand book of Soil, Fertilizer and manure 2nd enlarged edition 2004 Bharat printing press, Jodhpur, India.
51. Habib, G. (2004). Mulberry fruit based feed blocks–a key supplement for livestock in mountainous regions. *Mountain research Development*. 24: 106-109.
52. *Hand Book of Silkworm Rearing,* Published by Fuji Publishing Co. Ltd, Tokyo, Japan (1979).
53. *Handbook for Extension Workers,* Edited by K. V. Benchamin, Published by Director, CSRTI, Mysore, (1994).
54. *Handbook of Sericulture Technologies,* Edited by S.B.Dandin *et al.*, Published by Central Silk Board, Bangalore, (2000).
55. Healthy Lifestyle Magazine (2006). G.G.Enterprise, pp.34-36.
56. Hewitt, E.J. and Smith, T.A. (1975). Plant mineral nutrition, English Universities Press, London.
57. Hicks, P.K. (1990). Report on Round-table on Standardization of Design, Principles for silkworm rearing house and Instruments for Sericulture Development- Published by Regional Office for Asia and pacific, Bangkok, Thailand.
58. Himantharaj, M.T., Kamble, C.K., Rajan, R.K. and Datta, R.K. (1994). Silkworm rearing house construction: An ideal approach. *Indian Silk*, pp.19-21.

59. Hou, D.X. (2003). Potential mechanisms of cancer chemoprevention by anthocyanins. *Current Molecular Medicine.* 3:149-159.

60. Hurpin, B. (1962). Super-Famille des Scarabeoidea. *In* A.S. Balachowsky, ed. *Entomologie appliquée à l'Agriculture. Tome I. Coléoptères,* pp. 24-204. Paris, Masson.

61. Illustrated Hand book on silkworm Disease control technology, Edited by K. Kawakami, PPPBST Project, JICA, CSRTI, Mysore, (2002).

62. Illustrated working process of new bivoltine silkworm rearing technology, Edited by K. Kawakami, PPPBST Project, JICA, CSRTI, Mysore, (2002).

63. Ingham, R.E., Trofymov, J.A., Ingham, E.R. and Coleman, D.C. (1985). Interactions of bacteria, fungi and their nematode grazers: effects on nutrient cycling and plant growth. *Ecol. Mono.,* 55: 119-140.

64. Isaiarasu, L. and R. Ganesan (2005). Weed flora in a mulberry garden near Sivakasi, Tamil Nadu. *Bionotes* 7(2): 64-65.

65. Ito, T. and Arai, N. (1965). Nutrition of the silkworm *Bombyx mori,* Amino acid requirement and nutritive effects of various proteins. *Bulletin of Sericultural Experimental Station,* Japan. 19(4): 345-369.

66. Jaiswal, K., R. Goel, R. Kumar and S. K. Gangwar (2006). Effect of different soil mulches on mulberry leaf yield and leaf moisture content. In: Abstr. of Natl. Semi. on Soil Health and Water Management for Sustainable Sericulture, Regional Sericultural Research Station, Kodathi, Bangalore, India, 27-28 Sep., 2006, p. 30.

67. Jane, Y.H. Aw and Merlita A. Dacayanan (2012). A survey on usage of mulberry leaves for controlling treatment. *International Conference on Management, Behavioral Science and Economics Issues,* Penang, Malaysia.

68. Junliang, Xu, Shurlun, Lu, Yungen, Miao, Zhang Chuanxi, Shi Zuhiu and Zhang (1994). *Silkworm Physiology.* Bulletin of Sericulture Hanghour, China.

69. Kamal Jaiswal, Shashir Gangwar and Ravinder Kumar (2006). Soil to Silk (A text book of Sericulture) Subham Media Publications, Agra.

70. Kamble, C.K. (2003). *Improved Technologies for Silkworm Seed Production.* Silkworm Seed Technology Laboratory, Central Silk Board, Bangalore.p.6.

71. Kamli Affifa, S. and Masoodi, M.A. (2000). Principle of Temperate Sericulture, Kalyani publishers, Ludhiana, India.

72. Kawakami, K. and Yanagawa, H. (2003). *Illustrated Handbook on Silkworm Disease Control Technology,* published by JICA, Mysore.

73. Kitahara, N. (1999). Utilization of fodder tree for the production of milk and meat (3). *Live stock Research.* Vol. 53(9):969-972.

74. Kotikal, Y. K., Reddy, D.N.R. and Subbarayudu, B.V. (1989). Role of disinfection in silkworm management. *Indian Silk,* 27 (11), 31-32.

75. Krishnaswami, S. (1988). Chawki-The crucial input for success of Sericulture. *Indian Silk,* 27(2): 82-87.

76. Krishnaswamy, S. (1993). Special features of tropical sericulture and five crucial steps to successful silkworm rearing. *Indian Silk*, 31(9), 287-295.

77. Lal, E.P., Tom, B. And Barche, S. (2003). Studies on the effect of sewage water on the growth attributes and yield of four solanaceous vegetables. *Bioved.* 14(1/2):115-116.

78. Lavelle, P. And Spain, A. (2001). *Soil ecology*. Dordrecht, Netherlands, Kluwer Academic Publishers.

79. Lavelle, P. (1981). Strategies de reproduction chez les vers de terre. *Acta Oecol.*, 2: 117-133.

80. Lee, K.E. and Wood, T.G. (1971). *Termites and soils*. London, Academic Press.

81. Lee, K.E. (1985). *Earthworms: their ecology and relationships with soils and land use.* New York, USA, Academic Press. P. 411

82. Li Long (2011). Why Sericulture.

83. Liu, L.K., Chou F.P., Chen Y.C., Chyau, C.C., Ho, H.H. and Wang C.J. (2009). Effects of mulberry (*Morus alba* L.). Extracts on lipid homeostasis in vitro and in vivo. *Journal of Agriculture and Food Chemistry*.57:7605-7611.

84. Manual on Mounting and Harvesting Technology (1997). R.K.Rajan. *et al.*, Published by BSTD Project, JICA, CSRTI, Mysore.

85. Manual on Scientific Management of Multi-Bi grainages (1993). Dept. of Sericulture Govt. of A. P.

86. Miyashita, Y. (1986). A report on mulberry cultivation and training methods suitable to bivoltine rearing in Karnataka.

87. Mohsim, V., Sarkar M. A. and Mathur, B.S. (1995). Acid soil Management. Kalyani Publishers. Ludhiana.

88. Muniyappa, T. V. and H. R. Shivakumar (2000). Crop weed competition in mulberry. In: Proceedings of the National Seminar on Tropical Sericulture, 1999, Department of Sericulture, University of Agricultural Sciences, GKVK, Bangalore, India, 28- 30 December 1999, 1: 76-78.

89. Narayanaprakash, R., Periasamy, K. and Radhakrishnan, S. (1985). Effect of dietary water content on food utilization on silk production in *Bombyx mori* L., *Indian Journal of Sericulture*, 24(1):12-17.

90. Oosterbaan, R.J. (1981). Rice Polders Reclamation Project, Guinea Bissau In: ILRI Annual Report 1980, ILRI, Wageningen, The Netherlands. pp. 26–32.

91. Oosterbaan, R.J. (1992). Agricultural Land Drainage: A wider application through caution and restraint. In: ILRI Annual Report 1991, ILRI, Wageningen, The Netherlands., pp. 21–35.

92. Pallavi, S.N. and Kamble, C.K. (1997). Disinfection and hygiene in sericulture–A review. *Sericologia*, 37 (3):401-415.

93. Paul, D.C., Rao. G. C. and Deb, D.C. (1992). Impact of dietary moisture content on nutritional indices and growth of *Bombyx mori* L., and concomitant larval duration. *Journal of Insect Physiology*, 38(3):229-235.

94. Perur, N. G. and Mithyantha, M.S. (1985). Soils of Karnataka and their management. In soils of India and their management. The fertilizer Association of India, New Delhi.

95. Philip, T. (1989). Mulberry Fruit an Ideal Food. *Indian Silk*, 28(8):13-14.

96. Ponge, J.F. (1991). Food resources and diets of soil animals in a small area of Scots Pine litter. *Geoderma*, 49: 33-62.

97. Prabha Shekar and Frances Sinha (1992). Raw Silk Market in India EDAl Delhi and Gurgaon and Samuha Karnataka -ITDG. UK.

98. Rajan, R.K. and Himantharaj, M.T. (2005). *A Text Book on Silkworm Rearing*, published by Central Silk Board, Bangalore.

99. Ram Kumar (2007). *"Economics of silk Industry in India"* Tamil Nadu Agriculture University.

100. Reelers Training Manual (1993). Department of Sericulture, Government of Andhra Pradesh.-Quality Counts -The importance of Raw Silk. Testing and Grading-Silk conditioning and Testing House, CSB, Bangalore.

101. Report of The working group on Textiles and jute industry for the eleventh five year plan (2007-2012). Government of India Ministry of Textiles.

102. Rija, H., Siddiqui, Z.S. and Arif Uzzaman (2005). Changes in chlorophyll, protein and carbohydrate contents of *Vigna radiate, Cicer arietinum* and *Lens culinaris* after irrigation with sewage water. *International Journal of Biology and Biotechnology*. 2(4): 981-984.

103. Sandhya Rani, G. (1998). *Sericulture and Rural Development*. Discovery Publishera House, New Delhi, p.143.

104. Satyasai, K.J.S. and Ratna Babu, G.H.V. (2004). Report on integrated sericulture development project for Andhra Pradesh.

105. Sengupta, K. and Yusuf, M.R. (1974). Studies on the effect of spacing during rearing of different larval and cocoon characters of some multivoltine breeds of silkworm, *Bombyx mori* L. *Indian Journal of sericulture*, 23: 11-16.

106. *Seri Business Manual–A User's Guide Farm Sector*, (2003). Published by Central Silk Board, Bangalore.

107. Sericulture New Horizon for Rural Development in.U.P. (2007). Department of Sericulture Govt of U.P. Sonwalkar, T.N., Glossary of Silken Terms - CSTRI, Bangalore.

108. Setua, G. C., M. Setua, A. K. Dutta and B. Saratchandra (2008). Botanical weed management in irrigated mulberry: A new approach. *Indian Silk*. 46(11): 15-17.

109. Shailesh Soni, Sahu, K.R., Dewagan, S., Yogita Soni and Sanjeev Katre (2009). Medicinal value of (*Morus alba*) mulberry plant. *International Research Journal*. Vol. II, (5). 449-451.

110. Shankar, M.A. (1990). Nutritional Management of Mulberry and its effect on silkworm growth, development and silk quality. Ph.D. Thesis. University of Agricultural sciences, Bangalore.

111. Shivakumar, H. R., N. C. Prthibha and T.V. Muniyappa. (1994). Effect of chemical weed control on nutrient uptake by common mulberry (*Morus australis*) and associated weeds. *Indian Journal of Agronomy.* 39(2): 277-281.

112. Singh, G.P., Mathur, V.B., Kamble, C.K. and Datta, R.K. (1998). Yong age rearing of silkworm, *Bombyx mori* L., A Review. *Sericologia,* 38(2):199-213.

113. Soltner, D. (1978). *Phytotechnie Générale. Les bases de la production vegetable.* Tome 1, Le Sol. 7éme édition. Collection sciences techniques agricoles. Angers.

114. Sonwalkar, T.N. (1990). Manual for Reelers-CSTRI-Bangalore. 1993 - Technical Compendium-Charka Silk Reeling; Technical Options Intermediate Technology Development Group - Rugby, UK. and Economic Development Associates-Gurgaon.

115. Sonwalkar, T.N. (1993). Influence of Softened Water in Mulberry Silk Reeling - CSTRI - Bangalore.

116. Sreekumar, S., B.B. Bindroo, A.K., Saha, Jalaja, S. Kunar, H.Lakshmi, N. Suresh Kumar, G.K. Chattopadhyaya and N. Lalitha (2012). Mulberry fruit in table delicacies. *Indian Silk,* Vol.3 (51 old) No.6.p.13.

117. Srikanth, R., Khanam, A. And Rao, V. (1994). Cadmium levels in the urine of male sludge farmers in India. *Journal of Toxicology Environment Health.* 4:1-6.

118. Swift, M.J., Heal, O.W. and Anderson, J.M. (1979). *Decomposition in terrestrial ecosystems.* Oxford, UK, Blackwell Scientific Publications.

119. Tammanna, S.Sonwalkar (2001). *Hand book of Silk Technology.* Published by New Age International (P) Limited Publishers, New Delhi.

120. Tazima, Y. (1978). *Silkworm Egg.* Scientific Brochure 1. (Pub.) Central Silk Board, Bangalore. pp.24-25.

121. Tewary P.K. and Subba Rao, G. (1990). Mulberry By- products and their Utilization. *Indian Silk,* 29, 43-44.

122. Toshiyuki Kimura (2011). Development of mulberry leaf extract for suppressing postprandial blood glucose elevation. *Hypoglycemia-Causes* and *Occurrences,* Everlon Cid Rigobelo (Ed.) Japan.

123. Ullal, S.R. and Narasimhanna, M.N. (1994). *Handbook of Practical Sericulture.* Published by central Silk Board, Bangalore.

124. Usha Rani (2007): Employment Generation to Women in Drought Prone Areas: A Study with Reference to the Development of Sericulture in Anantapur District of Andhra Pradesh, *Journal of Social Science.* 14(3), 249-255.

125. Vermananda Reddy, G., Venkatachalapathy, M., Manjula, A. and Kamble, C.K. (2004). Impact of mountages and larval density on cocoon quality and egg production. *Indian Silk,* pp.14-16.

126. Vigneshwara Varmudy (2011). *Silk Industry: Need to Become Competitive*. Market Survey.

127. Vinod Mathur, B. and Qadri, S.M.H. (2010). *Manual on Mountages, Mounting and Harvesting Technology for Quality Cocoon Production*. Central Silk Board, Bangalore, pp.5-6.

128. WU Pang-Chuan and Chen Da (1988). Chuang translated by Chen Zuo - Pu, Liu, Ping. - Zhang and Tang He -FAO Agriculture Bulletin 73/2, Silkworm rearing.

129. www.yourhealthyourherbs.com (2009). Mulberry herbal tea.

130. www.znaturalfoods.com (2009). Mulberry fruit powder.

131. Yellamanda Reddy, T. and Sankara Reddi, G. H. (1992). Principles of Agronomy, Kalyani publishers, Ludhiana, India.

132. Yokoyama, T. (1962). *Synthesized Science of Sericulture*, published by Central Silk Board, Bangalore, India.pp.210-223.

Index

D

E

P

Q

R

S

T